Engineering Victory

ENGINEERING VICTORY

VICTORY

The Union Siege of Vicksburg

Justin S. Solonick

Southern Illinois University Press
Carbondale

18 17 16 15   4 3 2 1

Jacket illustration: color lithograph, *Siege of Vicksburg—13, 15 & 17 Corps, Commanded by Gen. U. S. Grant, assisted by the Navy under Admiral Porter— Surrender, July 4, 1863*, by Kurz and Allison, 1888. *Library of Congress Prints and Photographs Division.*

Library of Congress Cataloging-in-Publication Data
Solonick, Justin S., 1982-
Engineering victory : the Union siege of Vicksburg / Justin S. Solonick.
    pages cm
Includes bibliographical references and index.
    ISBN 978-0-8093-3391-2 (cloth : alk. paper)
    ISBN 0-8093-3391-0 (cloth : alk. paper)
    ISBN 978-0-8093-3392-9 (ebook)
    ISBN 0-8093-3392-9 (ebook)
1. Vicksburg (Miss.)—History—Siege, 1863. 2. United States— History—Civil War, 1861–1865—Engineering and construction. 3. Military engineers—United States—History—19th century. I. Title.
E475.27.S73 2015
973.7'344—dc23   2014026918

Printed on recycled paper. ♻

To my wife, Jinanda, whose boundless love, support,
and encouragement made this book possible

Contents

Illustrations and Table

Pictures

Maps

Diagrams and Figures

Table

Acknowledgments

It is a pleasure to call attention to those who made the publication of this book a reality. First, I would like to thank my major professor, mentor, and friend Steven E. Woodworth. Dr. Woodworth supervised this project from the beginning, providing valuable organizational suggestions and a careful eye to detail during the editing process. My gratitude for his constant support and patience is without limit. Next, I would like to thank Professors Richard Lowe, Todd Kerstetter, and Kenneth Stevens, who all provided valuable suggestions about how to improve the manuscript. Dr. Charles D. Grear did a wonderful job generating the maps included in this book during the final phase of the project. Special thanks go to my acquisitions editor, Sylvia Frank Rodrigue, for guiding me through the editing process and offering many useful suggestions. I would also like to thank my copy editor, Julie Bush, for her careful attention to detail.

Many individuals aided in my search for primary sources. Terrence J. Winschel, former chief historian at Vicksburg National Military Park, and park ranger Dr. David Slay were invaluable contacts who made my visits to the park both informative and enjoyable. Curator George "Bubba" Bolm and research historian Neal Brun aided my research at Vicksburg's Old Court House Museum. I would like to thank Michael Ballard for bringing to my attention the location of the Hickenlooper Collection at the Cincinnati Museum Center. Special thanks go to Christine Schmid Engels, the archives manager at the museum, who aided in my navigation of Hickenlooper's papers. Nan Card, curator of manuscripts at the Rutherford B. Hayes Presidential Center, provided access to information pertaining to James B. McPherson. The manuscript curator and librarians at the Abraham Lincoln Presidential

Library and Museum, namely Cheryl Schnirring, Dr. Glenna Schroeder-Lein, and Debbie Hamm, aided in the location of letters and diaries written by Grant's Illinois soldiers. Peter Harrington, curator of the Anne S. K. Brown Military Collection at Brown University, gave permission to reprint several period illustrations in this book. I would also like to thank the manuscript librarians at the United States Military Academy at West Point who provided access to sources pertaining to antebellum military engineering while I attended the Summer Seminar in 2012.

I would like to close with a special acknowledgment thanking the family members who provided moral support throughout this long journey. My father and mother, William R. and Teresa N. Solonick, fostered my interest in history from an early age and provided valuable words of encouragement. And there are not words to express the gratitude for the love and support that my wife, Jinanda, gave throughout this endeavor. That is why this book is dedicated to her.

Engineering Victory

Introduction:
With a Spade in One Hand and a Gun in the Other

----

emembering his Civil War service in the Army of the Tennessee, one Iowa soldier, writing in the twilight years of his life, reflected on the Union ordeal during the siege of Vicksburg—the Gibraltar of the Confederacy. Attempting to describe this peculiar form of warfare, which turned out to be the largest siege in U.S. military history, the Iowan wrote, "Every man in the investing line became an army engineer day and night. . . . The soldiers got so they bored like gophers and beavers, with a spade in one hand and a gun in the other."[1]

It is interesting that this observation, often cited in popular histories, describes a topic that historians have neglected for over a century. Yet the story of Vicksburg beleaguered remains an unwritten tale of engineering problems met with improvised solutions. Today, a visitor to Vicksburg National Military Park will be awestruck by the commanding earthen Confederate defenses and the footprint that remains of the Union besiegers. Exactly how the Army of the Tennessee, an almost all-volunteer army badly deficient in trained engineers, successfully concluded the largest and most elaborate siege in American history is a worthy topic of discussion. According to one Illinois soldier, "The siege of this place [Vicksburg] was the longest at this time of any in our history. . . . The mere fact that it was, in many respects, a new experience, having all the power of first impressions, gave it an exceptional position in the minds not only of the participants, but, I take it, of the people at large."[2]

The fact remains that a transformation occurred during the siege of Vicksburg. The soldiers who hastily dug in after the failed attempt to take the city by storm on May 22, 1863, were not the same men who triumphantly marched into Vicksburg on July 4. Although none of them would ever wage

Union soldier detailed to work in the trenches surrounding Vicksburg. *"Going to the Trenches,"* from *"Vicksburg Campaign," National Tribune, August 9, 1888.*

a siege like this again, the troops of the Army of the Tennessee received a crash course in military engineering as the siege progressed. Both enlisted men and engineer officers present at the time of Vicksburg's capitulation recognized this coming of age. Many years after the war, writing an article for the veterans' publication the *National Tribune*, First Sergeant Charles A. Hobbs, former Company B, Ninety-Ninth Illinois, recalled, "When we began the siege of Vicksburg we . . . knew very little ourselves how to proceed. When the [white] flags went up July 4 we had learned much, and could have managed better in every way. . . . Before the siege ended there were many volunteer officers who could have quickly chosen the best position, and with no little skill have constructed works of defense . . . and it happens to be the truth—that there was just as many privates who could have done as well or better." Such observations were not limited to enlisted personnel. The engineers themselves, in their after-action reports, also praised the fighting men of the Army of the Tennessee for their ingenuity and adaptability in the face of adversity. "At many times, at different places," one of the engineer officers wrote, "the work that should be done, and the way it should be done, depended on officers, or even on men, without either theoretical or practical knowledge of siege operations, and who had to rely upon their native good sense and ingenuity."[3]

Perhaps the "can-do attitude" of the midwesterners in the Army of the Tennessee facilitated victory. This confidence, which grew over time with each successive victory, allowed the army to experience "nothing but victory." Or, perhaps it was "improvisational ingenuity . . . the ad hoc engineering organization of the Army of the Tennessee" that allowed Major General Ulysses S. Grant's army to rise to the occasion. Contemporaries often commented on differences between eastern and western soldiers (what we would today refer to as midwesterners) during the Civil War. Writing to his father during the Vicksburg siege, William Lucius Rand of the 118th Illinois expressed contempt at the Washington authorities' favoritism toward the Army of the Potomac. Commenting upon Major General Joseph Hooker's defeat at the May 1863 Battle of Chancellorsville in Virginia, Rand penned, "We hear now that Hooker is repulsed and forced to recross the river[.] Why is [it] that Grants army is victorious [*sic*] while the army of Virginia is defeated in every movement?" "The eastern army is near at home," the hardened westerner's query continued, "and has had all the men and supplies that they have asked for while the western army is very remote from civilization . . . and its supplies are limited and we have driven the enemy at every point."[4] A distinct sense of pride mixed with a hint of jealousy permeated the Army of the Tennessee.

This feeling of western exceptionalism, though originating during the war years, became even more prevalent after the conflict. Lucien Bonaparte Crooker, an Illinois soldier who served in the Army of the Tennessee, commented on the improvisational adaptability of the midwesterners in Grant's army. "The Western volunteer became on occasion a pack mule, a fighting machine [and] an intelligent thinker and talker upon the tactics of armies," Crooker wrote. He further praised the army, relating that "when circumstances demanded he built bridges, repaired roads, ran engines or steamboats, printed newspapers, stormed forts, captured cities, killed men, or stole chickens. . . . To that end these sturdy men of the Northwest . . . discovered new principles, invented new theories and applied them to the practical purpose of saving a great republic." In short, the western fighting men during the Civil War were a special breed of "thinking bayonets" who made ultimate Union victory in the War of the Rebellion possible.[5]

Yet, ingenuity and western exceptionalism alone do not account for Union success during the Vicksburg siege. Although few engineer officers were present, those who directed the siege craft had received training at the nation's premier engineering institution, the United States Military Academy at West Point, or had served in some type of engineering capacity during their prewar careers. American military engineering on the eve of the Vicksburg Campaign was sophisticated, but the shortage of engineers in the Army of the Tennessee forced that particular Union army to mix its by-the-book siege techniques with western soldier improvisation. As a result, it was the marriage of western improvisation and ingenuity and West Point engineering theory, in the tradition of Sébastien Le Prestre de Vauban, as interpreted by Dennis

Hart Mahan, that allowed the Army of the Tennessee, with its deficient numbers of engineers, to wage a successful siege and force the capitulation of Vicksburg. Contrary to popular "Lost Cause" mythology, Lieutenant General John C. Pemberton and the beleaguered Confederate garrison at Vicksburg were not starved out, they were dug out. This is that story.

Of course, it is true that all sieges are improvised. History's great engineers, including the father of the art of the attack, Vauban, understood the need to adapt to terrain and changing circumstances. This understanding—that engineering is an applied science—trickled down through the centuries and into the classrooms of nineteenth-century West Point, the repository of America's knowledge pertaining to siege craft. Both the Academy's engineering guru, Dennis Hart Mahan, and the chieftain of the practical engineering department, James C. Duane, understood the need to improvise. Yet, despite this truism, the Vicksburg siege must be perceived through a different lens.

In the traditional sieges of the past, professional engineers improvised by selecting from a repertoire of techniques handed down from the engineering masters of their respective eras. At Vicksburg, this time-tested and unwritten rule failed. There were far too few engineers to wage the last traditional Vaubanian siege in the history of the Western world. As a result, the most that the Army of the Tennessee's professional yet numerically deficient engineering arm could do was to provide broad guidance to the army's common soldiers. These midwesterners, young men who had grown up scarcely a generation removed from their frontier fathers who had settled the young republic's Old Northwest, embraced conventional engineering maxims and adapted them to meet the needs of this particular siege upon which the fate of the Union hinged. For example, this study discusses a queer form of sap roller—the "land gunboat." While its function smacked of late seventeenth-century Vaubanian siege principles, its specifications were the spawn of western soldier innovation. Another example considers a peculiar observation tower designed to provide plunging sharpshooter fire into the Confederate defenses. While the theory of pouring on plunging fire from an elevated position was not new to Vicksburg, its uncharacteristic construction speaks volumes about the ingenuity of Grant's westerners.

Since this study examines the excavation of large quantities of dirt, some might be inclined to claim that the Vicksburg siege was a harbinger of the later trench warfare that plagued Europe during the First World War. It was not. Far too often has the War of the Rebellion been used to mark the middle of a false evolutionary spectrum bent on connecting the dots of Napoleon Bonaparte's brand of early nineteenth-century warfare with the "modernity" of World War I. If forced to choose, the siege of Vicksburg stands closer to its Enlightenment Vaubanian predecessors than it does to Ypres, Verdun, or the Somme. Nevertheless, it is important to remember that the American Civil War was neither purely Napoleonic nor exclusively modern but rather a transitional period in military history that held to previous maxims while foreshadowing the future. In short, the war was its own military event with its own defining characteristics.

The reason for this study's emphasis on the Union must be addressed. A thorough examination of the Confederate's stalwart efforts to hold Vicksburg is not only a worthy topic but also in need of a fuller and more careful analysis than the length of this volume will admit. Perhaps in the future another book will appear that adequately addresses this extremely interesting topic. Nevertheless, for the sake of space and focus, this book will concentrate on the Union engineering efforts to topple the Gibraltar of the Confederacy. With regard to standard nineteenth-century nomenclature, a siege, by definition, is an offensive tactic characterized by cutting the enemy's lines of communications and prosecuting forward-moving approach trenches. Thus, in short, the story of the *siege* of Vicksburg is the story of the Union, while the engineering of the *besieged* is that of the Confederacy. Despite the technicalities involved with terminology, the Confederates are still a part of this story. They will appear as "thinking obstacles" and are addressed in terms of their response to the Union's offensive siege techniques.

In addition, Major General William T. Sherman's defensive line along the Big Black River will not be examined in this study. While Sherman's role providing rear-area security for the Army of the Tennessee was important, it was not part of the offensive siege tactics that toppled Vicksburg. Rather, this is the story of a specific group of blue-clad midwesterners who fronted the Vicksburg defenses and who, by wielding "a spade in one hand and a gun in the other," methodically brought the Confederacy one step closer to surrender.

1. *The Engineer's Art*

At about 2 P.M. on May 22, 1863, Captain J. Harvey Greene of the Eighth Wisconsin spied a group of Union officers conversing about the present crisis that faced the Army of the Tennessee. But this was no ordinary group of officers: the intimate circle contained army commander Major General Ulysses S. Grant; his assistant adjutant general, Lieutenant Colonel John A. Rawlins; Fifteenth Army Corps commander William Tecumseh Sherman; Sherman's subordinate Brigadier General James M. Tuttle, Third Division commander; and one of Tuttle's brigade commanders, Brigadier General Joseph A. Mower. Grant, with his typical penchant for the casual, sported a slouch hat, a torn military blouse, and a pair of binoculars dangling across his body. As the group of generals talked within earshot, Greene could make out their conversation despite the shrieking artillery shells and rifle fire that pummeled the landward defenses of fortress Vicksburg, the final obstacle between the hitherto victorious Army of the Tennessee and the Gibraltar of the Confederacy.[1]

This informal meeting congealed just in front of the Eighth Wisconsin in order to discuss a peculiar message that had arrived from another of Grant's corps commanders, Major General John A. McClernand of the Thirteenth Army Corps. Until the middle of the afternoon of May 22, the Union assault against the Confederate defenses guarding Vicksburg had proven a failure. Sherman, to whom Grant had entrusted the task of striking the northern part of the Vicksburg entrenchments along the Graveyard Road, one of the primary arteries leading into the city, had been stopped. Just to Sherman's south, Major General James Birdseye McPherson, Grant's Seventeenth Army Corps commander, too had failed to penetrate the Confederate defenses in the sector of the Jackson Road, the narrow dirt path that ran all the way from the Mississippi capital, through the rebel defenses, and into the heart of Vicksburg. The failure of the assault in the sectors of Sherman and McPherson, Grant's most trusted lieutenants, made McClernand's message even more dubious.

According to McClernand, his troops had penetrated the Confederate defenses and were on the way to success. However, he could not exploit this temporary foothold unless Grant quickly dispatched more troops to the Thirteenth Army Corps sector on the left flank of the Union line. With more men, McClernand was certain he could succeed. Grant, however, was unsure of the situation and doubted the extent of McClernand's gains. He suggested that the Thirteenth Army Corps commander draw on his own reserve to exploit the purported foothold. McClernand replied that he had none and continued to plead for more men from other parts of the line. Grant eventually conceded and shifted Brigadier General Isaac F. Quinby's division of the Seventeenth Army Corps to McClernand's assistance.[2]

It was at this point that Captain Greene overheard Grant expressing his doubts to Sherman and Tuttle about McClernand's reported success. According to Greene, "I hear Gen. Grant say that he did not think it was true—but it might be so, and in order that the enterprise might not fail for lack of support he would order another charge to be made immediately; and turning to Gen. Sherman he said: 'General, send in your reserves.'" Sherman proceeded to commit more troops to his sector in order to draw Confederate attention away from McClernand's alleged success while Grant ordered McPherson to dispatch Quinby. But McClernand, even with reinforcements, could not maintain his tiny foothold inside the Confederate defensive work dubbed the Railroad Redoubt, which guarded the Baldwin's Ferry Road into Vicksburg. Grant's suspicions proved correct. McClernand had exaggerated his success, and while a handful of his men did briefly breach the imposing redoubt, he had not achieved a true breakthrough. James Curtis Mahan, of the Fifty-Ninth Indiana of Quinby's division, later recalled the march to support McClernand's alleged "breakthrough." Taking a circuitous route out of Confederate view, the brigade filed into a ravine fronting the forts that McClernand's troops supposedly occupied. But, to Mahan's surprise, the situation was not as the Thirteenth Corps commander had described. On arrival, the men of the Fifty-Ninth Indiana "then learned that McClernand's troops had made a charge on the two forts and only reached the embankment—and was holding the outside, while the rebs held the inside. This is how General McClernand had 'taken two forts.'" As was rapidly becoming painfully obvious to everyone in Grant's army, no Union troops would be entering Vicksburg on May 22.[3]

All along the line Grant's attacks fizzled and the Army of the Tennessee men poured back to the safety of Union lines in disarray. Those who had made it to within range of Confederate rifle fire or even as far as the ditches fronting the rebel forts themselves were forced to hunker down and wait for nightfall to make their escape. One soldier of the Sixty-Seventh Indiana who had participated in the assault on the Railroad Redoubt later recalled, "Those in the ditch are left, and while the hours slowly pass away they watch for the going down of the sun, that they may, in the shades of darkness, make their escape; and the hour arrives and, one by one, they crawl out and sneak their way through pools of blood, over the dead, and among the wounded; and finally reach the lines."[4]

During the night Isaiah Richards, of the Seventeenth Ohio Light Artillery, worked to help rescue the wounded who now lay on the open expanse of no-man's-land between the Union lines and Confederate earthworks. Richards's battery had fired from just north of the Baldwin's Ferry Road in support of the attack on the Railroad Redoubt, and throughout the afternoon, during lulls in the firing, the moaning of one particular Union soldier on a ridge near the battery tormented the Ohio artilleryman. Once darkness descended, Richards rushed to the man's assistance and, with the help of his fellow artillerymen, carried the wounded soldier back to the Seventeenth's guns. The invalid requested water and quaffed down the remaining drops of an artilleryman's canteen. After discovering that the failing soldier had been wounded in the chest, Richards asked what else he could do to comfort his fallen comrade. "He placed his hand to his blouse pocket," Richards recalled, "and muttered letter—Mothers name—tell her how I died." Richards "again asked him if there was any-thin [sic] else; he moved his lips feebly muttering saying—Jesus lover—of my soul." The nearly heartbroken Richards "with several comrades, sang that beautiful hymn for him." Before they could reach the final verse, the man had expired. Scenes such as this occurred all along the Union line as anger gave way to frustration and eventually to melancholia.[5]

Hindsight decrees that Grant bungled when he ordered the May 22 assault on Vicksburg, but events leading up to Grant's decision had suggested there might be a chance for victory. Until the evening of May 22, the Army of the Tennessee had experienced an unprecedented degree of success during the campaign. After several months of unsuccessful attempts to strike at Vicksburg from the north, Grant had decided to attack the fortress city from its eastern, landward, side. In order to do this, Army of the Tennessee troops departed Milliken's Bend on March 29, 1863. Marching south along the natural levies that formed the western bank of the Mississippi River, Grant's troops hacked their way through the Louisiana wilderness, building corduroy roads and bridging bayous.[6]

Meanwhile, Union soldiers, manning and piloting civilian steamboats, ran the Vicksburg batteries on April 22. Grant reached Hard Times on the western side of the Mississippi and crossed the river to land at Bruinsburg on the eastern bank on April 30. Thereafter Grant proceeded to engage Confederate forces under the overall command of Lieutenant General John C. Pemberton in five consecutive battles at Port Gibson, Raymond, Jackson, Champion Hill, and the Big Black River. At each engagement Grant, though he had fewer men than Pemberton in Mississippi, managed to bring more troops to the battlefield and won five stunning victories. After the Union victory at the Big Black on May 17, Pemberton decided to hole up in fortress Vicksburg and wait for relief from General Joseph E. Johnston's Confederate army lurking somewhere northeast of Jackson.[7]

And so, by May 22, only the landward defenses of Vicksburg stood between Grant and control of the Mississippi River. With New Orleans already in Union hands, Vicksburg and Port Hudson remained the only two major Confederate strongholds along the river. Once these obstacles fell, the Union stood to gain complete access to the Mississippi, and once again Union commerce could flow up and down the river unmolested. Meanwhile, with the river in federal possession, the Confederacy would be cut in two, leaving Richmond deprived of abundant trans-Mississippi resources.[8]

Fast on the heels of the retreating Confederates, Grant ordered an attack on May 19 against the Vicksburg defenses with Sherman's Fifteenth Corps, the first troops to arrive at the gates of Vicksburg. After the Union army handily swept aside the Confederate forces guarding the Big Black, Grant believed, despite the fact that the Confederates were well entrenched, that their poor morale would allow an easy victory. But the attack failed. According to General Sherman, an informal meeting between Grant, McPherson, McClernand, and himself on May 20 revealed why. The nature of the ground, primarily steep ravines, funneled the attackers against the strongest part of the Confederate lines, which guarded the three main roads leading into the city. Continuing to believe that a firm push against weak Confederate morale would win the day, the generals concluded that a larger, more carefully planned assault should be launched on May 22.[9]

Grant also believed the May 22 assault was necessary because future Union morale depended on it. Flush with victory, the soldiers of the Army of the Tennessee would engage in the drudgery of siege warfare, Grant believed, only as a measure of last resort. Once the failed assault proved the impossibility of an easy victory, the mundane task of siege craft would become more palatable. Nevertheless, the fact remains that Grant probably should never have attempted to take Vicksburg via direct assault.[10]

Although the attack failed, the commanders of the Army of the Tennessee did not hurl their men against the rebel fortifications nonchalantly. Careful planning went into the assault. The handful of engineer officers, where available, reconnoitered their respective fronts in order to determine the best points of attack—typically, the salients that guarded the main roads into the city. Where engineer officers were unavailable, generals and staff officers stepped forward to reconnoiter their fronts. Next, artillery officers placed batteries in favorable positions designed to provide covering fire for the attackers. Meanwhile, the soldiers of the pioneer corps constructed crude scaling ladders designed to assist the infantrymen in crossing the rebel ditches and surmounting their works.[11]

As the appointed hour, 10 A.M., approached, the men began to strip down to the bare essentials, toting only arms, accoutrements, a single day's rations, and their canteens. With advance parties selected, scaling ladders in hand, and the remaining men in reserve, all waited for the inevitable preliminary artillery bombardment. As one Indiana soldier recalled, "The Heavens trembled and the earth shook, while this heavy cannonading continued. . . . The skirmish line and sharp shooters were working their way well up to the forts, while the main line lay awaiting the signal of that awful moment." When ten o'clock arrived, the men charged. Yet despite these laborious preparations, the Union troops could not penetrate Vicksburg's defenses. According to one after-action report, "The attacks were gallantly made . . . but the fire both of artillery and musketry from the enemy's line was so heavy, and the loss in moving over the rough and obstructed ground so severe, that the assault failed at all points." When the smoke cleared, of the 40,000 troops engaged, Grant suffered the loss of 502 men killed, 2,550 wounded, and another 147 unaccounted for. As a soldier of the Forty-Second Ohio penned that night,

"General Grant Sealed the fate of Hundreds of his best Soldiers. It was not a charge; it was not a Battle, nor an assault; But a slaughter of Human Beings in cold Blood."[12]

Numerous reasons emerge for the failure of the May 22 assault. First, the ground itself, a series of undulating ravines, limited the assault routes to the most level paths into the city. According to a soldier of the 124th Illinois, "The hills were . . . very steep, running in nearly every direction, but mainly parallel to the rebel lines. Twisting and torturous [sic] were the snake-like defiles between them." But at the points where traverse proved possible, Confederate fire had been concentrated atop mutually supporting salients that swept the channels with a deadly crossfire from cannons, rifles, and muskets. In addition to well-sited earthworks and natural defenses, the Confederates had placed a series of artificial obstructions such as abatis—felled trees with lopped and sharpened branches fronting the enemy—as well as telegraph wire entanglements and chevaux-de-frise, all bent on deterring a rush attack and forcing assailants into the carefully prepared fields of fire.[13]

And so Grant, disappointed but undeterred, decided that he must lay siege to Vicksburg, or, as he termed it, "out-camp the enemy." His decision, however, did not come to the army as a shock. Writing to his "dear Kate" on May 23, Jefferson Brumback of the Ninety-Fifth Ohio outlined events to come. "Vicksburg cannot be captured by direct assault," Brumback stated. "The works in front of us are no doubt as formidable as any in America." As a result, "the place must be re duced [sic] by regular siege." "As soon as the Generals mature a plan," Brumback further explained, "we shall doubtless set to work and dig and approach in a scientific manner until the place surrenders." And so the Army of the Tennessee would have to consult its engineers and, for that matter, defer to anyone else on the Union lines who had been exposed to military engineering.[14]

- - - - - -

America's third president, Thomas Jefferson, an ardent republican who abhorred large standing armies, backed the establishment of the United States Military Academy in 1802. Although supporting the congressional move toward military professionalism contradicted Jefferson's political philosophy, it played to his appreciation of institutions of higher learning. The future founder of the University of Virginia now, in 1802, believed that a central repository of the country's military knowledge would produce a small cadre of specialized officers fit to lead the military in times of war. But the institution's original aim transcended establishing military professionalism. The Academy, in addition to creating a professional officer corps, sought to instill students with engineering knowledge that they could apply to civilian life and help build the new republic. As such, Congress decided that the engineer corps would take primary responsibility for maintaining West Point.[15]

The War of 1812 revealed the need for a more professional officer corps. So, shortly after the conflict with Britain, President James Monroe appointed Captain Sylvanus Thayer, an officer who had studied the latest French military doctrine in Europe, to become West Point's superintendent in 1817. Before Thayer, the Academy lacked uniformity and offered courses only in mathematics, fortification design, defense and attack, surveying, the French language, and sketching. Drawing proved an essential skill in generating fortification plans, drafting, and surveying. West Point operated without a rigid curriculum, and many students simply sauntered in and out of the Academy at will since the institution operated sans graduation requirements. All this changed in 1816 when the Academy adopted a four-year program. With this, students who wanted to achieve a commission in the army were required to undergo four years of intense study in a program that heavily weighted mathematics and engineering, a trial that became known as the "Thayer Method." The new structure divided students into small sections and forced them to master complicated topics for examination via recitation. Keeping pace with current European trends, the science of building and taking fortifications figured prominently into the Academy's new curriculum. Higher-ups continually tweaked the program, and by 1863 West Point had become the center of America's engineering knowledge.[16]

The Department of Engineering at the United States Military Academy went through its own process of development as the institution became the nation's premier citadel of engineering knowledge. Military engineering had been part of West Point's history since before its official founding in 1802. Prior to becoming an institution of higher learning, West Point was the sight of a Revolutionary War–era fort that guarded the mouth of the Hudson River. It continued to serve in this capacity after the war, protecting against unwanted foreign egress into New York. During the 1790s, the fort began to adopt an educational pose when, between 1795 and 1798, two former French army engineers built a replica of a fortification section face, based on the latest European style, on what would later become the campus grounds. This mock fortification section, combined with selected lectures, became the primary tool of engineering instruction until Congress established the Department of Engineering in 1812. Subsequently, Captain Alden Partridge, class of 1806, became the department's first official professor of engineering in 1813. But even with the creation of the department, principles of military engineering continued to be basic as the institution charted a course toward professionalism.[17]

Around the time Thayer became superintendent in 1817, Professor Claude Crozet, educated at France's premier engineering institution, École Polytechnique, replaced Partridge as the head of the department. With Thayer at the helm and Partridge in the department, the quality of engineering education at the Point improved. Under Partridge, French colonel Gay de Vernon's *A Treatise on the Science of War and Fortification* became the standard textbook. De Vernon, the Polytechnique's leading fortifications professor, represented the cutting edge of military engineering theory.[18]

A major development in the Department of Engineering occurred in 1831 when Professor Dennis Hart Mahan became head of the department. Mahan, born of Irish immigrants in 1802, did not enter the world a son of privilege. Prepared for a future career in medicine, Mahan deviated from this path and uncovered an early childhood love for drawing. On learning that the United States Military Academy cultivated drawing, Mahan eagerly sought an appointment, which he obtained, and entered West Point in 1820. Mahan showed unusual talent and became an "acting assistant professor of mathematics" during his second year (third classman). Graduating first in his class of 1824 and commissioned in the prestigious Corps of Engineers, Mahan eventually taught at his alma mater as professor of civil and military engineering until his tragic suicide, a result of forced retirement, in 1871.[19]

Described as "slight in frame and of an intensely nervous organization," Mahan proved a strict teacher. In fact, many first classmen (seniors), forced to attend their engineering classes with Mahan during their last year at the Academy, loathed him. "In the section room," an acquaintance once wrote, "Professor Mahan usually exhibited the earnest and military rather than the kindly side of his character. . . . He had no mercy for idleness and but little for stupidity . . . and in forcing the unhappy offender from his untenable positions the professor often chose stones rather than grass. . . . He was regarded as cynical rather than sympathetic."[20]

Cadet Cyrus B. Comstock, West Point class of 1855 and later chief engineer of the Army of the Tennessee at the end of the Vicksburg siege, recorded in his journal unpleasant memories of tutelage under Mahan. Comstock, in his diary, went to great lengths to mock the professor, whom he disparaged as "Denny." On one particular day, Mahan chose to mercilessly ride Comstock's classmates Edward L. Hartz and Henry W. Freedley. Hartz, despite this rebuke, would eventually graduate with Freedley in 1855. The former ended his career at the Point twenty-fourth in his class of thirty-four graduates, while the latter finished a few steps behind in twenty-ninth place. Their mediocrity, no doubt, collided with Mahan's nervous perfectionism. "Stand at attention, Mr. . . . Hartz!" Mahan belted out. "First Class officers should always observe rules & set an example for thos[e] in the Corps, ehem, ehem, but I have made the observation, ehem, ehem, that they are the first, ehem, ehem, to infringe them. Stand attention!! Sir!! . . . Mr. Freedley, if you are a snake, squirm; if you are a man stand still."[21]

Comstock further related another incident in which Mahan condescendingly corrected one student, George D. Ruggles, who made a technical error. Ruggles, though eventually graduating nineteenth in his class of 1855, was the object of Mahan's wrath this particular day. "All but our section [were] reciting in field fortifications," Comstock recorded, when "Dennis asked [Cadet] Ruggles What the use was in having the parapet of the particular height that is given to it." Ruggles shot back, "So the men can fire over it." Mahan, dissatisfied with the response, retorted, "Oh, Mr. Ruggles! The men fire over it, ehem, ehem, if it was fifty feet high. So they can fire at the enemy! over it!"[22]

In a later incident, Comstock recorded his horror at having been reassigned to a section under Mahan's tutelage. When assistant professor of engineering Gustavus Woodson Smith, class of 1842, retired from the Academy in order to pursue a civilian career, West Point reassigned his classes, dividing them into sections under the command of the remaining engineering professors. On finding out that he had been chosen for Mahan's section, Comstock recorded, "Good Lord deliver us! G. W. [Smith] was bad enough . . . but Denny's ehem, ehem! is far worse." But as Comstock's time at the Point was ending, he came to respect Mahan. At one time he even commented on the lucidity of the old engineer's lectures. Despite Mahan's gruff methods, his long tenure at the institution ensured that every Civil War officer who attended the United States Military Academy (USMA) during the antebellum period was exposed to his writings and teachings.[23]

Before Mahan became a professor of civil and military engineering at West Point, a position he held for forty-one years, the army sent him to

France in order to learn the latest engineering techniques. While abroad from 1826 to 1830, Mahan studied at the prestigious Military School of Application for Engineers and Artillerists at Metz for two years, and on returning to the United States, he began creating a reading list for the West Point engineering department.[24]

During his travels, Mahan purchased a French lithographic press and vigorously began printing his study notes in an attempt to create course materials. Eventually Mahan refined these notes and wrote his own engineering and military science books for use at the Academy. First, in 1836, Mahan published his most famous work, *A Complete Treatise on Field Fortification*. This book would later be refined and reappear in six editions, some with subtle changes to the title. According to one critique, this book proved "the best work on the subject in the English language." His other books, which became staples at the Academy, included *Course of Civil Engineering* (1837), *Permanent Fortifications* (1847), *Industrial Drawing* (1855), an American translation of *Mosley's Mechanical Principles of Engineering*, and *Treatise on Fortification Drawing and Stereotomy* (1865). Many of these books, like his famous 1836 field fortification treatise, passed through multiple editions. Both the breadth and depth of Mahan's publications illustrate a master of the military art. Throughout his tenure as professor of civil and military engineering and of the military art, Mahan became the sentinel of engineering knowledge at West Point while his published textbooks made up the entire curriculum. Together, Mahan and Thayer imported French professional military engineering standards to the United States and established an engineering curriculum that remained almost unchanged until Mahan's death in 1871.[25]

But despite West Point's emphasis on engineering, the majority of student course work focused on other areas of study such as mathematics and French. Meanwhile, during a cadet's third year at the Point, while he was a second classman, educational horizons were expanded to include natural philosophy and chemistry. But there was a method to this seeming instructional madness. Establishing the basic tenets of mathematics during the early years at the Academy paved the way for an intense final year of schooling in various aspects of civil and military engineering.[26]

During a cadet's fourth year, he was at last exposed to Dennis Hart Mahan and the rigors of the USMA engineering curriculum, which focused on both civil and military engineering. Students studied military engineering during the second term just prior to graduation. During this semester, cadets learned the details of waging siege warfare. Although the courses borrowed heavily from French military engineering theory and theoretical textbooks, Mahan emphasized applying "common sense" to every situation. In fact, this emphasis on using one's head led many students to cast upon Mahan the playful title "Old Cobbon Sense," a behind-the-back joke that smacked of Mahan's basic principle while mocking his manner of speaking.[27]

Despite the emphasis on military engineering, Mahan's treatises tended to focus on building field fortifications and permanent defensive works. This was most likely an attempt to teach course work in line with the larger national goal of coastal defense. Attacking such positions, although treated in some detail, remained secondary. Mahan's *A Complete Treatise on Field Fortification* was a prime example of this priority. Evolving through several editions over the course of the nineteenth century, the book became the foundational document of Mahanian fortification principles. In the fourteen chapters that make up the manual, instructions on how to attack permanent works appear only in the last half of the final chapter.

Mahan provided step-by-step instructions on how to besiege an enemy. Yet this instruction existed in a vacuum, a theoretical realm where an attacker approached an idyllic Enlightenment-era Vaubanian fortification and was allowed to implement all of the steps necessary to reduce a permanent work. Although "Old Cobbon Sense" preached adaptation in the classroom, it would be up to the engineers in the field to improvise and adapt his maxims to individual circumstances. Interestingly, Mahan's 1863 edition of *Summary of the Course of Permanent Fortification and the Attack and Defense of Permanent Works* provided a more detailed discussion of how to wage offensive siege warfare. In this rendition, in addition to commenting at length on specific offensive topics, Mahan broke down the science of siege craft into steps that an engineer was instructed to implement over a series of forty days. But, once again, this information appeared at the end of a much larger work dedicated to the history of the great military engineers and fortifications of Europe.[28]

Under Mahan's tutelage, cadets learned the science of attacking permanent works. Interestingly, this method had changed little since the brilliant French engineer Sébastien Le Prestre de Vauban (1633–1707) refined the art of constructing and attacking fortresses under the patronage of King Louis XIV. According to Mahan, "The science and experience of engineers since his day have added nothing of marked importance." Although taking an enemy fixed position appears as an afterthought in the 1836 edition of

A Complete Treatise on Field Fortification, instructors instilled students with detailed and specialized knowledge broken into methodical steps aimed at conducting a successful siege. Thus, after professors instructed cadets on how to build field fortifications and permanent works, students proceeded to master how to attack fortifications. In order to accomplish this, they learned the art of the siege.[29]

According to Mahan, "A *Siege* is the operation of cutting off all communication with a work, and attacking by *regular approaches*." First, the besieging force needed to invest the enemy, in effect cutting off all communication and preventing escape. The besieging army then established camp around, and out of range of, the enemy's defensive fortifications. After the besieging army settled in, it created lines of circumvallation and countervallation on either side of its encampments. Lines of circumvallation consisted of a connected line of works facing the enemy, while lines of countervallation made up a sporadic chain of "detached works" and protected the rear of the besieger from the possible approach of an army of relief attempting to lift the siege and save the fortress (or at least facilitate the besieged garrison's escape).[30]

Meanwhile, the besieging army, now ensconced between the lines of circumvallation and countervallation, built roads to connect the different camps while engineer officers conducted surveys in order to determine where the army should attack the beleaguered enemy. According to Mahan, "The object of the survey and plan is to enable the general, superintending the siege, to select the most suitable point to approach the work. This point was termed the *Point*, or *Front of Attack*." In short, once the commanding general decided to conduct a siege, engineers took over and applied their specialized skills in order to guide their superiors to the best points of attack. Typically, the engineer chose the salients—outward bulges or projecting angles—of the enemy's fortifications, as these protrusions from the defenders' lines usually proved the weakest point of any fortification.[31]

Next, the attacker entered the approach phase of the siege in which the besieging army steadily inched toward the enemy fortifications under cover (see figure). The purpose here, according to Mahan, was to get across the no-man's-land between the attacker and defender while incurring the fewest possible casualties. "The whole of their measures," he wrote of the besieging army, "should tend to the attainment of this end." In order to accomplish this goal, the attacker needed to first "approach the work under shelter; its fire must be silenced; and a breach be made in its rampart."[32]

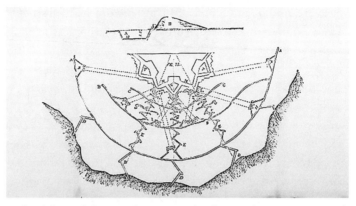

Mahan's "Attack by Regular Approaches." Note the zigzag approach trenches directed toward the capitals of the defenders' salients and the use of supporting parallels. The top of the image provides a cross section of a trench. *D. H. Mahan, A Treatise on Field Fortification, 1862 ed., plate 12, figure B.*

The decision to break ground and initiate the approach phase was termed *"Opening of the Trenches."* In order to cross no-man's-land safely, the besieging army, under the close supervision of engineers, dug trenches. These trenches fell into two categories: parallels and boyaux. The former, first employed by Vauban during the siege of Maastricht in 1673, were, as their name suggested, dug parallel to the enemy fortifications.[33] According to Mahan, "The parallel is a long line of trench, concentric with, or parallel to, the works of the point of attack, which it envelops." Typically, the "point of attack" referred to an opposing enemy salient. Most sieges contained three parallels. Engineers labeled each the first, second, and third parallel. Soldiers dug the first, the longest parallel that covered the broadest front, the farthest from the enemy salient, some six hundred yards as the crow flies from each point along the parallel to the protrusion in the besieged line. Subsequent to the excavation of the first parallel, soldiers dug the second and third. The second, established within three hundred yards from the enemy line, proved shorter than the first. The third, excavated within approximately sixty yards of the salient, covered less front than that of the second. These parallels provided cover for soldiers guarding the workmen. Meanwhile, soldiers dug boyaux, zigzag trenches that connected each parallel to its previous lateral trench. These served as communications trenches. Each type of trench, whether parallel or boyaux, contained the following parts: "a ditch, or trench, of uniform depth, and a parapet of uniform height, formed of earth taken from the trench, thrown up toward the work attacked." It fell to the engineer, with his specialized knowledge, to chart a path across no-man's-land that made the best possible use of terrain and to ensure that each soldier, typically sans engineering training, was able to dig his section correctly.[34]

In order to aid soldiers in the construction of parallels and boyaux, engineers first drove stakes outlining the direction of the trench and then connected the stakes with either rope or tape, thus illuminating the course of the proposed trench. Then soldiers spaced equidistantly, under the supervision of engineers, excavated trenches of uniform depth and width. The dirt from these was tossed toward the enemy so as to make an earthen parapet. In this way the besiegers established the first and second parallels, at specified distances from the enemy—the second closer than the first—along with their connecting, zigzag boyaux trenches.[35]

As the besiegers thus approached the defenders atop their defensive works, batteries of artillery were to be established along the way to provide covering fire and batter the enemy's works. It was to be expected that the soldiers and engineers would often conduct these different steps simultaneously. For example, while one group engaged in digging the first parallel, another might excavate the boyaux that would connect this parallel with the second parallel closer to the enemy works. But a difference existed. Those digging the second parallel, now exposed to enemy grapeshot, had to dig behind gabions, intricately woven wicker baskets filled with earth.[36]

With the second parallel now established and connected with the first farther to the rear, a specialized excavation crew called sappers took over. Sappers then proceeded to dig a sap (a trench that used gabions) toward the enemy. While the sappers excavated the sap, they crept forward under the protection of a sap roller, a larger version of a gabion placed on its side, lined with fascines (tight bundles of sticks), and rolled toward the enemy as the excavators dug forward, providing continuous cover from the defenders' fire. While the sappers inched forward, shorter half parallels were dug between the second and third parallels, the latter being established after the sappers reached within sixty yards of the enemy's works.[37]

At this point, the attacking general needed to make a decision: either to attempt to storm the enemy works or to adopt the more patient method of gradual approach with the ultimate goal of sinking a mine under the opposition's fortification. The first promised a quick, though costly, result, but the second, slower and more methodical, was most likely to bear fruit. Either way, at this point, Mahan instructed engineers to erect stone mortar batteries designed to lob projectiles over the enemy's parapets in hopes of softening up the defenders. Conversely, if the investing general decided to go for the sure thing, the gradual approach, a few more steps were required. The sappers had to keep on digging until they reached within thirty yards of the enemy and then dig a two-pronged fork with the interior acute angle situated directly across from the tip of the enemy's salient angle. Here, they raised mounds of dirt called trench cavaliers, designed to provide the attacker with artificial high ground from which to direct plunging fire on the defenders and drive them from the covered way, a step for defending infantrymen excavated into the front face of the ditch that composed the outermost part of the enemy's defenses. Once the defenders fled, sappers continued to dig an arc right up against the enemy glacis, the sloping ground that led up to the covered way. This trench hugged the extreme tip of the salient. This was called "crowning the covered way." Only then could the besiegers begin to sink a mine.[38]

Mining was perhaps the most complicated step in siege warfare. It required digging a tunnel on a descending slope underneath the enemy's fortifications. Depending on the stability of the soil, the besiegers might have to shore up the tunnel with wooden frameworks and linings in order to prevent collapse. This process was called "descent of the ditch." Once the sappers had dug the tunnel to its desired length, so that its end was directly under the defenders' fortifications, they dug galleries, or side tunnels, on either side and packed them with explosives. Engineers did not conduct this step haphazardly. Cadets learned to use equations that took into account different soil types in order to obtain the optimal breach in the defenses when the mine exploded. Once the engineer ordered the mine fired, soldiers, who had previously assembled in the trenches leading to the gallery, rushed into the breach and attempted to secure a lodgment that they or their comrades might be able to exploit further. If it all worked, the besieger took the enemy fortification.[39]

Careful analysis of period West Point engineering texts suggests several themes. First, military engineering, as taught at the Academy, was heavily rooted in French military theory. Second, building strong permanent fortifications to protect the nation trumped instruction on reducing enemy fieldworks and fortifications. Finally, American military engineering instruction on the eve of the Civil War was detailed and sophisticated, requiring intricate knowledge and specialization.

Yet although the institution instructed all students in civil and military engineering, only a few would obtain the ultimate prize, a commission into the prestigious Corps of Engineers. Many strove to attain this goal in order to prepare themselves for profitable civilian careers or to gain cushy, better-paying military assignments. James B. McPherson of the Army of the Tennessee, Seventeenth Corps commander at Vicksburg, taught sections on field fortifications and engineering drawings at West Point during the late 1850s. While a cadet at the Academy, a few years before, McPherson commented, "I have . . . concluded to go into the Corps of Engineers as I will have better pay, very good stations and, if I chose to resign after being in the service sometime I can get into more profitable business in all probability than if I went into any other Corps in the Army." West Point during the antebellum period was a technical school. The best and brightest, who scored the highest over their time at the Point, became engineers. The second-best group entered the artillery, while those considered below average became either cavalry or infantry officers. Nevertheless, as one historian astutely notes, "although the majority of each graduating class was destined for the line army, all cadets received an engineering education just the same." Thus cadets, despite their standing, aspirations, and future assignments, received an education that exposed them to the principles of military engineering.[40]

With Mahan's courses emphasizing the theoretical nature of fortification and fieldwork design, there was a need for a separate emphasis on practical military engineering. Prior to 1842 the all-encompassing Department of Engineering (which also taught military science classes) provided instruction in practical military engineering. During the summer of 1842 the Academy appointed Captain A. J. Swift of the Corps of Engineers to head up a new Department of Practical Military Engineering. First classmen, in their final year at the Academy, studied this discipline. The origins of this particular West Point department remain muddy. According to *The Centennial of the United States Military Academy at West Point*, Swift's course signaled its origins. Meanwhile, West Point historian James L. Morrison Jr. states that Joseph Totten taught the first class in practical military engineering at the Academy in 1851. Regardless of who pioneered the first practical engineering class at West Point, the fact remains that Mahan's courses, though exemplary when explaining fortification and fieldwork theory, left something to be desired when it came to the practical aspects of military engineering. In short, cadets needed hands-on instruction that supplemented theoretical classroom principles. As a result, due in large part to the creation of the Department of Practical Military Engineering, cadets, during their fourth and final year at the Academy, participated in field exercises that emphasized skills such as surveying positions, outlining traces for fieldworks, and commanding work details.[41]

One of the most prominent engineers to serve as an instructor in this new department between 1858 and 1861 was James C. Duane. Duane, who graduated near the top of his West Point class in 1848, did the Academy unprecedented service when he compiled the *Manual for Engineer Troops*. This manual, an English translation and synthesis of earlier British and French manuals, provided instruction in the minutiae of siege warfare. Under Duane's instruction, cadets learned specialized skills such as weaving gabions, launching full saps, and mining enemy fortifications. Interestingly, both Mahan's and Duane's reliance on European sources suggests that the USMA's engineering departments, although small, kept pace with their European counterparts.[42]

The practical engineering program provided hands-on experience, reinforcing what students learned in the classroom. Cyrus B. Comstock often recorded his experiences in practical engineering during his last year as a cadet. During their senior year at the institution, cadets spent substantial time conducting fieldwork in order to learn the details of siege warfare. Just below the cemetery, cadets gathered and received instruction in how to construct fascines and gabions, both of which were used to shore up trench walls and saps, and how to construct sap rollers. After cadets mastered these minor skills, they proceeded to the Washington Valley, where they engaged in simulated siege operations, including "experiments on different materials for embrasures," mounting siege guns, and observing the correct procedures for outlining and digging parallels and boyaux. In short, the marriage of classroom theory and practical hands-on experience was meant to ensure that all cadets exited West Point with at least a reasonable competence in siege operations.[43]

Despite the fact that West Point had improved considerably since its founding in 1802, problems still existed. The institution's emphasis on mathematics and engineering came at a price. While students graduated with top-notch engineering training, those pegged for artillery, cavalry, or infantry service were at a disadvantage. For example, cadets trained on dated equipment and tended to report to their first assignments ill prepared. In short, West Point trained engineers first and soldiers second.[44]

In order to correct deficiencies in military training, Secretary of War Jefferson Davis in 1854 authorized the creation of a five-year program. Adding another year to the curriculum would, in theory, allow the incorporation of more humanities and military courses that might correct the overemphasis on engineering and mathematics. This, however, did not bear fruit, and efforts to deviate from the institution's engineering focus met with limited success. Although expansion of the five-year program witnessed such developments as the introduction of William J. Hardee's new tactics manual, West Point remained an engineering school.[45]

Grant's professional engineers, as well as some of his officers, were graduates of the United States Military Academy, the nation's premier engineering institution. Indeed, the USMA sported one of the finest engineering departments in the world. Although the Academy's overall instruction in military strategy and tactics was lacking, its engineering curriculum was top-notch. Under the care of professors such as Dennis Hart Mahan and James C. Duane, the engineering program at West Point flourished. Cadets both received training in the theoretical aspects of siege warfare and became masters of the hands-on minutiae necessary to implement a successful siege. Thus, those officers in the Union army fronting the rebel defenses outside of Vicksburg in May 1863 who had received exposure to the engineering curriculum at West Point were more than adequately prepared to implement a scientific siege and reduce the Gibraltar of the Confederacy.

2. America's Early Sieges

P rior to the Civil War, the U.S. Army had experienced limited opportunities to besiege its foes. The first American involvement in offensive siege warfare came at Yorktown during the American Revolution. After rough campaigning in the southern colonies, British general Charles Cornwallis moved north into Virginia, eventually encamping on the Yorktown Peninsula in the Chesapeake Bay. This decision proved the undoing of the British army in North America once Continental army commander George Washington capitalized on this mistake. Washington convinced his French allies that they could trap Cornwallis at Yorktown. A French fleet blocked relief by the British navy while a combined Franco-American force approached the unfinished line of entrenchments Cornwallis had established on the landward side of Yorktown. By early October 1781, with British communication and supply cut off, French and American armies began conducting offensive siege operations against the beleaguered redcoats inside Yorktown.[1]

After settling in outside of Yorktown, the Continentals opened the trenches, commencing zigzags, and broke ground on the first parallel on October 6 approximately six hundred yards from the British line of works. The parallel faced the British fortifications and stretched about four thousand feet. Continental soldier Joseph Plum Martin recorded the early phase of the siege. "We now began to make preparations for laying close siege to the enemy," Martin wrote. "We had holed him, and nothing remained but to dig him out." "Every precaution" was made "to prevent his escape."[2]

Approximately one-third of the American investing army worked in the trenches. Officers and engineers marked the outline of the trenches using strips of wood and supervised the manual labor of the Continental soldiers who worked alongside the sappers and miners. When their labor was finished, redoubts anchored both sides of the line and batteries had been established. From these positions the French artillerists, better schooled in their trade than the Americans, achieved fire superiority and provided adequate cover for the next round of work parties. The accurate and devastating French gunnery forced the British to withdraw their artillery from their embrasures during the daytime.[3]

By October 11 the American forces, occupying the right of the siege line, commenced work on the second parallel approximately three hundred yards from the British earthworks. Under the guard of Continental pickets and suppressing fire of American artillery, workers completed the second parallel after assaulting and capturing two British redoubts that obstructed their path on October 14. On that day, after the sappers and miners cleared paths through the artificial obstructions that the British had placed in order to thwart a direct assault, the signal was given for the assembled Continentals to make their attack, and the Americans successfully stormed the two re-doubts. After incorporating these two redoubts into the American parallel, the Continentals prepared their position as a stepping-off point for a final assault against the main British fortifications. With the Americans and French closing in, Cornwallis attempted to escape. On the night of October 15, the British general attempted to skulk away to Gloucester on the opposite side of the York River. Poor weather made escape futile, forcing Cornwallis to seek peace terms with Washington, and on October 19, 1781, Cornwallis officially surrendered Yorktown to Washington.[4]

The next time the United States dabbled in offensive siege warfare was during the Mexican War. Although the U.S. military had achieved a series of successes early in the war, the Mexican government continued to rebuff American peace overtures. As a result, during the summer of 1846, U.S. president James K. Polk began thinking forward to another expedition that would force Mexico's hand at the peace table. In order to achieve his war aims, Polk believed that the United States should take Mexico City. The first step toward that goal would be to capture the Gulf Coast port city of Vera Cruz, with its impressive permanent fortifications. Polk delegated responsibility for planning this operation to his most talented subordinate, Major General Winfield Scott. Scott's logistical planning of the amphibious assault so impressed Secretary of War William Marcy and the rest of the cabinet that Polk, though concerned about transforming Scott into a potential political rival, gave Old Fuss and Feathers command of the entire operation.[5]

After painstakingly consolidating his men and necessary siege materials, Scott sent his first wave of troops, riding in specially built low-draft landing craft, to land on the beaches south of Vera Cruz on March 9, 1847. Believing that Scott's first wave outnumbered his garrison, Mexican general Juan Morales allowed the American forces to land virtually unopposed. After the initial landing party secured the beaches, the shallow-draft crafts continued to ferry more U.S. troops to shore. Overall the operation, which ultimately placed between eighty-six hundred and ten thousand American troops on the beaches by day's end, proved a textbook amphibious assault.[6]

Yet Scott's task had just begun; he still needed to reduce Vera Cruz, whose masonry walls, though deteriorating and containing dated artillery pieces, held a garrison of 3,360 Mexican troops. Complicating matters, the Mexican fortress of San Juan de Ulúa, built on the Gallega Reef just northeast of the seaward side of Vera Cruz, protected the city's harbor. Desiring the fewest possible casualties, Scott, after conferring with his most trusted staff officers, a group dubbed the "little cabinet," decided on March 10 to invest Vera Cruz and commence siege operations. Scott, who earned his laurels during the War of 1812, did not attend the United States Military Academy at West Point. Although Scott issued the order to reduce Vera Cruz via siege, overseeing the details of the operation was the work of reliable subordinates who had graduated near the top of their USMA classes and received commissions as engineers. These men included Captain Robert E. Lee (class of 1829) and Lieutenant George B. McClellan (class of 1846). McClellan and Lee were part of an elite team of ten engineering officers traveling with the army who inherited the responsibility of reducing Vera Cruz.[7]

Landing south of Vera Cruz, American troops slogged across the sandy and broken terrain to take up their positions around the inland sides of the city. By March 13 the investment line was complete. Meanwhile, engineers such as Lee and McClellan ventured into the dangerous no-man's-land between the lines in order to reconnoiter the best positions for the placement of artillery. On one such scouting endeavor, McClellan caught the eye of his superior, Colonel Joseph Totten, when he and engineer officer Lieutenant Gustavus W. Smith located and destroyed the aqueduct that supplied Vera Cruz.[8]

Engineers proceeded to oversee the details of offensive siege warfare, and by March 18 Colonel Totten, the commanding engineer of the army, had ordered McClellan to organize the engineers' depot then located on the beach and containing enough tools to outfit a two-hundred-man working party.

McClellan, implementing techniques learned in his West Point engineering courses and practical engineering classes, the latter of which emphasized field experience, proceeded to arrange "the tools for [the] working party . . . on the beach in parallel rows of tools for 20 men each and about four feet apart, so that they might take up the least possible space. Each man was provided with a shovel and either a pick, axe, or hatchets. . . . The party was conducted in one rank, by the right flank." With such attention to detail, engineer officers like McClellan used their West Point training to ensure that the siege of Vera Cruz proceeded in a timely and efficient manner.[9]

Vera Cruz, however, was not Scott's primary goal but rather a stepping-stone for his campaign inland against Mexico City. As a result, he wanted to bring about Vera Cruz's capitulation quickly in order to move on to bigger and better things. Also forcing his hand was the fact that his army could potentially face disaster should the siege become protracted. The threat of the approaching yellow fever season and the possibility of the arrival of a Mexican relief force also influenced Scott's actions. After posting skirmishers in the sandy dunes of no-man's-land in order to protect workers, engineer officers searched out the best positions for batteries. Interestingly, it appears that Scott did not intend to sink a mine below Vera Cruz. With the city's dated coral walls acting as the garrison's primary covering mass, Scott set out to breach the fortification with his artillery and then launch an assault through the breach, should the enemy not submit beforehand. As a result, the majority of the zigzags and parallels constructed during this siege were simple passageways connecting the different batteries as they crept forward, a peculiar by-the-book game of martial connect-the-dots.[10]

In contrast to what would be the case at Vicksburg some sixteen years later, the small size of Scott's army combined with the commander's efforts to limit the conduct of the siege to the southern sector of the investment line allowed the engineers to directly oversee the majority of the construction projects. Gustavus W. Smith, part of Company A, Corps of Engineers, described the hands-on spirit of Scott's engineers, writing that "the officers of the engineer company, including myself, were placed on general engineer service—supervising the construction of the siege works. All the engineer officers then with the army, except the Chief, were in regular turn detailed for that duty; each having some of the men of the engineer company to assist him." Thus, military professionals, schooled in the science of offensive siege craft, directed all aspects of the Vera Cruz siege.[11]

Meanwhile, the construction of Mortar Batteries No. 1 and 2 represented a microcosm of the professional conduct of engineering operations during the siege of Vera Cruz. According to McClellan, the engineers sited Battery No. 1 in order to mount mortars that would lob ordnance into the city. Detailing the construction of this particular battery, he wrote, "No. 1 was formed by cutting away the side of a hill, so that we had merely to form the epaulments [side walls] and bring the terreplein [floor of the battery] down to the proper level. The hill sheltering us from the direct fire of the Castle and Santiago." At the same time, engineers constructed Battery No. 2 a short distance to one side of No. 1 and connected the two emplacements with a parallel. Details are scarce regarding the construction of the platforms for these two guns, but engineers probably used the same technique as in other batteries at Vera Cruz, spiking down timber planks, carried over from the beachfront depot, and setting the guns atop them. After workers finished building these two batteries, they erected sandbag defensive walls, known as traverses, on the sides of the batteries in order to protect the artillerists from enfilade fire. Shortly thereafter, engineers oversaw the construction of magazines that would house powder and shell for the guns. The magazines were somewhere to the rear of the battery and propped open with a wooden framework. Concurrently, to the left of these batteries, on the other side of the railroad that led into Vera Cruz, Robert E. Lee and other engineer officers oversaw the construction of another battery.[12]

The engineer officers not only laid out the parameters of batteries but also micromanaged their excavation and construction. While overseeing the erection of Battery No. 3, McClellan directed every detail. "I employed four sets of men on the battery at the same time," he wrote, "one set throwing the earth from the rear of the parallel upon the berm, a second on the berm disposing of this earth thrown on the berm, a third set working at the rear of the battery, excavating toward the front (these threw the earth so as to form slight epaulments), and in rear." Meanwhile, "a fourth set were employed in making the excavations for the magazines. . . . At daylight the parapet was shot proof and the battery required about one hour's digging to finish it." Thus, under the watchful eyes of the engineer officers, batteries sprouted on the hills to the southeast of the city throughout the siege.[13]

But while the engineers employed their West Point skills efficiently, work on the batteries, zigzags, and parallels did not always come along smoothly. Sometimes the rowdy volunteer troops, who supplemented Scott's regulars, refused to engage in manual labor. At other times windstorms refilled trenches with sand shortly after their construction, causing delays. Nevertheless, operating under the cover of darkness, the work crews, with the engineers supervising, made steady progress, inching their zigzags forward and establishing batteries as they went.[14]

Problems with Scott's ordnance became apparent by late March. With mostly light field pieces, Scott's artillery proved incapable of battering large holes in the enemy's defenses. Without larger guns, Old Fuss and Feathers could not achieve his coveted breach. So on March 21 Scott met with Commodore David Connor and his soon-to-be replacement, Commodore Matthew Perry, and the three officers agreed that the army needed more firepower. In order to provide this, the navy loaned Scott six large thirty-two-pound naval guns. And so while the light batteries and Perry's ship-based guns provided covering fire, Lee supervised the construction of the emplacements that would support a battery known as the Naval Battery. This project was an engineering marvel. The task employed some fifteen hundred men who were charged with moving the guns. Soldiers erected tripods in order to distribute each cannon's load and safely crane the pieces from ship to shore. Once on land, Scott's men lifted the monster guns onto prefabricated wooden wheels designed to roll the ordnance to its designated battery position. Despite the convenience that the wheels provided, it still required two hundred men to move each gun to its appropriate spot on the siege line some seven hundred yards from the Mexican defenses. According to McClellan, the construction of this battery occurred under the nose of the beleaguered Mexican garrison on the night of March 19, 1847, and the heavy fire it unleashed on Vera Cruz was, in the words of Lieutenant McClellan, "fine music for us."[15]

With the large naval guns in place, bombardment began in earnest with the hope of achieving a breach in the Vera Cruz defenses. The battering continued to exact a heavy toll on the defenders as American engineers went on erecting batteries for additional field pieces. Yet each day brought Scott closer to yellow fever season and placed unrelenting strain on his supply lines. With his men succumbing to boredom and Morales not ready to surrender, Scott, on March 25, began to consider the prospects of ordering a costly assault. Yet the condition of the soldiers and civilians inside Vera Cruz proved much worse than Scott had imagined. Meanwhile, things inside the city looked grim as it became clear that outside help would not come to relieve the garrison. Much of the hardships that the Mexicans pent up in Vera Cruz endured came as a result of the work of the American engineers. On March 25 Colonel Totten ordered McClellan to report directly to General Scott. McClellan, upon arriving at Scott's headquarters, found him penning a report that gave credit for the successful siege to his "indefatigable Engineers." Meanwhile, the situation inside Vera Cruz continued to deteriorate. Not wanting to be the one to surrender directly to the Americans, the weak-kneed Morales handed over command of the city to his subordinate, Brigadier General José Landero. After several rounds of negotiations, Scott paroled the defenders and permitted the battered Mexican garrison to evacuate the city on March 29. Scott was now ready to move on Mexico City, completing a campaign that the victor of Waterloo, the Duke of Wellington, would later laud as "unsurpassed in military annals."[16]

Scott's prosecution of offensive siege operations against Vera Cruz illustrates a successful, traditional, textbook military siege. His relatively small army, roughly ten thousand men, operated efficiently under the direction of his West Point–trained engineers. Since Scott's army was small and confined its operations to the sector of the investment line just to the south of the city, the engineers were able to directly oversee the details of the operations and wage a by-the-book reduction of the enemy's fortifications, work that would have warmed the heart of Dennis Hart Mahan, then still teaching at the nation's premier engineering institution along the banks of the Hudson.

Shortly after the Mexican War, Company A, Corps of Engineers, returned to its home base at West Point, where the company continued to hone its practical engineering skills and found a new commander in McClellan. In September 1849, Walter G. Bartholomew, then serving in Company A, "the only Engineer Company in the U.S. service" and "composed of 100 young men who were picked principally from New England," described the unit's hands-on training. The company constructed mock fortifications, fashioning the gabions and fascines used in their construction. Once the defensive structure was complete, the engineering unit "approached them by sapping and mining as if they belonged to the enemy and blew them up." Then the unit would "level" what remained of the structure and build "some other kind."[17]

America's next experience with siege operations occurred in 1855 when then secretary of war Jefferson Davis (West Point class of 1828) ordered three U.S. Army officers to Europe in order to observe the latest military developments. With the Crimean War in full swing, Davis believed that studying this conflict would inform the United States as to the latest martial technology and techniques then being employed overseas. In order to conduct this mission, Davis selected an elite team of West Point graduates who had gone on to pursue successful military careers.

Desiring to make the research team as efficient as possible, Davis ordered each man to pay particular attention to his present area of specialization. To lead the team, the secretary of war chose Major Richard Delafield. After graduating at the head of the class of 1818, Delafield went on to pursue a successful career in the Corps of Engineers. It fell to Delafield to report on the state of military engineering in Europe. Next, Alfred Mordecai, first in his West Point class of 1823, drew the assignment of studying the latest developments in European ordnance. A member of the Corps of Engineers early in his career, Mordecai had later transferred to the Ordnance Corps. Finally, Davis settled on the youngest member of the commission, the bright and talented Mexican War engineer and West Point graduate of 1846 George B. McClellan. McClellan, though entering the Corps of Engineers upon graduation from the USMA and serving in that capacity during the Mexican War, had become a captain in the Second U.S. Cavalry Regiment in March 1855. As a result, McClellan's mission focused on European cavalry developments.[18]

After what was supposed to be a brief sojourn in Europe studying the latest in military science, the Delafield Commission planned on traveling to the most recent site of Crimean War conflict, the siege of Sebastopol, where British and French forces had trapped the Russian army in this Black Sea port city. After a series of diplomatic delays, the commission did not reach Sebastopol until after the Allies compelled the Russians to abandon the city. As a result, they did not witness the British and French siege operations firsthand but rather explored the labyrinth of trenches and artillery emplacements that had worked their way up to the Russian defenses. Throughout their observations, the differences from past sieges stood out to the American observers. For the first time, rifled artillery had been employed in large numbers, and the commission learned of this new weapon's devastating effects. The commissioners also recorded the increased use of rifle-muskets during the siege. The new infantry weapon, which loaded as quickly as a musket but fired as accurately as a rifle, appeared in large numbers for the first time during the Crimean War.[19]

One new innovation, lacking during both the siege of Vera Cruz and earlier Vaubanian sieges in Europe, was the rifle pit, a small shallow hole, with dirt thrown up to form a low embankment on the side facing the enemy, for a single marksmen or excavated wide enough to accommodate a few shooters. From the cover of these fieldworks, Russian soldiers, stationed in front of the main line of fortifications, fired on advancing Allied troops. Mahan later commented on the use of rifle pits at Sebastopol, writing that "the Russians . . . also used with great advantage small . . . pits for sharpshooters, in advance of their line, from which both the workmen at the trenches and the artillerists of the besiegers were greatly annoyed. These were in some cases connected and formed into a continuous trench of counter-approach, from which they were subsequently driven only after considerable loss to the besiegers." This new feature, the rifle pit, first used during the Crimean War, became a hallmark of later sieges, including Vicksburg. Marksmen placed in rifle pits offered new challenges that forced the Allies to adopt new tactics to methodically traverse no-man's-land. According to Mahan, in order to protect those digging the siege trenches around Sebastopol "from the annoyance of the sharp-shooters of the besieged," who were ensconced in their "advanced rifle pits" and managed to keep "up a very deadly and incessant fire," the attacking French created "companies of sharp-shooters, and placed them in rifle pits in advance of the ground on which they were working" so as "to keep down this fire."[20]

The traditional art of the siege appeared to have evolved. Rifle pits afforded cover against improvements in artillery and small arms. Meanwhile, nineteenth-century industrialization yielded larger armies, which in turn expanded the size of siege operations. In fact, according to one report, the British and the French dug a combined network of trenches spanning some fifty miles and "consumed about 80,000 gabions, 60,000 fascines, and over a million of sand-bags." Yet while some of the details of siege craft had changed, the overall concept smacked of the Vaubanian Enlightenment as zigzag and parallel trenches continued to provide sunken roads across no-man's-land. Nevertheless, the commission believed that siege warfare had entered into a new, more modern era.[21]

In truth, the commissioners, whose experiences and education had been rooted in the theories and principles of Enlightenment siege warfare, had for the first time glimpsed a new peculiar form of siege craft, one that blended older techniques with new technology, signaling a transitional period in such operations. Other military contemporaries, however, shared different opinions. Reflecting on the siege of Sebastopol in his later treatises, America's leading authority on military engineering, Dennis Hart Mahan, while acknowledging some of the new techniques employed, such as the widespread use of rifle pits, drew different conclusions than the commissioners had. According to Mahan, not only did the Russians add very little to the overall knowledge of fortifications, but the Allies too conducted a siege via traditional maxims. "From the very ample records of the siege of Sebastopol . . . no very marked deviations were made, either by the French or the English, from the methods of attack used in previous sieges," Mahan wrote. The Allies opened their initial parallels some seven hundred to a thousand yards from the Russian defenses, the traditional distances that Vauban had prescribed during the late seventeenth century. Battery construction remained relatively the same. In addition, "the French, after meeting with serious losses in the earlier stages of the siege . . . finally adopted" the traditional tactics for repelling enemy sorties. This involved "withdrawing the guards from the position of the trenches upon which the sortie was directed, with the view of assailing the enemy [as] soon as they [the Russians] had got within them." This time-tested practice "met with full success." The siege craft practiced at Sebastopol, as studied by Mahan along the banks of the Hudson River, appeared to have maintained the status quo.[22]

Mahan, after detailed discussion, concluded that the siege of Sebastopol stood closer to its earlier Enlightenment counterparts rather than foreshadowed the future conduct of trench warfare. In Mahan's analysis, the Allies implemented textbook techniques and deviated only when such variations were "imperatively demanded by the circumstances of the locality." While the Russian fortifications were not that remarkable, Mahan conceded that they were the only feature of the siege that deviated from previous methods. According to "Old Cobbon Sense," the "temporary character of the besieged works . . . having no permanent defences of any value, but only a line of earth works hastily thrown up," was the primary hallmark of the siege. Thus, in Mahan's opinion, the widespread use of temporary earthworks was the only noteworthy deviation from Vaubanian siege craft.[23]

Despite the lessons of the Crimean War and the siege of Sebastopol, the Union army contained a deficient engineering component at the beginning of the Civil War. This contingent, containing only 43 officers and some 100 enlisted men, reflected the overall unpreparedness of the Union forces in April 1861. In fact, the total paper strength of the Union army after the Confederates fired on Fort Sumter was only 16,400 men.[24]

President Abraham Lincoln, realizing the inadequate size of the U.S. Army, took action. On April 15, 1861, the day after Fort Sumter fell, the president, copying a precedent that George Washington had followed during the Whiskey Rebellion in 1791, issued a call for 75,000 ninety-day volunteers in order to quell the rebellion. Subsequently, on May 31, the president issued a second call for volunteers. This time, Lincoln requested 500,000 volunteers, a quota that was easily filled. Anticipating a short war, the president focused on raising infantry, artillery, and cavalry units. Congress did not make efforts to expand the Corps of Engineers as the Union army grew exponentially.[25]

With the Confederate victory at Bull Run on July 21, 1861, it became clear that the Civil War would not be ended in one dramatic battle. As a result, on August 3, 1861, Congress finally decided to bolster the Union's small engineering arm and increased the Corps of Engineers to 49 officers and 550 enlisted personnel. A second congressional bill authorized the commissioning of 6 more engineer officers. At this time, the Corps of Engineers and the Corps of Topographical Engineers existed as two separate groups within the Union army. In order to increase efficiency, Congress passed a bill on March 3, 1863, that allowed the Corps of Engineers to absorb the Corps of Topographical Engineers. This merger led to the formation of a new Corps of Engineers, which contained some 105 officers.[26]

With the Union and Confederate capitals just under one hundred miles apart, the eastern theater became the center ring of the Civil War. As a result, both Lincoln and Congress dumped most of their wartime resources into this seemingly important expanse in northern Virginia. Among these resources was the North's limited number of engineers. In fact, the most professional engineering component of the war, simply known as the Engineer Battalion, accompanied Major General George B. McClellan's newly formed Army of the Potomac. In order to augment the limited number of professional engineers in the Union army, Congress authorized the raising of volunteer engineer regiments during the summer of 1862, two of which, the Fifteenth and Fiftieth New York Volunteer Engineer Regiments, served with McClellan on the Peninsula. Not surprisingly, of the seven volunteer regiments created, four served in the eastern theater, with two being directly attached to the Army of the Potomac. Only one regiment, the First Missouri Engineers (also known as the Engineer Regiment of the West), served with Major General Ulysses S. Grant's victorious Army of the Tennessee at Vicksburg. Thus, when McClellan embarked on his Peninsula Campaign in March 1862, he brought with him the largest concentration of engineering troops of any of the Union's serving field armies.[27]

Between the Mexican War and 1861, American study of siege craft remained limited to theory and observation, but that changed with the outbreak of the Civil War. In the spring of 1862 McClellan landed his 120,000-man Army of the Potomac at Fort Monroe on the tip of the Yorktown Peninsula, from whence he planned to advance northwestward up the Peninsula formed by the York and James Rivers toward the Confederate capital at Richmond.[28]

In his path stood several lines of semipermanent Confederate fortifications that bisected the Peninsula. These earthworks have been dubbed "semipermanent" because they contained characteristics of permanent fortifications and temporary field fortifications. Prior to and during the landing phase of McClellan's operation, the Confederates had been building a series of field fortifications and earthworks running across the Peninsula roughly from northeast to southwest. With only eleven thousand Confederates reporting for duty as of April 5, Major General John Magruder, then in charge of Confederate forces on the Peninsula, deemed the first defensive line closest to McClellan's advancing army, the Poquosin River Line, untenable and retreated northwestward to the more formidable Warwick Line. Although the renowned Confederate general Edward Porter Alexander would later in his memoirs characterize these earthworks as "mere ditches with dirt thrown out in front . . . in many places nearly filled with water . . . [forcing] the troops . . . to sit & stand day & night," the line was actually formidable. It sported semipermanent fieldworks around Yorktown that extended southwest after arching around the city. As the fieldworks continued in the direction of the James River, they hugged the Warwick River, which the Confederates were able to flood by improving several preexisting dams. The river thereby created a type of moat just in front of their defensive line.[29]

Luckily for McClellan, his army contained the finest engineering component of any field army during the entire course of the war. It not only sported three official engineer companies (the U.S. Engineer Battalion under West Point professor of practical engineering Captain James C. Duane) but also included the Fifteenth and Fiftieth New York Volunteers, regiments "which contained an unusual number of sailors and mechanics in their ranks." Some fourteen officers presided over McClellan's engineering arm, which initially fell under the overall command of Colonel B. S. Alexander, and included the officers of the volunteer engineer regiments Colonel John McLeod Murphy (Fifteenth New York) and Colonel Charles P. Stewart (Fiftieth New York). At their disposal was the Army of the Potomac's engineering train, which contained materials for bridge building and thirty wagons of other engineering equipment.[30]

Despite McClellan's numerical superiority, he moved at a glacial pace up the Peninsula, allowing the Confederates to reinforce their position. McClellan interpreted intelligence reports in early April to credit the Confederates on the Warwick Line with forty thousand men, soon reinforced to about one hundred thousand. Convinced he faced overwhelming odds, McClellan charted a cautious course up the Peninsula. In truth, however, even after the arrival of Confederate general Joseph E. Johnston's Army of Northern Virginia in the Peninsula fortifications, Confederate forces still numbered only about fifty-six thousand men, roughly half of McClellan's opposing force. A sharp decisive attack by McClellan against the Warwick Line, before Johnston's reinforcements had arrived and before the Confederates were able to finish beefing up their fieldworks, probably would have prevented the quasi-siege that ensued.[31]

Believing himself outnumbered and facing insurmountable fieldworks, McClellan decided to undertake a quasi-siege in mid-April 1862. Although many have described McClellan's efforts against Yorktown as a siege, the term "quasi-siege" best describes McClellan's operations in front of the Warwick Line and, more specifically, in the sector fronting Yorktown. According to historian Earl J. Hess, McClellan himself misused the term "siege" in his description of operations outside Yorktown. Rather than engage in protracted siege operations, Little Mac simply desired to plant his heavy artillery at advantageous positions in order to create breaches in the Warwick Line. This mislabeling was common throughout the Civil War, with contemporaries often calling any action involving earthworks outside of cities a siege. According to Mahan, a siege by definition required cutting the enemy's line of communications "and attacking by regular approaches." Since McClellan never accomplished the former and attempted not to rely on the latter, the operations conducted outside the Warwick Line are best classified as a quasi-siege.[32]

In some ways, it appeared as though McClellan wanted a replay of the successful Vera Cruz siege, in effect relying on artillery superiority to implement a breach. Despite forfeiting his early opportunity to sweep over the Confederate defenses, once implementing siege tactics was decided on, the Army of the Potomac prosecuted a professional siege-type offensive rooted in the latest military principles. Engineers spotted adequate places for artillery and supervised the construction of connecting trenches between them. Meanwhile, engineers directed soldiers in building corduroy roads in order to transport their enormous siege artillery from transport ships to gun emplacements. Even McClellan himself visited the lines and checked on the status of operations. On spotting deficiencies in the state of the siege craft, he appointed Fifth Corps commanding general Fitz John Porter "Director of the Siege," thereby centralizing authority over construction and excavation. Prior to this decision, brigadier generals, operating under the title "General of the Trenches," supervised engineering efforts for their respective divisions. With the consolidation of command under Porter, Union efforts moved forward unhampered, and under unrelenting pressure, Johnston decided to evacuate the Warwick Line on May 3.[33]

With such careful oversight and attention to detail, it would be false to accuse McClellan of incompetence in conducting the quasi-siege of Yorktown. His experience as a West Point–trained engineer, active participant at Vera Cruz, and observer at Sebastopol ensured that Little Mac implemented textbook siege tactics. Work proceeded under the watch of professionally trained engineers who had access to a well-supplied siege train. In fact, had the quasi-siege of Yorktown been an actual siege, McClellan would merit high marks for his attention to detail and organizational abilities in conducting it. Where McClellan is open to criticism, however, is in his failure to act decisively during the early stages of the Peninsula Campaign. Had McClellan not submitted to faulty intelligence and to his tendency of overcaution, he might have been able to force his way through the Warwick Line while the defenses proved incomplete and undermanned, thereby bypassing the quasi-siege that ensued. Nevertheless, the quasi-siege of Yorktown, like the previous sieges that occurred throughout American history up until that time, bolstered the observation that the U.S. Army contained an intimate knowledge of siege craft via firsthand experience on the eve of the Vicksburg Campaign.[34]

Examining America's involvement in siege warfare from Yorktown through the Peninsula highlights the state of military engineering on the eve of the Vicksburg siege. The American effort outside of Yorktown during the Revolutionary War, prosecuted with the aid of the French, smacked of Vauban. Meanwhile, Scott's siege of Vera Cruz illustrated how, during any siege, the specialized knowledge of the engineer magnified his rank. Lieutenants and captains, typically overlooked during regular operations, became the primary consultants for waging a successful siege. This particular siege highlights the importance and sophistication of West Point engineering firsthand. Men such as McClellan and Lee, graduates of the Academy and educated in both the broader aspects of siege craft and siege minutiae, were capable of transforming theory into practice. The siege of Vera Cruz underlines the importance of professionals in waging offensive siege warfare and suggests that armies that lacked such trained engineers would have to find ways to blend professional knowledge with the common soldiers' improvisation in order to overcome obstacles.

Later, during the middle of the nineteenth century, the Delafield Commission's firsthand observations of the immediate aftermath of the siege of Sebastopol suggested a shift in the nature of siege warfare. The commissioners believed that the new technology used during the siege and the overwhelming scale of the event signaled a more modern, larger, and exceedingly violent form of siege craft. On the other hand, Mahan's post-Crimea analytical writing tended to downplay Sebastopol's modernity. The truth exists in the middle. In effect, the siege of Sebastopol, like the later siege of Vicksburg, was both a blending of older Vaubanian siege craft with more modern technological adaptations magnified by the nature of warfare during the years following the Industrial Revolution.

Finally, McClellan's quasi-siege on the Peninsula offered a glimpse into the nature of Civil War siege craft that Grant's men would employ at Vicksburg on a much larger scale. Little Mac's quasi-siege, though the result of his overcaution, exemplified the harmonious blend of new technology, modern war, and Vaubanian dogma that Vicksburg demonstrated. In addition, McClellan's quasi-siege, similar to the siege of Vera Cruz, depended on a team of professionally trained military engineers proportionate to the size of the besieging army. As a result, both sieges tended to be more by-the-book affairs. By contrast, an army that was short of engineers would have to adapt and blend theory with improvisation.

3. *Preparing to Dig Them Out*

The failure of the May 22 assault at Vicksburg completely changed the situation for the Army of the Tennessee. With the hope of a quick victory dissipating by the evening of May 22, Union troops began to make preparations for a long and arduous siege. One Illinois soldier, reflecting on this change, later recalled, "It now became very evident that the works at Vicksburg could not be carried by storm. . . . There was but one resource left, and that was to dig them out. . . . Henceforth, spades would be trumps." This feeling of change permeated the Union line. As one member of the Sixty-Eighth Ohio later wrote, "We began to settle down to a new life." With protracted siege warfare now a reality, preparations needed to be made before the Army of the Tennessee could "Attack by Regular Approaches" and "Open the Trenches."[1]

This first phase of the siege, beginning with the decision to besiege the enemy and ending just before soldiers broke ground on the first approaches dug toward the Confederate defenses, might best be described as one of laborious preparations. After the investment of Vicksburg, troops began to establish and strengthen their line of circumvallation with artillery and connecting rifle pits while maintaining their line of supply and communications and establishing their camps in the ravines behind the line of circumvallation, concealed from Confederate artillery projectiles and rifle fire. For the most part, West Point doctrine pertaining to the conduct of siege craft carried the day, with improvisation being limited to the micro-aspects of siege warfare. Yet even with these limited initial tasks, "the work to be done," as Major General Ulysses S. Grant put it, "was very great." Grant, a graduate in the West Point class of 1843 and familiar with Mahanian doctrine, knew that he must default to a protracted siege. In order to maintain clarity, it is best to break down this broader phase of the Vicksburg siege into two subphases. The first, considered in this chapter, involved the reorganization of the Army of the Tennessee from a field army of maneuver into an army of investment. The second, examined in the next chapter, encompassed the construction of the line of circumvallation designed to trap the Confederates inside Vicksburg.[2]

The investment of Vicksburg—the process of preventing Confederate escape and cutting off the garrison's supplies and communication—began on May 19. At this early date, the Union could prosecute only a partial investment of the line. With only three corps present by May 22, totaling approximately thirty thousand men, Grant could invest only the northern and central parts of the line. Major General William T. Sherman's Fifteenth Corps fell in on the north, and Major General James B. McPherson's Seventeenth Corps guarded the middle. With Chickasaw Bayou lying just to the north of Vicksburg, where it emptied into the Yazoo River and acted as a supply depot for Grant's army, investing the northern segment of the city was paramount. That was why Grant gave it to Sherman, his most trusted subordinate. Grant charged Major General John A. McClernand's Thirteenth Corps with investing the southern portion of the line. But even with the Army of the Tennessee's three corps in position, want of troops made complete investment impossible. A large gap in the line still existed to the south of Vicksburg.[3]

Meanwhile, Admiral David Dixon Porter's Mississippi squadron, upon learning that the Army of the Tennessee was driving the Confederates back into Vicksburg's defenses, moved in to support Grant's army. According to Porter, "As soon as the Army appeared, driving the Confederates into Vicksburg, all the gun-boats below the city were ordered up to attack the batteries, which fire was kept up for three hours." After Sherman's small preliminary assault on May 19 failed, Porter's gunboats, under the cover of darkness, bombarded Vicksburg that very night. Shortly thereafter, on May 22, Grant requested that Porter shell Vicksburg's river defenses in order to take pressure off of the army's eastern landward assault. The navy fought valiantly. According to Porter, "The gun-boats had done what was required of them by General Grant, and more." While Grant had initially only requested "an hour's attack to annoy the garrison, while his Army assaulted from the rear," the navy stretched is ammunition supply and poured on fire for two and a half hours. After the botched attack, Porter continued to assist the army and invested Vicksburg from the west, thereby establishing

Grant's line of circumvallation on the city's river side. While the Army of the Tennessee's investment line did not yet extend all the way to the river below Vicksburg, the inhospitable terrain to the city's south, combined with the assistance of Porter's gunboats, hemmed the Confederates into their Gibraltar. Confederate general John C. Pemberton was trapped. The function of the once mighty fortress Vicksburg quickly transformed. Originally hailed as a southern asset, the man-made sentinel of the Mississippi, it now became a Confederate liability. With Grant's strong investment beginning to tighten the noose around Pemberton, a tactical breakout appeared unlikely. Only a relief army could save the beleaguered garrison now.[4]

The Confederate landward defenses hugged approximately seven miles of ridges, stretching from the east bank of the Mississippi River to the north of Vicksburg, all the way around the eastern side of the city. Union troops, orced to curve their line concentrically around the Confederate defenses, needed to man a line of investment over fifteen miles long from Haines Bluff just north of the city to Warrenton to the south. According to the engineers traveling with the Army of the Tennessee, the investment of Vicksburg was not completed until Major General Francis J. Herron's division arrived on June 11. Thus, by the time the siege ended on July 4, the dispositions along the Union siege line, from north to south, consisted of Sherman's corps; McPherson's corps; McClernand's corps, later under the command of Major General E. O. C. Ord; Brigadier General Jacob Lauman's division, dispatched from the Sixteenth Corps; and General Herron's division, dispatched from the Army of the Frontier.[5]

Determining the order of operations for this phase of the siege, from the investment and subsequent establishment of the line of circumvallation to the opening of the trenches and attack by regular approaches, becomes difficult. According to Grant, "The first thing to do was to get artillery in batteries where they would occupy commanding positions; then establish the camps, under cover from the fire of the enemy but as near up as possible; and then construct rifle-pits and covered ways, to connect the entire command by the shortest route." But this statement, from Grant's memoirs, contradicts descriptions that he provided earlier in his reminiscences. In these earlier accounts he wrote that camps were established between May 19 and 20 while, at the same time, soldiers constructed roads to the rear of his investing army in order to connect the Yazoo River to Chickasaw Bayou. Meanwhile, Captain Frank Swigart of the Forty-Sixth Indiana, who, like Grant, recorded

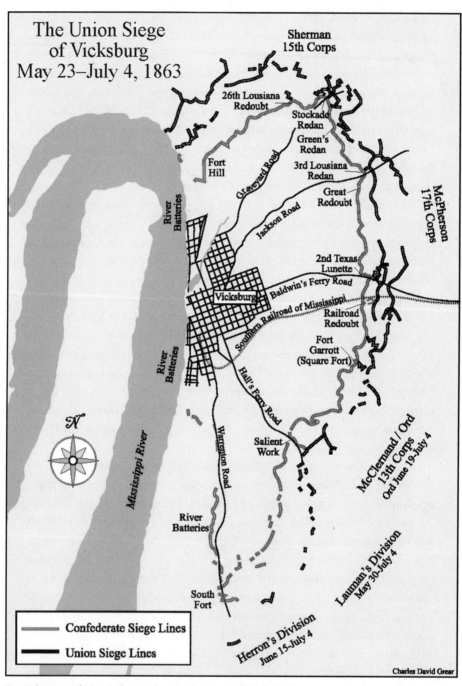

The Union Siege
of Vicksburg
May 23–July 4, 1863

Sherman
15th Corps

26th Lousiana
Redoubt

Stockade
Redan

Green's
Redan

3rd Lousiana
Redan

Great
Redoubt

Fort
Hill

Graveyard Road

Jackson Road

River
Batteries

McPherson
17th Corps

2nd Texas
Lunette

Baldwin's Ferry Road

Vicksburg

Southern Railroad of Mississippi

Railroad
Redoubt

Fort
Garrott
(Square Fort)

River
Batteries

N

Hall's Ferry Road

Mississippi River

Warrenton Road

Salient
Work

McClemand / Ord
13th Corps
Ord June 19–July 4

River
Batteries

Lauman's Division
May 30–July 4

South
Fort

Confederate Siege Lines
Union Siege Lines

Herron's Division
June 15–July 4

Charles David Grear

Distribution of Union forces during the siege of Vicksburg.

his reminiscences after the war, wrote that after May 22, "the siege began in earnest, Rifle-pits were dug for the protection of infantry in front, and earthworks were thrown up for the artillery in the rear, while camps were prepared for men and horses in the hollows or ravines."[6]

The reason for the discrepancy in the order of operations is that these events occurred simultaneously before Union soldiers commenced zigzag approaches toward the Confederate defenses. In Dennis Hart Mahan's theoretical siege model, which existed in an intellectual vacuum, the attacking army arrived, invested the enemy, and then commenced siege operations. But the May 22 assault slightly reconfigured the steps of the siege outside of Vicksburg. With the investment in place before the assault, sites for artillery positions, rough investment lines, and camps had already been chosen. What remained after the attack failed was to make these positions more permanent for the upcoming siege. Despite this minor deviation from West Point doctrine, Union engineers prosecuted a Mahanian-style siege during this phase as the army, in Grant's words, engaged in work designed "to make our position as strong against the enemy as his was against us."[7]

Although Grant did not issue Special Orders No. 140, decreeing the reduction of Vicksburg via regular approaches, until May 25, the beginnings of the siege may be found on the evening of May 22 and the morning of May 23. After the failed assault, many troops simply dug shallow pits where they were in order to escape the hail of Confederate gunfire. Without a special order from Grant, it was left to corps commanders to decide the proper course of action. Sensing the next step, Sherman late on May 22 ordered Major General Francis P. Blair's division to hold its ground and prepare fieldworks in anticipation of a siege. Micromanaging the brigades, Sherman, a West Point graduate of the class of 1840 familiar with Mahan's teachings, ordered Brigadier General Hugh Ewing and Colonel Giles Smith to "construct in their front a rifle-pit or breast-height of logs, and lay out a covered road to the rear, to be constructed as soon as tools can be procured." Next, the meticulous Sherman ordered his artillery to maintain its present positions and begin stocking ammunition for the days to come. After making these arrangements, Sherman informed Grant, who had established his headquarters just in rear of the Fifteenth Corps on the northern part of the siege line, of his new dispositions and further explained the potential to commence a sap with the ultimate goal of undermining the Confederate works. As Sherman prepared to wage offensive siege warfare, Grant informed his superior, Major

General Henry W. Halleck, that, despite the failed assault, Vicksburg was "now completely invested" and could "only be taken by a siege."[8]

The next day, May 23, the true work of siege craft began. Despite the lack of a special order, Grant's headquarters began contacting corps commanders in order to prepare for siege operations. The need to coordinate the efforts of the entire army and to guard against any potential relief attempt by Confederate general Joseph E. Johnston forced Grant to delegate to his subordinates the responsibility of executing the siege. One of these subordinates was Thirteenth Corps commander John A. McClernand, a political general lacking West Point training. To McClernand, whose troops held the southern part of the line of investment, Grant wrote, "Hold all the ground you have acquired; get your batteries into position, and commence regular approaches toward the city." Over the next few days, the soldiers widened and extended once-shallow rifle pits to form trenches. They left in position and fortified the batteries that had supported the failed assault.[9]

Meanwhile, troops established their encampments in the ravines behind the line of circumvallation in order to shelter from Confederate small arms fire and artillery projectiles. In short, the siege began in earnest on May 23. Lieutenant Colonel James H. Wilson, a member of Grant's intimate staff, recorded the actual start date of the siege. Wilson, who graduated near the top of his West Point class of 1860, entered the army as a topographical engineer. Like McPherson, Wilson was assigned to serve on Grant's staff as an engineer in 1862 due to the lack of professionally trained engineers then serving in Grant's inner circle. On May 23, 1863, Wilson penned in his journal, "The troops rested to-day from the excessive fatigue of yesterday. There was little firing. The Preparations for siege works began."[10]

Meanwhile, Grant did not sit idle. He visited the siege lines and directed operations. Soldiers frequently recorded Grant sightings throughout the siege. As a captain of the Eighth Wisconsin, the famed Eagle Regiment, casually observed, "We see him [General Grant] every day as [common] as a private soldier—but he always seems to be thinking." While troops commenced siege operations on May 23, Grant, early that morning, visited Major General McPherson of the Seventeenth Corps and Brigadier General A. J. Smith of the Thirteenth Corps. The group proceeded up a shallow trench to the front where the Seventeenth Ohio Light Artillery had set up its guns. The three officers, all West Point graduates and familiar with Mahanian siege craft, began to survey the ground and discussed the situation aloud. Artilleryman

I. Richards overheard their conversation. "I heard them say, that there would have to be a great amount of work done, with the pick and shovel, [and] that they would have to run rifle pits[,] dig trenches and do undermining," Richards wrote. "They were calm and cheerful, and gave no sight of worry." Grant, as "he started away," attempted to bolster the midwesterners' confidence and hailed, "Boys keep in good spirits, for we will get Vicksburg and its army in a short time." So far, the siege of Vicksburg was off to a textbook start.[11]

The situation now congealed. Why Grant waited until May 25 to issue Special Orders No. 140 to his corps commanders remains unclear. This has led some contemporaries to conclude that the siege did not officially begin until May 26. Nevertheless, on May 25, Grant ordered each corps commander to begin "the work of reducing the enemy by regular approaches," adding, "Every advantage will be taken of the natural inequalities of the ground to gain positions from which to start mines, trenches, or advance batteries." While engineers serving on the staffs of their respective corps would direct the operations on their individual fronts, Grant held each corps commander responsible for the progress, or lack thereof, made in their own sectors. This yielded uneven results later during the siege. Sherman and McPherson, both West Point graduates, implemented macro-textbook theory from the beginning. Meanwhile, farther down the line, McClernand, a general who received his rank based on political connections rather than on his military pedigree, bungled during the first half of the siege. Although all three generals managed to construct adequate works that made up the line of circumvallation, the transition from hemming in the enemy to digging forward-advancing approach trenches was easier for Sherman and McPherson than it was for McClernand. But for now, all three corps commanders proved capable enough for this first phase of engineering operations. Realizing that the task at hand required the work of a professional taskmaster, Grant concluded that all corps commanders would defer to the army's chief engineer, Captain Frederick E. Prime, who would "have general superintendence of the whole work."[12]

Prime, born on September 24, 1829, displayed promise at an early age. Graduating at the top of his West Point class of 1850, he entered military service as an engineer and worked on different East Coast fortifications. When the Civil War broke out, Prime continued in the army. He contributed to the building of the elaborate defenses around Washington and even took part in the Battle of Bull Run. Shortly thereafter, Prime was transferred to the western theater, where he served as "Chief Engineer of the Departments of the Kentucky, of the Cumberland, and of the Ohio." During his tenure in the Department of the Ohio, Confederate soldiers captured Prime while the engineer conducted a reconnaissance just outside of Mill Spring, Kentucky. The rebels eventually released him, and he was reassigned to Grant's army during the spring of 1862. Prime then served with distinction in the Battle of Corinth, where he received a brevet promotion to the rank of major.[13]

Despite the can-do attitude of the Army of the Tennessee and its talented officer corps, this particular army sported a rather deficient engineer component. According to Grant, only four engineer officers traveled with the Army of the Tennessee. These included Prime, First Lieutenant Peter C. Hains, West Point class of 1861; Captain William L. B. Jenney, a graduate of the École Centrale des Arts et Manufactures in Paris in 1856; and Captain Andrew Hickenlooper, a prewar civil engineer and former artillery officer. The first two officers, Prime and Hains, were the only engineer officers traveling with the Army of the Tennessee officially detached from the Corps of Engineers, the former serving in the capacity of chief engineer while the latter operated under McClernand's Thirteenth Army Corps. Meanwhile, Jenney and Hickenlooper served as corps engineers, with the title Chief Engineer of the Corps, on the staffs of Sherman and McPherson respectively.[14]

Andrew Hickenlooper, the youngest of seven children, was born in either 1836 or 1837 in Hudson County, Ohio. His father, an engineer of public works and a contractor, specialized in bridge building and road construction, a profession that demanded long stretches of time away from home and decreed that young Andrew would spend the majority of his formative years in the care of his mother and sisters. With the senior Hickenlooper's work demanding constant movement, the family eventually moved to Cincinnati in 1843, after a brief stint in Circleville County, in order to join their father, who for some reason had changed his occupation and become an employee in a wire manufacturing plant.[15]

Hickenlooper, an ambitious youth, was never able to complete his education. While young Andrew attended St. Xavier's College and later Woodward College, the future Seventeenth Corps engineer left school when his brother Edward died in 1848. After Edward's passing, Andrew went to work in order to help support his family. Fortunately for the Hickenlooper family, Edward had built a strong relationship with his previous employers at the local newspaper, the *Dispatch*. Taking pity on the family, the owners of the *Dispatch* hired young Andrew as a "Mailing Editor," a fancy title for a messenger. Meanwhile, Hickenlooper Senior had become ensconced in his latest employment adventure with a Cincinnati insurance company. Though a kind man, he lacked business sense, spent whimsically, and often succumbed to the temptation of liquor. Moral weakness dictated that his contribution to the Hickenlooper household declined. This placed additional fiscal responsibility on young Andrew. Despite his father's irresponsibility, Andrew drew strength from his mother, "a refined Christian woman of religious instincts," and charted a course toward a successful career.[16]

Andrew Hickenlooper was not destined to become an engineer. In fact, little evidence exists suggesting that this was his preferred career. Despite Hickenlooper Senior's inability to hold a steady job, the father held high aspirations for his youngest son and encouraged him to become a lawyer, although this did not bear fruit. As a result, Andrew's father obtained a job for his sixteen-year-old son as a surveying "rodman" under Cincinnati's city civil engineer A. W. Gilbert, who was then managing the city's topographical survey. Andrew proved successful at his profession and managed to endure the rigors that nineteenth-century surveying demanded.[17]

Although forced to work, young Andrew never abandoned his education. He continued to attend "Night High School" and received tutoring in his new profession from the head topographical engineer of the survey, J. T. Hogan. Andrew eventually acquired enough skill to become a draftsman, a position that yielded a higher salary. But just as Andrew achieved some success, his world came tumbling down. In 1855 Samuel W. Irwin, the Democratic Party candidate for the post of city civil engineer, was elected and replaced Hickenlooper's supervisor, A. W. Gilbert. Despite Andrew's skill, Irwin removed him in order to give his position to one of his Democratic cronies. Fortunately for Andrew, his firing could not have come at a better time. As the despairing youth wandered down the Cincinnati streets, he bumped into his previous employer, Mr. Gilbert. Gilbert, sorry to hear of the boy's troubles, immediately hired Andrew to act as his assistant in his lucrative private surveying company. Hickenlooper served in this capacity until he accepted a position under R. G. Phillips, a surveyor the federal government had hired to conduct a survey of an Indian reservation located in Michigan. On returning to Cincinnati, Gilbert hired Hickenlooper again, but this time as a partner in the new firm Gilbert and Hickenlooper, Surveyors and Civil Engineers. In 1859 the city again elected Gilbert city civil engineer. Although the loyal Gilbert offered his

Captain Andrew Hickenlooper in a photograph dated 1861. Before becoming the chief engineer of the Seventeenth Army Corps, Hickenlooper served as captain of "Hickenlooper's Cincinnati Battery," later renamed the Fifth Ohio Independent Battery of Light Artillery. *Cincinnati Museum Center–Cincinnati History Library and Archives.*

partner the position of first assistant, Hickenlooper preferred to take the more prestigious job of city surveyor. When Hickenlooper's professional rivals, jealous of the prosperity of his business, campaigned to have the position of city surveyor eradicated, Hickenlooper continued to run the lucrative business that he and Gilbert had established.[18]

It was as the head of Gilbert and Hickenlooper, Surveyors and Civil Engineers, that Andrew presided when the Civil War broke out in 1861. After the Confederates fired on Fort Sumter, the Union hired Hickenlooper to conduct a survey and generate a subsequent map of the part of Kentucky just opposite his home city of Cincinnati. This project, however, did not pan out. Kentucky's insistence on neutrality forbade the survey, since its military mapmaking might place the Bluegrass State in a precarious position. During the spring and summer of 1861, Hickenlooper sought a direct role in the Civil War. Andrew, then about twenty-five years old, began to read up on military science and joined a local military unit dubbed the "Teachers Rifles." After Lincoln issued his call for five hundred thousand troops to enlist and fight against the Confederacy for either three years or for the duration of the war, Hickenlooper moved to form his own artillery battery. He declared himself battery captain and transformed his engineer office into a recruiting station. He obtained approval for a unit, originally dubbed "Hickenlooper's Cincinnati Battery," from Governor William Dennison. Union authorities soon renamed this unit the Fifth Ohio Independent Battery of Light Artillery.

Hickenlooper fought with distinction at Shiloh and during the subsequent siege of Corinth, where he served as chief of artillery for the Sixth Division. Hickenlooper would not enjoy this post for very long. With the Army of the Tennessee suffering a lack of experienced engineers, headquarters ordered Captain Hickenlooper to report to McPherson's headquarters, then in Bolivar, Tennessee, to serve as chief engineer on the corps commander's staff.[19]

A deficiency in the number of engineers was not new to the Army of the Tennessee as it prepared to lay siege to Vicksburg. In fact, Henry Halleck had dispatched Seventeenth Corps commander James McPherson to serve under Grant earlier in 1862, when McPherson was a lieutenant colonel of engineers in the regular army, in order to bolster the engineering capacity of Grant's army. It was not talent that the Army of the Tennessee's engineer contingent lacked but sheer numbers. As one engineer officer reported, "Thirty officers of engineers would have found full employment." The four whom Grant credits in his memoirs simply were not enough. The lack of engineers prompted Grant to order "that all officers who had graduated from West Point, where they had necessarily to study military engineering, should in addition to other duties assist in the work." While there is no efficient way to quantify exactly how many West Point–trained engineers stepped forward (see appendix), one famous anecdote tells of an Academy officer who stepped back. According to Grant, the chief commissary traveling with the army, a heavyset fellow, although a graduate of the USMA, informed Grant with chagrin that not only had he been a poor engineering student but "there was nothing in engineering that he was good for unless he would do for a sap-roller."[20]

Despite the commissary's quip, Grant's headquarters compiled a list of aides-de-camp and line officers who had been exposed to some degree of

Brigadier General Andrew Hickenlooper, postwar photograph. *Cincinnati Museum Center–Cincinnati History Library and Archives.*

engineering instruction and then distributed those men to the various head-quarters of the corps and divisions encamped outside Vicksburg. The lack of engineers ensured that even Grant himself, burdened with the function of the entire army, would have to step forward at times and supervise mundane engineering tasks. According to the official reports that the consecutive chief engineers submitted at the close of the campaign, the lack of engineers gave the siege "one of its peculiar characteristics." Chief engineers Prime and Cyrus B. Comstock reported:

> Over a line so extended and ground so rough as that which surrounds Vicksburg, only a general supervision was possible.... Many times, at different places, the work that should be done, and the way it should be done, depended on officers, or even on men, without either theoretical or practical knowledge of siege operations, and who had to rely upon their native good sense and ingenuity. Whether a battery was to be constructed by men who had never built one before, a sap-roller made by those who had never heard the name, or a ship's gun carriage to be built, it was done, and, after a few trials, was done well. But while stating the power of adaptation to circumstances and fertility of resources which our men possess in so high a degree . . . officers and men had to learn to be engineers while the siege was going on.[21]

The Army of the Tennessee, as it had thus far done on so many campaigns, was forced to make do. Eventually the army proved able to divide its engineering talents. Captain Prime served as chief engineer until June 27, when illness forced him to take leave of the siege. Captain Cyrus B. Comstock, transferred from the East, had arrived on June 15 and presided over McClernand's Thirteenth Corps front, which, at that time, included supervising the divisions of Lauman and Herron. With Prime's health in decline, Comstock then received a promotion and acted as chief engineer until the end of the siege. Meanwhile, Captain Miles D. McAlester replaced Comstock as head of his former sector on the southern part of the Vicksburg line. But although McAlester replaced Prime, First Lieutenant Peter C. Hains, one of the original two official members of the Corps of Engineers, continued to oversee the minutiae of siege craft on the Thirteenth Corps front.[22]

Meanwhile, headquarters shuffled Lieutenant Clemens C. Chaffee of the Ordnance Corps to Sherman's front, and a Lieutenant Patrick Hopkins of the Third Infantry served "with the chief engineer for a few days." At the same time, Union captains and aides-de-camp William L. B. Jenney, William Kossack, Henry C. Freeman, and Arnold Hoeppner "were assigned, respectively, to Sherman's corps and Lauman's and Herron's divisions, as engineer officers." Jenney, born in Fairhaven, Massachusetts, on September 25, 1832, was, like Hickenlooper, a civil engineer before the war. Jenney did not attend the United States Military Academy but received his early schooling at the Phillips Academy in Andover, Massachusetts, and later entered the Lawrence Scientific School at Harvard, transferring eventually to the École Centrale des Arts et Manufactures in Paris. While attending this institution he pursued studies in engineering and architecture. Young Jenney completed his education in 1856 and graduated this prestigious school on the heels of Gustave Eiffel, a graduate of the class of 1857 and future architect of the Eiffel Tower. He eventually became an engineer on Grant's staff and served at both Fort Donelson and Shiloh. By the time of the Vicksburg siege, he was the chief engineer of Sherman's Fifteenth Corps.[23]

Meanwhile, Freeman, originally from Newark, New Jersey, attended both Old Woodward College in Cincinnati and the Columbia School of Mines during the antebellum period. By the time of the Vicksburg siege, Freeman had been promoted to captain and served as the acting engineer officer of the Fourth Division, Sixteenth Army Corps (Lauman's division). In addition, Grant dispersed various aides-de-camp with some knowledge of engineering among Sherman's corps and the divisions of Herron and Lauman. Herron had been sent down from the Department of Missouri to bolster Grant's army during the siege, and Lauman had been dispatched from the Sixteenth Corps while its headquarters remained in west Tennessee. In fact, one of Grant's personal staff members, none other than Lieutenant Colonel James H. Wilson, provided informal supervision of some of the engineering activities on the Thirteenth Corps front, probably due to want of experienced engineers and Grant's distrust of McClernand, which grew to a crescendo after the May 22 assault.[24]

The Thirteenth Corps front would prove troublesome throughout the siege. The men of the Thirteenth Corps started the siege under a corps commander, McClernand, who lacked formal West Point engineering training. With First Lieutenant Hains in charge of the right wing of the Thirteenth Corps, McClernand, in an unexplained move, placed Private Frank Holcomb Mason in charge of engineering on the left flank. Mason authored his regiment's history after the war and commented upon the siege of Vicksburg. "Generals Sherman and McPherson were themselves educated engineers, and kept an intelligent supervision of their own operations," Mason wrote, "but McClernand knew nothing of such work." As a result, "the trenches of his right wing were in charge of a Lieutenant of Engineers, a graduate of the class of 1861 at West Point [Hains], and those of his left wing were managed by an enlisted man of the Forty-Second Ohio [Mason], who studied 'Mahan' and the work of McPherson's Engineers as the siege progressed."[25]

The mundane labor fell to pioneer companies attached to various divisions, hired African American laborers under the direction of the pioneers, and work details formed from the line infantry. Each brigade formed an ad hoc "Brigade Pioneer Corps," composed of fifteen to thirty pioneers, skilled mechanics or ax-men, complemented by anywhere from thirty to fifty paid African American laborers, under the command of a junior officer, typically either a lieutenant or captain, familiar with "knowledge of bridge and roadway construction." The only formal pioneer organizations serving with the Army of the Tennessee were the Second Battalion of Colonel Josiah W. Bissell's Engineer Regiment of the West and Captain William Franklin Patterson's Independent Kentucky Company of Engineers and Mechanics.[26]

Bissell formed the Engineer Regiment of the West during the summer and fall of 1861. According to Bissell, these men, recruited from Illinois, Missouri, and Iowa, were to "be, all of them, either mechanics, artisans, or persons accustomed to work as laborers under mechanics." Their duty was to be "chiefly consistent in building bridges, the mechanical work on fortifications, etc." When the entire regiment was finally gathered at St. Louis at the end of October, the regimental roll listed 907 enlisted men. Prior to the Vicksburg siege, Bissell's regiment gained experience at New Madrid and Island No. 10. Although they arrived too late to take part in the Battle of Corinth, Companies B and H participated in the construction of that city's defenses in October 1862, which "were soon declared impregnable." They also participated in the fighting at Holly Springs and engaged in various construction projects throughout the Vicksburg Campaign. Bissell's Engineer Regiment took part in many of the engineering tasks that became the hallmark of Grant's early Vicksburg Campaign. They explored and opened bayous, constructed bridges, and built batteries at Young's Point facing across the river toward Vicksburg. The majority of Bissell's men, however, would not take part in the actual siege. In April, Union higher-ups ordered six of the ten companies to Memphis, Tennessee, in order to open the Memphis and Charleston Railroad. After accomplishing this task, this contingent was sent to Pocohontas and stayed there from May 11 to October 3, 1863.[27]

The smaller of the Army of the Tennessee's pioneer units, Patterson's Independent Kentucky Company of Engineers and Mechanics (sometimes referred to as Patterson's Independent Company), formed at Camp Haskins, Kentucky, in October 1861. The company served in various armies throughout the western theater until Washington assigned it to the Department of the Tennessee in November 1862. The company served in Sherman's Yazoo expedition from December 20, 1862, to January 3, 1863. During the Vicksburg Campaign and subsequent siege, Patterson's company served with the Ninth Division, Thirteenth Army Corps. Present for the failed assault at Chickasaw Bayou (December 29, 1862), Patterson's company participated in the expedition to Arkansas Post (January 3–10, 1863) and built the floating bridge across Bayou Roundaway on April 1, 1863. All other pioneer contingents were informally organized at the brigade or division level. Despite Bissell's and Patterson's organizations, the lack of formally trained engineers and the fact that pioneer units remained few and far between dictated that West Point theory would have to be blended with western improvisation in order to achieve success. Often, where engineer officers were absent, a project's success or failure depended on "the energy and engineering skill of the division or brigade commander who furnished the working party for it." A closer examination of McClernand's corps as it existed on May 31 highlights the disparity between pioneers and regular line troops. Of the 1,101 officers and 17,285 men present for duty in the Thirteenth Corps on May 31, only 6 officers and 272 men belonged to the pioneer corps, simply not enough to wage offensive siege warfare on that corps' front in the largest siege in American history.[28]

This constituted Grant's engineering force at the beginning of the Vicksburg siege. The men of the Army of the Tennessee, while experienced battlefield veterans by 1863, were novices when it came to siege warfare. Engineers and those with a modicum of engineering training stepped forward to grapple with the task at hand. With any luck, these men would be able to act as force multipliers and convert Grant's rugged midwesterners into an army of siege. So far, things were off to a good start. Now that the workforce had been successfully organized, Grant's engineers moved to construct a line of circumvallation bent on hemming in the Confederates.

4. *Earthworks Rose as by Magic*

With the Army of the Tennessee now organized to wage the largest siege in American history, Major General Ulysses S. Grant's dogged engineers stepped forward to apply their trade. They proceeded to outline profiles and sited areas "to be secured" for both artillery batteries and rifle pits that would come to form the line of circumvallation designed both to protect the Union forces encamped in the ridges behind the line and to prevent Confederate egress from the city. At the same time soldiers dug communication trenches leading to the rear in order to provide cover as men traveled from their camps to the front line. The line of circumvallation, composed of a series of detached works, would also provide initial covering and counter battery fire as Union troops began the next phase of the siege, digging approach trenches across no-man's-land.[1]

Constructing the line of circumvallation was the engineers' first task. According to Dennis Hart Mahan, this line "is usually a continuous line [of works]" designed to "prevent succours"—that is, outside help reaching the besieged force. The terrain on the landward side of Vicksburg, however, made the construction of a continuous Mahanian-style line of circumvallation nearly impossible. Textbook practice called for the creation of a single line of uninterrupted trenches or breastworks, but steep, undulating ravines did not allow Union soldiers to implement conventional doctrine. Constructing one long, connecting rifle trench around Vicksburg would force Grant's troops to position themselves not only on the commanding hills but also in the bottom of deep ravines. To do so would expose Army of the Tennessee men to plunging fire from Confederate artillery and small arms. On the other hand, if the Union soldiers constructed a line that followed the contours of the ground, attempting to stay at the same altitude, parts of the line would become deeply re-entrant, thereby making them superfluous. Furthermore, if the Union lines ran all the way back along every ravine, the line of circumvallation would become too long and completely impractical. In short, the problem of topography forced soldiers and engineers alike to improvise and construct a line of circumvallation consisting of a series of detached works that took advantage of commanding hills and avoided potentially troublesome ravines. Lack of engineers and local peculiarities of topography forced Grant to improvise.[2]

The Union line of circumvallation contained a series of detached works with two parts. For each such detached work, soldiers constructed artillery batteries and then dug trenches for riflemen that connected the batteries. All of this, of course, occurred only where the terrain permitted. From ranges within six hundred yards of the rebel works, Union troops, in the words of Grant's staff member Lieutenant Colonel James H. Wilson, began "strengthening batteries, digging rifle pits, [and] extending and widening parallels" with Major Generals William T. Sherman and James B. McPherson's corps being the "furthest advanced." Thus, before the Army of the Tennessee could begin working approaches toward the Confederate defenses, it needed to "build a complete chain of forts and rifle pits" that trapped the enemy in Vicksburg. As one soldier vividly explained after the war, "Earthworks rose as by magic. At first a line of mere rifle pits was drawn around the enemy; then forts with heavy redoubts, linked together by lighter works, so that, from one end of the line to the other one could pass with little danger." Thus, Union engineers depended on defilade, using the natural defiles in the terrain to shield troops, in order to protect the federal camps from Confederate fire.[3]

The construction of early artillery batteries during this phase of the siege illustrates the ingenuity and improvisational ability of the troops serving in the Army of the Tennessee. The unusual terrain on Vicksburg's landward side—undulating steep hills and ravines—dictated how and where the army placed its batteries. According to Grant, "No commanding point within range of the enemy was neglected." Thus, as one Union soldier correctly observed, "The first thing the commanding officers were after was to get their artillery well protected where it would do the most good—or harm, as you choose to view it."[4]

In some ways, battery placement at Vicksburg conformed to Mahanian teachings. According to Dennis Hart Mahan, "The batteries should be as far asunder as practicable, so as not to invite a concentration of the fire of the defences upon any point by the accumulation of a large number of pieces on it." Old Cobbon Sense's emphasis on practicable artillery placement provided some wiggle room for commanders to adapt their tactics to particular situations. But the Army of the Tennessee did not abide by Mahan's dictum of avoiding battery concentration. According to one Vicksburg historian, "Sometimes the Union besiegers carried the doctrine of concentration to extremes." For example, Union forces at one time or another during the siege assembled some one hundred artillery pieces aimed at providing counter-battery suppressing fire and battering the Confederate Third Louisiana Redan, the principle rebel fort that guarded the Jackson Road into Vicksburg. Although Mahanian dogma might consider this overkill, converging fire often suppressed the Confederate guns.[5]

With regard to distance from the enemy line, Union troops were able to conform to Mahanian maxims. According to Mahan, artillery batteries placed at "ranges between 300 and 700 yards [from the enemy works] are the best." Thus, Union batteries established within six hundred yards of the rebel defenses were within textbook range. However, the nature of the terrain forced the Army of the Tennessee to reject Mahan's demand for artillery dispersal: Union artillery graced the top of hills and ridges that provided a clear field of fire to the Vicksburg defenses. Guns were grouped closely together on narrow hilltops out of necessity in order to take advantage of the high ground. Unlimbering their guns at the bottom of the steep ravines between the ridges and hills would have drawn Confederate plunging fire and led to disaster. Placement of these pieces proved a masterful blend of Mahanian West Point teaching and the ability of the westerners to adapt to Vicksburg's unusual topography.[6]

The rough topography even influenced the placement of batteries and individual guns in the line of circumvallation. According to Mahan, the ideal battery during any siege was to contain between three and seven guns, and on some parts of the Vicksburg battlefield, long ridges allowed engineers and artillerists to conform to Mahan's teaching by spacing artillery positions well apart from each other. Often, however, the limited surface area of a particular hilltop determined how artillerists placed their guns. According to one Yankee artilleryman of the Sixteenth Battery of Ohio Light Artillery, part of Brigadier General Alvin P. Hovey's division of the Thirteenth Army Corps, an elevated position approximately one-quarter of a mile to the south of the Jackson Railroad sharply dropped on its left-hand side, forcing the battery to crowd "the guns . . . together much closer than the regular distance."[7]

The steepness of the hills posed other interesting problems. If artillerymen failed to buttress the wheels of one of their guns, troops encamped in the ravines to the rear were in for a surprise when the cannon's recoil rolled it right off the hilltop and sent it rumbling down the slope. One member of the 124th Illinois Infantry, part of Brigadier General Mortimer D. Leggett's brigade, Major General John A. Logan's division, Seventeenth Army Corps, recalled one day when a twenty-four-pounder howitzer fired and then "recoiled over the bank . . . tearing down among the 'chebangs' [soldiers' shacks] for some distance." In a similar incident, Charles A. Hobbs of the Ninety-Ninth Illinois recalled an artillery piece stationed next to his regiment, part of Brigadier General Eugene A. Carr's line of the Thirteenth Army Corps, recoiling off of the battery's platform and down into the ravine to the rear, an event that "raised a shout of merriment in all directions."[8]

Deficiencies in the Army of the Tennessee's artillery arm forced the westerners to make do. According to Mahan, the best artillery with which to prosecute offensive siege operations were "18 and 24-pounders, and 8-inch howitzers." Lacking proper siege artillery, the men of Grant's army used the same field pieces that had accompanied them throughout the maneuver campaign. This artillery, some 180 guns, lighter in caliber than heavy siege artillery, needed to be supplemented. The need for larger guns forced Grant to appeal to Admiral David Dixon Porter, commander of the Mississippi Squadron, for heavy naval guns that might prove more effective in reducing Vicksburg. Porter obliged when he could and eventually supplied the Army of the Tennessee with heavier artillery, including nine-inch Dahlgrens, some of which came complete with their own experienced naval crews to operate them. Batteries McPherson and Selfridge, both consisting of naval guns, proved two of the most famous batteries during the siege. The former, emplaced on the Seventeenth Corps front near the Jackson Road, concentrated its fire on the Confederates' Third Louisiana Redan. The latter, under the command of Lieutenant Commander Thomas O. Selfridge, U.S. Navy, sported two eight-inch columbiads operated by a crew of naval personnel. Selfridge's blue-jackets set up shop on Sherman's Fifteenth Corps front and trained their big guns on the Confederate defenses on the northern part of the siege line.[9]

Getting these larger guns into position was a monumental feat. Although naval personnel sometimes hauled their own guns into position, as was the case with Battery Selfridge, Army of the Tennessee men often bore the brunt of the manual labor. John Jackson Kellogg of the 113th Illinois, part of

Sketch of Battery McPherson, which was on the Seventeenth Corps front. *Frederic B. Schell,*
"Siege of Vicksburg—Battery McPherson," May–June 1863; courtesy of the Becker Collection, Boston College.

Sherman's Fifteenth Army Corps, recalled after the war the day of May 29,
when superiors dispatched him and his comrades to haul siege guns up from
Chickasaw Bayou north of Vicksburg. On arriving at Chickasaw, Kellogg
and the rest of the regiment found that the navy had offloaded the guns on
the wrong side of the bayou. Ever resourceful, the Army of the Tennessee
men had already rigged up a "temporary pontoon bridge." Kellogg and his
companions then harnessed the guns to ropes and hauled them across the
makeshift bridge. Even then the weight of the guns was almost too much.
"Although we supplemented the strength of the bridges with thick plank
laid lengthwise, and pulled the guns across them on the run," Kellogg wrote,
"still their immense weight broke almost every plank in the bridges as we
snaked them across. Had we allowed one of them to stop a second midway
on the bridge it would have crushed and gone to the bottom of the bayou."
Nevertheless, the Union men successfully hauled the guns to their designated
positions. As a soldier of the Forty-Second Ohio on the Thirteenth Corps
front wrote, "Volunteers who had never trod a deck in their lives, hauled

them up, put the mysterious navy carriages together, mounted the guns, and worked them with consummate skill."[10]

Brigadier General Jacob Lauman's troops, on the extreme left of the Union siege line, provided the most striking example of improvisation in upgrading their artillery firepower. Lacking proper siege guns, men of Lauman's division mounted a captured thirty-two-pound rifled artillery piece that the Confederates had emplaced at Warrenton, where the rebels had once maintained batteries and threatened river traffic half a dozen miles downstream from Vicksburg. Lieutenant Anthony B. Burton of the Fifth Ohio Independent Battery described in his diary how Lieutenant Isaiah Denness of the Twenty-Eighth Illinois orchestrated the project: "He [Denness] got up a carriage with an old farm wagon braced with timbers, and drawn by 10 mules, went down to Warrenton with it and hauled the gun up there." Although "there was no carriage for it," Denness "had seen an old barbette carriage lying somewhere else" and, as a result, "took a wagon and went and hauled it up." Since "there were no wheels for it and no chassis," Denness "went to work and rigged up a chassis to slide on the traverse circle and made the carriage slide on the chassis."[11]

The gun, an old Model 1852 smoothbore that the Confederates had altered into a rifled piece, bolstered the southern part of the Union line. Although the gun's new rifling increased its range, the lack of proper sighting tools limited its potential. This probably would not have been a problem, but on that particular day the division's engineer, Captain Henry C. Freeman, reported sick. Undaunted, Union troops, with the help of Captain Herman Klostermann of the Third Missouri and a navy officer, improvised. According to Burton, "An old gunboat officer was up here today and gave us some good hints about working it [the gun]. He made a graduated scale on the right trunnion [sic] to show the degrees of elevation, and says this is the manner of pointing universally at the rebels." With this improvised gadget, Union troops succeeded in lobbing shells at Vicksburg's defenses.[12]

Individual battery construction was part of establishing the line of circumvallation, and West Point cadets received detailed instruction in the minutiae of battery construction. For example, Mahan provided information on the exact specifications of the various parts of individual batteries, including the proper dimensions for gun platforms and the correct technique for reveting (shoring up) the interior face of both parapets and embrasures (including what materials were most suitable). In their official report, consecutive chief engineers Frederick E. Prime and Cyrus B. Comstock stated that battery construction along the line, and throughout the siege, lacked uniformity. Often working under the cover of darkness, soldiers and pioneers created batteries using whatever materials were readily accessible. According to Prime and Comstock, "The style of work was very varied, both reveting and platforms depending on the materials which could be obtained at the time. In some cases they were well and neatly reveted with gabions and fascines, and furnished with substantial plank platforms, while in other, reveting of rough boards, rails, or cotton bales was used, and the platforms were made of boards and timbers from the nearest barn or cotton-gin house." Because of what Prime and Comstock characterized as "the feebleness" of Confederate artillery fire, Union parapets seldom needed to be more than six or eight feet thick. Thus at times Union batteries conformed to Mahanian precepts, while at other times Grant's men improvised gun emplacements as their peculiar local circumstances either required or allowed.[13]

In order to revet the inner face of battery parapets and embrasures, soldiers constructed both conventional gabions and fascines or improvised using items on hand, such as cotton bales. Sometimes, where Vicksburg's loess soil allowed, artillerists simply excavated sunken batteries and disregarded artificial revetment. Loess is highly porous, impermeable to water when undisturbed, light, and easy to excavate. According to the Union engineers' reports, "The fine soil, when cut vertically, will remain for years." While loess soil might appear to be an excavator's ideal, it can be problematic. Disturbed loess soil erodes quickly. It is this process of erosion that gave the ground around Vicksburg its undulating ranges of steep hills with flat-topped plateaus that suddenly drop into deep ravines. Although fortifications made of loess soil and lacking artificial revetment appeared formidable, they were in fact vulnerable to artillery fire, since the lightweight soil was not very effective at stopping incoming shot and shell.[14]

The use of loess soil decreed that the dimensions of parapets set forth in period engineering manuals were inadequate for the fighting at Vicksburg. Calculated for construction in sandy East Coast soils, the specifics provided in engineering manuals would be of limited value when besieging the Confederate Gibraltar. Loess, a fine silt consisting of smaller grains than that of East Coast sand, is more susceptible to destruction. As a result, parapets made of loess needed to be thicker if they were to withstand artillery fire. With the siege still in its infancy, some soldiers had yet to learn this and continued to build structures sans revetment. According to Anthony B. Burton, commander of the Fifth Ohio Independent Battery serving in Lauman's division, his crew made "two small embrasures . . . for the pieces by digging into the hill, thus making the parapet consist of the solid earth of the hill—a very good plan."[15]

Despite the special qualities of loess, other soldiers, in many cases, constructed gabions and fascines to be used as reveting material. A gabion was a wicker basket lacking a bottom. Once placed in its desired location, the gabion would be filled with earth and used as a retaining wall. Captain Andrew Hickenlooper described the process of gabion construction at length after the war. "Gabions," Hickenlooper related, were "substantially willow, twig or cane woven cylinders about two feet in diameter and three feet in height." Soldiers took "straight twigs or tree branches from 1½ to 2 inches in diameter" and "trimmed" the sticks "to 3½ feet lengths with one end sharpened." The sharp ends were then "driven loosely in the ground in a circle about 6 inches apart," and "around these" were "woven in and out willow, cane or pliable twigs on the top, thus forming a light cylinder, which when filled with earth formed a protection from the enemy's fire." Trying to explain the peculiarities of this new form of protracted warfare to loved ones back home, Jefferson Brumback described the purpose of gabions. "Gabions," the soldier wrote, "are set on end in rows . . . and filled with earth. . . . [They] are used to make the inside facing of earthworks, called revetment and to form the sides of embrasures for guns." Although Union troops used grapevines extensively for gabion construction throughout the siege, this particular material proved burdensome. Many of the vines were simply too thick and led to the construction of gabions that were too heavy. Thus the engineers improvised. Later in the siege, farther to the south, Captain Henry C. Freeman "experimented with cane as material for wattling, and found by crushing the joints with a mallet the rest of the cane was split sufficiently to allow it to be woven between the stakes of the gabion yet be strong enough, making a good and very neat gabion."[16]

Meanwhile, in addition to gabions, soldiers fabricated fascines. A fascine was a tight bundle of sticks tied together. It could be used for revetment on its own or in conjunction with gabions, being placed horizontally on top of the earth-filled wicker baskets. The lightweight cane that grew in abundance around Vicksburg proved ideal for fascine making. According to Hickenlooper, "fascines" were "cylinders of twigs about 9 inches in diameter and from 12 to 15 feet in length strongly bound around with wire, cord, or vines." At Vicksburg

Union soldier standing next to gabions at Vicksburg. *"In the Rear at Vicksburg, Showing Style of Gabions Used," from "Letters from the Trenches," National Tribune, July 31, 1902.*

they were "used in revetments on the inside of the parapet or embrasures of batteries to maintain the earth backing in a vertical position." Similarly, Brumback described fascines to those back home as "made of canes, the same used at the north for fishing rods, and being cut into proper lengths are used for the same purpose as gabions. The reeds are laid together in bundles about a foot in diameter, and then fastened by wires tied together around them at short intervals."[17]

West Point engineering courses instructed cadets in the finer points of constructing both fascines and gabions. Although professional military men might eventually master the minute steps filled with military jargon, such practices were foreign to the average infantryman serving in the Army of the Tennessee. On Hickenlooper's Seventeenth Army Corps front, "details from the Pioneer corps of the several brigades, aided by colored laborers, were set to work . . . making gabions [and] fascines." The lack of professionals meant that line soldiers often had to build these necessary items. After the war, Charles A. Hobbs, who had served in the Ninety-Ninth Illinois at Vicksburg, described the difficulty that the volunteer troops faced when constructing artillery batteries and how lack of knowledge among the average infantrymen forced soldiers to improvise. "The preparation for a battery was new work for most of us," Hobbs wrote.[18] "We could dig a ditch as well as anybody, for there were few that had not at some time tried their hand at it; but we had never put guns into fixed positions." Hobbs went on to describe that "the part of making the embankment of dirt thicker than a common rifle-pit was well understood, and the way to put in the embrasures, or rather to leave the openings in the embankment, so that the guns could be run out and fired at the enemy, was not a thing very hard to master." Lack of experience dictated that "the way the inside of the bank was braced or lined . . . varied in different places." Thus, both traditional techniques and improvised solutions on this part of the line ensured that forward progress continued. According to Hobbs, "Sometimes the men took those baskets we have spoken of, made of grapevine often, and filled them with dirt, and with them lined the inside of the fort." At other times "bundles of twigs or cane were made 18 to 24 inches in diameter, and set up to do the same work." Sometimes, in a deviation from traditional maxims, "cotton-bales would be used thus, and sometimes rough boards, secured from any place affording them, would take their places against the inside of the wall of dirt." Meanwhile, "the platform for the cannon, upon which the wheels stood, was fashioned from heavy plank when it could be secured; and when not, by anything that would do as a substitute." Hobbs concluded that "the sides and openings through which the guns were thrust to fire were fixed with canes, and occasionally with hides, which some kindly ox, willing to die for his country, having given his flesh to the hungry, yielded up to the cannoneer." Hence, lack of previous exposure to siege minutiae forced many western soldiers serving in Grant's army to improvise solutions.[19]

The shortage of professionally trained engineers even prompted high-ranking officers to assume lesser roles and instruct soldiers in the finer art of siege craft. Reflecting on the lessons of the Civil War, William T. Sherman stated, "It was one of Prof. Mahan's maxims that the spade was as useful in war as the musket, and to this I will add the axe." Sherman's time at Vicksburg no doubt influenced his decision to add the ax to the list of necessary modern martial impedimenta. In one entertaining anecdote, related by Colonel John B. Sanborn after the war, Sherman, a corps commander who graduated from West Point in 1840, took it upon himself to instruct the western troops besieging Vicksburg in the finer points of constructing gabions and fascines. On his way to confer with Brigadier General A. J. Smith, Sherman stumbled upon a group of soldiers that had been ordered to construct "fifty gabions and fifty fascines." Sherman approached the officer commanding the detail and asked, "For what are you ordered out, what are you doing?" The officer handed Sherman a written copy of his orders. After reading the orders, the major general further queried, "Do you know how to make gabions and fascines?" The officer in charge, attempting to save face, replied, "We have been in the service less than a year, and have not been engaged in any sieges, and do not feel very well posted in regard to these matters." Sherman, ever the energetic, hands-on commander, got down from his horse and demanded,

"Have you got an axe? Give me an axe." One soldier obliged and "an axe was handed to him." Sherman proceeded to "cut down small trees in the canebrake" and "with his own hands . . . cut them into stakes, and drove them into the ground himself." The Thirteenth Corps commander "then cut a grapevine, and showed the enlisted men how a gabion was made, and how fascines were made." Sherman, throughout the process, never ordered "an enlisted man to do it for him, but [did] the work with his own hands." Thus, "in five or ten minutes, [Sherman] had at least a hundred men as well informed upon these matters as if they had been in the regular army for five years in time of war." The ability of Army of the Tennessee officers to swallow their pride and at times take on lesser menial tasks contributed to the success of the siege. Without an adequate number of engineers present, two-star generals willingly engaged in grunt work typically reserved for junior officers or enlisted men. They improvised.[20]

At times, the Army of the Tennessee men took improvisation to silly extremes, as becomes evident in the case of the Second Illinois Cavalry's Ben Boyce, who, out of sheer boredom, rigged up his own "battery of two guns made from stalks of sugar-cane, wound with marline [two pieces of rope or twine loosely twisted into a single strand] and mounted upon small trucks." Many onlookers found this a comical release that "served to divert our minds from the more serious and grewsome [sic] happenings around us." Sporting a paper cap and using a length of cane stalk as a telescope, Boyce organized a crew of four like-minded pranksters to man the guns. Amazingly, the makeshift cannons actually worked. According to one spectator, "his guns were phenomenal" and "required only about half the charge used for a Sharp's carbine." Grant's westerners, battling boredom as well as rebels, engineered their own entertainment.[21]

Overall, most batteries at Vicksburg, once finished, were impervious to enemy fire. According to one soldier of the Seventeenth Ohio Light Artillery on the Thirteenth Corps front, "Our works proved impregnable[;] their shot and shell would strike in front of our works, bound over and fall on the Jackson railroad that ran to our left and rear." These mini-artillery forts were "as good as those of the Johnnies." With these batteries constructed, a perfect wedding of Mahanian doctrine to western improvisation, the Army of the Tennessee guns could provide covering fire to workers digging approaches and hurl accurate suppressing counter-battery fire at the rebels holed up in Vicksburg.[22]

During this early phase of the siege, Union artillerists achieved fire superiority in a contest the soldiers came to call "giving them their coffee." As one soldier quipped, "We cannot call this fighting, it is merely artillery practice." Firing went on both day and night and exacted a heavy toll on the Confederate artillery as "the Union artillerists attained almost perfection in the precision of their fire." In fact, Union fire proved so accurate that it was not uncommon for federal artillerymen to send shells directly into Confederate embrasures. As Jefferson Brumback observed during one firing session, "The shot and shell tore up dirt at a terrible rate. . . . One of the rebel guns[,] st[r]uck apparently full in the muzzle, topple[d] over backward and fall [*sic*] to the bottom of the parapet like a log. In 30 minutes we had dismounted every gun." The fire often became so intense that the artillerymen in opposing Confederate batteries decided to close up shop and fill in their embrasures "with logs and earth" or "bales of cotton." The precision of Union fire even made an impression on General Grant himself. During one visit to the Thirteenth Corps front, Grant questioned the men of an Ohio battery as to "why it was that the enemy had no artillery in their fort before [them]." The artillerymen gaily replied, "Because we had taken the priveledge [*sic*] of moving it for them." Thus, the artillery batteries, a blend of professional engineering and improvisation, provided adequate cover from which the Army of the Tennessee could achieve fire superiority.[23]

Successful Union suppressing fire also silenced rebel marksmen. If artillery crews spotted Confederate sharpshooters firsthand, they would fire "raking shot on top of their works," a practice that proved successful in "quieting them." Often the artillerymen, with the help of a spotter, would locate enemy snipers and proceed to shell them into oblivion. As Captain Joel W. Strong of the Tenth Missouri Infantry recalled after the war, "the Rebels had some pretty annoying sharp-shooters who were always well secreted behind bags of sand or some other protection." One officer of the Tenth, William B. White, "would sometimes locate them by their gunsmoke then report their positions to the battery of Parrot[t] guns. The gunner with his field glasses would view the situation, and, after about the third shot, [there] would be no more trouble from that point."[24]

Another Confederate sharpshooter terrorized Logan's sector where the 124th Illinois was stationed. Fed up with the rebel fire, the officers of the 124th "scanned the Rebel territory" with their binoculars in order "to locate Mr. Sharpshooter." The officers, after a diligent search, "found him perched up in a tall tree concealed by a heavy foliage." In order to dislodge the Confederate marksman, "they soon brought to bear on this sharpshooter a six pound brass rifle piece. After taking deadly aim, distance one-half mile, they fired." The first shot found its mark and "Mr. Johnnie came tumbling to the ground. That put an end to his mischief." In short, throughout the siege, it proved nearly impossible for the Confederates to return artillery or rifle fire. This fire superiority resulted from the successful blending of Mahanian principles with western improvisation applied to Union battery placement.[25]

While some soldiers built batteries, others excavated lines of rifle trenches that contemporaries dubbed "rifle pits" or simply "the trenches." Typically strung along ridges running parallel to the enemy's works, these trenches, where the ground permitted, connected the different gun emplacements and were part of the line of circumvallation. Rifle trenches served two purposes. As one Union soldier astutely noted, "The main object in their construction [was] so to locate them as to have the works of the enemy in full view, and so to build them as to afford the best possible protection to our men from the Rebel bullets." According to Chester Barney of the Twentieth Iowa serving in Major General Francis Herron's division, "They were placed on such grounds as afforded the best security against the enemy's sharpshooters, and the most commanding view of the pits occupied by the rebels." Rifle trenches served a dual function. First, they protected the Union troops from enemy sorties. Second, they provided safe positions from which Union marksmen could lay down covering fire as their comrades dug approaches toward the enemy's works. As one Union soldier later recalled, "I need not tell you that men will work like beavers when they know each spadeful of dirt is liable to stop a bullet."[26]

Rifle trenches underwent their own evolutionary process, often beginning as shallow rifle pits and then developing into wider, deeper, and longer trenches. The use of rifle pits for either an individual or a small group of soldiers began even before the May 22 assault. After the failed May 19 attack, troops began "throwing up rifle pits as a precautionary measure in case of a sortie from the enemy." Burrowing small, shallow pits within enemy rifle range in order to gain cover was done before soldiers tackled the task of digging more elaborate trenches. This practice of resorting to hasty entrenchments, in effect those "being constructed generally in the actual presence of the enemy, often under musketry fire," also occurred shortly after the May 22 assault when Union soldiers, "with their bayonets and a tin plate, dug little holes in the ground and on top of the earth placed a few fence rails. Between these rails our men could pick off the sharpshooters of the enemy." But over time these temporary hasty shelters "were much improved." Charles Hobbs of the Ninety-Ninth Illinois, in Carr's division of the Thirteenth Corps, summarized this evolutionary process for interested laypeople after the war. According to Hobbs, the rifle trench, typically excavated at night, "at first . . . was a rough ditch, from 18 inches to two feet wide, and about three feet deep." The dirt, removed under the cover of darkness, was "thrown up toward the side of the rebels" in order to "protect the head and shoulders of the men." During the early phases of construction, nearly all of the "rifle-pits were thus narrow to begin with" making it "difficult for men to pass each other." Nevertheless, "as time went by," the trenches were "made large and convenient."[27]

Where possible, engineers marked "profiles and positions to be secured." This involved tracing "the direction of the trench" with "pickets [wooden stakes], connected by white tape," and identifying valuable pieces of terrain. If the engineer lacked tape or cord, "pickets alone" could be used to determine the position of the trench. But with engineers in short supply, line officers and soldiers were often left to their own devices. Typically, under the cover of darkness, a line officer escorted a detail of soldiers or hired freedmen to a predetermined location and began excavating rifle trenches behind a screen of advanced pickets, some of whom concealed themselves in "individual rifle-pits." As one soldier later recalled, "The men were placed as close together as they could work and wield a pick and shovel. The hot sun had baked those clay hills until they were almost as hard as cast iron. . . . Every man had to put in his best licks all night long or morning would find the workers without sufficient protection." As the men dug, they tossed the dirt toward the enemy in order to form a small parapet with the object being to make "it . . . thick enough to stop a bullet." Typically, during the first night, all that "could be accomplished would be a trench that sloped to a sharp point at the bottom, and not over two feet deep."[28]

As the soldiers excavated their trenches, they created a firing step on the front part of the trench that allowed them to fire and then step down out of sight in order to load their rifles. For added protection, most soldiers, or the officer in charge of a particular section, devised some sort of added head protection laid lengthwise across the parapet with holes cut out from which to loose sharpshooter fire. The most common version of this improvised head protection was the "headlog." Grant, in his memoirs, generalized when he

Union soldiers detailed to sharpshooter duty. Note the use of headlogs for protection and wooden planks as revetment. *"Shooting behind Breastworks,"* from Charles A. Hobbs, *"Vanquishing Vicksburg: The Campaign Which Ended in the Surrender of America's Gibraltar,"* National Tribune, March 17, 1892.

recalled that "additional protection of sand bags, bullet proof, were placed along the tops of the parapets far enough apart to make loop holes for musketry. On top of these, logs were put. By these means the men were enabled to walk about erect when off duty, without fear of annoyance from sharp-shooters."[29]

This, however, is an oversimplification as soldiers often improvised different types of head defenses. In the Forty-Second Ohio, in Brigadier General Peter J. Osterhaus's division of the Thirteenth Corps, soldiers formed a parapet out of the earth they had excavated from their trench. Then, as Ohio soldier W. F. Jones recalled, they laid a plank "on the top of the dirt, and a piece of timber 12 inches square [was] laid upon it, with holes on the underside of the timber, so that we could thrust our guns through to shoot." W. R. Eddington described a different process used in his regiment, the Ninety-Seventh Illinois: "As we laid up the first tier of [sand]bags we left about two inch spaces between each of the bags. Now we would lay another tier of bags on top of this one and this would leave a smallhole [sic] through which we could put our guns. [W]e would lay more bags on top of these until we had them away over our heads so that we were entirely hid from the Rebels."[30]

Soldiers used both conventional and unconventional means to devise adequate head protection. Hobbs of the Ninety-Ninth Illinois recalled, "Occasionally, if we could get a great log . . . we lifted it bodily on top of the dirt we had thrown up. [T]hen we could punch holes through the dirt immediately under it, and have a row of portholes without further trouble. . . . Generally, where we could get sandbags we used them. Sometimes then a log would go on top of the sand-bags. But the sand-bags—enough of them—with dirt even over these occasionally, could be best arranged for portholes." Even camp rubbish might be improvised into head protection. "We made one porthole, at least, out of . . . wooden cartridge boxes—top and bottom knocked away, of course," Hobbs noted. "We smoothed down the bank a little, and set it in the upthrown dirt; then we piled dirt around it and on top of it. It was quite a roomy porthole, but as we threw the dirt over it more, it gradually narrowed its outward opening to proper size."[31]

Similarly, Thomas B. Marshall of the Eighty-Third Ohio, serving in A. J. Smith's division just to the north of Hobbs's position, described how he and his comrades did it. "On our side, as the pits were completed some would take an ammunition box which was some 14 by 12 by 8 inches, and fill it with dirt. When this was placed on [top] of the bank, the dirt would be dug from under it and from this open place as a kind of port hole, a gun could be fired with the head protected." In some sectors of the siege lines, however, soldiers did not use any head protection on top of their parapets and opted to use what Mahan termed a "simple trench," in effect, a trench with a parapet "formed of earth alone." Although the concept of the head-log was not exclusive to the western theater, Army of the Tennessee soldiers improvised and used a variety of objects in order to rig up this essential piece of trench defense.[32]

All along the line, soldiers continued to ply their deadly trade and provided lethal suppressing fire that "practically silenced many of the guns." Throughout the siege, a portion of any given group ordered to act as sharpshooters stood on the firing step while their comrades lounged in the recesses of the trench awaiting their shift. One soldier recorded, "We placed our muskets across the rifle pits, pointing towards the fort, and then lay down and ran our eyes over the gun, with finger on trigger, ready to fire at anything we might see moving." As any given soldier waited, he could hear other sharpshooters all along the line who had loosed their rounds, creating a concert that "sounded much like popping corn" to some and like "a party of wood choppers at work" to others. When a Confederate soldier finally dared lift his head above an opposing parapet, Union sharpshooters throughout the sector fired, sending "a dozen bullets . . . flying at it." From their position in the rifle trenches, it was not uncommon for each Union soldier on duty to fire from fifty to one hundred rounds at the enemy.[33]

Inside the safety of their rifle trenches, many Union soldiers became proficient marksmen. One soldier recorded early in the siege, "If this siege is to last a month there will be a whole army of trained sharpshooters, for the practice we are getting is making us skilled marksmen." As Captain

William Franklin Patterson, head of the Independent Kentucky Company of Engineers and Mechanics, related to his wife on May 28, 1863, "Would you know what we are doing now[?] . . . A man in a ditch earth thrown up in front of him watching intently an opportunity to shoot any one who may be so daring to show himself, men 6 miles in a line just in this condition, and a battery every 300 yards and all day lone [*sic*] where ever you may go." Thus, from the protection of their carefully adapted rifle trenches, Union soldiers poured on suppressing fire that silenced enemy guns and rifles, allowing their comrades to dig in relative safety.[34]

But headlogs and other devices did not provide absolute protection. According to Hobbs, the "log might be splintered some even by minie-balls, and if a cannon-ball struck it, one would prefer not to be behind it." In another example, Hobbs described how one comrade "had been neatly scalped by a rebel bullet . . . while in the act of sending a ball from his musket through the very porthole penetrated by the enemy's missile," an event that made Hobbs leery of sharpshooting even with the protection of head cover. Similarly, W. F. Jones of the Forty-Second Ohio, serving in Osterhaus's division, commented after the war that timbered portholes provided relative safety, "although a ball occasionally would find its way through a porthole, and some one would be hit."[35]

Although Mahan provided precise widths and depths for trenches, the dimensions of the finished Union trenches at Vicksburg varied across the line. According to one soldier serving in the Ninety-Seventh Illinois, the trenches in his part of the line, A. J. Smith's division of the Thirteenth Corps, were approximately four feet from front to back and approximately three feet deep. Meanwhile, W. F. Jones of the Forty-Second Ohio reported that the trenches were "about three feet deep, and the same in width." Still, Charles A. Willison of the Seventy-Sixth Ohio, serving in Major General Frederick Steele's division of the Thirteenth Corps front, described his rifle trench as "just high enough for a man to stand over and fire over." Meanwhile, the length of the trenches varied due to the nature of the terrain. According to one soldier, "Trenches were hard to connect with, either on the left or the right because of the interrupting ravines." Later in the siege and farther to the south on Lauman's front, "the pits were from four to six rods apart, and in each there were from six to ten men on duty at all times." Still, in Herron's division on the extreme left of the Union line, Captain Chester Barney of the Twentieth Iowa reported that their "rifle pits were constructed . . . of a length sufficient to accommodate two hundred men." Adaptability and improvisation proved the key to successful trench placement. Once soldiers began digging approaches toward the enemy, these "reserve" rifle trenches continued to provide soldiers with positions from which to snipe at the enemy.[36]

With the investment of Vicksburg, Union forces cut Confederate communications and supplies, but in order to wage a successful siege, the Union army needed unlimited access to northern resources if it were to "out-camp the enemy." The process of reestablishing supply lines began before the May 22 assault. With Sherman's forces the first to arrive outside Vicksburg on May 19, the Fifteenth Corps commander immediately seized Haines Bluff to the north of town and reestablished Union communication with the Mississippi by way of the Yazoo.[37]

Up to this point, for the past twenty-three days, the Army of the Tennessee had been surviving on quarter rations. Deprivation, however, came to an end on May 23. One soldier of the Forty-Second Ohio remembered that on this day the army received its first government-issued rations since landing at Bruinsburg on the eastern side of the Mississippi on April 30, when they "drew them for five days, consisting of five large crackers, some sugar, and coffee." The lack of rations during the march through Mississippi had forced the Army of the Tennessee to implement the age-old practice of foraging. According to one member of the Thirty-First Illinois, "everything along the line of march from water mill to farm house had been eaten. Everything that grunted, squa[w]ked, gobbled, or crackled had found its way into the mess pan, or had been stewed in the camp kettle, or roasted on the ramrod."[38]

Nevertheless, despite the need to forage, the Army of the Tennessee had traversed approximately two hundred miles on foot and defeated the Confederates in five consecutive battles. Thus, reestablishing communications and supply with the navy, now docked at Haines Bluff, lifted morale as soldiers could now receive not just food but also information from the North, including dated mail and newspapers. Even more important to the siege, restoring communication with the navy allowed the Army of the Tennessee to tap into the Union's seemingly unlimited supply of ammunition. As Grant later recorded in his memoirs, "We had an inexhaustible supply of ammunition to draw upon and used it freely."[39]

Reestablishing supply and communications would not be enough, however. A difficult task still remained ahead. With supplies landing to the north of the city, engineers, pioneers, and soldiers needed to build roads in order to transport the goods to the army settling in around Vicksburg. Captain William L. B. Jenney, acting engineer officer, Fifteenth Corps, described the labor involved. The first step required a reconnaissance to determine the path of the road. Jenney had conducted just such a survey on May 19 with the intention of connecting the army with the Johnston Place landing, located on the Yazoo River, just above its mouth on the Mississippi. This road, which was supposed to hug Chickasaw Bayou, proved difficult to construct. After pioneers cleared the trees Confederates had felled in their efforts to obstruct Union movement the previous December, the finished road bridged a series of small bayous.[40]

On May 20, Captain Herman Klostermann's pioneer company, supplemented with labor from the Eighty-Third Indiana Infantry, discovered an easier path to allow the army to move supplies by way of Thompson's Lake. By 11 A.M. on May 20, this road proved stable enough to allow wagon transport. In addition to this route, Klostermann also established another road that, after originating just above Mint Spring Bayou, hugged Chickasaw Bayou and connected with the Yazoo.[41]

Nevertheless, despite Klostermann's "short cut," workers and pioneers from what remained of Colonel Josiah W. Bissell's Engineer Regiment of the West, under the command of Major William Tweeddale, continued to build and clear the main road that Jenney had scouted. This road opened to transport on May 22. These well-conceived roads, serving as Grant's logistical artery to the North, extended from the Yazoo River along the rear of the Army of the Tennessee. As a soldier of the First Iowa Battery lucidly wrote after the war, this feat ensured that the Army of the Tennessee's "base of supplies could run up the river and land within a few miles of our lines," allowing the besieging army to tap into "the whole Northland with its bounteous harvests." In addition to planning the route, engineers constructed these highways in such a way as to facilitate a smooth flow of traffic. According to a Union soldier of the Ninety-Ninth Illinois, "Attention was paid to cutting out roads to different landings on the Yazoo River, and also to the different corps. Two roads were generally constructed in the same place to avoid interference in travel."[42]

While roads provided smoother surfaces for supply transport, soldiers strung telegraph wires to connect Grant's headquarters, just behind Sherman's headquarters on the northern sector of the line, with the river fleet. First successfully demonstrated by painter-turned-amateur inventor Samuel

Finley Breese Morse in May 1844, the telegraph had become a communication staple by the middle of the Civil War. Ineffective if buried, telegraph wires, if placed above ground, could transmit information in a matter of minutes. Although during pitched battles Civil War commanders relied upon older, time-tested methods of communication, such as handwritten orders entrusted to couriers, in the controlled setting of a siege the electromagnetic telegraph proved paramount. Not only did Grant establish telegraph communications between his headquarters and his supply depots on the river, but he also had the various corps headquarters connected to his command tent in order to facilitate quick communication and coordination. As one soldier during the siege observed about Grant's communication network, "He [General Grant] has telegraphic communication along the whole line encircling the city, and also with Haines' and Snyder's Bluffs, and with Chickasaw Bayou Landing."[43]

Meanwhile, to the south of Vicksburg, the Union army had established a supply depot at Warrenton on the eastern bank of the Mississippi. This spot provided much-needed supplies to Major General John A. McClernand's corps, later supplemented with the divisions of Lauman and Herron, holding the southern part of the Union investment line. With the investment completed, Lieutenant Colonel John A. Rawlins, of Grant's staff, wrote on May 25 to Sixteenth Corps commander Major General Stephen A. Hurlbut at his headquarters in Memphis, Tennessee, "The investment of Vicksburg is complete, and supplies for our Army are drawn from Chickasaw Bayou on the Yazoo, above, and Warrenton on the Mississippi below the city." Everyone, from corps commander down to humble private, understood the significance of establishing solid bases of supply and opening communications. As Sherman wrote to his wife, Ellen, on May 25, "We have now perfect Communication with our supplies, plenty of provisions, tools, and ammunition. . . . Vicksburg is ours as sure as fate." Similarly, William Winters of the Sixty-Seventh Indiana penned to his wife on June 9, "We will go into the city of Vicksburgh [*sic*] after awhile, that is shure, for we can live outside of their works longer than they can inside of them, that is certain for we can get everything we want, and they can get nothing atall." And so the Union, with its logistical network in place, thanks largely to the efforts of the handful of engineers with the army, could prosecute the largest siege in American history.[44]

Meanwhile, just behind the line of circumvallation, officers directed soldiers in establishing their camps in the deep ravines in order to protect them from Confederate rifle and artillery fire. Here the soldiers relied on defilade, using the natural recesses in the terrain to shield them. Forced to strip down to a campaign kit consisting of bare military essentials in preparation for Grant's march through the interior of the state, most soldiers had arrived on the outskirts of Vicksburg without tents. As a result, they had to "engineer" their own improvised shelters.[45]

Typically, soldiers excavated dugouts, sometimes called "dog nests," which could house up to four men. As one soldier explained, "A place was dug against the hill, and in many cases, into it, forming a sort of cave. Poles were put up and covered with oil cloths, blankets or cane rods, of which an abundant supply was near at hand." In another soldier's morbid imagination, these improvised shelters looked "very much like graves with one end out." Often, soldiers covered the openings of these dugouts with tattered Confederate tents that the rebels had discarded on their retreat into the safety of the Vicksburg defenses.[46]

With cane abounding in the ravines around Vicksburg, this potential resource quickly caught the eye of the industrious westerners. Some used this plentiful material to rig up beds. Fastening a few swatches together and propping them up with whatever was at hand allowed soldiers to rest in relative comfort off of the wet Mississippi ground. An Iowa soldier wrote extensively about how he and his comrades constructed these ingenious beds. "We had also got our beds raised from the ground by setting crotches and laying poles in them for the ends and carried canes (such as some have for fish poles in the North) and put them on the poles and then got corn husks or corn leaves for budding. It makes a bully bed for the cane springs just enough to lay easy."[47]

But, despite residing in the relative shelter of the ravines, camp life could be dangerous at times. A soldier of the 113th Illinois in Sherman's corps later recalled, "I put in a half day of solid work building me a cane palace which, when I had it enclosed and nearly finished, was instantaneously wrecked by a piece of rebel shell." On a more somber note, Colonel William H. Raynor of the Fifty-Sixth Ohio recorded in his diary on Sunday, May 24, "An occasional ball finds its way, however, into the camps and several have been wounded while a few have been killed."[48]

Only a generation or two removed from their frontier fathers who had settled the present day Midwest, Army of the Tennessee soldiers, roughing it for most of their formative years, were able to engineer dwellings that most would consider primitive. In an attempt to explain their new surroundings to those on the home front, removed from the hardships of army life, Sergeant

Sketch of Union shelters constructed during the Vicksburg siege. *Frederic B. Schell, "Siege of Vicksburg—Life in the Trenches," May–June 1863; courtesy of the Becker Collection, Boston College.*

James H. Lewis of the Twenty-Fourth Iowa described their new homes as being constructed in a fashion similar to the "cattle shades in Iowa—that is by setting crotches and covering with boughs of trees, but leave it open at the sides and ends so that air can get through." Humble, like their commanding general, these rugged westerners were willing to live in bovine quarters if need be in order to ensure the fall of the slave empire and to restore the Union.[49]

At the same time, soldiers excavated wells in order to have access to water, a siege necessity, especially under the torturous rays of the Mississippi summer sun. Often, these soldiers dug circular holes, approximately eight feet deep, and then placed barrels in the holes in order to act as receptacles for the water. Once soldiers established camps and dug wells, Union troops built roads in order to connect all of the separate camps in the ravines, thereby allowing the unobstructed flow of information and soldiers from one part of the line to another. The inspiration for this final step, connecting the camp via an elaborate road network, came courtesy of Mahan.[50]

With all of these preparations in place, the Army of the Tennessee was now ready to commence prosecuting zigzag approach trenches toward the

Engraving, *Siege of Vicksburg,* from an original painting by Alonzo Chappel. Soldiers' shades in the foreground would have been farther to the rear in the ravines behind the Union trenches. *Johnson, Fry, and Company, New York, 1867; Anne S. K. Brown Military Collection, Brown University Library.*

enemy fortifications. As an Illinois soldier observed while his comrades undertook the daunting endeavor of establishing preliminary defenses, "Men [are] in good spirits and prefer the spade and pick to charging breastworks." The Union line now had the rebels trapped within Vicksburg via "a semi-circle . . . of rifle pits and batteries extending from the river above to the river below." And so, as Sherman observed on the dawn of May 31, "Vicksburg was completely beleaguered. . . . We were in a splendid condition for a siege." Describing the situation once his line of circumvallation was complete, Grant later recalled, "We were now as strong for defence against the garrison of Vicksburg as they were against us." Writing confidently to Department of the Gulf commander Major General Nathaniel P. Banks on May 31, Grant stated his belief that he could "effect the reduction of Vicksburg within twenty days." Little did he know that the largest and longest siege in American history had just started.[51]

This phase of siege craft involved elaborate preparation. Establishing a line of circumvallation protected the Union army and acted as a jumping-off point for attacking via regular approaches. The lack of engineers and pioneers yielded uneven results. At some points along the line, Mahanian engineering theory dominated. Where engineers could not directly supervise construction, the industrious westerners improvised. With the extreme topography dictating the nature of the line of circumvallation, engineers and soldiers alike improvised. While a traditional line of circumvallation typically encompassed a single line of works, Grant's army rigged up an adequate line of defense that contained artillery emplacements attached via rifle trenches atop commanding positions wherever the topography allowed. These artillery emplacements and trenches could be either textbook or improvised. Regardless, the engineers and soldiers camped outside of Vicksburg were able to establish an improvised series of detached works that served a textbook function. Although the details of every battery or trench may not have conformed directly to Mahan's teachings, their ultimate function did. From these positions, whether textbook or improvised, soldiers and artillerists provided splendid suppressing covering fire that allowed workers to dig in relative safety. Despite the lack of engineers traveling with the Army of the Tennessee, Grant was able to establish an adequate line of circumvallation, a result of Mahanian West Point teaching wedded to western improvisation.

Meanwhile, soldiers rigged up camps connected with roads, set up an effective communication network, and established a supply line with the North via the Yazoo and Mississippi Rivers that would allow Grant to wage a successful siege. Although the principle of establishing camps between the lines of circumvallation and countervallation came straight out of Mahan's manuals, the individual types of shelters that the westerners excavated provide prime examples of improvisation. Despite the lack of engineers and pioneers, the Army of the Tennessee hacked out a successful series of roads that allowed the army to tap into the nearly inexhaustible supply of northern war resources. If unable to reconnect with these resources, the achievements of Grant's soldiers during the maneuver campaign and their ability to construct an adequate line of circumvallation would have been for naught. Now, with no Confederate relief army in sight and a virtually unlimited supply of food and ammunition pouring into Grant's camps, the fall of Vicksburg appeared to be only a matter of time. The adaptation of Mahanian principles and western improvisation so far in the siege had proved of paramount success.

5. *More Roads to Rome Than One*

ome 36,325 Illinoisans served the Union during the Vicksburg Campaign. Back in the heart of the Prairie State, on the banks of the Illinois River, stands a two-hundred-foot sandstone butte. There in the late eighteenth century, as local legend has it, a band of Illini took refuge from their deadly enemies, the Ottawa and the Potawatomi. The latter two tribes, bent on avenging their murdered chieftain Pontiac, camped around the butte, cutting off all escape for the beleaguered Illini. Eventually, as the story goes, the Illini starved. Half a century later, when neither Illini nor Ottawa nor Potawatomi inhabited the rich farmlands of the upper Illinois valley, residents nevertheless still referred to the prominent butte as Starved Rock, and so Major General Ulysses S. Grant's Illinois soldiers would have known it. The men of the Fifty-Third Illinois, in Brigadier General Jacob Lauman's sector, had been raised around the rock, and their first lieutenant colonel, Daniel Gitt, owned the rock and the land around it. Gitt had resigned and gone home the preceding December, but his men and others would have been no less conscious of the old legend.[1]

More important, they and virtually all of the citizen-soldiers of Grant's army, whether or not they knew about Starved Rock and its legend, held the same general concept of siege warfare that the Ottawa and Potawatomi had practiced there. In frontier warfare, besieging an enemy meant that if an attacker cornered his opponents but could not take them by storm, then he sat down and waited for the beleaguered defenders to run out of food. Hem them in and starve them out was the only method in the soldiers' culture for dealing with such situations, and beyond that, Grant's amateurs—from privates in the ranks all the way to corps commander Major

General John A. McClernand—had only the vaguest of ideas as to what the next steps might be.

By contrast, for professional officers, trained in military engineering, the methods of Vauban, as interpreted by Dennis Hart Mahan, offered clear steps toward conquering the enemy stronghold before its defenders starved. For the handful of such officers in Grant's army, the challenge would now be to teach these steps to the citizen-soldiers and direct them in carrying out the progressive stages of the siege. Once the midwestern amateur soldiers recognized what needed to be done, they brought to bear on the task their own ingenuity, born of two generations, at least, of carving farms and towns out of the wilderness. This applied to the second phase of the siege that would see Grant's army digging steadily closer to its quarry. Similar to the way the troops established the line of circumvallation, this phase of the Vicksburg siege illustrates the wedding of West Point siege theory to western improvisation. Although the Army of the Tennessee implemented textbook siege theory, the lack of trained military engineers forced improvisation.

The next step, now that the line of circumvallation was complete, was the creation of approaches and parallels. In order to maintain clarity, it is best to subdivide this process. Thus, this chapter will consider forward-moving approach trenches and lateral parallel trenches. The next chapter will examine a special type of approach trench termed a "sap."

Traditionally, engineers regarded the line of circumvallation and parallels as two different types of works. According to period manuals, the former typically consisted of "a continuous line [of works]," while the latter fell into Mahan's broader category of "trenches." According to Mahan, "The term *trench* is applied to an excavation or ditch made by the besiegers, by means of which, and of the earth thrown from it, they are enabled to obtain speedy cover from the fire of the defences, and to approach them with security." In Mahan's realm, trenches contained precise dimensions and fell into two categories: parallels and approaches (also called "boyaux" in the Francophilic military literature of that era). Mahan explained, "The parallels are designed as stations for troops to guard the trenches, and the workmen employed in their excavation, from the sorties of the garrison. . . . [They run] parallel to, or concentric with, the line connecting the most salient points of that portion of the defences attacked." Meanwhile, "the approaches serve simply as covered communications which lead to the parallels, and toward the points of the defences upon which the attack of the besiegers is directed. . . . [They] are run in a zigzag, or in a straight line." The main difference between the line of circumvallation and the parallel was each feature's function. While the line of circumvallation served a defensive purpose, protecting the besiegers against sorties by the besieged, the parallel served an offensive tactical function, part of what Mahan termed "Attack by Regular Approaches." Approach trenches brought attackers closer to the enemy. Meanwhile, successive rows of parallel trenches facilitated lateral movement along the lines and provided protection for marksmen. Parallels existed in order to support the forward-moving approach trench.[2]

The terrain at Vicksburg provided natural cover for Grant's troops and allowed them to begin the siege at a relatively close distance. As a result, Union soldiers established their line of circumvallation at Vicksburg at the distance typically reserved for the second parallel. From the parapets of the Confederate semipermanent works, Major Samuel H. Lockett, chief engineer of the Army of Vicksburg, reported that on "the morning of the 23d [May] . . . the enemy . . . soon had possession of a line of hills on the main roads, not exceeding 350 yards distance from our salient points. These hills they crowned with heavy batteries and connected as rapidly as possible with their second parallel." What Lockett described is not a true parallel in the Mahanian sense but a hybrid—a line of circumvallation containing batteries and connecting rifle trenches constructed at the textbook distance typically reserved for the opening of the second parallel. With the initial Union investment line (line of circumvallation) well within six hundred yards of the Confederate defenses, the first parallel, as prescribed by Mahan's texts, became unnecessary. According to Mahan, in a textbook siege, "the *First Parallel* is six hundred yards from the most advanced salients [of the defensive works]," while the second parallel is "less than three hundred yards" from the first. At Vicksburg, however, most of the approach trenches began "within three or four hundred yards of the enemy's line" and "in some cases these distances were less than one hundred yards." Thus, as the approaches were begun this close to the Confederate works, "the first and second parallels incident to ordinary sieges being thus rendered unnecessary were omitted." Due to the short distance from the enemy defenses and the detached nature of the Union fieldworks, the line of circumvallation, completed on May 25, took on an improvised form that served a textbook function at the distance traditionally reserved for the second parallel.[3]

Although it was not until May 25 that Grant issued Special Orders No. 140, delegating the "reducing of the enemy by regular approaches," the order to begin "regular approaches toward the city" trickled down from Grant's command tent on May 23. Signaling this shift from establishing a line around Vicksburg to moving toward the rebel defenses, Major General William T. Sherman wrote to John Sherman on May 29, "We are now approaching with pick and shovel." While engineers and line officers oversaw the construction of the line of circumvallation, they also began planning the possible routes for zigzag approaches. Soldiers of differing skill levels understood the purpose of these zigzags. Sherman, writing to his wife, Ellen, explained on May 25 that "the men are making Roads and ditches to enable us to get close up to the enemys parapet without crossing within full view and fatal effect of their well-prepared forts and trenches." Seventeenth Army Corps brigade commander Colonel Green B. Raum recalled years later that the purpose of the zigzags was "to get up to the very front of the Confederate fortifications, undermine them, blow them up, and carry the works by assault through the breaches." Both Sherman, a professional, and Raum, a prewar lawyer without formal military training, adequately summarized the basic principle of this phase of Mahanian siege craft. With the ultimate goal being to traverse no-man's-land while suffering the fewest possible casualties, the Union army devised approaches that blended West Point training with western soldier improvisation.[4]

The Union army dug thirteen major approach trenches toward the Vicksburg defenses. These included five on Sherman's front, two on Major General James B. McPherson's front, and five on McClernand's front (later under the command of Major General E. O. C. Ord). The thirteenth approach was excavated by Major General Francis J. Herron's division and was not under the jurisdiction of the aforementioned corps commanders. Those on the fronts of Sherman and McPherson were better coordinated and prosecuted with more vigor during the early part of the siege. According to the reports of Captains Frederick E. Prime and Cyrus B. Comstock, ten of the thirteen zigzag approaches may be labeled as "principal approaches" receiving "their names from the brigade or division commanders who furnished the guards and working parties." Sherman's Fifteenth Corps, on the Army of the Tennessee's right flank north of Vicksburg, contained the approaches of Brigadier General John M. Thayer, Brigadier General Hugh Ewing, Brigadier General Ralph P. Buckland, and Colonel Giles Smith. Buckland's Approach, halted on June 22, reopened on June 28 under the name Lightburn's Approach. Later in the siege, Lightburn's Approach would be connected to Ewing's. To Thayer's right, and closest to the river, Colonels Francis H. Manter and Charles R. Woods's brigades began their own approach, but, as Prime and Comstock explained, "It met a deep ravine, precluding further progress." Next on Sherman's left, in the center of the Union line, McPherson's Seventeenth Corps dug two approaches, Brigadier General Thomas E. G. Ransom's and Major General John A. Logan's. On McPherson's left, farther south, the Thirteenth Corps front contained the approaches of Brigadier General A. J. Smith, Brigadier General Eugene A. Carr, Colonel James R. Slack, Brigadier General Alvin P. Hovey, and Brigadier General Jacob Lauman. Herron's Approach secured the southern flank of the Union siege line.[5]

On Sherman's front, Ewing's Approach became the dominant approach. Meanwhile, just to the south, in McPherson's sector, Logan's Approach evolved into the major approach of the Seventeenth Corps. On McClernand's front, the approaches of A. J. Smith and Carr, started after those on Sherman's and McPherson's fronts, were primary until engineers opened Hovey's Approach late in the siege. When possible, the approaches hugged the roads leading into Vicksburg, since, as Grant's later military secretary Adam Badeau pointed out in a military biography of Grant, "these roads had originally been built on the most suitable and even ground for ingress to the city." For example, Ewing's Approach followed the Graveyard Road into the city; Logan's Approach, the Jackson Road; A. J. Smith's, the Baldwin's Ferry Road; Carr's, the railroad leading into Vicksburg; Lauman's, the Hall's Ferry Road; and Herron's, the Warrenton Road. Thus, these thirteen approaches became the primary Union avenues of assault toward the Confederate Gibraltar. As one soldier quipped, "More roads to Rome than one."[6]

Attacking via regular approaches involved charting a path of zigzag trenches across no-man's-land. The purpose of advancing via this angular route was to provide cover for the besieging army as it slowly worked its way into a favorable position from which to break through the enemy's defenses. Digging a zigzag trench achieved defilade (cover) for the attackers and prevented enfilade (flank fire), thereby providing a relatively safe way for the attacking army to cross the ground between the line of circumvallation and the enemy defenses.

Soldiers all along the siege line clearly articulated the form and function of the zigzag approach trench, though they sometimes used their own homelier expressions to describe them. According to Albert O. Marshall of the Thirty-Third Illinois, "The trenches we were making were approaching the objective point diagonally from each direction, and in such a manner that they would meet at a sharp angle, directly in front of the main rebel fort;

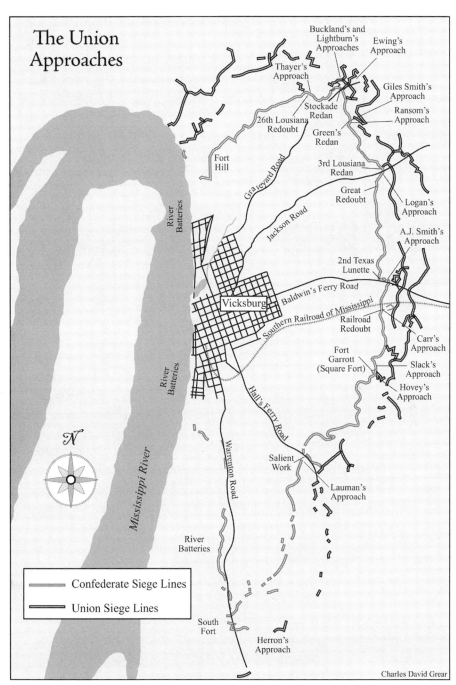

The Union Approaches

Buckland's and Lightburn's Approaches
Ewing's Approach
Thayer's Approach
Giles Smith's Approach
Ransom's Approach
Stockade Redan
26th Lousiana Redoubt
Green's Redan
Fort Hill
3rd Lousiana Redan
Great Redoubt
Logan's Approach
A.J. Smith's Approach
Graveyard Road
River Batteries
Jackson Road
2nd Texas Lunette
Baldwin's Ferry Road
Vicksburg
Southern Railroad of Mississippi
Railroad Redoubt
Carr's Approach
Fort Garrott (Square Fort)
Slack's Approach
Hovey's Approach
River Batteries
Hall's Ferry Road
N
Warrenton Road
Salient Work
Lauman's Approach
Mississippi River
River Batteries

Confederate Siege Lines
Union Siege Lines

South Fort
Herron's Approach

Charles David Grear

Approximate locations of the Union approaches at Vicksburg.

Zigzag approach trench at Vicksburg. *"Approaching by Parallels," from Charles A. Hobbs, "Vanquishing Vicksburg: The Campaign Which Ended in the Surrender of America's Gibraltar," National Tribune, March 17, 1892.*

that is the two trenches would meet in a V shape with the point resting on the rebel hill." Joseph Thatcher Woods of the Ninety-Sixth Ohio related, "Roads were slowly cut deep into the face of the hills, proceeding in a zigzag course, but always presenting the side of the ditch or cut to the enemy, and then turning at an angle present the other side." The reason for this angular route was, as Granville B. McDonald of the Thirtieth Illinois explained, "to keep the enemy from shooting along" the approach trench.[7]

Writing for a general audience unfamiliar with siege craft around the turn of the twentieth century, Myron B. Loop of the Sixty-Eighth Ohio and Charles A. Hobbs of the Ninety-Ninth Illinois, both veterans of the Vicksburg siege, best summarized the purpose of the zigzag approach. "If we dug a trench straight toward the enemy," Loop wrote, "either infantry or artillery would get in a position to shoot through the whole length of it. But if we dug the trench crooked and threw the dirt up high on the side next to the enemy, we increased our chances of living a while longer, which most of us preferred to do. We never dug our trench far enough in one direction to make it possible for the enemy to rake it with his deadly fire, but made frequent turns." Similarly, Hobbs explained, the approach trenches were "dug in a zigzag fashion. . . . If you dug a trench straight, some foeman would get at a place where he could shoot through it from end to end. . . . But if they made a trench crooked, then the [enemy rifle] ball would strike the dirt first." In short, the zigzag approach trench, providing defilade and avoiding enfilade, allowed soldiers to traverse no-man's-land in relative safety.[8]

While the army's professional military engineers understood what their targets should be, coordinating the effort proved difficult due to the limited number of professional engineers then serving in the Army of the Tennessee. According to Mahan, the enemy "salients are usually the weakest part of the work, because they are easily enveloped by the . . . approaches." Although this principle appeared simple enough, the lack of professional engineers made it difficult for chief engineer Prime to personally direct all of the Union approaches. According to Sherman's corps engineer William L. B. Jenney, "There were so few engineering officers that Chief Engineer Captain Prime did not attempt to control the approaches, but let each brigade dig as they chose toward the enemy, remarking that they were ready enough to dig in that direction." Chief engineers Prime and later Comstock defended their lack of direct supervision in their official report, writing that "superintendence at any particular point was impossible, without neglecting the more important general superintendence of the whole line." Lack of centralized authority led to unequal results along the siege lines. Not surprisingly, the approaches prosecuted along the fronts of Sherman and McPherson were the most professional and best coordinated during the early part of the siege. According to Private Frank Holcomb Mason, who was later promoted to captain during the siege for his engineer services on the Thirteenth Corps left flank, "Generals Sherman and McPherson were themselves educated engineers, and kept an intelligent supervision of their own operations; but McClernand knew nothing of such work." Thus, with a lack of direct supervision from the chief engineer, corps commanders became responsible for the approaches in their respective fronts.[9]

The failed May 22 assault had left many Union dead dispersed throughout the no-man's-land between the Union lines and the Confederate works. By May 25 the rancid smell of the decomposing blue-clad bodies had become too much for the Confederates to endure. Humanity, decency, and practical necessity demanded that the fallen federal troops be buried. On May 25 Lieutenant General John C. Pemberton, commanding the Confederate army now trapped inside Vicksburg, requested a temporary truce in order to allow the Union men time to remove their fallen comrades. Grant agreed and declared a two-and-a-half-hour truce to commence at six that evening.[10]

A ghastly scene greeted the Union troops detailed to bury the dead. According to John Jackson Kellogg of the 113th Illinois, "The dead were buried by simply throwing earth onto the bodies where they had fallen. . . . The victims [were] laying scattered over the field as far as the sight could reach. The bodies were bloated and swollen to the statue [*sic*] of giants." Not all of the wounded

Union soldiers were dead; many wounded had become trapped between the lines. Those badly injured and unable to crawl to safety themselves had waited helplessly for their fellow soldiers to come and rescue them. Albert O. Marshall of the Thirty-Third Illinois later remembered that "the saddest part of all was to find some of our wounded boys still alive who had lain helpless upon the field since Friday noon. What they suffered during those three long days, helpless and uncared for, with the guns of both sides continually firing over them, can only be imagined; it can never be told." The sights and smells proved so grotesque that some soldiers, such as Joseph Stockton of the Seventy-Second Illinois, preferred to wait behind the Union lines for the siege to commence rather than witness firsthand the morbid panorama in no-man's-land.[11]

Union soldiers of all ranks took advantage of the truce. Some enlisted men seized upon the opportunity to collect war souvenirs and practical items, including pocketknives and watches. Kellogg, blending sentimentality with practicality, picked up a picture "of a woman and two children which some soldier had lost" and upgraded his shoulder arm to "a splendid Springfield rifle" that had been discarded on the battlefield. While enlisted men scored items of value, engineers used the lull to prepare for the upcoming siege. Captain Andrew Hickenlooper, supervising engineering activities on the Seventeenth Corps front, believed this to be a splendid opportunity to conduct a reconnaissance and survey the possible avenues of approach toward the Vicksburg defenses. According to Hickenlooper, the truce "afforded . . . the opportunity of closely inspecting the ground to be passed over, of fixing [identifying] salient points, and of determining upon the general direction of the various sections of the sap."[12]

In a traditional siege, the path that a zigzag charted across no-man's-land was not haphazard. Engineers decided which part of the enemy defenses to target. They typically pegged the capital, or tip, of enemy salients as the best line of attack. According to Mahan, "The boyaux are run in a zigzag direction across the capitals; because this is the shortest line to the salients of the work attacked which are the points first reached; and in this position they are less exposed to the fire of the work, and are less in the way of the other works of the attack." After a preliminary survey, engineers were instructed to plant stakes marking the proposed route of the zigzag. Sometimes those stakes were connected with easily visible white tape or cord designed to aid the work parties when excavating. But, with a formal truce in place, this textbook procedure would have to wait for now.[13]

In Hickenlooper's front, the decision to strike at the Third Louisiana Redan appeared the logical choice since this fort guarded the Jackson Road that ran through the rebel defenses into the heart of Vicksburg. In order to facilitate easy travel before the war, the road ran along a ridge that pointed like a finger through the Confederate works. If the Union could dominate this ridgeline that almost connected the two opposing lines, the Army of the Tennessee could virtually walk into Vicksburg. According to Hickenlooper, the redan "was only approachable over a broad, flat ridge, forming a comparatively level plateau, extending eastwardly from the fort for a distance of almost five hundred yards before descending into one of the numerous ravines or depressions which extended in almost every conceivable direction over the ground lying between the contending armies." But the Federals could not dig directly toward the redan along this road as such practice would draw enfilading fire down the length of the trench. As a result, the Union troops, in textbook fashion, needed to dig zigzag trenches that cut at angles in order to shield them from Confederate fire as they advanced.[14]

With this goal in mind, Hickenlooper sauntered into the no-man's-land between the Shirley House (also known as the White House) and the Third Louisiana Redan for the purpose, in his own words, of "inform[ing] myself very th[o]roughly as to the topographical features of the ground over which he would have to pass with our saps between the White House and Fort Hill." While between the lines, Hickenlooper began to eye possible routes for his approach toward the Third Louisiana Redan. He immediately spotted "a peculiar and sharp bend in the direction of the ridge over which" his workers would have to dig their approach trench. Unable to mark the potential path in textbook fashion with stakes and tape, as such an act would violate the truce, the Ohio engineer improvised. Taking up an "old musket" with a fixed bayonet that had been carelessly discarded in no-man's-land, Hickenlooper stuck the shoulder arm into the ground stock-end up in order to provide an easily identifiable marker for his soldiers to dig toward "in the dark at some future time." Hickenlooper's trick, however, failed. A Confederate officer lurking on the redan's parapet saw what the engineer was up to and shouted, "Put down that gun." Hickenlooper, surprised, called back, "Oh! . . . It's only a broken and abandoned musket." The unconvinced gray-clad officer insisted, "Put it down I say!" The Seventeenth Corps engineer, outgunned and unwilling to violate the truce, immediately complied.[15]

James and Adeline Shirley's house, near the route of Logan's Approach. Many Union soldiers referred to the house as the "White House" both during and after the siege. *Library of Congress.*

But not all attempts to mark the best path of an approach were as dramatic as Hickenlooper's foray into no-man's-land, and after the May 25 truce, some engineers adopted traditional methods for marking approach lines. On the right flank of McClernand's front in Carr's Approach, work commenced after darkness descended on June 2. Charles A. Hobbs of the Ninety-Ninth Illinois noted that an engineer officer proceeded in front of the working party, driving stakes into the ground to mark the path the zigzag trench was to follow. As Hobbs recalled, "There was no trouble to follow the marking." Thus, Union engineers let circumstances dictate whether or not to implement textbook procedure or to improvise.[16]

Back on the Seventeenth Corps front, Hickenlooper "at once reorganized [his] operating force." He chose Captains John W. Powell and Frank C. Sands of the artillery along with Captain Meritt, "a citizen employe[e]," to carry out engineering details. Powell reported to Ransom's division just to the north of the Jackson Road, while Sands went to work with Brigadier General Isaac F. Quinby's division to the south of the road. At the same time, Hickenlooper dispatched Captain Meritt to serve as his direct voice in Logan's command tent. This organization, in the end, allowed Hickenlooper to direct his personal attention to the main approach against the Third Louisiana Redan, what he considered "the most prominent and formidable work along the entire line." Thus Hickenlooper personally oversaw Logan's Approach, which commenced at first light on May 26.[17]

Not all encounters during the May 25 truce were as hostile as that between Hickenlooper and the rebels on his front. Across the line, Union and Confederate troops "mingled in conversation over the scenes which had transpired." Spying an officer atop the "Jackson road redan," Sherman dispatched a messenger and invited the Confederate to speak in the open spaces of no-man's-land. This particular rebel, as it turned out, was none other than Confederate chief engineer Major Samuel H. Lockett, a graduate of the United States Military Academy class of 1859. As Lockett arrived at the spot where Sherman and his entourage had stopped "some two hundred yards in front of our line," the Union general initiated the conversation. Sherman began, "I saw that you were an officer by your insignia of rank, and have asked you to meet me, to put into your hands some letters intrusted to me by Northern friends of some of your officers and men. I thought this would be a good opportunity to deliver the mail before it got too old." Lockett shot back with wit, "Yes, General, it would have been very old, indeed, if you had kept it until you brought it into Vicksburg yourself." Sherman then nonchalantly replied, "So you think then . . . I am a very slow mail route," to which Lockett quipped, "Well, rather . . . when you have to travel by regular approaches, parallels, and zigzags." Sherman, not to be outdone, retorted, "Yes . . . that is a slow way, and I was determined to deliver those letters sooner or later."[18]

The playful banter ceased for a moment, and Sherman and Lockett proceeded to seat themselves "on an old log near by." Sherman, a brilliant man with an inquisitive mind, carried on the conversation and began to talk shop with Lockett. Although Sherman had graduated from the USMA as an artilleryman in 1840, he had been exposed to West Point engineering classes similar to those Lockett had taken and began discussing the more technical aspects of the siege. Complimenting Lockett, Sherman said, "You have an admirable position for defense here, and you have taken excellent advantage of the ground." Unbeknownst to Sherman, this feat had not been accomplished easily and had actually proven very onerous for Lockett before Grant's campaign.[19]

During the summer of 1862, Confederate higher-ups had decided that the landward side of Vicksburg needed to be fortified. This immense task had fallen upon the shoulders of Lockett, the chief engineer. The rippling, undulating hills with steep ravines plagued with timber and brush made it difficult for Lockett to ascertain the best location for the Confederate defenses. According to Lockett, "No greater topographical puzzle was ever presented to an engineer." At first, the problem appeared nearly insolvable. But, after nearly a month of painstaking reconnaissance, "careful study gradually worked out the problem." In the end, Lockett decided to erect a series of "redoubts, redans, lunettes, and small field-works" atop the "most prominent points," the majority of which dominated the roads that entered the city. The spots for these fortifications, once designated, were then to be connected with a series of rifle trenches. With his plan firmly established in his mind, Lockett broke ground on what would by September 1, 1862, evolve into the Confederate defenses guarding the eastern side of Vicksburg. Lockett, however, did not let on to the difficulties that Vicksburg's topography had given him the previous summer. To Sherman's compliment he frankly responded, "Yes General . . . but it is equally well adapted to offensive operations, and your engineers have not been slow to discover it." Sherman agreed. Shortly thereafter the truce came to a halt, each side posted its pickets, and "the sharp-shooters immediately began their work," which continued "until darkness prevented accuracy of aim."[20]

Lockett was correct. The ground around Vicksburg, although appearing intimidating, could be used to the attacker's advantage. According to Frank Holcomb Mason, "In front of nearly every division was a natural covered approach, through some defile, to within three of four hundred yards of the enemy's line—in some cases these distances were less than one hundred yards." As one Union soldier described it, "The ground around here is very much broken and the lay of the land is favorable for our protection while it gives the enemy a fine chance to fortify." In either case, even the common soldier recognized that the Union approaches were at the mercy of the terrain. Charles A. Willison, serving in the Seventy-Sixth Ohio, observed, "Approaches advanced wherever the nature of the ground admitted." Similarly, Albert O. Marshall of the Thirty-Third Illinois later recalled that the approaches "were governed by the lay of the land."[21]

Union soldiers could either view the steep hills and ravines between the lines as obstacles or as naturally covered highways. Soldiers tended to describe the ground in both ways. Some perceived the rough terrain as an impediment. Engineers were forced to run their parallels over undulating bluffs with open tops, devoid of foliage, and sharp sides that made them "difficult to scale." The Confederates, in preparation for a possible Union attack, had recognized the advantages of the rough Mississippi terrain and used them. Confederate axmen cleared fields of fire for their artillery and felled remaining trees in no-man's-land, thereby creating "a perfect labyrinth of fallen timber, with trunks and limbs entwined and interlaced." This, combined with the mutually supporting fire from the rebel's network of fortifications, intimidated many Union soldiers. But others, like John Quincy Adams Campbell of the Fifth Iowa, understood the hidden benefits of the terrain. "The topography of the country is thus very favorable to us, in approaching the rebel works," he wrote.[22]

More important, those in charge who were trained professionals, such as Sherman, recognized the hidden benefits of the terrain. Writing to his wife, Ellen, on May 25, Sherman explained, "We are now hard at work with roads and trenches, taking all possible advantage of the Shape of the ground."[23] Although Sherman's description might have held true for approaches such as Ewing's along the Graveyard Road, where engineers used the ground to their advantage, Sherman's right flank experienced problems. Here, the ground did not allow the construction of approaches. Charles A. Willison belonged to the Seventy-Sixth Ohio, which was in turn part of Major General Frederick Steele's division, charged with guarding the extreme right flank of the Union line to the north of Vicksburg. Willison described how the terrain stymied federal approach in this sector. "Owing to the deep ravine in our front," he wrote, "nothing of this kind [advancing approaches] could be done, so that our efforts were mainly devoted to sharpshooting."[24]

Meanwhile, all the way down on the southern end of the siege line, First Lieutenant Peter C. Hains wrote that between June 2 and June 7, "the approaches to the salients in front of Generals Smith's and Carr's Divisions were commenced, the ravine on the right of the wagon road was taken advantage of as an approach." Incorporating this natural depression in the ground into the forward-moving trench meant that "much labor" was "avoided." Further reporting on A. J. Smith's Approach, Hains wrote on June 10, 11, and 12 that "the ravine [in Smith's front] will be used itself as an approach." As Lucius W. Barber, serving in the Fifteenth Illinois excavating Lauman's Approach, similarly wrote, "The ground was cut up by deep ravines, winding around in such a manner that we could march almost to their lines without being seen." In sum, all along the siege lines, the ground determined the avenues of approach. While the topography could act as a deterrent in some sectors, those trained in the engineer's art, and even some common soldiers, recognized its potential benefits in many other parts of the line.[25]

Soldiers engaging in sharpshooting during the Vicksburg siege. This image appeared in
Harper's Pictorial History of the Civil War under the title "The Investment of Vicksburg—
Sherman's Extreme Right on the Mississippi." The steep ravines on Sherman's right flank
and the commanding position of Fort Hill made it impossible for the Fifteenth Corps commander to prosecute approach trenches in this vicinity. As a result, sharpshooting became
the predominant activity of Union soldiers on this part of the line. *Anne S. K. Brown Military
Collection, Brown University Library.*

On parts of the line where the terrain could not provide natural defilade,
soldiers improvised. On May 30 Captain Prime ordered Captain Herman Klostermann to organize a fatigue party to dig an approach toward the Twenty-Sixth
Louisiana Redoubt. Klostermann organized a detail consisting of General
Steele's pioneer company and line troops from General Thayer's brigade. The
approach, dubbed Thayer's Approach, began in earnest under cover of darkness
later that night some three hundred yards from the Louisianans' salient work.[26]

The ground in front of Thayer's position lacked the undulating hills and
ravines that characterized most of the ground around Vicksburg between
the opposing lines. While Union troops occupied a small ridge fronting the
Confederate works, the ground approaching the rebel defenses gave way to
a ravine that suddenly rose on the opposite side. Atop this higher position,
Lockett had designed the Confederate defenses to dominate the high ground,

thereby allowing the city's defenders to pour plunging fire on attackers. The inability to find defilade via natural cover forced the engineers and troops excavating Thayer's Approach to implement a technique typically reserved for crossing the enemy's defensive ditch. According to Prime and Comstock, "It was difficult to defile this approach." As a result, "blinding was resorted to." Details constructed "fascines made of cane" and "placed [them] across the trench, which was about 6 feet deep." The cane fascines were impervious to small arms fire and "formed a roof which hid the movements of our men." Luckily for the Union troops, the rebel defenders did not direct artillery fire against this approach. Such a concentration "would have soon destroyed [the covered trench]." In this way, Union soldiers in Thayer's Approach crept toward the Confederate defenses.[27]

While the sharpshooters claimed the day, the engineers and their work parties owned the night. Although some approaches, such as Logan's Approach, began on the morning of May 26, the opportunity to conduct work during the daylight hours eventually faded. With the Confederate and Union lines within artillery and rifle range, it became necessary to dig under the cover of darkness in order to avoid exposure to enemy missiles. As Private Daniel G. Winegar of the Ninety-Fifth Illinois, working on Ransom's Approach on the Seventeenth Army Corps front, wrote to his wife, Elvira, on May 31, "We have to work nights, because we are in reach of the rebel sharp shooters." Transitioning from daytime infantryman to nighttime excavator struck some soldiers as new and peculiar, "a queer phaze of war."[28]

On the northern segment of the Union line, a soldier of the Ninety-Fifth Ohio excavating Buckland's Approach (which commenced under the cover of darkness on May 30) described to his wife the soldiers' new role as siege laborers. "At night a working party set out and by day have dug a long, deep, narrow trench in such direction that the enemy can only fire across it, throwing the dirt towards the enemy," the soldier wrote. The work was typically done underneath the rebels' noses so "quietly, that the enemy know nothing of it until next morning." Sometimes, however, the Confederate defenders would hear a Union worker and otherwise grudging attitudes toward manual labor fell to the sideline. The midwesterner further wrote to his wife that "if the enemy fire, it is astonishing how quickly a man with a pick and shovel will dig a hole deep enough to screen himself. . . . Once down in the ground far enough to be safe, he . . . works forward or back to connect with his neighbors so that a trench is soon completed."[29]

Both details of infantry and hired African American laborers, predominantly escaped slaves, provided the muscle for the construction of zigzags. According to consecutive chief engineers Prime and Comstock, "The labor in the trenches was done by men of the pioneer companies of divisions, by details from the line, or by negroes. Several of the pioneer companies had negroes attached to them, who had come into our camps. These negroes were paid $10 per month, in accordance with law, and proved to be very efficient laborers when under good supervision."[30]

Although using a combination of soldier and African American labor appeared on all corps fronts, the work conducted in the Thirteenth Corps sector on the south of the Union line is most illustrative of the practice of utilizing the labor of freed persons. Up until this point in early June, progress on the Thirteenth Corps front had moved at a glacial pace. While McPherson's and Sherman's corps prosecuted vigorous approaches, McClernand appeared to take the phrase "out-camp the enemy" to a literal extreme. Although the activities of both A. J. Smith's and Carr's Approaches fell under the competent and scientifically trained West Point engineer First Lieutenant Peter C. Hains, McClernand's meddling and micromanaging style stymied progress. While some of the soldiers in Carr's division began to press forward across no-man's-land, George A. Remley of the Twenty-Second Iowa, working in Carr's Approach, observed the redundant work that had been conducted in this sector. Rather than pushing forward the approach trenches, black laborers were set to strengthening the already formidable rifle trenches constituting the line of circumvallation. According to Remley, "We are daily extending and strengthening our earthworks, working only at night and using all the available 'black help' we can procure."[31]

Attitudes toward black laborers varied, with some reports revealing the inherent bigotry of many of the western troops. A member of the Seventeenth Ohio Light Battery recorded an incident in which rebel fire proved "to[o] strong for the Negroes courage [forcing them to drop] their picks and shovels, and [flee] . . . down the hill. . . . This ended the work of the Negroes on our part of the line [and] a company of the 83d Ohio came up and pushed forward the work." Biased reports such as this, however, detract from reality as the work of the pioneers and the freed African American laborers tended to outpace that of the details formed from the line regiments. According to the chief engineers, Prime and Comstock, "The labor performed by the details from the line, as is usual in such cases, was very light in comparison with that done by the same number of pioneers and negroes. Without the stimulus of danger or pecuniary reward, troops of the line will not work efficiently, especially at night, after the novelty of the labor has worn off."[32]

Meanwhile, E. H. Ingraham of the Thirty-Third Illinois wrote to his aunt from the siege lines on June 16 about his changing attitudes toward Mississippi's African American population. Before the war, Ingraham admitted, "I knew very little about them but have slowly arrived at the conclusion that they are superior to the Irish and far more likely to make useful citizens." Of course, Ingraham sought fit to qualify this statement, adding, "Of course I refer to the well known lower class [of Irish]. The protestant Irish are many of them superior to the Scotch and English." Thus, with all hands on deck, the midwesterners of Grant's army and hired African American laborers methodically worked their way closer to the beleaguered Confederate garrison.[33]

6. *The School of the Sap*

As the midwesterners of Major General Ulysses S. Grant's army pressed forward, the sap became the most popular form of advancing under cover. Yet the term "sap" becomes difficult to define. According to James C. Duane, who borrowed heavily from French sources and included in his manual an entire segment titled "School of the Sap," a sap was simply a trench, whether it be an approach or a parallel, that employed the use of gabions. Meanwhile, Dennis Hart Mahan reserved the term only for approach trenches with gabions, dug within enemy "musket range" or under the range of "case shot." Once under enemy fire, specialized engineer troops known as sappers took over and pushed forward the approach trench, now called a sap, both day and night. Since they were now completely exposed to the defenders' fire, Mahan instructed sappers to excavate "on their knees" behind "a large gabion stuffed with fascines, or wool, termed a *Sap-Roller*," which was moved ahead of the advancing work party. Thus, in Mahan's view, any trench that sappers dug using gabions, beginning from the second parallel and pushing forward toward the enemy, was termed a sap.[1]

Despite the nuances in definition, both Mahan and Duane agreed that engineers should adopt this method of approach once working parties were within range of "small arms" fire. According to Mahan, this usually occurred at the distance traditionally set aside for the second parallel. The second parallel, the second lateral trench facing the enemy's works and the first to employ the use of gabions, typically rested within three hundred yards from the first parallel, which was closer to the besieging force's camps and the farthest parallel from the enemy.[2]

Mahan identified different types of saps in the engineer's repertoire, including the flying sap, the full sap, and the double sap. Mahan stated that when soldiers reached within range of enemy case shot, the simple trench, a trench with a basic earthen embankment, would no longer provide enough protection. As a result, engineers were to begin to construct a flying sap. For this building project, engineers and pioneers furnished ordinary line troops with two gabions, "which [they were] required to fill." The flying sap was then constructed "by placing a row of ordinary gabions in juxtaposition, along the direction of the trench; these being filled with the earth from the trench, the parapet [then being] completed by throwing the

Union soldiers excavating behind a sap roller at Vicksburg. *"The Sap Roller," from Charles A. Hobbs, "Vanquishing Vicksburg: The Campaign Which Ended in the Surrender of America's Gibraltar," National Tribune, March 24, 1892.*

remaining earth over and beyond them." The process was termed the "flying sap" from the rapidity with which the work was to be done.[3]

If the enemy's fire proved hot enough to break down the flying sap, Mahan instructed engineers to implement the full sap. According to Mahan, "The full sap . . . is resorted to when the fire becomes so destructive that the flying sap cannot be used. The trench is pushed forward by engineer troops alone; for this purpose a working party, termed a *brigade*, of eight sappers is requisite." This elite team of sappers, with each man knowing his specific job, carried forward the sap under heavy fire. In terms of construction, one primary difference between the flying sap and the full sap was that the latter warranted the placing of "sap-fagots along the berm [top of the trench], at the junction of the gabions," and demanded that "trench fascines [be] placed upon the gabions."[4]

Meanwhile, Mahan instructed his students to use the double sap when circumstances negated the use of either the flying sap or the full sap. As stated by Mahan, the double sap "consists of two heads of sap [the front-most part of the approach trench which sports the sap roller] pushed forward by two

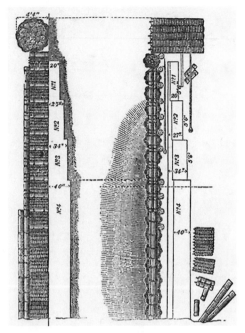

"Full Sap," as depicted by James C. Duane. *J. C. Duane, Manual for Engineer Troops, 150.*

brigades working abreast." The purpose of the double sap was to push a trench into an area that could be swept by enemy fire from both sides. According to West Point's practical engineering guru James C. Duane, a sap became "*double* when the fire, coming in two different directions, requires a gabionade [a row of gabions] on each side of the trench, which is effected by conducting two simple saps side by side, whose parapets mutually protect each other." Unlike the types of saps previously described, the head of the double sap contained two sap rollers "placed end to end."[5]

Despite Mahan's and Duane's specific criteria for what is properly classified as a sap, the term itself loses meaning when discussing the Vicksburg siege. First, there exists the issue of proximity. As discussed in earlier chapters, Union soldiers established their line of circumvallation around Vicksburg at the traditional distance typically reserved for the second parallel (between three hundred and six hundred yards from the enemy salients). Union troops, digging within rifle range from the beginning of the siege, adopted saps early on. Thus, with Grant's soldiers prosecuting forward-approach trenches within six hundred yards of the Confederate works, the sap became the preferred type of forward advance.[6]

Due to the close proximity of the opposing lines and the nature of the soil, saps at Vicksburg tended to blend both Mahanian dogma and soldier improvisation. According to Captains Frederick E. Prime and Cyrus B. Comstock, "In close approaches the sap was reveted with gabions, empty barrels, or with cotton bales, or sometimes left unreveted, it being difficult to prevent the working parties from sinking the sap to the depth of 5 or even 6 feet when the enemy's fire was heavy, and reveting then was unnecessary." Thus, as Prime and Comstock reported, "compactness of the alluvial [loess] soil" allowed soldiers to dig saps both with and without artificial revetment as circumstances demanded. For example, Joseph Thatcher Woods of the Ninety-Sixth Ohio described how Union troops in A. J. Smith's Approach opted for artificial revetment: "Baskets, about the size of but much longer than a barrel, constructed out of withes and filled with cotton, were rolled over the works. Men lying down pushed [these forward] as a protection until reaching the desired spot, then they instantly began securing themselves by throwing over them earth enough to make a bullet and cannon shot proof embankment." Nevertheless, despite the technical jargon and subtleties, the term "sap," as defined in this text, and keeping with Prime and Comstock's observations, refers to any approach trench leading toward the enemy defenses.[7]

Yet, some sources attempt to classify the type of saps used at Vicksburg. According to Confederate Major Samuel H. Lockett, the Union besiegers advanced "regular double saps" against various Confederate "salient works" from June 15 until the end of the siege. These rebel salients included the Stockade Redan fronting Sherman's Corps, the Third Louisiana Redan guarding the Jackson Road, the Second Texas Lunette protecting the Baldwin's Ferry Road, the Railroad Redoubt in front of Brigadier General Eugene A. Carr's division, the Square Fort (later named Fort Garrott) in front of Brigadier General Alvin P. Hovey's division, and the salient obstructing the Hall's Ferry road. Those prosecuted against the Stockade Redan guarding the Graveyard Road, the Third Louisiana Redan aside the Jackson Road, and the "lunette on . . . [the] Baldwin's Ferry road" were commenced by June 4. Lockett's observations suggest that the approaches of Brigadier General Hugh Ewing, Major General John A. Logan, Brigadier General A. J. Smith, Carr, Hovey, and Brigadier General Jacob Lauman all eventually implemented the double sap.[8]

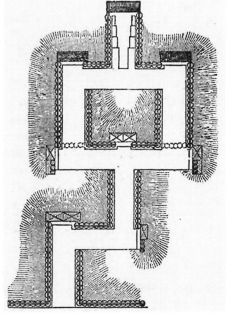

"Double Sap," as depicted by James C. Duane. *J. C. Duane, Manual for Engineer Troops, 158.*

Lockett's report, however, appears to contradict Union sources. According to Thirteenth Army

Corps commander John A. McClernand, A. J. Smith drove a "flying sap" toward the Second Texas Lunette on June 13–14. Meanwhile, to the north of Smith, Captain Andrew Hickenlooper described the use of a "flying-sap" in Logan's Approach until June 22, "when the head of the sap reached the outer ditch surrounding the fort." With conflicting reports, it becomes difficult to ascertain exactly what types of saps Union engineers drove toward the Vicksburg defenses. The truth probably lies somewhere between the Confederate and Union descriptions. Different saps were most likely used at different times, depending on the terrain and the specific circumstances. As the manuals suggest, direction and intensity of fire determined which type of sap Grant's soldiers built. With regard to saps, engineering theory, which stressed improvisation, dominated.[9]

Either writing to loved ones during the siege or recording their experiences after the war, Union soldiers struggled to paint pictures with words that described the process of digging a zigzag approach trench or sap. Overall, the methodology for digging a zigzag was the same all along the line. On Major General James B. McPherson's front, one soldier wrote with regard to Logan's Approach, "The trench was constructed about six feet deep and eight feet wide, with a parapet and banquette [firing step] to be occupied by infantry. On the parapet sand-bags and head-logs were placed, through which embrasures were made of suitable size for sharpshooters." Similarly, S. C. Beck of the 124th Illinois serving in Logan's division described the same approach trench as "twelve feet wide, six feet deep and some seven hundred feet long commencing at our left rear and extending up to a Rebel Fort in our front." Beck elaborated on the details of the trench, writing that "it was made very crooked so that the Rebels could not rake it from any direction. The loose dirt from the ditch was thrown on the side of the Rebel fire. Square timbers were placed on top of this dirt with gains [holes] cut on [the] bottom side for us to look through and shoot through without exposing ourselves to their fire." In an interesting deviation from Mahanian principle, the approach trench served as both an avenue of advance and a place from which to provide suppressing fire atop firing steps and through loopholes.[10]

Like all the Vicksburg approaches, Logan's Approach had different dimensions at different points. Nevertheless, the majority of the Vicksburg trenches were the same. Both approaches and parallels were wide and shallow, with the former cutting at sharp angles in order to guard against enfilading fire. But, unlike their World War I counterparts, these trenches were "never dug so deep that [they] required long ladders to climb out [of]." In short, the trench needed to be just deep enough to cover a man but wide enough to facilitate troop movement. As one soldier in the Thirteenth Army Corps, working on A. J. Smith's Approach, explained, "The . . . approaches had [to be] deepened and widened until four men would march abreast or a field-piece could be moved from point to point unobserved."[11]

Similarly, to the north, in Buckland's Approach, Jefferson Brumback of the Ninety-Fifth Ohio wrote to loved ones back home on June 21 about the process of digging a zigzag toward the enemy. "At night," Brumback wrote, "a working party set out and by day have dug a long, deep, narrow trench." The trench ran parallel to the enemy works, and the dirt excavated from the ditch was thrown to the front, forming a small berm. In this case the trench was narrow and "only wide enough for one man to stand in." Stealth was paramount. According to Brumback, "The work has perhaps been done so quietly, that the enemy know nothing of it until next morning. Or if they do hear the noise of working, they cannot fire with any certainty, so that the working party is comparatively safe." Brumback further humorously described that "if the enemy fire, it is astonishing how quickly a man with a pick and shovel will dig a hole deep enough to screen himself perfectly from musketry." "Once down in the ground far enough to be safe," Brumback continued, the soldier "is at his leisure, works forward or back to connect with his neighbors so that a trench is soon completed." The next day, "working parties leisurely widen the trenches so that the road is two and a half or three feet wide and two persons can easily pass each other." In some cases, the trenches were dug wide enough to allow for the movement of wagons and artillery. According to Brumback, "These ways and zigzags cross each other, and run in every direction so as to enable us to plant guns or station sharpshooters wherever it may be deemed best." And so, by this method, the Union soldiers methodically moved "closer and closer towards the enemy." In fact, the crossing of the zigzags became more elaborate than most of the midwesterners ever thought possible, prompting Brumback to comment that "the trenches and streets and ways are more tortuous and bewildering than the streets of Boston."[12]

One of the best descriptions of the process of digging a rifle trench, however, comes from an officer in Brigadier General Hovey's division in the center of the Thirteenth Army Corps front. Hovey's Approach, although not commenced until the night of June 23, stands out as a textbook example of Mahanian siege craft at Vicksburg.[13]

On June 18, Grant dismissed Major General John A. McClernand as head of the Thirteenth Army Corps. A little over a week earlier, on June 10, the *Missouri Democrat* and *Memphis Evening Post* printed an inflated congratulatory order in which McClernand gave the Thirteenth Corps the lion's share of the credit for the campaign's success. This was an especially audacious gesture considering the fact that by June 10 only one approach on McClernand's front, Carr's, had been opened. Grant, irked with McClernand's inflammatory order, the submission of which to a newspaper was a violation of army regulations, replaced him with Major General E. O. C. Ord on June 18.[14]

Ord, although a graduate of the West Point class of 1839, was not a rising star while at the academy. Graduating seventeenth out of a class of thirty-two, Ord had been anything but a stellar student. Yet even this former mediocre cadet, exposed to Mahan's teachings, could see that things were not right on the Thirteenth Corps front by June 18. According to Charles A. Dana, a special commissioner sent by Secretary of War Edwin M. Stanton to spy on Grant, "Ord reports that it will require about ten days to bring the siege works in his front to the same general efficiency and safety as those of McPherson and Sherman," who by this time had made steady advances against the salients on their front. This, however, is not to say that all had been for naught on the Thirteenth Corps front. On the right wing of the Thirteenth Corps, First Lieutenant Peter C. Hains had opened A. J. Smith's Approach within one hundred yards of the Second Texas Lunette on June 11. About a week and a half earlier, Hains had broken ground on Carr's right approach on June 2. Then, on June 7, Carr's men had commenced a second approach branch, dubbed Carr's left approach, toward the Second Texas Lunette. But when compared to the rest of the siege line, the Thirteenth Corps gains had been limited.[15]

On McPherson's front, Hickenlooper had by June 8 pushed Logan's Approach to a point fewer than seventy-five yards from the Third Louisiana Redan. By June 16 the approach was within twenty-five yards of the Confederate fort. Farther north, the Fifteenth Corps had also made steady progress and outpaced the approaches on the south of the siege lines. As early as June 2, Sherman confidently wrote to his wife that he had "approaches and parallels within 80 yards of the Enemys Line." Displaying contempt for McClernand, Sherman wrote to Ellen on June 11 about the deficiencies on the southern part of the line. On that day Sherman described to her a jaunt that he had taken to McClernand's front, where he "found that he [McClernand] was digging his ditches & parallels further back from the enemy than where I [Sherman] began the first day [of the siege]." Sherman did, however, have a right to brag. On the day after he wrote Ellen, June 12, Ewing's Approach had reached a point within twenty yards of its target, the Stockade Redan. A few days later, the Union and Confederate lines were within hailing distance of one another. Closer to the river, Brigadier General John M. Thayer, also under Sherman's command, had made only slightly less impressive progress. By June 8 the Union troops pushing forward this approach were within one hundred yards of their objective, the Twenty-Sixth Louisiana Redoubt.[16]

Stagnation on the southern part of the siege line, however, was not the fault of the Thirteenth Army Corps' energetic engineer officer, First Lieutenant Hains. Throughout the first part of the siege, Hains had attempted to conduct a professional siege on the northern sector of the Thirteenth Corps front, but McClernand's meddling had made this impossible. According to Dana, Ord was unimpressed with what he found when he took command on June 18, describing the trenches that McClernand had opened as deficient "rifle pits 3 or 4 feet wide," incapable of allowing "the passage of artillery" and unable to accommodate "the assemblage of any considerable number of troops." Furthermore, Ord reportedly complained that the Thirteenth Corps artillery batteries were "with scarcely an exception, in the same position they apparently held when the siege was opened." While it is commonly accepted that Dana was a Grant supporter and a McClernand detractor, the fact remains that Ord inherited a sector where approaches, when compared to Sherman's and McPherson's fronts, were behind schedule.[17]

Interestingly, Ord exempted the engineer in charge of these operations, First Lieutenant Hains. According to Ord, as reported by Dana, "The corps commanders and generals of divisions were not willing to follow his [Hains's] directions, either as to the manner of opening the lines of advance or the positions of the batteries to protect those lines." Thus, prior to Ord's rise to corps command, all Hains could do was to mark time and improve the line of circumvallation.[18]

Nevertheless, progress in the Thirteenth Corps front was slow. On June 8, Hains reported to McClernand's headquarters that on the northern part of his front, details "enlarged and improved that part of the rifle pit on the same line already begun." Similar activity occurred on Hovey's front, where on June 9, "details still [worked] at widening . . . trenches and making the batteries . . . stronger." In fact, as late as June 17, McClernand reported to

Lieutenant Colonel John A. Rawlins, the assistant adjutant general on Grant's staff, that, instead of concentrating on forward approach, "Genl. Hovey was employed in improving and strengthening his position." From the beginning of the siege until this late date, the blue-clad midwesterners of Hovey's division simply sniped at the enemy from their rifle pits. As a result, "the excellent ground in front of Hovey's Division was not utilized" until Hains broke ground there during the last week of June. Meanwhile, a little farther north, 120 black laborers under Brigadier General Stephen G. Burbridge's command in A. J. Smith's division simply "cut a rifle pit 150 yards in length." All of this occurred against Hains's protest. The Thirteenth Corps chief engineer, no doubt frustrated, had insisted that "this part of the field offers eminent facilities for successful approach to the enemy line." His superiors ignored him. It took McClernand three days to acknowledge this suggestion, and soldiers did not break ground on A. J. Smith's Approach until June 11.[19]

Yet, Dana's observation is only partially accurate. Interestingly, although McClernand was himself a political general without formal military training, he commanded a corps that contained more division commanders who were graduates of West Point than those of either McPherson or Sherman. Of McClernand's four original division commanders—Brigadier General Peter J. Osterhaus, Hovey, A. J. Smith, and Carr—Smith and Carr were graduates of the United States Military Academy. Meanwhile, on McPherson's front, aside from the corps commander himself, only Brigadier General Isaac F. Quinby, Brigadier General Marcellus M. Crocker's replacement, was a West Point graduate. Similarly, of Sherman's three division commanders, only Major General Frederick Steele was a USMA graduate. It is not a surprise, therefore, that the first approaches on the Thirteenth Corps front were Carr's and A. J. Smith's, which were opened on June 2 and 11 respectively. Both had been educated in the school of Mahan.

Despite the presence of trained engineers, effective leadership at the corps level was needed in order to prosecute effective, offensive siege warfare. On Sherman's front, corps-level micromanagement worked because Sherman was a graduate of the USMA who understood the science of siege warfare. On McPherson's front, where corps-level micromanagement does not appear to have occurred, the decision to concentrate on one approach, Logan's, allowed for a controlled environment and the successful prosecution of an offensive siege. In McClernand's sector, this politician-turned-general's corps-level micromanagement led to the waste of valuable time. When Hains was allowed to work with other professionals, such as Carr and later Smith, success ensued. This success, however, was limited and late in the game. McClernand simply dumped too much responsibility on the young lieutenant, and then, when the junior officer, fresh out of the Academy, attempted to take control of the situation, McClernand meddled. Thus, Dana had it partially right. It was not only the division commanders who stifled Hains but also McClernand's unwillingness to support the young engineer's informed decisions that led to stalemate on the Thirteenth Corps front.

With Ord in command, Hains was permitted to execute the professional type of siege warfare that West Point and Mahan had trained him to implement. On June 22, Hains ordered the construction of Hovey's Approach and set Union troops to work on this favorable ground. Despite the lack of engineer officers and pioneers, the work on this zigzag highlighted the synchronized marriage of soldier motivation, improvisation, and professional know-how. The result: a textbook approach, one that a professional engineer directed and amateurs prosecuted with vigor. Captain Frank Swigart of the Forty-Sixth Indiana described this flawless execution. "A favorable place on the hill-side was selected and a line for a trench marked out," Swigart wrote, and "if the place was not exposed, no temporary shelter was put up to protect the men." But, if enemy fire endangered the federal excavators, "cracker-boxes and barrels were put on the side next the city to shield the men." During the daytime, "an engineer officer" would examine "the ground" to be traversed "and marked out the [trench] line." Once nightfall descended upon the siege lines and held the potential for cloaking the work party, "men were distributed along the line, and each one, besides his gun, had a pick or spade. He then laid down his gun and used the pick or spade until relieved by another detail." By the time the sun came up the next day, a "ditch or trench would be dug about two feet wide and as deep as possible." The excavated soil was not wasted. According to Swigart, "The dirt taken out of the trench would be thrown up on the Vicksburg side, so that it aided in sheltering the men who were then at work or on guard." After one trench was excavated to the point where the work party could dig in safety, another was started, and thus the Union besiegers "worked up closer to the enemy works."[20]

As in Logan's Approach, engineers and soldiers working on Hovey's Approach designed both the "zig" and the "zag" to double as a rifle trench from which to pour on suppressing fire. As the work party dug forward on its angular course, other soldiers in back of them, closer to the Union lines, began to place headlogs on top of the dirt mound that had been formed when the excavators shoveled earth out of the trench toward the Confederate defenses. According to Swigart, "We would place a heavy log on top of the earthworks with notches cut in the lower side for portholes, through which the men on duty could fire without danger to their heads." But at times, these firing portholes could prove dangerous. When the competent rebel marksmen proved able to place well-aimed rounds through the sniper ports, Union troops improvised and closed off the holes with lids taken off boxes of hardtack. And so the men of Hovey's division, although off to a late start, snaked their way across no-man's-land toward the Confederate lines.[21]

As it had been in the age of Vauban, the sap roller became at Vicksburg the distinguishing feature of the sap. According to Mahan, once the sap reached within "musket range" of the enemy defenses, an elite team of sappers was to take over. These specially trained "engineer troops . . . advance the end of the trench, working on their knees, and shielding themselves in front from the enemy's fire by a large gabion stuffed with fascines, or wool, termed a *Sap-Roller*, which is rolled forward as they gradually advance." At Vicksburg, however, with professional sappers in short supply, ordinary line troops worked the trenches behind the sap roller.[22]

In Mahan's theoretical realm, sap rollers had very precise measurements. As stated by Mahan, a sap roller should be "a large gabion, 7'6" in length, and 4'4" exterior diameter. It requires for its construction fifteen stakes, each from 1½" to 2" in diameter. After it is completed, it is stuffed compactly with fascines 7'6" long. The sap roller is sometimes made of two concentric gabions, the diameter of the smaller 2'6". The space between the two is compactly stuffed with fascines." Such precise figures, ideal in theory, were impossible to conform to in the field. With few engineer officers on hand at Vicksburg to supervise such minutiae, soldiers constructed a diverse array of sap rollers. Some were traditional and attempted to model Mahan's maxims. Others were the product of soldier improvisation. The construction of sap rollers during the Vicksburg siege clearly illustrates the wedding of West Point theory to western soldier adaptation that allowed Union troops to engineer victory.[23]

A sap roller, or what Union soldiers at Vicksburg commonly called "a bullet-stopper," appeared at the head of most saps. According to Captain Cyrus B. Comstock, "The sap-roller was used in all close approaches, one of cane with a central cavity being found best." Andrew Hickenlooper, chief engineer of the Seventeenth Army Corps, described traditional Vicksburg sap

Haas and Peale photograph of Union soldiers excavating a full sap on Morris Island, South Carolina, in 1863. Similar types of sap rollers were also used at Vicksburg. *Library of Congress.*

rollers. They were "larger and stronger [than gabions]," Hickenlooper wrote, resembling "basket woven cylinders" typically "about 6 feet in diameter and 12 feet in length." In order to make them maneuverable yet bulletproof, "the inside [was] filled with some light material effective in resisting the passage of musket balls." Once constructed, "they [were] used by being rolled along the surface in the direction, and at the head of the sap or trench, as a protection to the men engaged in making the necessary excavations." Behind these sap rollers "the men, with spade and pick, dug away, pushing the [approach] closer and closer [toward] . . . the Confederate works." As one soldier described, "By keeping this [the sap roller] in front of a couple of men, they could dig a trench directly toward the enemy's lines, and still be protected from the deadly minnie-balls [*sic*]." Although sap rollers differed from gabions in size and dimension, they also deviated from their smaller counterparts in function. As one Union soldier succinctly explained, "The sap rollers are larger than the gabions, and are to be used by the ditch dig[g]ers. [T]he gabions are to be used by our sharp shooters" along the sides of the trench.[24]

Some approaches used traditional, Mahanian-style sap rollers. This became typical on the Thirteenth Corps front where Hains, a West Point professional, was allowed to prosecute a textbook-style siege after Ord replaced McClernand on June 18. But it would be inaccurate to blame McClernand alone for the late implementation of sap rollers on the Thirteenth Corps front. According to Hains, rugged terrain in front of A. J. Smith's Approach made it very difficult to employ sap rollers. Finally, on June 18, the approach had reached level ground and Hains could order the construction of "a large roller made of bundles of cane, placed directly across the designated approach and rolled forward as the ditch lengthened." Similarly, in Hovey's Approach, soldiers devised traditional "cane brake rollers" that "the men kept rolling before them as they worked" in an attempt to protect themselves from "enfilading fire from the enemy."[25]

Between A. J. Smith's and Hovey's Approaches, Carr's Approach too made use of traditional sap rollers "twelve to fifteen feet in diameter" and made of "wild cane stalks, such as are shipped from the South and used by the Northern boys for fishing poles." They were slowly rolled forward "with hand spikes . . . in advance of the work in the trench." Charles A. Hobbs of the Ninety-Ninth Illinois working in Carr's Approach lucidly described the process of making one of these traditional sap rollers. According to Hobbs, the size and dimensions of individual sap rollers varied across the Union line with the width of each sap trench determining the apparatus's specific length. Nevertheless, the sap rollers, despite their variations, contained similar characteristics overall. They were "round basket-sort of affairs" without a bottom and woven from grapevines, which grew in abundance behind the Union siege lines. The thick diameter of the grapevines, however, resulted in a basket-like structure that contained spaces throughout the walls of the sap roller. In order to fill in these gaps so as to keep dirt from leaking out, soldiers improvised. They used wooden mallets to split thinner cane reeds into strands that could then be woven through the spaces of the grapevine sap roller. Once soldiers completed weaving the basket, they packed the hollow shell with dirt, tipped it onto its side, and rolled it along in front of them as they dug their sap. These rollers adequately shielded work details and, according to Hobbs, could stop any Confederate bullet.[26]

Sometimes, however, where those without the requisite knowledge of sap roller construction were not present, soldiers were forced to dig saps without sap rollers. During these instances, soldiers crouched down on their knees and dug in an attempt to present smaller profiles to rebel sharpshooters. "I will admit that I preferred to have the sap roller, though," recalled Hobbs, "even if we did sometimes get along without it. Where the trench was liable to be very much exposed to the enemy's fire, the sap roller would be larger."[27]

But even under Hains's professional and watchful eye, sap rollers went through a process of trial and error. In A. J. Smith's front, once soldiers reached level ground on June 18, engineers began considering the employment of sap rollers. On June 19, Thirteenth Corps soldiers, under Hains's careful supervision, constructed three different types of sap rollers. Although the first two traditional variants failed, the third, a product of ingenuity and improvisation, proved a monumental success. According to Hains, the first "was made of solid cane and of the usual dimensions, but was found too heavy to use." The second attempt "was of the usual dimensions, but made with an interior gabion." This sap roller, like the first, failed. It was "crushed, of its own weight, in being rolled." The third roller "was made by taking two barrels" and "placing them head-to-head." They were connected with "bracing" on the "inside" of the barrels. A "row of fascines" was tied "around the outside by means of wire." In order to help the sap roller "roll easily, the space between the outside fascines, on the circumference, was filled with smaller bundles of cane, and well lashed together with telegraph wire." One soldier in Carr's division later recalled that this final type of sap roller was not only lighter and more maneuverable but also stout enough so that "no bullet could get through it."[28]

Cotton, a cash crop abundant in antebellum Mississippi, provided another resource soldiers used when experimenting with sap rollers. In one incident, a member of the Seventeenth Ohio Artillery wrote to his family of an unusual event. On May 20, before the siege officially began, the Ohio artillerist and his battery were waiting for the rest of the army to arrive. He "was much amused" when he saw soldiers of the Twenty-Third Wisconsin "rolling their cotton bales in front of them making an advance on the enemy." The soldiers made it partway into no-man's-land and proceeded to dig a trench from which to observe the enemy. In another, more common example, W. R. Eddington of the Ninety-Seventh Illinois, A. J. Smith's division, wrote to his father describing the process of making a sap roller stuffed with cotton. "We got a lot of sticks," wrote Eddington, "about one inch in diameter and six feet long." A circle was then drawn on the ground in order to provide an outline for the diameter of the roller. The soldiers proceeded to "sharpen one end of the sticks and drive them in the ground around [that] circle." Each stick was "about three or four inches apart." The Illinoisans would then weave

Cotton bale being used as a sap roller. *"A Some-what Notable Picket Post," from Charles A. Hobbs, "Vanquishing Vicksburg: The Campaign Which Ended in the Surrender of America's Gibraltar," National Tribune, March 24, 1892.*

smaller brush or grapevines "around these poles [in order] to keep them together." They then topped off the sap roller by filling "it full of cotton and tramp it down solid. [W]e would push it over on its side and make a roller of it."[29]

In Hickenlooper's front in the Seventeenth Corps sector, a perfect meshing of West Point theory and western soldier improvisation occurred early in the siege. With the initial Union line only approximately five hundred yards away from the Third Louisiana Redan, the main fort guarding the Jackson Road that ran into the city in this sector, Hickenlooper immediately began work on the sap that would become known as Logan's Approach. At first light on May 26, Hickenlooper ordered a group of three hundred men to begin work on this approach. In danger of enfilading fire, "recourse was had to the sap-roller." According to Hickenlooper, once darkness fell, Union skirmishers would move forward to engage Confederate vedettes guarding their works. In nearly every case "a lively fight generally ensued but always resulted in the enemy being crowded back." With the Confederate skirmishers pushed back, soldiers would prosecute the approach under the safety of the sap roller. This, however, was not a typical sap roller. Although it prevented enfilading fire and therefore conformed to Mahanian dogma, its construction and schematic reflected western soldier improvisation in its purest form.[30]

Soldiers both during the siege and in the years following the Civil War wrote in depth about the unusual sap roller that spearheaded Logan's Approach. In fact, it went by a variety of names. To some, it resembled a shallow-draft watercraft. Those who perceived the sap roller in this light labeled the device the "land gunboat," "dry-land Gun-boat," or, simply the "gun Boat." To others, it looked more like a "moving fort." Then there were those soldiers who just called it "Logan's Car" or the "go devil." Despite the diversity of names, these soldiers wrote about the same peculiar sap roller: a wheeled device whose axles supported a platform that contained a cotton barricade from behind which sharpshooters harassed the enemy.[31]

The details of the construction of the "land gunboat" vary. According to S. C. Beck, "In digging a trench from our lines up to the Rebel fort our men had a flat car covered with cottonbales which they rolled in front of the sappers." Providing more detail, William A. Lorimer of the Seventeenth Illinois described the sap roller as one with "four wooden wheels about three feet in diameter and one foot thick . . . connected with wooden axles . . . propelled by wooden crowbars." Atop this base rested "a platform . . . surrounded with cotton bales" that housed "armed men from the division." One of the most detailed descriptions of Logan's "gunboat" came from a mounted trooper attached to Logan's headquarters. As stated by Samuel H. Fletcher of the Second Illinois Cavalry, "A platform of heavy timbers about twelve feet wide and sixteen feet long, was built and supported upon strong wheels." Sitting atop the "platform were mounted two large wooden guns." In order to provide a more realistic appearance, each was "painted black and varnished" as to provide the illusion of "a ten inch bore." The "formidable engine of war" reminded Fletcher of the Homeric "wooden-horse at the siege of Troy" as it was steadily rolled in front of the Union excavators, serving "to shield them and their work from the enemy."[32]

The men excavating Logan's Approach made steady progress shielded behind the "land gunboat." With enfilading fire threatening Hickenlooper's trench, the Seventeenth Corps engineer decided to drive forward a flying sap with a single row of gabions on the side of the sap wall facing the enemy. But the western soldiers, despite their capacity for ingenuity and inventiveness, could not implement this building project alone. The line

Improvised sap roller used at the head of Logan's Approach, dubbed by some Union soldiers as Logan's "Land Gunboat." *Osborn Hamiline Oldroyd, A Soldier's Story of the Siege of Vicksburg, 47.*

troops carrying out the manual labor depended upon the engineer's expertise as well as his bravery.[33]

As stated earlier, saps did not chart random and haphazard courses across no-man's-land. Engineers, in addition to surveying the best avenue of approach, were responsible for physically marking with pickets and white cord the precise direction that the sap would travel. Hickenlooper, despite his formal training as a civil engineer, understood this invaluable art and exposed himself to personal danger in order to ensure that his sap followed the correct path across no-man's-land. Just before midnight, under the cover of darkness, the Seventeenth Corps engineer crawled into the exposed ground between the lines with "three or four detached bayonets" and several yards of cord in order to stake out the sap's planned direction for that night. As Hickenlooper sidled along his predetermined path, he would, at variable distances, plant one of his bayonets, tie the cord to its shank, and continue to drag the cord to the next point, where he would repeat the process. Once all of the bayonets were gone, Hickenlooper returned to the safety of the Union trenches.[34]

The evening's work, however, was not complete. Upon Hickenlooper's return to the Union lines, he had a party of soldiers advance the sap roller to the farthest point in the mapped-out line where he had placed his final bayonet, closest to the Confederate defenses. Meanwhile, a line officer commenced organizing the night's work detail. Each soldier in the detail snatched up an unfilled gabion (which had been fabricated earlier that day) and either a shovel or a pickax. Armed with their excavation implements, the soldiers formed into a single-file line and entered into the darkness, following along Hickenlooper's newly laid cord-bayonet line. The officer in charge then ordered the soldiers to halt at four-foot intervals. Once in position, each soldier stuck one of the open ends of his gabion into the ground and commenced filling the basket by digging a hole on the side of the gabion away from the Confederate fortifications. After he had filled his basket, the now fatigued soldier expanded his hole, digging along the bayonet-cord line backward toward the soldier to his rear, thus creating a continuous trench line. At sunrise the night detail left the trench, now a shallow gully lined with gabions and a sap roller in front, and a second detail filed in with the mission of widening and deepening the trench.[35]

In this way, the men on Logan's front inched closer to the Confederate works, reaching within seventy-five yards of the Third Louisiana Redan on June

8. Work had thus far proceeded so smoothly that Hickenlooper reduced the number of men working on the approach first to 150 men on June 2 and then to a skeleton force of 100 soldiers on June 3. This changed a few days later.[36]

The rapid progress of Logan's Approach alarmed Confederate chief engineer Major Samuel H. Lockett. With nothing to lose, Lockett decided to entertain a "novel experiment" that a Confederate private proposed. According to Lockett, the private "took a piece of port-fire [a fuse tube], stuffed it with cotton saturated with turpentine, and fired it from an old fashioned large-bore musket into the roller, and thus set it on fire." The fire alarmed the Federals and, after several attempts to extinguish the flames, forced them to abandon their coveted "gunboat."[37]

Nevertheless, determined to "recommence their operations . . . some distance back" the Union troops built a second sap roller. This version was more traditional. It consisted of a "wicker casing five feet in diameter by ten feet in length compactly filled with cotton." As added protection, the Union troops poured water on the sap roller in order to prevent future burnings. By June 13 the Union troops in Logan's Approach were once again "within 40 yards" of the Third Louisiana Redan. Despite their rapid advance, this last precaution, soaking the cotton in water, proved all for naught. According to Hickenlooper, "A little after midnight on the 18th [of June] the enemy succeeded in some mysterious manner in firing our sap-roller, causing its total destruction," but shortly thereafter, "another roller [of unspecified type] was substituted the next night, and the work continued to the end without any similar interruption." To ensure the success of this third sap roller and the approach that it protected, Hickenlooper also increased the work detail back to 150 men.[38]

All of this success, with its minor setbacks, took a personal toll on Hickenlooper. With a limited number of engineers present for duty, the Seventeenth Corps engineer assumed personal responsibility for Logan's Approach around the clock. For nearly a month he "never left the work before one or two o'clock in the morning, and never obtained over three or four hours sleep any one night." Working in the uncomfortable, sticky humidity of the Mississippi summer, Hickenlooper decided to make every hour of shut-eye count. After each exhausting day in the trenches, Hickenlooper would retire back to his tent sandwiched between Major General James B. McPherson's "on the left" and Colonel Clark's, McPherson's chief of staff, "on the right." In order to obtain quality sleep, the engineer ordered that "a tub of full clear water [be left] in the rear of [his] tent in which [he] could take a bath when [he] came down from the front."[39]

Although Hickenlooper shared a close relationship with both McPherson and Clark, Clark could be "at times . . . exceedingly nervous and irritable to an objectionable degree." In one particular incident during the siege, Clark interrupted Hickenlooper's ritual and displayed his irascible tendencies. According to Hickenlooper, "One morning as I was about to take my accustomed bath he [Clark] appeared upon the scene and vented his wrath upon me in no measured terms, informing me that I was thus disturbing the slumbers of the General and the entire staff, and the practice must be abandoned, or indulged in at a more seasonable hour, to which I made no reply." Hickenlooper let the issue drop. His superior, McPherson, did not. A former engineer who understood the difficulties of the profession and a savvy professional who recognized that men with Hickenlooper's talents were in short supply, McPherson was not about to let his most trusted engineer be reprimanded in such a way.[40]

The next day, the Seventeenth Corps commander ordered a meeting between Hickenlooper and Clark. When the three men convened, McPherson addressed the issue. "Gentlemen I overheard what was said last night, and I now desire to say to you Hickenlooper in Colonel Clark's presence that when you come down from the trenches at night you are at liberty to bathe and make as much noise in doing so as you please, and if any member of the staff is disturbed by your doing so, he had better remove his quarters to some other location." McPherson then excused himself, leaving the two men alone. According to Hickenlooper, "Neither the Colonel nor I made any comment or referred to the subject afterwards; but the bathing went on just the same."[41]

Hem them in, starve them out. The common western soldier, as well as those unacquainted with military science, came to Vicksburg with that perception of siege craft. It would take the efforts of the handful of professionals in Grant's army to correct this misinterpretation of siege warfare. As Sherman wrote to his wife on June 11, after boasting about the superiority of his approach trenches when compared to others in the field, "It will take some time to dig them out. The truth is, we trust to Starvation." Sherman, despite his military qualifications, understood that the Army of the Tennessee lacked experience in professional siege craft and contained a deficient engineering contingent. A professionally trained soldier, Old Cump immediately commenced offensive siege operations after the failed May 22 assault and pushed forward some of the most formidable approach trenches anywhere along the line. Unlike his colleague McClernand, who, for the most part, was ignorant of siege craft, Sherman understood the need for forward movement. Remaining idle would cause the Army of the Tennessee to deteriorate while encouraging an attack from a Confederate relief force against Grant's rear. But Sherman's vigor was not enough to move the entire army. While he could personally oversee operations in his own front, he recognized that much of the army, due to its engineering deficiencies, would have to sit tight and "trust to starvation" while Grant's handful of engineers picked up the slack and pushed forward textbook approaches wherever possible.[42]

While professionals realized the necessity and benefit of forward advance, novices took Grant's postwar phrase "out-camp the enemy" to heart. Waiting for starvation was not an option. Hunkering down and trusting that the enemy would eventually run out of food would be ill advised. This approach would allow an army of relief to gather and perhaps help the beleaguered garrison to break out of the city. Furthermore, sitting and waiting would put logistical strains on Grant's army while allowing disease and boredom to reduce the effectiveness of the Army of the Tennessee. Hemming the rebels in and starving them out was not a sufficient solution to the problem faced by Grant and his army. While the men serving in the Army of the Tennessee struggled to describe this new form of peculiar warfare to loved ones at home, they quickly adapted and mastered their craft. The successful blend of West Point engineering theory with soldier improvisation allowed the Army of the Tennessee to take the first forward steps toward conquering the no-man's-land between the lines.[43]

Progress was uneven during the early days of the siege. Sherman and McPherson, both West Point graduates, implemented macro-textbook theory from the beginning. Meanwhile, to the south of the line, McClernand, a general who had received his rank based upon his political connections rather than upon his military training, bungled during the first half of the siege. Although all three generals managed to construct adequate works that made up the line of circumvallation, the transition from hemming in the enemy to digging forward-advancing approach trenches was easier for Sherman and McPherson than it was for McClernand. Despite McClernand's meddling, his chief engineer, First Lieutenant Peter C. Hains, ably applied his West Point training where he could. Unfortunately, it would not be until Ord replaced McClernand that Hains would be able to conduct the scientific Mahanian siege that he wanted.

For the most part, the main approaches along the Union siege lines were very similar. Where possible, engineers attempted to use the undulating terrain and natural defiles in order to zigzag their way closer to the enemy salients. The same ground that protected the Confederates, if identified, could provide natural approach highways toward the rebel works. While the term "sap" contained specific meaning in the engineer's vocabulary, those serving at Vicksburg used the term rather loosely, thereby making it difficult to ascertain transitions from simple trenches to saps—forward-moving zigzags that used gabions and other artificial revetment. Despite the nuances of nomenclature, establishing a line of circumvallation close to the Confederate defenses allowed Union troops to skip the early parts of Mahanian siege craft and delve right into forward movement via saps.

The use at Vicksburg of the sap roller, in all its curious permutations, serves as a microcosm of the successful blending of Mahanian dogma and soldier improvisation that made the Vicksburg siege successful. At times soldiers used traditional sap rollers. When those proved inadequate, they improvised. Sometimes improvisation was basic, such as on the Thirteenth Corps front, where barrels with cane lashed around them proved lighter and more effective. At other times improvisation took on an extreme character, like Logan's "land gunboat." In short, this phase of the Vicksburg siege, the running of forward zigzag approaches, proved successful due to the harmonious marriage of West Point engineering theory and western soldier improvisation. This blending allowed the troops serving in the Army of the Tennessee to make the first forward advances toward the enemy as they engineered victory.

7. *The Body Snatchers*

The federal soldiers inched forward toward the Confederate defenses under relative safety. The zigzag approach, which utilized simple geometric principles, allowed the Army of the Tennessee to conquer no-man's-land while avoiding enfilading fire. Despite the fact that Vicksburg's natural loess soil allowed trenches to hold their shape, engineers and soldiers used artificial revetment such as gabions and fascines for additional protection. When a sap came within range of Confederate rifle muskets and its head fronted enemy works, the danger of enfilading fire became more pressing. In order to solve this problem, the western troops that made up Major General Ulysses S. Grant's army used both traditional and improvised sap rollers in order to protect workers as they advanced.

All of these precautions suggest that the besiegers were guaranteed safe passage across no-man's-land. They were not. Saps and general approach trenches, with all of their devices to protect excavators, were not foolproof. As those working in the trenches drew closer to the enemy works, artillery fire could obliterate even the best sap roller and gabion-reinforced trench. Adding to the hazards, the defenders' musket and rifle fire peppered the attackers as they made their advance. As one soldier recalled after the war, "It was the busy season for the snipers—the body snatchers." These problems, inherent to all sieges during the gunpowder age, threatened to derail Grant's methodical advance toward Vicksburg. But the Army of the Tennessee had an answer, one torn from the pages of tradition. Heavy suppressing fire would be needed in order to silence Confederate guns and rifles, with the ultimate goal, as Chaplain W. M. Baker of the 116th Illinois lucidly explained, "being to keep the enemy down so that they could not fire on our working parties."[1]

Suppressing fire during the Vicksburg siege, as during most sieges during the gunpowder age, broke down into two broad categories: small arms–suppressing fire and artillery-suppressing fire. Both sought to silence the enemy's guns and small arms. Placing unprotected sharpshooters and guns charged with this task in no-man's-land would be futile. Sharpshooters and artillery crews would come under direct fire and either be obliterated or become themselves suppressed. In order to deliver effective suppressing fire, engineers and common soldiers devised a diversity of contrivances that would allow them to deliver suppressing fire from relative safety. This chapter will examine how Grant's army engineered the sharpshooter war that contributed to federal victory. The engineers and soldiers of the Army of the Tennessee devised both traditional and improvised solutions to the problem of Confederate harassing fire that threatened to upset Union siege operations. These construction projects, some Vaubanian and others the spawn of western soldiers' imaginations, allowed Grant's army to achieve small arms fire superiority that allowed the federal troops to approach the Confederate defenses virtually unopposed.

The first and most obvious form of protection that allowed soldiers to deliver suppressing sharpshooter fire was the parallel trench. The parallel trench was not new to the Vicksburg siege. In fact, one can trace its origins back to the late seventeenth century and the French Enlightenment engineering master Sébastien Le Prestre de Vauban. When Vauban entered the service of Louis XIV in 1653, Enlightenment engineers were already using zigzag approach trenches. Although these approaches protected excavators from defilade, work details were still susceptible to enemy sorties. In order to remedy this problem, Vauban, in 1673, at the siege of Maastricht, devised a solution: the parallel trench. As workers prosecuted the zigzag approach toward the enemy's salients, other excavators dug lateral trenches. These lateral trenches extended from the zigzag on either side and ran parallel to the enemy defenses. It was in these trenches that Vauban placed soldiers charged with protecting the workers in the main zigzag approaches from enemy sallies. As the flintlock musket and later the percussion rifle-musket earned their places on the battlefield, soldiers in the parallel trenches began not only to guard those working the sap but also to provide suppressing fire against enemy marksmen and artillery. Thus, the defensive characteristics of the Vaubanian parallel gave way to the defensive-offensive sharpshooter parallel that dominated later sieges. Still charged with protecting the workers in the sap against sallies, nineteenth-century soldiers could, due to advances in small arms technology, provide offensive suppressing fire aimed at silencing enemy artillery and marksmen bent on putting the besiegers' work parties out of commission.[2]

The typical Vaubanian-style siege featured three parallel trenches. The parallels, as their name implies, extended like arms from the forward-moving, zigzag approach saps and lay parallel to the enemy defenses. These three parallels were labeled the first, second, and third with the final (third) being the closest to the enemy's fortifications. While approach trenches moved forward toward the salient, other workers labored to dig their lateral parallels and, if practicable, attempted to connect these trenches with the corresponding parallels of the other approach trenches targeting the same part of the enemy's defenses.

The science of the Vaubanian parallel was handed down to the West Point cadets of the antebellum period. According to Dennis Hart Mahan, "The object of [the] parallel is to protect the approaches as they are pushed forward upon the salients." Mahan, as in the age of Vauban, specified that there were to be three parallel trenches. The first parallel, if situated properly, was to be approximately six hundred yards from the targeted enemy salient. Next, the second parallel was to be traced "parallel to the first" and was situated about three hundred yards from the same targeted salient. Finally, the third parallel was to be parallel to the second and dug within sixty yards of the same enemy salient. The Army of the Tennessee, however, did not follow this prescription at Vicksburg.[3]

While the engineers at Vicksburg made use of parallel trenches, they did not conform exactly to Vaubanian and Mahanian maxims. First, there was the issue of distance. As stated in previous chapters, the besieging Union force established the initial line of circumvallation within 600 yards of the enemy. This meant that the approaches that the Federals began were well under the distance traditionally allotted for the first parallel in Mahan's and Vauban's theoretical realm. For example, Ewing's Approach, which hugged the Graveyard Road into Vicksburg, originated at a point fewer than 380 yards from the advanced salient of the Confederate Great Redoubt. Similarly, Logan's Approach, which began near the Shirley House (often known to the soldiers as the White House) and roughly followed the Jackson Road into the city, originated some 433 yards from the salient of the Third Louisiana Redan, commonly called "Fort Hill" by some of the Union soldiers.

Meanwhile, to the south, Carr's right approach began some 350 yards from the Railroad Redoubt while his left approach began some 280 yards from the same Confederate fortification. Even farther down the siege line, Hovey's right approach originated approximately 260 yards from the rebel Fort Garrott. The Vicksburg approaches, when compared to traditional siege doctrine, originated at close proximities to the Confederate lines.[4]

The relatively close distances that marked the origin of each approach trench support the observations of Private Frank Holcomb Mason. "In front of nearly every division," Mason wrote, "was a natural covered approach, through some defile, to within three or four hundred yards of the enemy's line." In certain isolated examples, "these distances were less than one hundred yards." Here, close to "these advanced points a sap began, and the first and second parallels incident to ordinary sieges being thus rendered unnecessary were omitted." Since the Union saps began so close to the enemy salients, precise conformity to Mahanian maxims was unnecessary. Union engineers and soldiers improvised. They cast off the shackles of Vaubanian dogma and opened traditional parallels only as needed.[5]

The issue of distance ties directly into the second problem that forced engineers to forgo the use of what Mason called "the first and second parallels incident to ordinary sieges": the issue of terrain. The ravines that provided essential defilade and allowed the Federals to begin their approaches closer to the enemy works also influenced how engineers constructed and connected parallels. Albert Chipman of the Seventy-Sixth Illinois wrote during the siege that "the ground is very uneven and as a matter of course the picket lines are very crooked." This "uneven ground" made it difficult for engineers to connect the parallels that extended from different saps and to create continuous lines of parallels, as suggested in Mahan's manuals. The extreme topography dictated that many parallels supporting the main approach trench were not continuous, similar to the fragmented nature of the line of circumvallation at Vicksburg. In order to combat this, engineers implemented the textbook practices of demi-parallels and half parallels, which were, in effect, shorter versions of the standard parallel. The use of demi-parallels and half parallels may be seen in the approaches of Brigadier Generals A. J. Smith, Joseph A. J. Lightburn, and Hugh Ewing. Yet, where possible, engineers seized the opportunity to adopt convention and connect parallel trenches. For example, down on the Thirteenth Corps front, engineer officer First Lieutenant Peter C. Hains succeeded in connecting "the second parallels . . . in front of Generals Smith and Carr," making them "continuous" on June 28. This parallel, once completed, ran some thousand yards in length. Meanwhile to the north, troops of Major General William T. Sherman's Fifteenth Corps dug a short parallel trench in order to connect Ewing's and Lightburn's approaches sometime after June 28.[6]

While the Federals opened their trenches at distances closer to the rebel defenses than those prescribed by Mahan, parallels appeared all along the siege lines. In many ways the parallels closely resembled the trenches that formed the line of circumvallation established after the failed May 22 assault. The primary difference between the parallels and the trenches that made up the line of circumvallation was that the parallel trenches extended laterally from the approach trenches. As William S. Morris of the Thirty-First Illinois explained, "From each side of these [approach trenches], and running lateral to them, rifle pits [parallels] were opened confronting those of the enemy. These grew up every night, always encroaching toward the front." As another federal soldier succinctly put it, "Each tier of rifle pits brought the contending forces closer together."[7]

For the most part, the construction technique and features of the parallels mirrored trenches that formed the line of circumvallation. Engineers or line officers typically escorted details to designated areas, where, under the cover of darkness, work parties began to excavate the profile of the intended trench. When daylight came, a second detail began deepening and widening the parallel. The result was "a heavy parallel trench, or rifle-pit . . . cut along the front" that was "wide and spacious, with banquettes for riflemen, who ingeniously protected their head with sand-bags, or by laying heavy green logs notched on the under side, along the parapets," according to Private Mason. Sharpshooters manned these ports and "stood with their rifles pushed out through the loop-holes, ready to shatter any head that appeared above the enemy parapet."[8]

Of course, some variations existed. While Mason described a trench that did not use revetment and relied on the natural properties of the surrounding loess soil, other parallels utilized gabions, cotton bales, and "empty bread and flour barrels" in order to shore up the sides of trenches. According to Lucius W. Barber of the Fifteenth Illinois, "The *modus operandi* of building these rifle pits [that made use of artificial revetment] was this: Long baskets, made of withes in the shape of a cylinder, were placed on line and filled with dirt, the man standing behind one while he filled the next, thus protecting himself from the enemy's fire." In addition, while Mason described a trench that used a headlog, a popular form of sharpshooter head protection, other trenches sometimes used different forms of upper-body defense, including sandbags (sometimes used in conjunction with headlogs in order to create firing ports for sharpshooters) and even, in more bizarre circumstances, empty wooden cartridge crates. In order to prevent headlogs from rolling back and hitting Union troops as a result of Confederate artillery fire, engineers placed the logs "in the notches of smaller ones that ran rearward across the trench" so that "when knocked off [the log] rolled backward over the heads of the men."[9]

Overall, firing ports for riflemen were kept narrow in order to protect sharpshooters from rebel marksmen. For example, Morgan Ebenezer Wescott of the Seventeenth Wisconsin described in a letter to his parents on June 20 that "we have sand bags on top of our pits, with little space between the sacks of about two inches, just large enough to put the muzzle of our guns through, and we watch, and if a Johnny shoes [*sic*] his head he gets a salute." Similarly, down in Brigadier General Alvin P. Hovey's sector, Thomas Wise Durham of the Eleventh Indiana wrote of similar construction techniques. "On the front side of our rifle-pits fronting the enemy," Durham wrote, "we placed large logs or bags of cotton." Under those different forms of head protection Union troops created "portholes just large enough to receive a gun barrel." Across the expanse of no-man's-land, "the enemy had the same on their forts." "For weeks," Durham recalled, "we would watch these port holes in the fort of the enemy and when we would see one darkened we knew someone was in front of it and would fire at the port hole."[10]

Similar to the trenches that formed the line of circumvallation, the Union parallels at Vicksburg—while containing all of the same features as Mahan's trench, including firing steps and parapets—differed in precise dimensions from those spelled out by both Mahan and James C. Duane. Although Mahan and Duane provided exact measurements for the dimensions of parallels, such precision became nearly impossible to replicate in the field. Both practical constraints and the fact that the Army of the Tennessee lacked professional engineers led to discontinuity in trench design all along the line. For example, Major General John A. McClernand reported to Lieutenant Colonel John A. Rawlins, Grant's assistant adjutant general, on June 12 that, on the previous day, "the second parallel trench in front of Genl. Smith was nearly completed" and was "now of sufficient width to allow troops to march through in two ranks without difficulty." In contrast, in Major General Francis J. Herron's

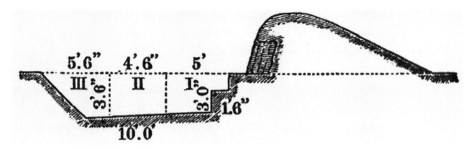

Cross section of a trench excavated to textbook specifications. *J. C. Duane, Manual for Engineer Troops, 121.*

front, one of the parallels resembling an extended rifle trench was only between three and five feet deep and long enough to shelter two hundred soldiers. The mundane realities of working in complete darkness or under enemy fire, combined with the lack of experienced engineer officers to guide the work, made it difficult to achieve consistent textbook dimensions.[11]

Of course, West Point professionals such as Mahan and Duane understood the need for improvisation. In fact, Duane, in his *Manual for Engineer Troops*, provided an entire section instructing students in how to adapt both parallels and approaches to different types of terrain. Duane realized that, up until this point in his text, "we have supposed the [enemy] fortress to be situated on a plain, and to have only that moderate degree of command over the country . . . [in addition] we have also supposed the soils to be favorable." This assumption, often deviating from reality, led the manual's author to instruct cadets to improvise. For example, "If the soil were unfavorable," Duane wrote, "it might be necessary to alter the profiles of both the parallels and approaches." Thus, the manual went on to teach students how to advance approaches and parallels in "marshy or rocky soil" and "in irregular ground." The second subsection, that of waging siege warfare over "irregular ground," demanded further investigation because, as previously stated, the terrain surrounding the landward side of Vicksburg was a series of undulating hills and steep ravines.[12]

Duane, assistant instructor of practical engineering at West Point during the 1850s, compiled a manual, synthesized from British, French, and Austrian textbooks, that taught students how to engage in the minutiae of siege warfare. Although this manual, like Mahan's, provided theoretical detail that would prove nearly impossible to carry out in the field, it did provide contingencies that stressed adaptability. Case in point: in his section on excavating parallels and approaches, originally published by British engineer Lieutenant Colonel

Charles Pasley as *Rules for Conducting the Practical Operations of a Siege* in 1829, Duane stressed that the profiles of these trenches would vary depending upon their relationship to the enemy's fortification, what he termed "the commanding eminence." For example, "If the [enemy's] fortress should be situated on a very commanding eminence," Duane wrote, "it is obvious that the trenches must be cut deeper and the parapets raised higher . . . [than if the profiles had been] constructed on level ground." "But," the West Point instructor continued to explain, "if . . . the ground on which these parallels and approaches must be made . . . slope regularly down on all sides from the commanding eminence crowned by the fortress, this ground being naturally defiladed, is not unfavorable, and may not require deeper trenches or higher parapets than usual."[13]

Ultimately, Pasley, as stated in Duane's compilation, concluded that it would be excessive to outline every engineering problem that a soldier might encounter in the field. "To investigate the farther modifications in the outline or profile of parallels or approaches, that might be required by other varieties of irregular ground not yet noticed," Duane wrote, "would be superfluous in a treatise of this kind, because the expedients necessary for overcoming or evading the difficulties thereby occasioned, will readily suggest themselves to an intelligent officer, on the scene of action." In sum, even those mandating engineering theory recognized the need for contingencies. Duane's improviser on the spot, however, was not a common soldier hailing from the farmlands of America's heartland. He was, to quote Duane, "an intelligent officer," a professional schooled in the art of the siege.[14]

Since this particular manual is a synthesis of English, French, and Austrian engineering treatises, one may conclude that engineering improvisation was not uniquely American. This leads one to question whether or not the Vicksburg siege was remarkable when juxtaposed against other sieges. It was. The lack of engineer officers in the nearly all-volunteer Army of the Tennessee and the degree of improvisation are what made Vicksburg different. Pasley's (and therefore Duane's) "intelligent officer, on the scene," able to adapt and overcome, was a professionally trained military engineering officer. The adaptability that professionals such as Pasley and Duane stressed required a foundation in basic engineering fundamentals that only a handful of engineers at Vicksburg possessed. Understanding how to lay siege to a "commanding eminence" on the opposite side of a valley required that one first master how to besiege an enemy under favorable conditions in an ideal setting. Although it might have been common sense to Pasley and Duane that "approaches should never be carried down the slope of a hill occupied by the besiegers, but should be carried round from the rear of the hill, so as to turn the flank of it," only those exposed to the fundamentals of military engineering would be able to carry out such a task.[15]

Yet, despite their inferior numbers, Union engineers overcame both the lack of professionals and the demanding topography. For example, while the enterprising and resourceful Captain Andrew Hickenlooper did not receive formal prewar training in military engineering, he did, on being appointed chief engineer of the Seventeenth Army Corps in February 1863, take "measure[s] to qualify myself for the service by the procurement of the best works on military engineering, and in close study of the requirements for such a position." Through such self-education, Hickenlooper was able to make the best possible use of terrain when establishing his parallels and prosecuting approach trenches that used the hills in order to achieve defilade.[16]

Nevertheless, Duane's professionals, those educated in the art of siege craft who could respond to specific contingencies, were few and far between at Vicksburg. While engineering theorists advocated improvisation, they never foresaw the special set of problems that Vicksburg possessed. Waging a large siege over irregular ground with a handful of engineers operating in a nearly all-volunteer army required an unprecedented degree of western soldier improvisation that, when blended with Vaubanian theory, held the key to federal success.

Meanwhile, some parallels, especially those on McClernand's front, were simply disappointing in terms of construction and progress. As Sherman wrote to his wife on June 11, "I rode away round to McClernands Lines the day before yesterday, and found that he was digging his ditches & parallels further back from the enemy than where I began the first day." As previously stated, when Major General E. O. C. Ord took command of the Thirteenth Corps on June 18, he was shocked to find parallels that resembled simple rifle pits deficient in both depth and width. Charles A. Dana reported this deficiency on the Thirteenth Corps front to Secretary of War Edwin M. Stanton on June 22. According to Dana, "Ord reports that it will require about ten days to bring the siege works in his front to the same general efficiency and safety as those of McPherson and Sherman." This not only included pushing forward approach trenches more vigorously (or in some cases starting them at all) but deepening and widening rudimentary parallels in order to provide "places for arms of troops" to assemble.[17]

Ord, upon taking command, immediately turned to First Lieutenant Hains, the engineer in charge of the front, for an answer to these appalling deficiencies. But upon interviewing Hains, Ord concluded that his predecessor, McClernand, was to blame for the lack of progress on the Thirteenth Corps front, since, according to Dana, "the corps commanders and generals of divisions were not willing to follow his [Hains's] directions, either as to the manner of opening the lines of advance or the positions of the batteries to protect those lines." Thus, McClernand's unhelpful micromanagement and failure to respect Hains rubbed off on his division commanders, who dismissed the young lieutenant's professional suggestions. As a result, the practical necessities of digging in the field combined with the lack of professional engineers made it difficult to create parallels that mirrored Mahan's guidelines. Nevertheless, the western soldiers of the Army of the Tennessee doggedly plodded forward.[18]

In addition to formal parallels, the Federals excavated informal rifle pits or, as one Union soldier aptly termed them, "a line of light works" designed to provide shelter while sniping at the enemy. Shallow pits for marksmen appeared shortly after the Union arrival on the outskirts of Vicksburg. After the failed May 19 assault, soldiers waited until the cover of darkness, withdrew from the enemy fortifications a few yards, and began to "cover themselves with rifle pits." Similar burrows for one to up to a handful of men appeared after the May 22 assault and soon became standard throughout the siege. Rifle pits, however, were not original to the Vicksburg siege. As stated in previous chapters, Mahan, in his *Summary of the Course of Permanent Fortification*, described how the Russians used rifle pits to great effect during the siege of Sebastopol. According to Mahan, "The Russians . . . also used with great advantage . . . pits for sharpshooters, in advance of their line, from which both the workmen at the trenches and the artillerists of the besiegers were greatly annoyed. These were in some cases connected and formed into a continuous trench of counter-approach."[19]

Mahan handed down knowledge of these informal excavations, and West Point cadets became aware of their construction and basic features. Evidence, however, does not indicate that engineers during the siege oversaw the placement of individual rifle pits. Rather, it is more plausible that line officers dispatched details to the front to form advance picket posts, and, under the cover of darkness, "each man dug a hole for himself and as self-preservation was his motive to work, he was not slow about it." One soldier in the Twelfth

Wisconsin described the process of rifle pit construction in detail. "Under cover of darkness," he recalled after the war, "we would quietly leave our pits, go as still as possible to the place of the proposed new rifle-pits, put a part of the men in a little advance as sentinels, and then go to work." The work was done quickly and methodically. In fact, "sometimes three or four [pits] would be constructed in a night by the same squad of men." The next morning, "the enemy would, quite to his surprise, find our lines nearer, and our firing a little sharper and more acute."[20]

Rifle pits served a dual function. They protected advanced pickets and provided skirmishers with a relatively safe position from which to provide suppressing fire while workers toiled away in widening and deepening approach trenches during daylight hours. As Charles A. Hobbs of the Ninety-Ninth Illinois wrote, "These rifle-pits, somewhat carefully dug in favorable places and protected, afforded the soldier a good place to shoot from." According to S. C. Beck of the 124th Illinois, Union vedettes eventually got so close to the Confederate works that "picket duty was abandoned" and "firing from the rifle pits took its place." Grant's midwesterners continued to pour on merciless rifle fire from their man-made martial depressions in Mississippi's loess soil, and the siege continued.[21]

Despite the fact that their function remained the same, the exact shape and size of rifle pits varied all along the line. According to a solder serving in Major General John A. Logan's division, the skirmishers on the picket line in front of his regiment, the Thirty-First Illinois, "protected themselves by lunettes [crescent-shaped mounds of earth a foot or two in height] that sheltered them from the fire in front, opening to the rear and thus affording a safe retreat when necessary." Meanwhile, a soldier of the Thirtieth Illinois, in the same brigade as the Thirty-First, wrote after the war, "Our rifle-pits were usually cut in the bank at the crest of a ridge, with head-logs or bullet-breaks laid up in front and in the sides where there was a cross-fire on us, with loop-holes or spaces beneath the log large enough to shoot through." The Illinoisan elaborated, writing that "the head-logs protected the head while in the act of shooting. . . . Those pits were of different sizes, varying in capacity from three or four to six or eight men, who went on and off duty about the middle of the night."[22]

The size of the rifle pits varied not only within brigades but also all along the siege line. They ranged in size from "individual rifle-pits," as described by Hobbs of the Ninety-Ninth Illinois on Brigadier General Eugene A. Carr's front, to the pits in Hovey's front that Edward N. Potter of the Twenty-Ninth Wisconsin recorded as being long enough to shelter "10 men." More simply, Anthony B. Burton of the Fifth Ohio Independent Battery, Brigadier General Jacob Lauman's division, described basic slit trenches similar to modern foxholes on his part of the siege line when he wrote on June 8, "This morning our boys had dug little pits for themselves . . . not more than 150 yards from the rebel works."[23]

Yet, perhaps the most extreme example of western improvisation bent at achieving suppressing fire occurred along the line of Logan's Approach. It was here that Second Lieutenant Henry C. Foster of the Twenty-Third Indiana, also known as "Coonskin" due to his nonregulation headgear, a coonskin cap, erected a structure that eventually became an icon of the Vicksburg siege—Coonskin's Tower.

Foster was perhaps the closest thing to a modern sniper lurking in the trenches around Vicksburg. Although the verb "to snipe" and the noun "sniper" had already entered the English language by the time of the Civil War, contemporary Americans referred to those who targeted individuals with shoulder arms as "sharpshooters." The fact that these men did not receive modern training in marksmanship, concealment, observation, or stalking raises debate as to whether or not Civil War sharpshooters were indeed "snipers." Typically, when commanders had luxury to do so, the "best shots" were "detailed to act as sharpshooters." In extraordinary circumstances, some soldiers were detached from their regiments to wander the lines and snipe at the enemy. Such was the case of the Twentieth Ohio's Private Lorain Ruggles, who, due to his "important service through the war as a spy, was presented by Grant with a Henry Rifle" and allowed to roam "along the lines sharp-shooting." Nevertheless, more commonly at Vicksburg, officers selected sharpshooters from the rank and file and formed them into "daily details from the entire brigade." They lined parallels and zigzags and hunkered in shallow advanced rifle pits in order to plink unsuspecting enemy soldiers while providing suppressing fire that would, they hoped, allow workers to dig in safety.[24]

Foster was different. His ability as "an unerring shot" earned him instant fame and the freedom to cruise the federal lines seeking the best fields of fire. According to one source, "Coon Skin . . . a fellow who wore a coon skin cap . . . [was] said to have been brought up on the Plains among the cow boys. . . . He was as bold and daring a young man as one would wish to see." One night Foster put his daring to the test and crept into no-man's-land between the lines and constructed "a burrow in the ground, with a peep-hole in it," a predecessor to the modern sniper's hide. "There," as a fellow officer recalled, "he would frequently take provisions with him, and stay several days at a time watching Confederates." Still dissatisfied with the lack of targets, Foster, sometime around June 8, decided to engineer his own device that would allow him to give plunging fire down into the Confederate Third Louisiana Redan and surrounding fortifications. One night, under the cover of darkness, Foster began directing "a volunteer detail of Companies E and B of the 23rd Indiana Regiment" in the construction of his "observatory." He chose for the site of his tower a spot "on the north side of the approach on the Jackson road" near Shirley's "White House" and some 550 feet from the Confederate Third Louisiana Redan (commonly called Fort Hill by Union soldiers). The structure was erected next to the advanced breaching battery dubbed Battery Hickenlooper in honor of former artillery officer and then Seventeenth Corps engineer Captain Andrew Hickenlooper.[25]

Descriptions of Coonskin's Tower vary. One point of conjecture among contemporaries and veterans was the exact height of the structure. According to one source, "When it was about 40 ft high, [Coonskin] placed some large mirror, so that by reflection he could see the enemy without raising his head above the top of his tower, which, if he did, would make a fine mark for the [Confederate] sharp shooters." Meanwhile, Osborn Hamiline Oldroyd of the Twentieth Ohio wrote on June 9, "Another Yankee device was contrived—a tower, ten or twelve feet high, with steps inside running to the top, where was hung a looking-glass in such a position as to catch and reflect, to a man inside the tower, the interior of the enemy's fort and rifle pits, and thus every man and gun could be counted." The purpose of this looking glass, as one soldier wrote at the time, was "to watch their operations and not be exposed at the loophole." Despite disagreement over the exact height of the structure, it was high enough "to see the city spread out, and the river shining beyond." While different accounts mince details about the stature of the tower, the fate of the "looking glass" that held a coveted place atop the tower remains undisputed. According to Granville B. McDonald of the Thirtieth Illinois, the looking glass was "worked with a string" and proved effective until "the Johneys . . . put a ball through it." As one Union soldier later wrote to his parents on June 30, the rebels "broke it [the looking glass] all to smash after about 100 rounds had been fired at it."[26]

The majority of the sources state that the tower was built out of loose railroad ties. Others describe its sides as constructed out "of timber, plank." Some sources maintain that the walls, thusly built, were hollow, "filled in with dirt," and contained "loopholes in the side to shoot from." Written descriptions of the tower's breadth, however, remain scanty. According to one soldier, the tower was "about six feet square with a ladder for climbing to the top on the inside." The ties were stacked in a "log cabin style." Some contemporary sources held the tower up as a paragon of western ingenuity and the brainchild of hard frontier living. According to one source, Foster piled up the loose railroad ties the way that he did because, "learned in backwoods lore, he [Foster] knew how to construct a genuine pioneer log-cabin." A letter from a Union soldier to his parents dated June 30, 1863, provides a vivid, and perhaps the most accurate, description of Coonskin's Tower: "We also have a lookout sharpshooter post, on the highest point of the ridge. This lookout is 20 or 25 feet high and is built of heavy timber and protects a man on three sides and had 3 loopholes in it. [One shooting port] had five large bullet-holes in the exposed side of it. . . . The outside is more than spattered full of holes."[27]

The exact purpose of Coonskin's Tower remains somewhat a mystery. One source related that Foster, who by this time had already gained a degree of fame in the army, requested permission to build his tower in order to "look right into Ft. Hill [in order to] give its strength and arrangement, and [ascertain] where [it would] be safe to make an attack." Meanwhile, other sources suggest that the purpose of the tower was to provide a platform from which to snipe at the enemy. In any case, Coonskin's Tower allowed for both tasks and drew considerable attention, becoming an instant attraction.[28]

Sketch of Coonskin's Tower, known to some as the "Yankee Lookout." *Osborn Hamiline Oldroyd, A Soldier's Story of the Siege of Vicksburg, 49.*

Soldiers from all over the line came to see Coonskin's Tower. On June 27, Seth J. Wells of the Seventeenth Illinois recorded in his diary, "We climbed the observatory and took a good look at Vicksburg, the river, and its surrounding works." Climbing the tower, however, could be dangerous. Its location only some six hundred feet from the Confederate lines placed careless visitors well within the range of rebel sharpshooters. The tower became so popular and its ascent so dangerous that a guard needed to be stationed at its base in order to prevent unauthorized personnel from climbing it and exposing themselves unnecessarily to "the enemy's sharpshooters."[29]

Even Ulysses S. Grant himself came out to see the peculiar contraption. On one of the more mundane days of the siege, the commanding general decided to visit the tower and take a look around for himself. On this particular day, the customary sentinel ordered to keep passersby from climbing the tower had temporarily neglected his post, and Grant managed to slip up the tower unnoticed. The guard, upon returning, looked up toward the top of the tower and, to his anger, spied a man. The irresponsible guard, ignoring his role in the mishap, proceeded to yell at the figure atop the tower, "What are you doing up there?" The man on top did not answer. The guard commanded, "You come down out of that you fool; you'll get shot." Still, no answer came. Not fazed, the unassuming man, still the object of the sentinel's curses, began slowly descending the tower and, upon reaching the ground, quietly walked away. One of the guard's comrades who had observed the whole affair approached his friend and said, "You've played with thunder I must say." Confused, the guard replied, "What have I done?" His comrade fired backed with chagrin, "You've been cussing General Grant black and blue." The befuddled guard muttered, "You don't say . . . I didn't know it was him." Despite the fact that Grant was now walking away and had refused to acknowledge the incident, the embarrassed guard, fearing punishment, ran after the commanding general in order to explain himself. The soldier, upon catching up with Grant, proceeded to nervously apologize, "I hope you will pardon what I said, General. I didn't know [that it was] you." Grant casually replied, "All right, my boy . . . but you must watch closely or some one will get shot there." And with that brief exchange, the two parted ways.[30]

The fate of Coonskin's Tower is also a point of debate in soldiers' accounts. According to S. C. Beck of the 124th Illinois, "Away on our right the Rebels had a twenty pound parrot[t] gun planted. . . . The first day they saw this observatory [Coonskin's Tower] they turned this gun on it and had a picnic knocking Foster's lookout to 'smithereens.' Don't think anyone was hurt. . . . Foster did not rebuild his tower so it was a failure." This account, however, is most likely false since other accounts testify to its longevity. In fact soldiers continued to write home about Coonskin's Tower as late as June 30, some four days before the siege ended. Meanwhile, other sources simply state the contrary. For example, Ira Blanchard of the Twentieth Illinois wrote, "Well, Bill set to work on an eminence before the fort to build his tower, and as it rose higher and higher, the 'Rebs' tried to batter it down with their guns, but Bill and his tower kept going up, and they never succeeded in hitting it, though at close range." Fortunately for modern readers, this historical mystery, unlike so many others, can be settled with concrete evidence. A photographer after the siege took a picture of Coonskin's Tower still intact, silent testimony that the observatory survived the siege. As for Second Lieutenant Henry C. "Coonskin" Foster of Company B, Twenty-Third Indiana, he would go on to fight with his regiment for the remainder of the war. Although rebels captured the wily Foster during the Atlanta Campaign, he was later exchanged and mustered out as a first lieutenant.[31]

The impact of Coonskin's Tower on the overall progress of Logan's Approach is conjectural. As one soldier correctly noted, Foster "could look down into their fort and see their movements; but whether any real good

Photograph of Coonskin's Tower, along the line of Logan's Approach. Battery Hickenlooper appears just to the right of the observatory. The trench in the foreground utilized gabions for revetment and headlogs with firing ports. *Photograph by Armstead & Taylor; Chicago History Museum, ICHi-68339.*

came of the thing I never knew." To say that the tower was the key to the success of Logan's Approach would be a gross overstatement. Certainly other factors, such as the tenacity of the workers, the persistence of Andrew Hickenlooper, and the covering fire provided by sharpshooters in the surrounding parallels and the advanced batteries, played a larger role. But to say that Coonskin's Tower itself was inconsequential would be unfair. From atop the tower, marksmen could gather intelligence about enemy movements and lay down plunging suppressing fire. Furthermore, it is no coincidence that this approach, the only one during the entire siege that made use of such a device, would later successfully detonate two mines during the siege. Nevertheless, while the impact of Coonskin's Tower is up for debate, the fact that the structure was a model of western soldier improvisation remains indisputable.[32]

Sharpshooters' small arms fire succeeded in suppressing Confederate marksmen and guns throughout the siege, making it possible for workers to dig vigorously toward the Vicksburg defenses. In fact, the report of shoulder arms became such a common feature of the siege that Union troops attempted to describe the sound using familiar analogies. One soldier of the Twenty-Second Iowa wrote to his wife on June 13 that "the men in the rifle pits keep it up so constantly that it sounds just like a chopping frolic where the aces [axes] are going continually." Similarly, Joseph Bowker of the Forty-Second Ohio described the sounds of constant sharpshooter fire as "like the ticking of a clock" and "similar to a large force of lumbermen at work in the pine forests, a continual chopping."[33]

Union fire superiority occurred from the earliest days of the siege and remained constant all along the line. Sylvester Rynearson of the Fifteenth Iowa in Brigadier General John McArthur's division on the Seventeenth Corps front wrote on June 6, "We have sharpshooters so near their forts that they have not been able to fire any of their large guns for several days." Just to McArthur's south in Brigadier General Isaac F. Quinby's division, John Quincy Adams Campbell of the Fifth Iowa had written the day before, "Early in the morning, the rebels showed themselves about their forts and rifle pits pretty freely but we put the minies in so thick about them that they soon learned better. . . . Their sharpshooters fired several times during the day, but never more than two or three shots from one place." Farther to the south, William Reid of the Fifteenth Illinois wrote to his father on June 24, "By day our riflemen keep the rebel work clear of anything living. . . . Whenever one of them dared fire, half a dozen of our boys sent a reply and kept up the thing until the rebel left his place." Thus, Union sharpshooters achieved small arms fire superiority throughout the siege. As Albert O. Marshall of the Thirty-Third Illinois summed up when writing about marksmanship activities in June 1863, "The record for the entire month runs about like this. . . . During the day our riflemen kept up a slow fire; the only return the enemy attempted was to occasionally fire a rifle in the air. It is not safe for them to raise up [from] their breastworks high enough to aim at us."[34]

Part of the reason for this effectiveness was distance. The ability to establish rifle pits and open parallels at less than traditional distances allowed the Federals to achieve fire superiority early in the siege. Since the early days of the siege, sharpshooters were able to plant themselves in trenches and rifle pits relatively close to the enemy. Reports of federal marksmen advancing "close up to the rebel forts" and preventing the rebels "from using many of their guns by picking off the cannoneers whenever they show themselves" appeared as early as May 24. According to W. B. Smith, serving in the Sixty-Eighth Ohio in Logan's division, by May 26, "our forces had dug large rifle pits within 20 rods [110 yards] of the [rebel] fort [Third Louisiana Redan]." Similarly, down in the Thirteenth Corps sector in A. J. Smith's division, J. A. Bering wrote to his brother on June 7, "We occupied the rifle pits within 100 yards of the rebel works." Meanwhile, to the extreme north in the Fifteenth Corps sector, Sergeant James H. Lewis of the Twenty-Fourth Iowa four days later reported the same distance between the advance rifle pits and the enemy's works.[35]

As Grant described the overall situation in a letter to his wife, Julia, on June 15, "I have the town closely invested and our Rifle Pitts up so close to the enemy that they cannot show their heads without being shot at short enough range to kill a squirrel. They dare not show a single gun on the whole line of their works." Soldiers in the rank and file confirmed Grant's statements in their own accounts of the siege. William Reid of the Fifteenth Illinois, part of Lauman's division, wrote to his father on June 8 that "in many places along the lines our riflemen have crawled up so near that the rebels dare not show himself above the works, and many of their guns have been silent for several days. It is death of any one to try to load or sight the cannon." Farther north in Carr's division, one soldier wrote to his wife on June 13, "Our rifle pits are now being extended within 40 or 50 yards of the reble breast works. We work in the rifle pits at night and then lay in them in the day time and if a reble shows himself we shoot him. We have got so close to them that they can not work their cannon and have not been able to fire more than 50 shots at us from their forts since I come here."[36]

Similar effects of close-range sharpshooter fire were also reported on the middle of the siege lines on the Seventeenth Corps front. Here, according to Colonel Green B. Raum, "in front of every Confederate battery the Union forces constructed strong rifle pits capped with timber, with loop-holes for firing; from these works a constant musketry fire was kept up into every embrasure; this steady firing practically silenced many of the guns." By June 23, nearly two weeks before the siege ended, Union parallels and rifle pits dominated no-man's-land. George A. Remley of the Twenty-Second Iowa, serving in Carr's division of the Thirteenth Corps, wrote to his father on that day, "The siege is still progressing favorably and our rifle pits are gradually encroaching on the enemy—being almost the whole line within 50 yards of the rebel works and some places within a few feet." Thus, the Federals' ability to plant sharpshooters close to the Confederate defenses provided invaluable suppressing fire that allowed Union workers to advance in relative safety.[37]

Despite their ability to achieve fire superiority, workers and sharpshooters still received occasional incoming Confederate rifle and artillery fire. Union soldiers all along the lines recorded isolated instances in which they took on rebel fire. To the north, in the Fifteenth Corps sector, Chaplain W. M. Baker, a regular visitor to the advanced parallels and rifle pits, reported on May 28, "Late in the evening . . . [I] went up to our rifle-pits within 50 yards of the enemy's works. The balls came pretty close, and fragments of shells passed over us." Meanwhile, on the Seventeenth Corps front, David W. Poak of the Thirtieth Illinois wrote in a letter to his sister Sadie on June 12 that the rebel "sharpshooters keep up a constant fire on our pickets, working parties &c and our sharpshooters and pickets return it the best they can. A man cannot raise his head on either side without being a special target for half a dozen guns."[38]

Soldiers also reported similar incidents in the Thirteenth Corps sector, where Union soldiers were forced to watch out for random Confederate fire. In Carr's division, Samuel D. Pryce of the Twenty-Second Iowa wrote, "Both sides had the range so perfectly during the latter part of June that it was almost a miracle to escape from the zipping bullets. . . . These crack-shots [on both sides] would put a bullet into a man's anatomy at almost any point he chose to put it." Farther south in Hovey's division, Thomas D. Williams recalled after the war that, during the siege, "we watched their port-holes so closely that it was unsafe for them to fire a gun. But they did take the risk and fired a load of grape and canister into the head of our trench. Knocking over the gabions we had at the head of the trench and covering several of us with dirt and rubbish. Some of the boys thought we were killed but none of us was seriously injured." Nevertheless, this Confederate fire was sporadic, and the Union ability to achieve fire superiority allowed those excavating the approaches to push vigorously forward. As S. C. Beck of the 124th Illinois summarized after the war, "The sharpshooters of Grant's army had made it so dangerous for the Rebels to use their artillery that it was practically silenced during the greater part of the siege."[39]

Despite accounts of impeccable marksmanship and iconic figures such as Henry C. "Coonskin" Foster, it was the volume of Union sharpshooter fire that suppressed rebel fire. After Grant secured his supply line by way of the Mississippi River on reaching Vicksburg, not only did nearly unlimited victuals flow into the Union camps but also a nearly inexhaustible supply of ammunition found its way down the Father of Waters. Lucius W. Barber of the Fifteenth Illinois recalled a memorable incident early in the siege when "General Grant rode along the line and told the boys that he had plenty of ammunition and not to be afraid to use it." Thus, it was not uncommon for Union sharpshooters in parallels and rifle pits to fire between eighty and one hundred rounds of small arms ammunition in their daily attempts to suppress Confederate rifle muskets and artillery.[40]

Firing a mere fifty rounds during a day of sharpshooting, when a soldier's cartridge box contained only forty rounds, was considered by some to be "quite economical" and frugal. In one extreme case, a federal infantryman reported that on one day of the siege, "some of the boys expended over two hundred rounds." With enough ammunition to go around, some soldiers took it upon themselves to engage in sharpshooting even when off duty. According to George Ditto of the Fifth Iowa, "Many of the men consider the sharp shooting fun and many when not otherwise engaged will take their pockets full of ammunition and go to [the] skirmish line." With cartridge boxes full and pockets stuffed with extra rounds, Grant's westerners plied their deadly trade.[41]

Although Union troops "poured a constant fire of musketry into the embrazures and over the parapets of the forts," most "daily casualties were not very numerous." The blue-clad Federals poured on heavy rifle fire, but most rounds did not find their target. This was true for the Confederate side as well. Taylor Peirce, writing to his wife on June 13, noted that "their sharp shooters still lay in their rifle pits and shoot at us if they get a chance but they seldom hit anyone." Despite the fact that Union sharpshooters were well within range of the rifle-musket and even musket range for most of the siege, the majority of small arms lead never found its mark. As Jefferson Brumback of the Ninety-Fifth Ohio aptly summarized in a letter written on June 11, "It is wonderful how few shots even of sharpshooters ever take effect. I have no doubt it takes a man's weight in bullets to kill a man in battles and sieges." It did. Soldiers in Civil War armies did not receive standardized marksmanship training, and as a result, the majority of Civil War soldiers were inferior marksmen. While the exploits of rank-and-file celebrities such as Henry C. "Coonskin" Foster have become ingrained in Civil War legend, the fact remains that proficient riflemen were few and far between during the War of the Rebellion. The crack shots of the war came into service already practiced marksmen, and their comrades celebrated them for their skills with a rifle. Hence, it was not the accuracy of Union small arms fire that suppressed Confederate sharpshooters and artillery but rather the sheer volume of lead that allowed the federal infantrymen to achieve fire superiority.[42]

Despite the use of both traditional and improvised shelter for federal marksmen and their ability to achieve suppressing fire superiority, sharpshooting duty could still be hazardous and often forced those manning the parallels and rifle pits to hide "like hares in burrows." The close proximity to the Confederate lines that helped federal soldiers suppress rebel artillery and riflemen also placed Union troops in danger. Colonel William H. Raynor of the Fifty-Sixth Ohio, Hovey's division, Colonel James R. Slack's brigade, wrote on May 29 that "being so very near the enemy it is very necessary for the men to be very careful about exposing themselves. To-day Private Graham of Co. G was hit in the head and instantly killed, and Spriggs of Co. F severely wounded in the shoulder."[43]

Adding to these dangers, the construction features in man-made sharpshooter cover that allowed Union troops to ply their deadly trade, such as firing portholes, led to Union casualties. On the Thirteenth Corps front in Brigadier General A. J. Smith's division, W. R. Eddington of the Ninety-Seventh Illinois had several "close calls" while on the firing line. In one incident, Eddington had to leave his "hole" in order to obtain rations for those serving alongside him in the trenches. Another man stepped in and took Eddington's place. Unfortunately for this second man, rebel sharpshooter fire found its way through the firing port and killed Eddington's replacement.[44]

Meanwhile, farther to the north on the Fifteenth Corps front in Major General Francis P. Blair's division, Colonel Giles Smith's brigade, Chaplain W. M. Baker of the 116th Illinois glumly reported on June 27 how Confederate sharpshooter fire struck his comrade and friend Captain Thomas White. According to Baker, White, after leading a nighttime "fatigue party," decided to whittle away the morning hours sharpshooting "from a port-hole." While hunting for Confederate sentinels, "a rebel ball cut the forward band from his gun." White, undeterred, returned to the safety of the Union lines and grabbed breakfast. After this brief respite, "he again went out" but "was soon afterwards brought in wounded." Baker recalled that White "had been making a port-hole by running the handle of the pick under some sand bags. Just as he withdrew the handle of the pick, he raised his eyes to the aperature [sic], and [at] the same moment was struck by a ball which grazed the top of his nose and entered just under his right eye, the ball lodging somewhere in his head." Baker remained pessimistic, writing that "it is a serious wound, and I fear will prove fatal." The chaplain, however, was wrong. Thomas survived his wound and continued to don the Union blue until he was cut down at the Battle of Dallas during the Atlanta Campaign in 1864. Nevertheless, the dangers that the federal sharpshooters endured reaped a valuable reward. By plying their deadly trade, they allowed excavators to dig forward toward the Vicksburg defenses in relative safety.[45]

The sharpshooter war that the Army of the Tennessee waged against the Confederates during the Vicksburg siege was integral to Union success. Although revetment and sap rollers provided a degree of protection, rebel marksmen and artillerists still posed a threat to the Union troops working in the approach trenches. Without the ability to silence the rebel guns and thwart the gray-and-butternut-clad marksmen, the Union saps would not have been able to traverse no-man's-land. Conversely, it was not simply heavy suppressing fire alone that allowed workers to push zigzags forward but the ability to do so from covered positions that made the difference. In other words, the Federals' ability to achieve fire superiority, however essential to Union success, would not have been possible without the structures that protected the sharpshooters. Exposed federal marksmen would have become easy targets and rendered ineffective. The fieldworks that shielded Union sharpshooters and allowed them to lay down a heavy blanket of suppressing fire were just as important as the riflemen who occupied them.

Meanwhile, the terrain and the lack of engineers determined the nature of the Union defenses that sheltered the marksmen. The irregular ground allowed the Army of the Tennessee to begin the siege at distances under those traditionally outlined in period engineering manuals. As a result, the traditional trench designed to protect the zigzag approach, the parallel, was adapted to meet the needs of the besiegers. While conventional Vaubanian approaches were supposed to contain three parallels, the Union soldiers at Vicksburg built parallels on an as-needed basis and let the lay of the land determine the length and number on each front.

In addition to parallels, soldiers also excavated informal rifle pits in order to provide protection for vedettes and to act as sharpshooter nests. Often in their writings, soldiers used the terms "parallel" and "rifle pit" interchangeably. They were, however, two separate features, parallels being a more formal trench and rifle pits acting as shallower, advanced quasi-trenches for an individual or a small group.

Nevertheless, despite the nuances of nomenclature, the dimensions of parallels and rifle pits lacked uniformity. Deficiencies in the number of engineers and the practical necessity of digging either at night or under enemy fire led to this lack of uniformity and the need for improvisation. Improvisation, however, could be taken to an extreme. The need to deliver suppressing fire, combined with the monotony of siege warfare, led Henry C. "Coonskin" Foster to build his sharpshooter tower. While one could argue over the effectiveness of this structure, it is undeniable that it reflected western soldier ingenuity in its purest form, a commonsense solution to a basic siege problem. Ultimately, the Federals' ability to weave Mahanian siege concepts with soldier improvisation allowed the Army of the Tennessee to win the sharpshooter battle that took place during the Vicksburg siege.

8. *Turning Loose the Dogs of War*

The Union artillery made its presence known during the Vicksburg siege. Although Major General Ulysses S. Grant's veteran Army of the Tennessee had, up to this point, fought in many engagements, the day-to-day struggle of siege warfare was new to the rank and file. While the sounds of war were certainly familiar, they had previously occurred only for relatively brief periods of time as a part of set-piece battles. Siege warfare around Vicksburg was different. The never-ceasing cacophony of martial acoustics contrasted with anything that the westerners in Grant's army had experienced before. Reuben B. Scott of the Sixty-Seventh Indiana encapsulated all of this when he wrote after the war that "at no time, day or night, did the firing on either side cease during the siege. . . . It became a practice on our side, at 10 o'clock each day, to turn all of these dogs of war loose upon the enemy for an hour or so. . . . During this time, the rebels . . . remained silent."[1]

Underneath the spectacular sound of artillery lay a practical purpose. Consistent and constant federal artillery fire, aimed at silencing Confederate guns and sharpshooters, would allow Union soldiers working in the approach trenches and parallels to excavate in relative safety. The effect of artillery-suppressing fire, however, is only half of the story. Before the federal artillery could unleash its deadly covering fire, engineers and artillerymen needed to construct earthworks that would protect gunners from Confederate artillery and sharpshooters. In order to accomplish this, Grant's engineers and artillerists erected battery emplacements that blended traditional Mahanian dogma with soldier improvisation.

As the federal besiegers pushed their advance via approaches and parallels, it also became necessary to establish enfilading batteries, counter-batteries, and breaching batteries. Zigzag approaches needed to be at least "five to six feet wide" so that cannons and their limbers could be "worked through them by hand" and placed at "commanding positions close to the enemy's works," either along the lines of approach or "on a line with the rifle pits."[2]

Each type of battery (enfilading, counter-, and breaching) served a specific purpose. According to Dennis Hart Mahan, enfilading batteries, those firing lengthwise down the enemy's flank, were to contain different types of guns, including "cannon, howitzers, and mortars." These types of batteries, sometimes grouped together with counter-batteries and aimed at silencing enemy guns, provided an array of suppressing fire with each type of gun carrying out a specific purpose. Artillerists and engineers employed regular cannons, firing on a relatively flat trajectory, in order to destroy the enemy's guns and traverses. Unfortunately for the attacker, the level trajectory of regular cannons, though effective at battering fortress walls, could not reach enemies hiding behind low-profile earthen fortifications. In order to strike at these defenders, attackers used high-trajectory, short-range howitzers and mortars. Howitzers and mortars allowed artillerists to harass enemy troops hiding behind the safety of their defenses. In short, enfilading and counter-batteries provided suppressing fire that, as Mahan described, was "used for destroying the [enemy's] artillery and silencing the fire of the defenses," a feat that would allow excavators in the approach trenches to prosecute a vigorous advance. Meanwhile, breaching batteries attempted to batter holes in the enemy defenses that might be exploited by infantrymen lying in wait in parallels.[3]

The Union engineers and artillerymen at Vicksburg understood the textbook prescription for correct battery placement. On the Thirteenth Corps front, First Lieutenant Peter C. Hains reported on June 8, three days before he opened A. J. Smith's Approach, that he had established a battery in this division's sector that had "an enfilading view" of the enemy defenses. Hains, a professional, continued to abide by this maxim and established enfilading batteries at points of tactical significance throughout the siege. On June 20, in Brigadier General Alvin P. Hovey's sector, Hains established another battery that could enfilade the salient in front of that division. The ability to place enfilading batteries in places of tactical importance, however, was not unique to Hains's jurisdiction. Farther to the north, Union artillerymen and engineers, some West Point–trained and others self-taught, continued to place their batteries in areas that would allow for enfilading fire. Although a

Mahanian maxim, placing batteries at points that allowed for enfilading fire was, in many ways, common sense. Both professionals and nonprofessionals at Vicksburg understood the value of achieving enfilading fire and placed their batteries accordingly.[4]

As with the line of circumvallation, terrain influenced battery placement. Steep hills lacking level tops and deficient in surface area forced engineers and artillerymen to break up batteries into sections in order to take advantage of desirable terrain while achieving their goals of delivering enfilading fire or establishing a "breaching battery" in a desirable location. For example, in Hovey's front, on June 20, the terrain limited Hains, allowing him only to "mount two 20-pounder Parrotts, taken from the four gun 20-pounder Parrott battery." Similarly, farther north, in front of Brigadier General Peter J. Osterhaus's division, Joseph Bowker of the Forty-Second Ohio reported on June 29, "Our battery now occupies three knolls, a section on each knoll, each of them within 300 yards of the rebel works." Thus, professional know-how, basic common sense, and terrain were all factors in determining battery placement.[5]

The construction of advanced batteries mirrored that of those built along the line of circumvallation. Unlike those batteries, however, these tended to be established at strategic points along approaches and parallels. Although Mahan provided rigid guidelines for battery construction, the engineering master did recognize the need for flexibility in siege operations. According to Mahan, engineers conducting an offensive siege needed to adhere to the limitations of the surrounding terrain when marking the outline for a battery emplacement. Engineers were to build artillery installations on top of commanding points that dominated the surrounding area and could support the methodical infantry advance across no-man's-land. Unfortunately, not every hill and knoll with a dominant vantage point offered adequate (or level) surface area on which to build a textbook artillery emplacement. As a result, Mahan stressed flexibility and instructed engineers to conform the dimension of their profiles to the surrounding terrain. But Mahan's dabbling with flexibility was evanescent. Larger emphasis in his treatises on precise measurements for specific battery features negated any cursory remarks about adaptability and resulted in maxims that become impractical, if not impossible, to replicate in the field. This inflexibility forced the Army of the Tennessee, a largely volunteer army deficient in engineers, to improvise.[6]

Without sufficient pioneers to engage in all of the laborious tasks that a siege required, it fell to details "from the different regiments to assist the pioneers" since there was "more work to be done than the [pioneer] corps can get along with." These details, supplemented with labor parties formed from free African Americans, engaged in the backbreaking work of establishing advanced batteries. Similar to other construction projects, advanced batteries were constructed at night and improved during the daytime.[7]

Although Mahan demanded that batteries be constructed to exacting dimensions and revetted with gabions, fascines, and sandbags, at Vicksburg the resources at hand determined what materials soldiers used to build what they termed artillery "forts." The few pioneer companies available tended to prepare gabions and fascines, fashioned from grapevines, for use in revetting battery walls. This bountiful material, however, proved heavy when woven into ga-

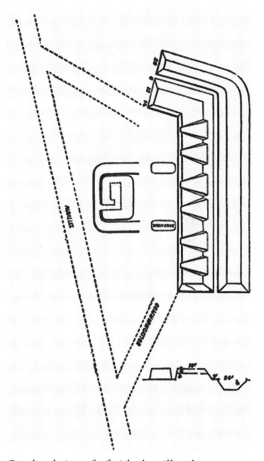

Overhead view of a finished artillery battery constructed to textbook specifications. *J. C. Duane, Manual for Engineer Troops*, 241.

bions, leading some to split the cane into thinner strands. Splitting the cane did not compromise the strength of the gabion and yielded a product that was easier to work with. On the whole, Union batteries and most approach walls were shored up with gabions. Despite this commonality, chief engineers Frederick E. Prime and Cyrus B. Comstock concluded after the siege that battery construction "varied" and depended "on the materials which could be obtained at the time." E. B. Bascom of the Fifth Iowa recorded similar observations on June 15, writing, "I was detailed to take charge of the erection of a new fort on high ground near the enemy's line and in plain view of their works. We got the material such as stakes, grape vines and anything we could use in ravines at rear of the location of this fort."[8]

But despite soldier ingenuity and resourcefulness, the lack of engineers began to take its toll. Lieutenant Anthony B. Burton of the Fifth Ohio Independent Battery recorded in his diary an incident on June 14 on Brigadier General Jacob Lauman's front where a battery could not be constructed because "the engineer was not there to lay the work out, so nothing could be done." Thus, where pioneers could not be obtained, line troops stepped in. If traditional building materials were fashioned, they were used. If customary materials could not be requisitioned, soldiers scavenged and improvised; however, if an engineer officer was not available to oversee complicated tasks, such as laying out profiles for batteries, construction could be stymied.[9]

Burton's report of delayed battery construction was atypical. Despite the lack of engineers present for duty, the Army of the Tennessee pushed forward and established many different types of improvised artillery "forts." Isaiah Richards of the Seventeenth Ohio Light Battery described to loved ones back home that "works of protection" were being constructed out of "cotton bales and earth." After the war, Richards wrote to former Army of the Tennessee veteran and Vicksburg Park commissioner William T. Rigby on November 27, 1903, about his battery having used "cotton bales . . . for revetments" in some artillery forts and "logs held in place by stout pickets" in others for the purpose of "retaining the earth banked against them."[10]

Upon first glance, it would appear that the use of cotton and earth in this simple structure conformed to Prime and Comstock's statement that access to materials determined battery construction. This, however, was only partially true. Richards also wrote to Rigby on July 13, 1903, that Brigadier General Stephen G. Burbridge, a brigade commander without formal military training, "personally ordered and superintended the construction of the Parapet and Traverse in which the 3d section was placed." Burbridge, lacking formal instruction in battery construction, improvised. He ordered the pioneer section of his brigade to advance behind cotton bales "rooling [sic] . . . them [ahead] until they reached [the] point" where Burbridge's battery was to be built.[11]

After reaching the desired location, the pioneers "excavated . . . to the depth of two and a half feet" and leveled the bottom of their hole in order to form the terreplein of the battery. The pioneers then proceeded to use the excavated earth to form the battery walls. According to Richards, "There was no rifle pits either to our right or left for some time into the seige [*sic*]. We were supported by a force of Infantry lying under cover of our works which was relieved each night by another like force." The structure itself was simple, containing traverses fifteen feet long, a front thirty feet long, and embrasures four feet wide on the side closest to the enemy, narrowing to two feet where the gun sat. Lacking West Point training, Burbridge designed and constructed a simple artillery placement that defied Mahanian maxims. Basic and unsupported by connecting rifle pits/parallels, it served as a mini-fort from which sharpshooters and artillerymen could hurl suppressing fire at the enemy. It was a creation that, as Prime and Comstock suggested, made the best use of the materials at hand, displaying the tenacity of the western fighting men.[12]

Other improvised artillery forts abandoned all types of revetment. Engineers and artillerymen at times made this decision for two reasons. First, the Union's ability to silence the rebel guns led to "the feebleness of the enemy's artillery fire," thus resulting in federal troops constructing "parapets often . . . not more than 6 or 8 feet thick." Second, there was the soil. The natural properties of Vicksburg's loess soil were such that, when cut vertically, it could stand on its own without artificial shoring. For example, in Lauman's front on the southernmost part of the Union siege line, Lieutenant Anthony Burton, commander of the Fifth Ohio Independent Battery, upon arriving on June 1 at the spot where his guns were to be deployed, "found two small embrasures made for pieces by digging into the hill, thus making the parapet consist of the solid earth of the hill—a very good plan." Also in Lauman's front, Captain Henry C. Freeman, acting engineer officer of the Fourth Division, Sixteenth Army Corps, described a similar practice on June 17 when he wrote, "Work commenced at night. In this battery, the terre-plein for each gun was cut down through solid earth to a depth of 7 feet, and no revetment used; the dirt thrown to the rear. The embrasures were cut through in a similar manner, and reveted only at the end next [to] the muzzle of the guns with sand-bags."[13]

Just to the north in Major General Francis Herron's division, artillerymen built batteries that lacked revetment. According to Captain Martin Welfley of the First Missouri Light Artillery, on June 18 "a more favorable position was selected [for our battery] on a hill. . . . A fatigue party was immediately set to work digging out places for two 12-pounders and one 32-pounder gun, thereby making the brow of the hill a natural breastwork for the pieces." Thus, in addition to available materials and lack of engineers, soil composition determined how the Federals constructed their batteries. Improvisation and deviation from Mahanian maxims meant not only constructing batteries of different dimensions and substituting conventional forms of shoring in the form of gabions and fascines but, at times, even forgoing revetment entirely.[14]

The lack of engineers affected battery construction in other indirect ways. It also meant that only a select few among the rank and file would receive the necessary on-the-job training to wage a textbook siege. This not only applied to artillery forts but also influenced the construction of approaches and parallels. As in the anecdote in which Major General William T. Sherman took it upon himself to instruct neophyte infantrymen in the details of gabion and fascine assemblage, many Army of the Tennessee men, like most soldiers during the nineteenth century, were unaware of the finer points of siege detail. Yet what made this particular siege different was its scale, scope, and the nature of the army fighting it. Unlike professional European armies or Major General George B. McClellan's Army of the Potomac during the quasi-siege on the Virginia Peninsula in 1862, the Army of the Tennessee lacked engineer officers, and this brought with it an inability to transmit and disperse engineering knowledge to the majority in the rank and file. Nevertheless, Grant's tenacious westerners prevailed. They learned from both engineers and those with former West Point training. Their ability to learn on the job, and improvise when necessary, allowed the siege to march forward.[15]

Despite the willingness of West Point–trained officers to provide engineering instruction, the involvement of senior Union commanders in mundane engineering projects was uneven. This contrast is best illustrated when examining the roles that Sherman and Major General James B. McPherson played during the siege. If Sherman fit the paradigm of a hands-on teacher, McPherson tended to distance himself from practical engineering tasks. According to George Ditto of the Fifth Iowa, McPherson did not take an interest in teaching the finer points of practical engineering to his soldiers. Ditto, frustrated at the inability to obtain adequate artillery pieces for a battery emplacement that he was helping to construct, blamed the Seventeenth Army Corps commander for the situation. "To me," Ditto wrote, in addition to "having a hard time to get our new fort armed," the Union troops serving in his corps appeared "to take less interest in their work than they use[d] to." He laid this blame at McPherson's feet because, from Ditto's perspective, the Seventeenth Corps commander "seems to have lost all interest in [the fort's construction] and to care but little how things go so as they do not interfere with his ease and comfort." In short, Ditto believed that McPherson should have been leading by example, for "how can men be expected to take an interest in what they have to do when those that have control of them take none[?]"[16]

Ditto, however, was incorrect. Mundane construction projects, such as the outfitting of a particular battery, fell under the jurisdiction of either an engineer officer or another junior officer. Corps commanders, as per Grant's orders at the outset of the siege, were to take responsibility for the entirety of their respective fronts and not for individual projects. Thus, this particular soldier's frustration, while understandable and perhaps a product of the drudgery of siege life, was misplaced.[17]

In retrospect, when one considers the role of corps commanders during the Vicksburg siege, Sherman's hands-on style tended to be the exception and not the rule with regard to practical engineering at the corps level. The Fifteenth Corps commander's micromanagement and instruction in gabion and fascine making was effective because it involved the dissemination of knowledge in appropriate doses. His tutorial in the details of constructing artificial revetment speaks to Sherman's ability to understand and implement the correct amount of hands-on instruction. Had Sherman spent the entirety of the siege ignoring his corps-level responsibilities and ensconced in the details of how to execute practical engineering details, he most likely would have failed as a corps commander.

Colonel John B. Sanborn's postwar anecdote, however, is not the only source that depicts Sherman as an effective micromanager. According to his own memoirs, Sherman kept his headquarters "close to the works, near the centre of my corps." In another incident, one soldier of the Fifty-Fifth Illinois reported after the war that he recollected seeing Sherman and Grant together inspecting the progress of the siege "almost every day." This type of effective micromanaging, unlike McClernand's tendency to thwart Hains on the Thirteenth Corps front, could yield great results, for, as Sanborn concluded his story, "in five or ten minutes, [Sherman] had at least a hundred men as well informed upon these matters [gabion and fascine construction] as if they had been in the regular army for five years in time of war." Such an act would have been unthinkable in a professional European army, such as the British army, where elite aristocrats used their influence to purchase officers' commissions until Edward Cardwell's army reforms abolished the elitist system in 1871.[18]

Conversely, McClernand's interference and lack of engineering training obstructed progress on the Thirteenth Corps front. His meddling and disruptive micromanagement style not only jarred Hains but also impeded battery construction. Jenkin Lloyd Jones of the Sixth Wisconsin Battery, part of the Seventeenth Corps, reported on the lack of advancement in McClernand's sector. On June 17, one day before Major General E. O. C. Ord replaced McClernand, Jones wrote, "Called at the 23d Wisconsin to see friends. . . . The line on the left we found much weaker than here. No battery planted as yet in [a] formidable position."[19]

As previously stated, this particular western army, a mostly volunteer army, lacked professionals. Few high-ranking Army of the Tennessee officers shared their expertise with soldiers, not because they did not want to but simply because they did not possess the requisite skills needed to wage an effective siege. For example, brigade commander Brigadier General Stephen G. Burbridge, a general without formal military training, compensated for his professional deficiencies by providing his troops with motivation and encouragement. As one soldier wrote home on June 15, "Gen Burbridge is . . . constantly on the firing lines with his brigade of men, giving his attention to the trenching . . . and dispositions of his forces. He stayed about one hour with us this afternoon, and jollied us . . . and also said he was makeing a place for us on the front line, so that we would be close enough to shake hands with the Johnies." Although this type of motivation kept soldiers moving forward, it was not enough. As Prime and Comstock's report concluded, "From the lack of educated engineer officers, the approaches and parallels were in some places badly located and much unnecessary work done." Nevertheless, the Union's ability to achieve fire superiority, the diligence of the army's few engineers, and the tenacity of the westerners serving in the Army of the Tennessee allowed the siege to move forward.[20]

Once the guns were in place, artillerymen rigged mantlets or "blinds" designed to "cover the gunners from the enemy's riflemen." This technique was not new to the Vicksburg siege. During the Middle Ages, besiegers made shields of woven wicker or wood from behind which they would loose arrows and other types of early artillery fire against the besieged. Once gunpowder and primitive cannons became part of the siege arsenal, besiegers designed mantlets that would hide artillerymen working the guns.[21]

While the concept of the artillery mantlet or "blind" was not a Vicksburg innovation, the materials readily available combined with the imagination of the common soldier gave rise to some interesting takes on an old concept. Some forms of protection were very basic. According to one artilleryman serving in the Sixth Wisconsin Battery on the Seventeenth Corps front, the "Pioneer Corps put up a brush screen to hide us from the view of the sharp-shooters, who of late became not only annoying but dangerous." These basic variations were often freestanding structures that soldiers would remove only after their pieces were loaded and primed and the gun was ready to be fired. According to Manning M. Force, commander of the Twentieth Illinois in Major General John A. Logan's division, "General Ransom had a battery so close that the embrasures were kept covered by mantelets. A gun would be loaded and pointed, and then fired just as the mantelet was removed. The first time a gun was fired from it a storm of rifle-balls poured through the embrasure. A gunner jumped on the gun and shouted back, 'Too late!'"[22]

Other variants of artillery blinds were more elaborate. The design of any given blind depended upon the proclivities of either the artillery officer or engineer in charge of construction. Nevertheless, the majority of the advanced batteries at Vicksburg used some type of artillery blind. Chief engineers Prime and Comstock reported after the siege that "in all close batteries the gunners soon found the necessity of keeping the embrasures closed against rifle-balls by plank shutters, sometimes swung from a timber across the top of the embrasure; sometimes merely placed in the embrasure, and moved when firing." In sum, while artillery blinds were not new to the siege of Vicksburg, the local materials combined with the imagination of the western soldier determined the type of mantlet used at any given part along the siege line.[23]

That Grant had never intended to besiege Vicksburg was evident from the fact that the Army of the Tennessee had not traveled with siege artillery during its maneuver campaign across Mississippi. As a result, when it reached the Confederate defenses guarding the city, the Federals had to begin their siege with the basic field guns that made up their artillery arm. Grant, however, was able to supplement his field artillery with heavier guns borrowed from the navy and with more specialized siege pieces from the North after he reestablished his line of communication on the Mississippi River.[24]

The arrival of heavy artillery, which held the possibility of hastening the end of the siege, elicited commentary from the rank and file. On June 7, Owen Johnston Hopkins of the Forty-Second Ohio on the Thirteenth Corps front wrote with joy that "guns of heavy caliber are daily arriving and being placed in position. This morning, two eleven-inch guns arrived off of the Gun Boats, and by night will peal their notes of thunder with their particular neighbors."

W. B. Smith of the Sixty-Eighth Ohio deemed it worthy to record on June 10 that, in front of Logan's division, "a 10-inch Dahlgren gun arrived yesterday from the landing which was mounted and put in operation today apparently with good effect." Similarly, Captain Andrew Hickenlooper reminisced with pride after the war that on June 11 he supervised the establishment of "two 9 in. Naval guns in battery just south of the 'White House' bearing directly against the Fort, with which most effective work was done." Heavy artillery continued to arrive as the siege progressed, and the Union arsenal began to grow into an arm that contained everything from Parrott rifles to "old fashioned long 32 pdr siege guns" and even "rifles and James guns, direct from Memphis."[25]

Despite the lack of uniformity among the guns in the Army of the Tennessee, the characteristics of surrounding loess soil negated need for specialized siege artillery. Although loess soil is easy to excavate and readily holds its shape without revetment, its natural composition makes it weak against artillery shells. This feature of Vicksburg's loess soil, as previously stated, led many Union engineers and artillerymen to shore up the inside walls of their artillery forts with gabions.[26]

One of the most famous makeshift artillery forts constructed during the Vicksburg siege was Battery Hickenlooper. Named after Seventeenth Corps chief engineer Andrew Hickenlooper, the battery, established some 130 yards to the east of the Confederate's Third Louisiana Redan, became the closest breaching battery established along the line of Logan's Approach. Workers began building the battery on June 3, and construction ended two days later. The battery, in its final form, proved formidable. It was approximately three thousand square feet and used traditional revetment in the form of gabions and fascines. By the time construction ceased on June 5, Battery Hickenlooper contained "two embrasures on [the northern side] and one on the west face [being] open to and covered by batteries in the rear."[27]

On June 6, Hickenlooper was ready to plant guns in what he later described as "a very strong work." The first guns put in place, two twenty-four-pound howitzers and one six-pounder, were too light to inflict any serious damage against the Confederate redan. As a result, on June 17 Hickenlooper began "building platforms for 30 pounder Parrotts" in his "advanced battery." Hauling these new guns into position proved daunting. According to S. C. Beck of the 124th Illinois, Union troops "succeeded in getting two thirty pound parrot[t] guns from Porter's Fleet from the Mississippi River. These guns were about fifteen feet in length, [and] perhaps eighteen inches in diameter at the breech. . . . These guns were taken by way of the sap or ditch that we had made to fort hill [the Third Louisiana Redan]." Proud of his achievement, Hickenlooper wrote after the war that the battery occupied "a prominent knoll distant less than 200 yards from the Fort."

Together, these guns devastated the Confederate defenses and silenced the rebel artillery. According to Hickenlooper, "They [the Confederates] were never able to work a gun on our front." From the protection of Battery Hickenlooper, sharpshooters and artillerymen provided invaluable suppressing fire that allowed the Union troops digging Logan's Approach to work in safety. As Beck recalled after the war, "Our officers watched with their field glasses [and] when the muzzle of the Rebel gun came into the porthole our guns were fired. One of our guns struck it in its muzzle, tore the end off and landed it to the rear about thirty paces down in the ravine."[28]

Meanwhile, on the Father of Waters, the navy tried to provide suppressing fire in support of Grant's army. Beginning at an early point in the siege, Admiral David Dixon Porter's Mississippi Squadron attempted to use the majority of its resources to help the Army of the Tennessee. Patrolling the

Battery Hickenlooper, as depicted in *Harper's Pictorial History of the Civil War*. *Anne S. K. Brown Military Collection, Brown University Library.*

Mississippi allowed an unobstructed flow of necessary food and ammunition to travel downriver from the north and right into the camps of Grant's investing army. Furthermore, Porter's vigil over the river eliminated any possibility of the Vicksburg garrison receiving aid from Confederate reinforcements that might have planned to enter the city via the river. The spirit of cooperation that Grant and Porter had shared throughout the early phases of the Vicksburg campaign carried into the siege and, for the time being, was contributing to Union success.

Porter's gunboats even tried to provide suppressing fire in order to help the Army of the Tennessee. While the navy scored minor successes in this category, it proved very difficult for the squadron's gunboats to elevate its guns high enough to score hits on the Confederate artillery situated on top of commanding heights such as Fort Hill. For the most part, all Porter's gunboats could do was to shell the city and attempt to take pressure off of Grant's army, as they had done previously during the May 22 attack.

Perhaps the best example illustrating the difficulty that Porter's gunboats faced when attempting suppressing fire occurred during the incident that ultimately led to the sinking of the *Cincinnati*. On May 27, Sherman asked Porter for naval support that could be used to destroy prospective batteries on his right flank, somewhere below Fort Hill. Porter immediately complied and dispatched a contingent of gunboats, including the *Cincinnati*. Four gunboats plodded upriver against the current and immediately engaged one of the Confederate batteries. Meanwhile, the *Cincinnati* steamed downriver and engaged a second rebel battery. Sherman attempted to use his artillery to cover the gunboat, but the hills masking the Confederate battery interrupted his line of sight.[29]

Upon approaching the battery, the *Cincinnati* fired its bow guns. They missed. Then a sharp current grabbed the *Cincinnati*, spinning it around approximately 180 degrees, negating the use of its primary guns on the craft's sides. As a result, George M. Bache, the boat's captain, loosed a sharp fire from his stern guns. They too proved ineffective. Bache then regained control of the boat and loosed a sharp broadside. This also did not elicit its desired effect. The Confederate guns now fired back from three different directions and tore holes in the ironclad. The acute rebel fire found its mark, and the *Cincinnati* sank in the shallow waters of the Mississippi. With the stern of the boat resting on the bottom of the river and the bow still visible above the surface, Bache ordered his crew to abandon ship. With this final order, the *Cincinnati's* very gallant yet very brief last voyage came to an abrupt end. As a result, it would be up to Grant's army, entrenched behind improvised artillery forts, to deliver the bulk of the Union's suppressing fire.[30]

The artillery superiority that the Army of the Tennessee's artillerymen achieved at the beginning of the siege on the line of circumvallation continued as Union troops mounted counter-batteries and breaching batteries. By June 30, the Federals would have eighty-nine batteries, secured behind "eighty-nine forts and redoubts," yielding a grand total of 220 guns. Thus, by the end of June, Union artillery was entrenched and ready to decimate the Vicksburg defenses.[31]

In addition to the enormous quantity of guns flowing into the Union lines via the Mississippi River was a nearly endless supply of artillery ammunition. As Captain Martin Welfley of the First Missouri Light Artillery, part of Hovey's division, reported after the siege, "The total number of rounds of ammunition fired by the pieces under my charge [during the siege] is 910." Similarly, just to the north in Osterhaus's division, one soldier reported earlier, on June 15, that the artillery on his front "fire our regular allowance of 100 rounds daily, and make it a splendid artillery practice."[32]

Artillery batteries on Hovey's front, sketched by A. E. Mathews, Thirty-First Ohio Volunteer Infantry. *Lithograph by Middleton, Strobridge, and Company, Cincinnati; Anne S. K. Brown Military Collection, Brown University Library.*

In contrast, the besieged Confederates could claim only 172 guns and were forced to stretch a fixed supply of ammunition. Yet according to engineer Captain Cyrus B. Comstock, this should have been enough to delay the Union approaches. Comstock wrote after the siege, "Although the enemy had over one hundred and thirty-guns of all calibers within his defenses, he made but slight use of artillery fire in delaying our approaches, the defense being almost entirely by musketry. Lack of ammunition was assigned as the reason for this by some of the Confederate officers, but we captured over 40,000 rounds of artillery ammunition, as reported to the Chief of Ordnance." Thus, from the Union perspective, the Confederates should have been able to offer stronger resistance, considering their stockpile of ammunition.[33]

The Army of the Tennessee's ability to bring more guns to bear on the Confederate defenses than their besieged counterparts were able to do, combined with superior logistics and exceptional gunnery, allowed the Federals to achieve a fire superiority that let workers traverse no-man's-land under relative safety. The quantity of Union guns and ammunition played an important role in silencing the Confederate defenses. As one Union soldier in Brigadier General Eugene A. Carr's division wrote on June 16, "They [the Rebels] have not succeeded in doing us any harm yet for as soon as they shoot one of their guns about 6 or 8 of ours lets off at them and makes it so hot that they have to dry up untill they can steal in and give us another sly shot." Charles A. Hobbs of the Ninety-Ninth Illinois confirmed such statements about fire superiority in Carr's front when he wrote that on June 5, "much of the artillery of the rebels was dismounted or withdrawn." Similarly, Albert O. Marshall of the Thirty-Third Illinois wrote that by June 26, "the Confederates . . . can not open with a single gun but that half a dozen or more on our side will immediately reply. They keep their port-holes closed with bales of cotton most of the time." Meanwhile, on Brigadier General Joseph A. J. Lightburn's front, near Ewing's Approach, a soldier commented, "Our artillery . . . was numerically so superior that when a rebel battery opened upon us it was quickly silenced by the fire concentrated upon it, and the guns had to be removed to new positions to save them from destruction."[34]

Thus, the Union's ability to build improvised artillery forts allowed them to bring more guns to bear on their Confederate counterparts, which in turn let the Federals lay down heavy suppressing fire that permitted fatigue parties to advance their approaches. As the Union engineers and artillerymen inched batteries closer to the Confederate defenses, the Federal's numerical superiority in number of guns became apparent. Chief engineers Prime and Comstock summarized the situation best when they wrote in their after-action report, "As our batteries were built and opened, their artillery slackened, until toward the close of the siege it was scarcely used at all, the enemy contenting himself with occasionally running a gun into position, firing two or three rounds, and withdrawing it again as soon as our fire was concentrated on it."[35]

In addition to being able to concentrate their guns, the Federals were able to deliver well-aimed fire from their improvised artillery emplacements. This fire, placed with surgical precision, provided effective counter-battery fire that would have otherwise impeded the Federals' approach trenches. As a soldier serving in the Twenty-Fourth Indiana on Hovey's sector recalled, in one particular incident on June 29 "the rebels planted a heavy gun to dismount our twenty-four pounders that lay to our rear. They had fired two shots which took no effect, when one of our twenty-pound Parrot[t]s in the rifle pits threw a shot which knocked the rebel gun out of existence." Similarly, a little farther north on the Seventeenth Corps front, a soldier commented that the guns "are all sighted nearly as fine as a rifle, and they can put a shot right where they want every time." Meanwhile, up in the Fifteenth Corps sector in front of Brigadier General Ralph P. Buckland's brigade, Jefferson Brumback of the Ninety-Fifth Ohio described to his "dear Kate" how the Federals were able to use precision fire to destroy enemy artillery. According to Brumback, "Every gun [the Confederates] put in position on the land side and attempt to use we have so far succeeded in dismounting. . . . I saw one of the rebel guns st[r]uck apparently full in the muzzle, topple over backward and fall to the bottom of the parapet like a log. In 30 minutes we had dismounted every gun."[36]

In addition to counter-battery fire, accurate federal gunnery also suppressed rebel sharpshooters posing a threat to excavators in the trenches. As Isaiah Richards of the Seventeenth Ohio Light Battery serving in Brigadier General A. J. Smith's division reported in a letter dated June 15, "Sharpshooters have hotly opposed our advances . . . [but] we frequently make raking shot on top of their works which I think has been ef[f]ective in quieting them." Yet despite the Union gunners' ability to provide accurate counter-battery fire and suppress the efforts of rebel marksmen, Union artillery was not able to cause a breach. Although artillery fire hit the Confederate defenses and inflicted destruction, the rebels patched their earthworks during the cover of darkness.[37]

On June 20 Grant decided that it was finally time to try to force Lieutenant General John C. Pemberton to capitulate. With nearly two hundred guns ensconced behind the Union's makeshift artillery forts and pointing at Vicksburg, Grant believed that a general bombardment all along the line might batter a breach somewhere in the rebel defenses. On June 19 Grant issued orders outlining the details of the bombardment. The guns were to begin firing at 4 A.M. and continue without hesitation until 10 A.M. Meanwhile, at 6:30 A.M., two and a half hours into the bombardment, Union infantrymen were to "be held under arms" and "ready to take advantage of any signs the enemy may show of weakness, or to repel an attack should one be made."[38]

Grant handed down lucid instructions designed to avoid a replay of the disastrous May 22 assault. So that his subordinates did not take it upon themselves to bring on a full engagement and so that his men understood that he was not being careless with their lives, Grant made his intentions clear. "It is not designed to assault the enemy's works, but to be prepared," Grant explained; however, "should corps commanders believe a favorable opportunity presents itself for possessing themselves of any portion of the lines of the enemy, without a serious battle, they will avail themselves of it." In short, Grant would try to batter the Confederate defenses and effect a breach. If somewhere along the line this succeeded, those closest to the breach were to be ready to exploit the opportunity and storm the rebel defenses so long as they did not bring on a large engagement.[39]

At 4 A.M. on June 20, 1863, the Union guns opened fire. Union troops all along the siege lines recorded this fantastic interruption of the otherwise mundane routine siege warfare. In the Fifteenth Corps sector, Lieutenant R. W. Burt of the Seventy-Sixth Ohio, part of Major General Frederick Steele's division, recalled after the war that "during all the six hours of the cannonading [the Confederates] did not dare to raise their heads to reply from their fort." Just to Burt's south in Lightburn's brigade, a soldier serving in the Fifty-Fifth Illinois later reported that "during the whole forenoon the roar was incessant and terrible, and the tornado of shot and shell tore the ramparts at some points into almost shapeless mounds." Farther down the line, two soldiers of the Seventeenth Corps commented about the Union fire superiority during the event. Sylvester Rynearson of the Fifteenth Iowa wrote to his friend Mollie on June 22, "While our men was bombarding the place, the Rebels threw only a very few shells compared to what our men threw." Similarly, John Quincy Campbell of the Fifth Iowa recorded in his diary on June 20, "While our batteries were firing, the rebels fired scarcely a shot."[40]

Farther to the south, in Hovey's division, Ephraim E. Blake of the Twenty-Eighth Iowa recalled after the war his experience during the bombardment. "I remember I had sat down in the pit and dozed off to sleep and was awakened from my dreams by the quivering earth beneath me and the vibrating air above and jumped up to see what had broken loose. A glance at the Confederate earthworks covered with splinters, flying dirt, and smoke from bursting shells with not a Johnny in sight." He further added that this display "demonstrated clearly that in case we wanted to charge their works our artillery could keep the enemy down until the charging columns were ready to scale the forts making a sure success if it became necessary to make the attempt." Blake, however, reflecting on this incident in hindsight and knowing that the siege was to end about two weeks later, overestimated the impact of the bombardment. Nowhere along the line was a sufficient breach made, and where holes *were* made, a "few cotton bales would repair all the damages done." Grant would have to keep pushing his approaches forward and try another siege tactic for creating a breach and entering Vicksburg.[41]

On the whole, the methods that engineers and artillerymen employed when building advanced batteries mirrored those that were used when erecting artillery forts in the line of circumvallation. Many relied upon traditional revetment in the form of gabions and fascines, while others used cotton bales to shore up walls. Some, due to the nature of Vicksburg's loess soil and feeble Confederate artillery fire, abandoned all forms of revetment. Most advanced batteries were constructed along the avenue of approach or in line with parallels and rifle pits. Others, such as Burbridge's battery, were not connected to rifle pits and best exemplify the independent artillery forts that popped up during the siege.

The lack of engineers and the materials at hand determined how batteries were built. Both resulted in the erection of artillery forts that blended Mahanian dogma in the tradition of Vauban with western soldier ingenuity.

Without the ability to improvise artillery forts, the Army of the Tennessee would not have been able to achieve the fire superiority that allowed those working in the trenches to traverse no-man's-land quickly and in relative safety. In other words, the ability of the men serving in the Army of the Tennessee to fulfill Mahanian maxims via improvised building techniques allowed for the construction of well-placed artillery batteries that in turn allowed the Federals to achieve fire superiority.

9. *Toiling Day and Night*

Up until this point in the siege, Major General Ulysses S. Grant's exuberant June 3 report to Major General Henry W. Halleck that "five days more should plant our batteries on their parapets" had not been fulfilled. Whether Grant believed this statement himself or fired it off with chagrin merely to satisfy Halleck remains uncertain. But despite Grant's early confident, if unrealistic, claims of instant success, the siege had been progressing quite well. As one soldier reminisced after the war, "As June began to draw to a close our lines around the beleaguered city began to draw tighter and closer and held their fortifications in close embrace." With nearly "every hill right up to their works . . . fortified," June 20 appeared as good a day as any to effect a breach with an artillery bombardment and potentially take the Vicksburg defenses by storm. Writing to his son William T. Sherman Jr. on June 21, the Fifteenth Corps commander stated with embellishment that "yesterday we again fired nearly twenty thousand Cannon Balls into the City." What Old Cump forgot to mention was that the bombardment did not have its desired effect. A breach had not been made, the rebel works had not been taken by storm, and the Confederates had not been forced to surrender. The siege would continue.[1]

To overemphasize the failure of the June 20 bombardment, however, would be unjust. As a soldier of the Ninety-Fifth Ohio penned to his "dear Kate" on the day after the bombardment, June 21, the Union "trenches and streets and ways are more tortuous and bewildering than the streets of Boston." Captain Cyrus B. Comstock later reported on June 27—the day he replaced Captain Frederick E. Prime as chief engineer after illness forced the latter to take leave—that the Union approaches "gave cover to within 10 feet to 200 yards of the enemy's works." This fact elicited exuberant commentary from the rank and file. Albert Chipman of the Seventy-Sixth Illinois wrote to his wife on June 22 that the Union "chord [*sic*] grows tighter every day." Six days later, the Eleventh Illinois's Cyrus E. Dickey quipped to his sister that the federal "'public works' . . . are getting uncomfortably close." In short, the siege, up to this point, had been making steady progress.[2]

Instead of effecting a breach via bombardment, the Army of the Tennessee would have to implement a different siege tactic. As Albert O. Marshall of the Thirty-Third Illinois later summarized, "The work now to be accomplished was to undermine the rebel forts. . . . The object was to run the tunnel under the enemy's fort and then, when all was ready, a wagon load of powder could be taken in and the fort blown out of existence." But, if the Federals were to achieve success via mining, they first needed to close the final distance between their lead trenches and the Confederate works. Pushing forward under the cover of their sap rollers, the blue-clad "toilers" would need to ply "their guns and spades" both "day and night." The successful formula of Mahanian siege craft and soldier improvisation that had so far proved successful would now propel the blue-clad besiegers over the final distance from the forward-most approaches to the base of the rebel works.[3]

Comstock's report stating that June 27 witnessed federal approaches within ten to two hundred yards from the enemy works reflects Union progress in the waning days of June. The situation on June 21, however, was different. While the Federals had made steady progress, such advances were not even all along the line. Some approaches had proceeded smoothly and needed only to close the short final distance between the heads of saps and the rebel fortifications. Meanwhile, others had just begun their journey toward the Confederate salients. Some had not even been started at all.

Progress along the Thirteenth Army Corps front was uneven at best, a fact that prompted special commissioner Charles A. Dana to fire off to Secretary of War Edwin M. Stanton a disparaging report of the progress, or lack thereof, made in this sector under Major General John A. McClernand's command. As previously stated, after Major General E. O. C. Ord replaced McClernand on June 18, Dana reported that the trenches in the Thirteenth Corps sector represented "mere rifle pits 3 or 4 feet wide." They were deficient, would "neither allow the passage of artillery nor the assemblage of any considerable number of troops," and remained "in the same position they apparently held when the siege was opened."[4]

While this may have been true for some approaches on the southern part of the Union line, those of Brigadier General A. J. Smith and Brigadier General Eugene A. Carr, the two approaches that engineer officer First Lieutenant Peter C. Hains directly supervised, appear to have been exceptions to Dana's generalization about Thirteenth Corps stagnation. In A. J. Smith's front, Hains by June 18 had already advanced the approach across the Baldwin's Ferry Road and cut to level ground, which allowed the use of sap rollers. Three days prior to this, on June 15, a Union soldier gleefully wrote, "Our forces are making excelant progress in advancing their entrenchments; In our immediate front our boys have got up quite close to the enemies line of works." Just to Smith's south, Carr's Approach established rifle pits approximately sixty yards from the Confederate Railroad Redoubt on June 19. The remaining approaches on the Thirteenth Corps front, however, tended to reflect Dana's disparaging remarks. Hovey's and Slack's Approaches would not be opened until June 23 and June 30 respectively, after Dana had written his report.[5]

Although the more gentle terrain in front of Brigadier General Alvin P. Hovey's division proved ideal for approach operations, Hovey's obduracy, combined with the stubbornness of his direct superior, McClernand, created stagnation on this particular front. After the siege Hovey penned a self-serving report about operations in his sector: "Receiving orders on the 23d [of May] to prepare for a siege," he wrote, "my [troops] commenced the work with spirit, and during the whole period prosecuted their labors with success, pressing our rifle-pits to within a few yards of the enemy's fortifications." While Hovey's Approach would eventually reach a point within approximately twenty feet of the Confederate parapet before the siege ended on July 4, the division commander conveniently omitted the fact that he did not even bother to begin approach operations until June 23. Responsibility for the failure to act did not rest solely with Hovey, though. His superior, McClernand, must bear the brunt of the blame.[6]

McClernand's unwillingness to defer to the better judgment of his superiors resulted in approach delays on the southern part of the Vicksburg siege lines. Although Grant had graduated with the West Point class of 1843 a mediocre twenty-first out of thirty-nine, he did understand the basics of Mahanian siege craft. Able to recognize the advantageous ground that lay before McClernand on the southern part of the Thirteenth Corps sector, Grant kept a close eye on the progress, or lack thereof, on this part of the line. While Grant had ordered McClernand on June 6 to "make all advance

possible in the approaches during my absence [to Mechanicsburg]," McClernand failed to comply. With limited progress on McClernand's front, Grant
outlined his intentions more specifically on June 15. On that day, Grant gave
McClernand more pointed direction. "The idea then is that two lines should
now be selected for mining perpendicular to our present line," Grant wrote,
"one from Lauman's [division] left in along Halls Ferry road and one from
Hovey's present left." McClernand continued to ignore Grant.[7]

On the night of June 23, five days after McClernand's departure, Hovey's men finally opened their approach. Colonel William H. Raynor of the
Fifty-Sixth Ohio reported on June 26, "Our men [are] still digging and
creeping clear to the rebel works," but he gleefully recorded in his diary
on the same day, "I shall look forward for a blow up in our front before
many days." Raynor had a right to be optimistic as the blue-clad toilers of
Hovey's division made immediate progress. By the night of June 26, Hovey
had "rifle pits extended to within forty paces of their large fort." On June 28
the Federals advanced to a point approximately ten to twenty yards from
the Confederate Fort Garrott, better known among Grant's troops as the
"square fort." Finally, Hains reported with confidence on July 1 that "in front
of General Hovey's division a sap has been started from the nearest point of
his advance trench, to reach the counterscarp of the ditch, at a point not apparently enfiladed." The speedy progress on Hovey's front had been amazing,
and Colonel Raynor's dream of "a blow up" of the square fort appeared to be
coming true. The same day that Hains made his report, Raynor recorded in
his diary that "I feel sure of being able to take our brigade inside the rebel
works on the 4th inst."[8]

Meanwhile, Brigadier General Jacob Lauman's second parallel was a
distant 275 yards from the rebel defenses on June 21. On the southernmost
part of the Union line, Major General Francis J. Herron's division, detached
from the Sixteenth Corps in west Tennessee and ordered to report directly
to Grant's headquarters, had by June 16 only established a series of rifle pits
some eight hundred yards from the Confederate fortifications. By June 25
another parallel would be excavated some two hundred to three hundred yards
from the rebel line. In Herron's front, the adage "hem them in, starve them
out" had been taken to an absurd extreme. As brigade commander William
Orme wrote on July 1, "We are doing all we can in the way of digging rifle
pits, earth works, [and] covered ways. . . . But I have more hope in starving
them out than in immediately taking the place by storm."[9]

At the same time, to the north, progress had been more rapid. In the Fifteenth Corps sector, Thayer's Approach, which had begun some three hundred yards from the Twenty-Sixth Louisiana Redoubt on May 30, was within sixty yards of that rebel fort on June 25. Although little progress had been made on Giles Smith's Approach, the principal approach on Sherman's front, Brigadier General Hugh Ewing's, moved forward rapidly and, by June 20, was some twenty feet from the counterscarp of the Confederates' Stockade Redan. Meanwhile, Buckland's Approach, which had been suspended on June 22 within sixty yards from the rebel works, was opened again on June 28 under the name Lightburn's Approach. Similarly, in the center of the Union line, while Ransom's Approach was not commenced until June 15, the principal Seventeenth Corps approach, Major General John A. Logan's, was on June 21 only a few yards from the Third Louisiana Redan. Thus, while the Union advance had not been even all along the line, it had been progressing nonetheless. The Army of the Tennessee now needed to press its approaches forward from the most advanced parallels and place itself in a position from which the men could dig mines under the enemy's fortifications. This stage of the siege, the final approaches before the mining phase, highlights the perfect wedding of Mahanian theory to western soldier improvisation, which would ensure the success of the Vicksburg siege.[10]

While the Union approaches continued to advance under a curtain of sharpshooter and artillery-suppressing fire, the absence of specialized siege equipment was felt as the Army of the Tennessee closed the distance between the heads of saps and the rebel works. The lack of mortars, and the Union response to this problem, provides an excellent example of the western soldier improvisation that contributed to the success of the Vicksburg siege. As previously stated, prior to May 22 Grant had never intended to lay formal siege to Vicksburg. As a result, when the Army of the Tennessee departed Milliken's Bend on March 29, it did not trail a siege train containing specialized artillery designed to reduce fortifications. If it had, the westerners would have dragged batteries of a special type of artillery known as stone mortars (also known as Coehorn mortars) in tow. But since besieging the Gibraltar of the Confederacy was not their primary objective they did not. As a result, once the Army of the Tennessee entered the final approach stage of the siege, the troops found themselves wanting for this invaluable piece of siege equipment.[11]

Mahanian engineering theory dictated that advanced approaches make use of small mortars. "To attack the covered way by storm," Dennis Hart Mahan wrote, "*Stone Mortar Batteries* are erected in front of the third parallel, for the purpose of throwing showers of stone into the covered ways." The Army of the Tennessee's engineers, and Grant himself, subscribed to this axiom but did not have any mortars with the army that could carry out this vital task. On June 20 Grant ordered his chief of ordnance, Lieutenant Stephan Carr Lyford (USMA class of 1861), to request mortars from the chief of ordnance in Washington, Brigadier General J. W. Ripley. On that day, Lyford wrote, "General Grant wishes twenty mortars for siege operations, with 400 rounds of ammunition, as soon as possible. I think of this number perhaps as half should be Coehorn and stone mortars, and the other 8-inch and 10-inch siege. Please have them come through by special messenger as quickly as possible." But, for whatever reason, Ripley did not fulfill Grant's request. The Army of the Tennessee would have to improvise.[12]

As the Union approaches neared the Confederate works, the blue-clad westerners found themselves in a precarious position. With the principal rebel forts erected to commanding heights, those in the Union approach trenches found themselves below their Confederate antagonists and therefore susceptible to Confederate plunging fire. Although the Federals lacked mortars, they did have one gadget in their arsenal that might prove effective—hand grenades. While considered primitive when compared to their modern grandchildren, Civil War hand grenades were, in actuality, state-of-the-art technology at that time. Many soldiers described these devices in letters as well as in their regimental histories. In a letter dated June 28, 1863, George O. Cooper of the Forty-Sixth Illinois described to a relative back home the properties of the weapon. "Hand grenades," Cooper explained, "are a small round shell weighing four pounds[.] [T]here is a cavity in the center which they fill with powder and then there is a piece of fuse running into it the same as a shell[.] [T]hey light the fuse and throw it by hand." Similarly, the Fifteenth Iowa's Oscar Eugene Stewart related after the war that, when "our zigzags [and] approaches . . . had been pushed forward until we were up to the very parapets of the enemy's works . . . hand grenades were thrown into the enemy's works." They were "ten or twelve inch shells, with short time fuses."[13]

It is worth pointing out, however, that Cooper's and Stewart's descriptions of hand grenade use applied to the point of the siege when the Union approaches had finally reached the Confederate works and a small berm was all that separated the hostile parties. Before this occurred, federal soldiers excavated at a distance close enough to the rebel works to take on plunging fire yet far enough that even the heartiest of the blue-clad midwesterners would experience difficulty in hurling a hand grenade on an inclined trajectory up and over the Confederate defenses. According to First Lieutenant Peter C. Hains, "Some naval hand-grenades were also procured . . . [but] even when the approaches were only 10 feet from the ditch, it required an extraordinary powerful man to throw one into the works."[14]

In order to hurl their grenades at high trajectories over greater distances, the inventive westerners of the Army of the Tennessee improvised. As stated by Hains, "In order to have some means of throwing our shells into the fort, I . . . directed Captain Patterson, of the pioneer corps, to construct spring-boards for this purpose." Meanwhile, another member of the Thirteenth Corps, W. F. Jones of the Forty-Second Ohio, fondly reported after the war that "one of the members of Co. C, 20th Ohio, invented a machine-like gun that would shoot hand-grenades, the propelling power being a spring." The dogged soldier "would creep or crawl through the brush and broken ground unseen by the rebels until he could get a good position where he . . . could use his machine." He would then throw "hand-grenades over into the enemy's lines with such accuracy that [the Confederates] were at a loss to know how to dislodge him."[15]

Farther to the north, in front of the Third Louisiana Redan, affection-ately called by Union troops "the rebel Fort Hill," the Army of the Tennes-see's westerners engineered a different device for hurling grenades over the Confederate works. "The principal business carried on while I was there," wrote a soldier serving in the Thirtieth Illinois, "was the throwing of a small bombshell into the fort, called a hand-grenade. These were a little fuse shell, the fuse being cut to so many seconds, lighted and like a firecracker, laid on the end of a board or plank, fixed like a teeter, and the other end hit with a maul, which threw up the end with the shell on it and sent it over to explode on the other side." These inventive devices, the product of western soldier ingenuity in the face of adversity, however, were not enough. As A. J. Smith's Approach finally reached the Confederate works, Hains reported on June 29 and 30, "In General Smith's front, the *saps* are now about as close as they can get without first clearing the rebel works in front by means of mortar shells. Cohorn mortars would be invaluable at the present time." Thus, as Prime and Comstock stated after the siege, "The want of Cohorn mortars was severely felt."[16]

The engineers in front of the Third Louisiana Redan, pushing forward Logan's Approach, adapted to adverse conditions and overcame. As Union troops worked in close proximity to the Confederate redan, the rebels harassed the Federals with hand grenades. One Union soldier summarized the problem when he wrote that "at Vicksburg, the Confederate Works were on slightly higher ground than those of the Union works, and the rebels annoyed our works by tossing lighted shells over the works." In order to counter the Confederate threat and achieve higher trajectories over greater distances than those offered by the various types of primitive "grenade launchers" then in use, the soldiers on this front adopted the use of wooden mortars.[17]

Although it is certain that wooden mortars first appeared on the Seventeenth Corps front, it is not clear who pioneered their implementation. After the devices proved their worth, many angled to be credited as the inventor of Vicksburg's wooden mortars. Captain Andrew Hickenlooper was one who claimed credit for introducing wooden mortars to the Vicksburg siege. According to Hickenlooper, his sap, at the head of Logan's Approach, reached the defensive ditch protecting Fort Hill (the Third Louisiana Redan) on June 22. With Union troops at the base of the Confederate fortifications, the rebels could not depress their firearms low enough to shoot at the Federals. As a result, the Confederates guarding the redan resorted to lobbing hand grenades and rolling artillery shells with "short fuses" down the fort's walls. According to Hickenlooper, this resulted in "a kind of warfare we had difficulty counteracting." The combined height from the bottom of the Union trench up to the top of the Confederate parapet was too high for the Federals to throw their own shells at the rebels. As a result, the clever Hickenlooper "devised a novel expedient for launching shells" at the Confederates. He ordered his subordinate Captain Stewart R. Tresilian, the assistant engineer of the Third Division, Seventeenth Corps, to carry out the details of the plan. Hickenlooper ordered Tresilian to take "sections of gum-trees of various diameters about 4 feet in length" and burn out holes in the logs "of diameters to suit the calibre of the shells to be used." After the holes were burned and the ashes scraped out, Hickenlooper instructed Tresilian to secure the width of the logs with iron bands in order to keep the pieces from exploding. The chief engineer of the Seventeenth Corps reported that the mortars were very effective and relieved the Union work details in Logan's Approach "from much serious annoyance and interruption of our work."[18]

Thus, according to Hickenlooper, he alone devised the "novel expedient" of bringing wooden mortars to the Vicksburg siege and Tresilian, his subordinate, was merely the mechanic who carried out the craftsmanship. This, however, contradicts Tresilian's own report, which stated that, previous to July 1, "I had constructed three wooden mortars, one 6-pounder and two 12-pounders, and put two of them into position about 100 yards from the main redoubt." Interestingly, Tresilian's report does not make mention of Hickenlooper as the instigator of the project. This version, casting Tresilian as the inventor of Vicksburg's wooden mortars, is reiterated in the Prime and Comstock report. According to the chief engineers, "Mr. Tresilian, civil assistant engineer, made some wooden mortars for 6 to 12 pound shells, which were very effective at from 100 to 150 yards."[19]

Although some regimental histories subscribe to the *Official Records* and recognize Captain Tresilian as the designer of the wooden Coehorn, others do not. Writing after the war, M. B. Loop of the Sixty-Eighth Ohio credited one of his fellow soldiers, Hanson Barr of Company C, as the inventor of Vicksburg's wooden mortars. Loop wrote in 1900 that "Comrade Barr served on detached duty with the Third Division Engineers, and to him was given the credit of devising and constructing two mortars made from a sweet-gum log. These wooden guns were placed in convenient locations in the trenches, and proved to be of service in tossing shells over the enemy's breastworks at short range." Later, in 1910, another Union soldier, John McElroy, stated that the improvised mortars were a common soldier invention that was later adopted by the engineers. According to this soldier, "Union troops found that if they would slightly hollow out a stump and place a couple of broken Springfield cartridges in it the force of the powder would throw the shell so that it would fall inside the rebel works. This proved so effective that the engineers began to improvise mortars by taking sections of a log, hollowing out a chamber in it and binding it with iron hoops." In short, a diverse array of sources credits different soldiers as the true inventor of Vicksburg's improvised wooden mortars.[20]

Nevertheless, while it may never be known who pioneered this project, it is clear that the device caught on and exacted a heavy toll on the besieged Confederates. First Lieutenant Hains on the Thirteenth Corps front, after ordering Captain William Franklin Patterson, commander of the Thirteenth Corps' pioneer unit, to construct his springboard grenade launchers, "learned that General McPherson was using mortars made of trunks of trees (gum trees being the best) to throw 6 and 12 pound shells . . . shrinking about three iron bands around the mortar." Learning of this device, Hains ordered Patterson "to make some of these also." Hains intended to put his mortars in place sometime after July 2, some fifty to seventy-five yards from the rebel works and in time for Grant's proposed July 6 assault.[21]

While engineers built wooden mortars on the Seventeenth and Thirteenth Corps fronts, evidence does not suggest that they were used at the heads of the Fifteenth Corps' approach trenches. Yet, where they were used, these "'Coehorn mortars' . . . made from short sections of gum-tree logs bored out and hooped with iron bands" raked the tops of parapets, inflicted casualties on the Confederate defenders, and "proved exceedingly effective." In fact, Union and Confederates soldiers alike gave testimony to the effectiveness of the Federals' improvised mortars. Osborn Hamiline Oldroyd of the Twentieth Ohio, part of Logan's division, wrote on June 22, "A wooden gun has been made which, charged with a small amount of powder, throws the shell inside the fort—a new device, but working well, for it can drop a missile where the cannon cannot." Edmund Newsome of the Eighty-First Illinois, also part of Logan's division, wrote on July 1, "Our men have made wooden mortars to throw small shells over the breastworks. . . . They just land them nicely over in the fort, among the enemy, in the deep ravine." Meanwhile, Francis R. Baker of the Seventy-Eighth Ohio, serving in Logan's Approach, reported on June 30, "The wooden mortars that our Pioneer Corps made are behaving satisfactorily." But Baker's glee was short lived: "On account of a defective shell, one of the wooden mortars was blown to pieces today," he glumly recorded on July 2. "Our boys escaped injury," but "another of the mortars became disabled [as well]."[22]

On the other side of the siege, Confederate chief engineer Major Samuel H. Lockett reported what it was like on the receiving end of the fire of the Union wooden mortars in the Third Louisiana Redan guarding the Jackson Road. According to Lockett, "A Cohorn mortar [played] upon this redan . . . [and] at least a dozen of its garrison were killed or wounded by the mortar alone." And so the Union implementation of wooden mortars was a product of western soldier ingenuity that allowed the fulfillment of Mahanian siege maxims.[23]

In the final stage of the siege, the Federals began constructing what were called "trench cavaliers" to enhance their ability to deliver suppressing plunging fire into the Confederate fortifications. According to Mahan, when the trenches were advanced via the full sap to within approximately "30 yards from

the [enemy] salient," it was time to
construct trench cavaliers, a raised
horseshoe-shaped structure that
hugged the salient. "This work"—the
trench cavalier—"[was] of a parapet
raised on a mound of earth, for the
purpose of obtaining a plunging fire on
the covered-way," Mahan explained.
"The mound should, in all cases, be
raised so high that the cavalier will
have a command of 4½ feet over the
crest of the covered way." There were
two different methods for erecting
trench cavaliers, depending upon
the soil type that the engineer had
to work in.[24]

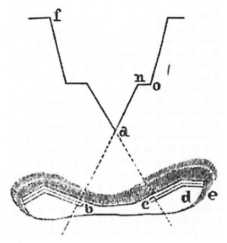

Overhead view of a trench cavalier. *D. H.
Mahan, Summary of the Course of Permanent
Fortification, 305.*

When the soil was such that, once excavated, "it can be easily made to
stand at any slope," one specific style of construction was used. This technique was the preferred method for constructing trench cavaliers because
it required fewer building materials and could be erected quickly. Despite
these advantages, erecting this type of trench cavalier required the engineer
to follow a series of meticulous steps. Using a double sap (an approach trench
that utilized two sap rollers and contained two different "heads of sap"), a
V-shaped trench was formed that hugged the enemy's salient.[25]

Next, excavators began raising the trench cavalier. This was, in short,
a mound of earth "sustained by several courses of gabions, against the interior of which steps [were] arranged to ascend to the upper course, which
[served] as a parapet." First, sappers planted and filled gabions on the front
of the trench facing the enemy. Soldiers then expanded this trench to six
feet in width and proceeded to construct a step on the floor of the trench
twenty-two inches high and extending some five and a half feet "within the
gabion [wall] of the parapet" facing the enemy. From the top of this platform,
the soldiers erected stepped levels of gabions and fascines some three tiers
high with each successive tier moving closer toward the enemy's parapet.
The first tier consisted of the gabions that made up the front of the approach
trench. Fascines were then placed on top of this wall of gabions, thereby
creating the next step in the trench cavalier. Between the first and second

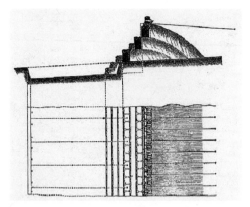

Cross section and overhead view of a textbook trench cavalier erected in "easy soil." *J. C. Duane, Manual for Engineer Troops, 185.*

tier, soldiers constructed a step made of dirt shored up with stacked fascines. From the top of this platform, soldiers planted the third tier (the top tier), which formed the parapet of the trench cavalier. On top of this tier, soldiers placed sandbags arranged with loopholes. Standing on the second tier of gabions and fascines, soldiers placed their guns through the loopholes atop the top tier and delivered plunging fire onto the enemy. Meanwhile, when engineers had to dig in soil that was loose, a similar but more complicated construction technique was used. Engineers made the first and second tiers wider, forming a pyramid-like structure, in order to evenly distribute the weight of the successive tiers over the unstable soil.[26]

In short, Mahan's and James C. Duane's meticulous steps, while fine in theory, proved overly complicated in the field. It would have been difficult even for West Point–trained professionals to have memorized and implemented these steps so close to the enemy's defenses while under enemy fire. Interestingly, one finds three examples of improvised trench cavaliers at Vicksburg, two constructed by nonprofessional engineers and one by a West Point–trained engineer.

On June 19 Captain William Kossak became commander of the trenches in the area around the Graveyard Road. Kossak, however, while serving on the Fifteenth Corps staff as an engineer officer, was not a professionally trained military engineer. Originally born in Prussia, Kossak entered federal service as a lieutenant in the Fifth Missouri

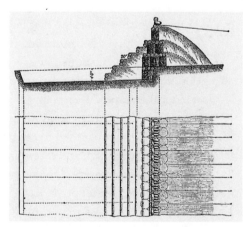

Cross section and overhead view of a textbook trench cavalier erected in unstable soil. *J. C. Duane, Manual for Engineer Troops, 187.*

Infantry shortly after hostilities broke out in 1861. By the end of the summer of that year, Kossak had become a captain and was made an "additional aide-de-camp" in the volunteer engineers. During the Vicksburg siege he served as an "acting engineer" on the Fifteenth Corps' staff.[27]

Immediately after taking charge of the trenches in the Graveyard Road area on June 19, Kossak found Ewing's Approach within twenty feet of the Confederate redoubt. But there was a problem. Kossak later reported that on taking command, he "found the work advanced within 20 feet of the enemy's counter-scarp, with such obstructions in front of the sap-roller as to make it impossible to move the roller one inch without having the party engaged in the moving killed outright." Kossak engineered a solution to the problem. "I therefore branched off to the right and left," Kossak wrote, "trying to raise trench cavaliers parallel to the enemy's counterscarp and get a plunging fire into his ditch." "The sap-roller," he continued, "I left in its position, crowning it with gabions and sand bags, so as to offer the pickets supporting the working party a proper shelter." The description Kossak left regarding his trench cavalier, built over the course of two days, June 20–21, indicates that he did not adhere to Mahanian principles. Its center contained the stalled sap roller, crowned with gabions and sandbags. Extending from this makeshift center like two arms hugging the capital of the Confederate salient were two "bastions" of unspecified dimensions.[28]

Meanwhile, farther south, West Point professional First Lieutenant Peter C. Hains also improvised a trench cavalier. Hains's cavalier, however, was not erected in order to provide suppressing fire. Rather, it proved an improvised solution to a desperate problem. On July 1 Confederate fire ignited the sap roller spearheading A. J. Smith's left approach. With the sap roller out of commission, Hains ordered it "covered at once with earth . . . [in order to] establish a trench cavalier at that point." This could not be accomplished. The rebels began lobbing "hand-grenades into the fire," an act that tore "it [the sap roller] considerably." According to Hains, "In about one-half hour it was entirely destroyed, exposing to their [the rebels'] view a portion of the trench." Thus, on July 2, with a hole now created in A. J. Smith's left approach, Hains "directed the head of the sap to be filled up with sand-bags, and the cavalier commenced a little to the rear of the point first intended" for the purpose of closing "the head of the sap." Thus, while engineers did use trench cavaliers at Vicksburg, they were on-the-fly improvisations that deviated from Mahanian specifications.[29]

The effects of Union engineering on Confederate morale became most apparent on Carr's front during this part of the siege. The nightly truces that occurred at various points all along the siege lines revealed the flagging rebel morale in Carr's sector. On June 20 Hains reported, "The enemy's pickets in front of General Carr's division have entered into an agreement with the latter's pickets not to fire on each other at night. They allow our men to work in full view, and make no attempts to stop it."[30]

Hains's observation, by itself, is not remarkable. Soldiers' writings on the siege are riddled with accounts of nightly truces and playful banter. Twilight ceasefires, however, were not the result of formal military agreements, and their character varied all along the siege lines. "Nightly truces," wrote Albert O. Marshall of the Thirty-Third Illinois, "were confined to different parts of the line" and "could only occur where each side had confidence in the enemy in his front." As a result, "a visitor, passing along the lines in the evening," might see "Union and Confederate soldiers peacefully looking at each other at one point and as he came to the next division, would find a fierce contest still raging." Truces, hence, were localized agreements among weary soldiers tired of the drudgery and boredom of siege warfare.[31]

Nevertheless, despite the commonality of nightly ceasefires, what occurred on the evening of June 21 in Hains's sector did, however, prove somewhat unusual. Here, Confederates posted to stymie Carr's advance simply gave up. Commander of the Thirteenth Corps' pioneer unit Captain William Franklin Patterson later related the incident to his wife. "I must say what the rebs said last night," Patterson wrote on June 22. A Union officer "moved his men out to a place where the rebels pickets stood." The officer "walked up" to the Confederate soldiers and said, "I am going to work here, to dig a riffle [sic] pit, just sit still we won't fire on you, Only if you think we are too close you can move back a little." The southern sentry walked back to the remainder of his company who were off duty sleeping and woke them up saying, "Get up boys wake up the Yankees want to dig a riffle [sic] pit here we must [get] out of the way wake up." The sleepy-eyed Confederates complied with the order and the Union colonel "went to digging leaving the Reb to move his men out of the [way]."[32]

Albert O. Marshall described this remarkable event in greater detail after the war. According to Marshall, as the Union troops on this front closed the final distance between their approach trench and the Confederate works, an unusual incident occurred. One night a few Federals, including Marshall and

an engineer officer, went out of their sap and reconnoitered the terrain that
their trench was supposed to traverse. The survey revealed that a Confederate
picket line interrupted their line of advance. Unable to skirt around the rebel
sentries, the scouting party approached the gray-clad sentinels. As related
by Marshall, "The Confederates were notified of the difficulty." The Union
reconnaissance party informed the rebels that "the trenches had to be dug that
night or else [they would] have to fight over the ground." Wishing to avoid a
"stubborn fight," the Confederates discussed the matter among themselves.
After a few moments of deliberation, they called for the Union engineer who
proceeded to "go over the ground with them [the Confederates] and marked
the course [that the Union] trenches would take." Once the Confederates and
the Union engineer officer finished their survey, the rebels left their post and
the Federals continued to dig their trench. According to Marshall, "It certainly
was a strange war scene, for the opposing men of a desperate contest to meet
and talk over the disputed ground just as though it was adjoining neighbors
who had met in a friendly way to establish their line fence."[33]

Other incidents also occurred suggesting that the Confederate defenders
opposite Carr's division experienced flagging morale during the latter part of
the siege. A short time after the Confederate pickets abandoned their post
in order to make way for Carr's Approach, Marshall reported another event
highlighting dampened Confederate spirits. While the Confederate sentries
allowed the Union excavators to proceed forward, they continued to send out
pickets that shadowed the federal advance. In fact, the rebels got so close to
the federal approach that discarded dirt from the Union trench began to land
near where the Confederate guards stood watch. Union troops excavating the
approach, including Marshall, "suggested that they move back." According
to Marshall, the Confederates complied and shouted back, "Oh, that don't
make any difference. You Yanks will soon have the place any way." Without
the prospect of General Joseph E. Johnston's intervention and cut off from
supplies, the weary rebel sentinels deployed to obstruct Carr's advance stepped
aside and allowed the Union besiegers to advance their approaches.[34]

To the north, Ewing's and Logan's Approaches emerged as the front-runners
during the final approach phase. Despite their comparable successes, only
the latter was able to "crown" the enemy's defenses before the first Vicksburg
mine was detonated on June 25 (a topic to be explored in the next chapter).
According to Mahan, after engineers erected trench cavaliers, it was time
to "crown the covered way." "When the besieged are effectually driven from

the covered way," Mahan wrote, "the sappers push forward the sap to within six yards of the crest of the glacis; and they make a trench entirely around the covered way, which is termed *Crowning the Covered Way*." Mahan went on to instruct that "after the covered way is crowned, breach batteries are erected around the salient places of arms, and from these positions breaches are made in the face of the demi-lune, and in the bastion faces." Once this was achieved, mining operations could begin in earnest.[35]

While Sherman issued orders on June 19 to his chiefs of artillery to "crown the enemy's works when the engineers report the work done," things on Ewing's front had not gone to plan. As previously stated, when Kossak took over engineering operations in the Graveyard Road sector on June 19, a series of problems greeted the engineer. Ewing's Approach, up to that point, had progressed smoothly. Sherman gleefully wrote to Admiral David Dixon Porter on June 15, "My 'Sap' is up to their Main Ditch and I have two Side parallels quite close up." Hugging the Graveyard Road, a level route into the city, allowed the work to move rather quickly, and it appeared as if mining operations would commence within a short period of time. But the evening of June 19 threatened to derail operations when the Union sap roller encountered "obstructions . . . [so] as to make it impossible to move the roller one inch without having the party engaged in the moving killed outright" approximately twenty feet (some six yards) from the enemy's salient. Kossak countered and erected trench cavaliers on June 20 and 21. Shortly thereafter, he commenced mining operations. Early in the excavation Kossak detected the "dull, deep sound of tamping." This could mean only one thing—enemy countermines. The newly appointed Union engineer officer parried and attempted to countermine the Confederate countermine, but the rebels beat him to the punch and detonated their countermine first on June 26. According to Kossak, "Some gabions in the trench cavaliers were thrown down; but the charge of the mines was too small to throw up any crater which we might have taken advantage of. The mines acted *a la ca-mouflet* [camouflet], which was probably the enemy's intention."[36]

The explosion, while small, filled Kossak's mines and "disintegrated the soil." This presented Kossak with a problem. Vicksburg's loess soil, though able to stand without bracing when undisturbed, became very unstable when shocked by an explosion. As a result, pulverized loess soil would require extensive bracing and shoring. In this particular incident the Confederate explosion damaged the soil to the "extent that further mining at that point

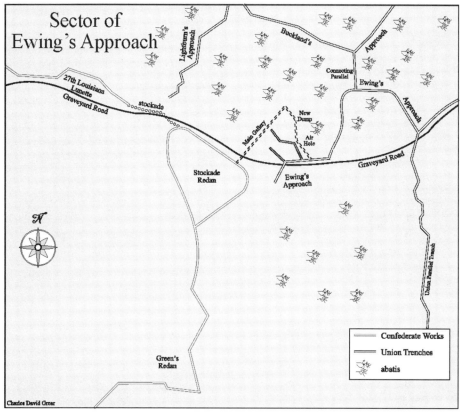

Sector of Ewing's Approach.

was out of the question." All of this would force Kossak to cut his approach to the right of the Graveyard Road into the deep ravine and attempt to undermine the left face of the Confederate salient.[37]

Meanwhile, to the south, in Logan's Approach, soldiers continued to gain ground on the enemy. While Hickenlooper had not raised formal trench cavaliers, advanced positions such as Coonskin's Tower and Battery Hickenlooper provided enough covering fire to allow excavators to push forward. Beginning his approach some 433 yards as the crow flies from the rebel Fort Hill (Third Louisiana Redan) on May 26, Hickenlooper's sap was by June 16 about twenty-five yards from this key Confederate fortification guarding the Jackson Road into Vicksburg. Making the final push from this point, Logan's Approach finally arrived near the base of Fort Hill on June 21, a feat that led Hickenlooper to "call for all miners in the command to report to

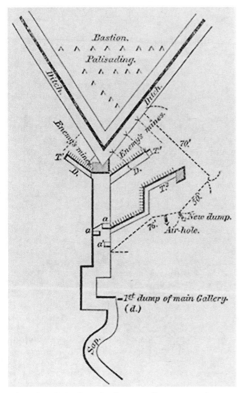

Sketch of the head of Ewing's Approach. *OR, vol. 24, pt. 2, 191.*

[him] in person." It now became time for the Federals to crown the Third Louisiana Redan's salient. Unfamiliar with engineering jargon, John Quincy Adams Campbell of the Fifth Iowa described this procedure the best he could, writing on June 21, "'*Logan's Ditch*' is still progressing—being now dug *around* the rebel fort." Thus on June 22 Hickenlooper confidently reported, "We reached the rebel fort to-day at 10 o'clock with main trench, and cleared away a place to commence mining operations." The self-taught Seventeenth Corps engineer was now ready to undermine the Confederate Fort Hill.[38]

Once it became clear that Grant's artillery could not effect a breach in the Vicksburg defenses, mining operations were the Army of the Tennessee's only alternative. Before they could do this, however, the blue-clad westerners needed to close the distance between their most forward approach trenches and the Confederate works. To this end, the perfect blending of Mahanian siege craft theory with soldier improvisation would, once again, have to carry the day. The Union's ability to achieve this unity becomes clear when one considers the use of wooden mortars and the erection of trench cavaliers during the final approach stage of the siege. As the Army of the Tennessee advanced through the heart of Mississippi, it did not trail a proper siege train for the simple reason that Grant never intended to lay formal siege to Vicksburg; such materials would have impeded his march. This meant that a vital siege tool, the Coehorn mortar, was not available during the final approach phase of the siege. Although soldiers rigged up a variety of grenade-throwing devices, these were not enough. Using the tools that the Mississippi environment afforded, namely the sweet gum tree, the crafty westerners of Grant's

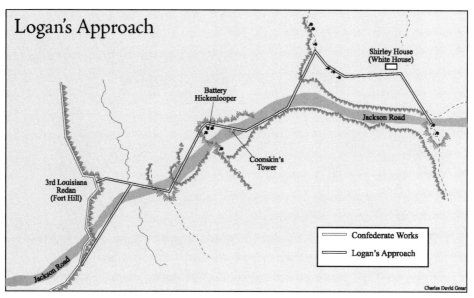

Logan's Approach.

army engineered wooden mortars capable of conforming to Mahanian maxims. Similarly, Grant's engineers erected improvised trench cavaliers not because Mahan demanded it but because they proved useful on-the-spot solutions to Confederate attempts to stymie the Federals' advance.

This stage in the siege also brought out the unevenness of approach operations along the Union line. Although stagnation on the southern part of the Thirteenth Corps front, the result of McClernand's obduracy, mandated that the near-perfect ground in front of Hovey's division was not taken advantage of until late in the siege, the Thirteenth Corps commander's northern approaches progressed in a timely fashion. On this part of McClernand's line, First Lieutenant Peter C. Hains pushed forward Carr's and A. J. Smith's Approaches with vigor. On Carr's front, Confederate morale flagged to the point that no attempt was made to stop his advance. Despite Carr's successes, it was the northern and central parts of the Union siege line, the sectors of the Fifteenth and Seventeenth Corps, where the greatest progress was made. Ewing's and Logan's Approaches emerged during the final approach stage as the preeminent Union saps, and it would be Major General James B. McPherson's chief engineer, Captain Andrew Hickenlooper, who would reach the rebel defenses first and commence successful mining operations.

10. *The Key to Vicksburg*

T he siege tactic of undermining an enemy's fortifications dates back to antiquity. In order to bring down the stout stone walls protecting an ancient city, besieging miners, also known as sappers, dug tunnels directly underneath the enemy works, shoring the subterranean cavity with large wooden timbers in order to prevent cave-ins. Once directly underneath the wall of the beleaguered city, miners built a chamber revetted with wood and filled with combustible materials. Then the sappers would set the chamber alight and scramble to safety. The burning of the shoring timbers would cause the chamber and the stone walls above it to collapse, causing a breach in the city wall that a besieging force of infantry could then exploit.[1]

With the advent of gunpowder, however, this tactic changed. Better and heavier siege artillery, developed during the seventeenth century, forced an evolution in fortification design. The angled-bastion fortress, with its low, thick earthen walls and interlocking fields of fire, became the European standard that influenced fortification design in the New World until the late nineteenth century. Keeping pace with changing defensive measures, offensive siege tactics also evolved. The concept of "bringing down" a stone wall during antiquity gave way to "blowing up" the earthen Vaubanian ramparts of the Enlightenment era, a practice that continued through and beyond the American Civil War.[2]

More than twenty years earlier, Albert O. Marshall of the Thirty-Third Illinois, part of Brigadier General Eugene A. Carr's division, reflected on the mining activities that occurred at Vicksburg some two decades before, during the summer of 1863. According to Marshall, it became known throughout the Union ranks that "General Grant [had] consented that the soldier who first [completed] the excavations under an important rebel fort may try the experiment of blowing it up." This news supposedly generated a wave of enthusiasm throughout the Army of the Tennessee, and as Marshall described, "the soldiers [became] anxious to win this race first." Whether or not Major General Ulysses S. Grant did in fact initiate such a friendly competition remains uncertain. Nevertheless, the can-do attitude of the Army of the Tennessee, which had carried the blue-clad westerners to the gates of Vicksburg, continued to generate momentum throughout the army as it embarked on mining operations against the Gibraltar of the Confederacy.[3]

Unfortunately for Marshall, Carr's division would not be the first to sink mines underneath the Confederate works. That honor would fall to Major General John A. Logan's division of the Seventeenth Corps, who, until late June, had been digging a zigzag approach trench that hugged the Jackson Road as it neared Vicksburg. The division's plan, however, did not go unopposed. Prior to the siege, the Confederates had constructed one of their most formidable forts in this road's path in order to prevent easy access into the city. To the Confederates, it was dubbed the Third Louisiana Redan, after the regiment that manned its defenses. To the Union troops digging toward the obstruction, it was simply Fort Hill. Since federal solid shot and Parrott shells had failed to obliterate the fort with multiple aliases, it was now time to try another tactic. As Wilber F. Crummer of the Forty-Fifth Illinois wrote after the war, "Fort Hill is said to be the key to Vicksburg. We have tried to turn this key, and have as often failed—in fact, the lock is not an easy one, but we soon shall try the burglar's plan, and with the aid of powder blow up the lock to 'smithereens.'"[4]

After having traversed some "one thousand five hundred feet" in "less than thirty days," the Federals excavating Logan's Approach finally reached the Third Louisiana Redan on June 22. At 9 A.M. the following day, Union troops began to undermine the rebel works. In brief, this involved tunneling underneath the enemy defenses and there digging a series of galleries and branches that ended in chambers. Once these excavations were completed, sappers packed the chambers with powder, backfilled the branches and galleries with earth, and tamped the opening in order to force the subsequent explosion upward to effect a breach that Union infantry could exploit. As Albert O. Marshall of the Thirty-Third Illinois summarized, "The object was to run the tunnel under the enemy's fort and then when ready, a wagon load of powder could be taken in and the fort blown out of existence. That is the idea. Time will tell how it succeeds."[5]

Despite Marshall's ability to capture the essence of military mining, Captain Andrew Hickenlooper had a large task ahead of him. Military mining during the Civil War lacked precedent. The fact that no American mine had ever successfully been detonated during wartime throughout the country's young history lends further credence to Marshall's innocent comment that the first Union troops able to reach the Confederate works would be bestowed the honor of "the experiment of blowing it up." This lack of precedent, combined with the lack of engineers and sappers during the siege, forced Hickenlooper to improvise. Recalling this grand undertaking after the war, Hickenlooper proudly declared that the mine on Logan's front was "the first one of the war, and one of but two mines of any importance successfully fired during that unpleasantness." The second mine that Hickenlooper referred to, excluding his later detonation at Vicksburg on July 1, would occur at Petersburg on July 30, 1864. Although not a professionally trained military engineer, Hickenlooper, by this point in the siege, had earned Major General James B. McPherson's complete confidence. According to one onlooker, "General McPherson believed in Hickenlooper, and allowed him to construct the work in his own way."[6]

Traditionally, engineers relied on professionally trained sappers to carry out mining operations, but the lack of such specialized troops in Grant's army forced Hickenlooper to improvise. In response to this problem, the Seventeenth Corps engineer sought help from those with prewar civilian mining experience and made "a call for all men having had practical experience in coal mining." Thirty-five men from the "Lead Mine, 45th Illinois Regiment," and "a number of coal miners in the 124th Ill[inois]" answered the call and were subsequently divided into three reliefs, with each detail assigned an eight-hour shift. Once his miners were divided, Hickenlooper placed the details under the immediate command of Lieutenant Thomas Russell of the Seventh Missouri and Sergeant William M. Morris of the Thirty-Second Ohio. Brigadier General Mortimer D. Leggett assumed overall command of the effort.[7]

With nightly fraternization occurring between Union and Confederate pickets, friendly scuttlebutt threatened to leak crucial details about the project. While the rebels atop the Third Louisiana Redan could clearly see that Union mining operations were afoot, the precise federal timetable and the nature of the mine itself remained something of a closely guarded secret. According to William H. Bently of the Seventy-Seventh Illinois, "Guards were placed at the entrance leading to the mine, with instructions to allow no one to pass under the rank of a general excepting the engineers and workmen carrying on the operations." Equipped with "drills, short handled picks, [and] shovels," each individual relief "worked an hour at a time, two picking, two shoveling, and two handing back the grain-sacks filled with earth." By the end of the day on June 23, a gallery some three feet by four feet had been excavated twelve feet under the Third Louisiana Redan. Subsequently, on June 24, Hickenlooper's miners drove their gallery "a distance of 40 feet" and "commenced on [a] branch gallery to the left." This "smaller gallery extended in on the same line 15 feet, while from the end of the main gallery two others were run out on either side at angles of 45 degrees for the distance of 15 feet." In short, Union mining operations on Logan's front progressed quickly, smoothly, and under relative secrecy.[8]

One of the reasons for Hickenlooper's rapid progress lay in the characteristics of the loess soil. Vicksburg's loess soil allowed the federal miners to excavate galleries and branches that did not require shoring or bracing, a step that professional military engineers considered the most difficult part of military mining. According to West Point engineer James C. Duane, civilian mining and military mining were two completely different tasks. Typically, civil mining was "carried on at greater depths below the surface of the earth, and in solid rock." Meanwhile, military mining "[was] what may be termed superficial, and consequently the miner [worked] through the more recent formations of earth and sands." The instability of looser soil in military mining required artificial support. As a result, military miners normally had to frame and shore up the mine with "wooden linings" as they advanced under the enemy's position. According to Duane, "It is [in] the adjustment and fittings of these linings that the chief art of the military miner [consisted]."[9]

The Army of the Tennessee's astute engineers recognized the serendipitous circumstances that loess soil afforded, characteristics that allowed them to skip an otherwise tedious, dangerous, and complicated engineering step. According to consecutive chief engineers Frederick E. Prime and Cyrus B. Comstock, "The compactness of the alluvial soil, [made] lining for mining galleries unnecessary, these galleries were formed with ease." Hickenlooper, at the forefront of Logan's mine, wrote after the war, "The soil of this locality consisted of a peculiarly tenacious clay, easily cut, self supporting, and not in the least affected by exposure to the atmosphere, thus rendering bracing and sheathing unnecessary." In other words, Vicksburg's loess soil favored the neophyte miners who were handicapped when it came to knowledge of the specifics of framing and sheeting mines in order to prevent cave-ins.[10]

Although Hickenlooper's mine progressed smoothly, Confederate countermeasures threatened Union success, and on June 24 the Union miners underneath the rebel fort could "hear the conversation and pick-strokes of the Confederates engaged in countermining." In effect, the rebels defending the Third Louisiana Redan attempted to intercept the Federals' mine in order to destroy it before it was detonated. Confederate chief engineer Samuel H. Lockett later recalled the rebels' attempts to thwart Union progress on this front: "The Third Louisiana was located on a very narrow ridge and had no ditch. The counter-mines for it were therefore started from within by first sinking a vertical shaft, with the intention of working out by an inclined gallery under the enemy's sap." The Confederates were coming for the Union tunnelers.[11]

Relaying the disturbing news back to headquarters, Hickenlooper reported to his superiors that his miners "can hear the rebels at work on counter-mining very distinctly. [They] appear to be above and to the left of our gallery." The federal miners "became frightened at the noise made in the rebel counter-mine and quit work" for fear of being entombed should the rebels fire their mine. A concerned Union soldier immediately sent for Hickenlooper, who quickly rushed to the mine and "by . . . presence, example and persuasion induced them to renew their labors with increased energy." With the Union troops back in the mine, "it thereupon became a race to see which side would get in the first blow, that is whether we would be blown out or they blown up." The blue-clad miners won.[12]

Hickenlooper completed the construction portion of his mine on June 25. With his gallery by this time far enough under the rebel Fort Hill (Third Louisiana Redan) and with concern for the Confederate countermine, the Seventeenth Corps engineer decided to begin packing his mine with powder. "Having reached a distance of 70 feet," Hickenlooper later reminisced, "and fearing that if we penetrated further the explosion might not destroy the easterly [that is, front] face, and being also admonished that the enemy's countermine if fired might destroy our gallery and thus defeat our purpose, I ordered the whole force in[to the mine]." He proceeded to divide the Union soldiers "into three separate detachments" and "began running branch galleries north, south and west." These "were completed for a distance of about fifteen feet, and properly prepared for the reception of the charge." Now all that remained was to pack the mine with powder, detonate the charge, and exploit the breach. Yet the state of the art of military mining at this time dictated that this would be a difficult and unpredictable task.[13]

Military mining during the mid-nineteenth century was a science based on assumption and trial and error. It existed in a theoretical vacuum. The sieges of recent memory, namely those at Vera Cruz and Sebastopol, had been brought to a successful conclusion without the implementation of mining techniques. At Vera Cruz, the U.S. forces under General Winfield Scott had used their artillery to force Mexican capitulation. At Sebastopol, the French storming of Fort Malakoff, one of the key strongpoints in the Russian fortifications, had signaled the end of this Crimean siege. Thus the sieges of the last twenty years had not yielded any empirical mining data.

Dennis Hart Mahan recognized the fact that military mining was still in its infancy and credited the problem to the lack of hands-on experimentation. According to the West Point engineering instructor, "But little advance by experiment has been made in the subject of mines, owing to the time, labor and expense, which a prosecution of the subject demands; and the practice has, therefore, undergone but slight changes since the earliest introduction of this means of attack and defence." For this reason, while it was possible to teach West Point cadets the finer points of choking sap fagots for fascines, weaving gabions for revetment, and excavating zigzag approaches and parallels in the Academy's Hudson Valley, experimental mining was impractical due to the associated costs and resulting potential damage.[14]

Nevertheless, during the period between the end of the Mexican War and the outbreak of the Civil War, some hands-on instruction in mining did occur at West Point. This, however, was reserved for the hundred men designated to Company A, Corps of Engineers, the U.S. Army's elite engineering unit. Training was limited and confined within the parameters of a peacetime military exercise. The engineers built small mock forts, sapped them, destroyed the structures with small mines, and then repeated the process. Unfortunately for theoreticians like Mahan, this exercise was carried out in order to perfect the company's skills in practical engineering, not for the sake of collecting scientific data pertaining to mining.[15]

Lack of experimentation in different soil types, in turn, yielded an imperfect pseudoscience. "The physic-mathematical theory of mines is still very imperfect," Mahan wrote. This was due to "the impracticability of ascertaining the exact effects of the explosion of powder in a medium [soil] which is seldom homogeneous." According to Mahan, the gases that a charge expended needed to overcome three obstacles before the desired crater could be created: the weight of the soil to be blown out of the crater, the "tenacity" of the soil type in question, and the atmospheric pressure pressing down on the surface of the crater radius before the charge exploded. Unfortunately for the military engineer, the lack of practical experimentation in different soil types had, up until that time, yielded little observational data. As a result, the equation that engineers used in Mahan's day to determine the weight of charge needed to blow any crater relied upon "approximations" that were "valuable as only guides that the miner [had] to refer to." Thus, with regard to mine detonation, a larger knowledge gap than usual existed between theory and practice. For the most part, successful mining, or lack thereof, rested on the tenacity and ingenuity of the engineer excavating beneath the enemy's defenses.[16]

Nineteenth-century military mining was a science rooted in assumption. In order to calculate the weight of the charge required to produce a finished opening, engineers needed to determine the volume and weight of the soil to be displaced from the crater. Computing this proved more an art than a science. As stated by Mahan, "The form of the crater in ordinary soils has not been exactly ascertained. The only use of the exact determination of this form would be to calculate precisely the quantity of earth thrown from the crater, and by that means the proportion of the charge to the effect to be produced." Consequently, nineteenth-century engineers working in this pseudoscience theorized as to the shape of the hole that a given charge might yield. According to Mahan, some engineers believed that the blast created a "cone, of which the centre of the powder was taken as the vertex." Meanwhile, other professionals concluded that the blast resulted in "a paraboloid, of which the centre of the powder was the focus." Drawing on these two hypotheses, Mahan taught cadets that, in order to determine the volume of a crater and the weight of the soil to be displaced, one needed to assume that the blast consistently resulted in an inverted right truncated cone.[17]

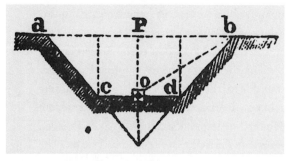

Mahan's perception of the idealized crater in the form of a right truncated cone. *D. H. Mahan, Summary of the Course of Permanent Fortification, 251.*

In order to determine the weight of charge required to displace a specific volume of soil, Mahan assumed an idealized crater in the form of a truncated cone. To provide a simple method of calculating the volume of the crater, Mahan additionally assumed that the radius of the lower circle, *oc* and *od*, was equal to one-half the radius of the upper circle, *Pa* and *Pb* (also called the crater radius). The line *oP*, a perpendicular line from the location of the charge *o* at the center of the base of the crater to the surface, was called the line of least resistance (hereafter referred to as *l*). This was, in theory, the shortest route that the exploded gas would travel on its journey from the center of the base of the crater to the surface. Mahan defined the lines *oa* and *ob* as the radius of the explosion. When an engineer blew a crater where the line of least resistance equaled the radius of the finished opening (*oP* = *Pa* = *Pb*), the engineer generated what Mahan termed a "common mine."[18]

In Mahan's theoretical model, the common mine provided a simulated standard. It represented an assumed condition designed to offer a basis of comparison against results in the field and provided engineers with a simple method of calculating the volume of soil to be displaced. This, in turn, permitted the engineer to determine the amount of charge needed to produce the desired result. Hence, in order to determine the amount of charge needed to produce a theoretical common mine, Mahan derived the following equation:

$$c = 11/6 \ q \ l^3$$

In Mahan's equation, the engineer needed to solve for *c*, the necessary charge (in pounds) required to blow the common mine in question. Meanwhile, the letter *l* referred to the line of least resistance (in yards), and the value *q*, in Mahan's words, represented "the [necessary] quantity [of] powder," measured in pounds, needed "to throw out one cubic yard of any species of soil." Unfortunately for Mahan's engineers, contemporaries knew little about the properties of different soils, and empirical data remained limited. Thus, according to Mahan, *q* was "found by experiment." Despite this shortcoming, Mahan compiled a table of various soil types and the necessary amount of charge (measured in pounds and ounces) "required to throw out a cubic yard of the soil in question."[19]

	Lbs	Oz.
Light sandy earth	1	13
Hard sand	2	00
Common earth	1	10
Wet sand	2	2
Earth mixed with pebbles	2	8
Clay mixed with loam	2	8
Rock	3	10

Weight of charge necessary to displace one cubic yard of each soil type. D. H. Mahan, *Summary of the Course of Permanent Fortification*, 256.

Already knowing the depth of the charge and therefore the line of least resistance *l*, the engineer simply needed to plug in the value of *q* in order to solve for *c*. This equation, of course, allowed an engineer to determine only the amount of charge necessary to blow a common mine when only the line of least resistance and the soil type were known.

The common mine, however, was not always the result that the engineer was trying to achieve. When an engineer wanted to blow a shallow mine with a wide opening (one in which the crater radius was greater than the line of least resistance), Mahan instructed students to detonate what he termed an "overcharged mine." Conversely, if an engineer wanted to blow a deep mine with a narrow opening (one in which the crater radius was less than the line of least resistance), Mahan taught cadets to explode what he called an "undercharged mine." Despite the negative implications of their names, both overcharged and undercharged mines were not terms assigned to negative results. Instead, they were simply definitions derived from the results of different explosions that deviated from Mahan's standard, idealized condition, the common mine. In order to provide an engineer with the ability to determine the charge size required to blow an overcharged or undercharged mine, Mahan derived separate equations for each based on the charge required to explode a common mine. These equations, however, are relatively complex, and it is beyond the scope of this study to examine them in detail. Nevertheless, their mere existence provides further proof that, in some cases, either overcharging or undercharging a mine could have been a desirable result.[20]

As stated in previous chapters, Vicksburg's defenses sat atop a thick layer of loamy, siltlike clay known as loess soil. Although Mahan's table did not contain this exact soil type, the composition of loess soil closely resembles what Mahan termed "Clay mixed with loam." According to the table, the charge required to blow out one cubic yard of this type of soil is 2 lbs., 8 oz. (that is, 2.5 lbs.). Yet, with regard to the Vicksburg siege, Mahan's equations and table of soil types remained of limited value. With Captain Andrew Hickenlooper, an antebellum civil engineer and wartime self-taught military engineer, the only soldier to successfully detonate a mine under the Vicksburg defenses, it is unclear how much Mahanian mining theory was used against the Confederate Gibraltar. While First Lieutenant Peter C. Hains on the Thirteenth Corps front and chief engineers Frederick E. Prime and Cyrus B. Comstock had been exposed to Mahan's tutelage, Hickenlooper had not. In addition, although Hickenlooper's superior, McPherson, had graduated from West Point as an engineer, he did not partake in the day-to-day minutiae of siege work. Thus, it is unlikely that the Seventeenth Corps chief engineer used Mahan's equations when packing his mine with gunpowder. This western, homespun engineer improvised.[21]

Despite the inherent problems of the pseudoscience of military mining and his lack of official military engineering training, Hickenlooper prepared the mine to receive its charge and sometime before 9 A.M. on June 25 "deposited 1,500 pounds of powder in three different branch mines (500 in each): and 700 pounds in [the] center; 2,200 pounds in all." Subsequently, he arranged fuses so "as to explode them all at the same instant." Following this step, the engineer tamped the mine "with cross-timbers, sand-bags, &c."[22]

On June 24, Hickenlooper informed McPherson that he would be ready to detonate the mine sometime before 3 P.M. the next day. McPherson relayed this news to Grant, who in turn ordered that the mine be fired at that time. Once the mine exploded, Union troops were to attempt to exploit the breach. In order to keep the rebel forces manning the Vicksburg defenses from reinforcing the Confederates defending the Third Louisiana Redan, Grant ordered a general bombardment all along the Union line for approximately fifteen minutes immediately after detonation. Union commanders were to place their troops in the rifle pits and trenches along their respective fronts at 2 P.M. and, with the sound of the mine detonation as their signal, were to unleash a hailstorm of iron and lead against the Vicksburg defenses.[23]

On Logan's front, the blue-clad troops began to make their preparations despite the stifling heat of the Mississippi afternoon, which, according to one Union soldier, "was 102 degrees above zero . . . in the shade." McPherson sketched out the general plan for Logan, who was to take advantage of the hoped-for breach in the line. According to McPherson, "If successful in destroying a portion of the enemy's works, it is important for us to take advantage of it." The division commander was therefore to place his "division under arms at 2 P.M." with General Leggett's brigade "in the trenches with fixed bayonets, [and] . . . advanced as near to the mine as they can go with safety." McPherson further ordered that Leggett's men advance under the cover of sharpshooter fire and be supported by a reserve force of three regiments, two from Brigadier General John E. Smith's brigade and another single regiment from Brigadier General Thomas E. G. Ransom's brigade. In addition, Logan was to assemble "a working party, provided with picks and shovels, [to] be in readiness to make a lodgment on the enemy's works should we succeed in getting in." That is, the working party was to create new Union entrenchments at the farthest point the attackers might reach as a result of the mine explosion. All of this, of course, was contingent on whether or not Hickenlooper's mine successfully detonated.[24]

With the general assault plan in place, the specifics of the attack congealed on Logan's front. Leggett placed the Forty-Fifth Illinois in the front behind "ten picked men from the pioneer corps" under Hickenlooper's direct command who were to remove blast debris from the crater and "move forward and take possession of the fort." Meanwhile "in the left-hand sap," Second Lieutenant Henry C. "Coonskin" Foster and a detachment of one hundred men from the Twenty-Third Indiana were situated and given "orders to charge with the Forty-fifth Illinois, provided they attempted to cross the enemy's works." Behind the Forty-Fifth Illinois and the Twenty-Third Indiana, the remainder of Leggett's brigade waited in close supporting distance.[25]

With the Union preparations in place, Grant's scheduled detonation time, 3 P.M., June 25, approached. Tension filled the air. Colonel William E. Strong of the Twelfth Wisconsin assisted Hickenlooper in lighting the fuse that held the promise of destroying Fort Hill. "We crept forward together on our hands and knees from the terminus of the covered way," Strong later recalled, "and fired the dozen strands of safety fuse; and how coolly yet eagerly Hickenlooper watched the burning grain until it reached an embankment, and how we hurried back to 'Coon Skin Tower,' and held our watches and counted the seconds! All was quiet along the entire line from right to left, save a shot at long intervals from some wary sharpshooter on the other side." Back at the foot of Coonskin's Tower, "where the head of the charging column rested," Hickenlooper and Strong waited with gut-wrenching anticipation. Private Jerome B. Dawn of the Twentieth Illinois also recollected the eerie silence that filled the air. "I remember seeing birds fly over us and noted the unusual quiet. . . . The heat was intense. . . . We waited, it seemed to me, a long time." Near Dawn's position, Jenkin Lloyd Jones of the Sixth Wisconsin Battery reported a similar stillness. "As the hour approached, all hands were anxiously waiting. Each desirous of witnessing the result. It was dull and very oppressive; all nature seemed drooping, and ominous silence prevailed on both sides; not a flutter of air, not a word was spoken, and you could hear naught but your own silent breath."[26]

Close by, Grant, McPherson, and Logan peered out from the protection of Battery Hickenlooper, awaiting the grand spectacle. Three o'clock came and went, and nothing happened. It appeared as if Hickenlooper had failed.

Time seemed to move slowly, and three o'clock eventually became three thirty. Meanwhile, back at the base of Coonskin's Tower, Strong observed the composure that cloaked what must by that time have been Hickenlooper's considerable anxiety. Hickenlooper "was leaning carelessly against the base of Coon Skin Tower, with his eyes intently fixed upon the hands of his watch," Strong wrote. "His face was white, and there was an anxious expression about his eyes." Despite his inner turmoil, the engineer adopted a cool demeanor throughout the stressful affair. "His reputation with that army was at stake," Strong later remembered, "and I pitied him from the bottom of my heart. What if it should fail? Three seconds more,—tick! tick! tick!"[27]

Just then, at about 3:30 p.m. on June 25, the first successful mine of the Civil War exploded. According to Strong, "The huge fort, guns caissons, and Rebel troops . . . were lifted high into the air; a glimmer, and then a gleam of light—a flash—a trembling of the ground beneath our feet, and great clouds of dense black smoke puffed up from the crater of the mine, like jets from a geyser!" Standing next to Strong, Hickenlooper observed how "the whole Fort and its connecting earth-works appeared to be gradually moving upward, breaking into fragments, and gradually presenting the appearance of an immense fountain of earth, dust and smoke, through which one could occasionally catch a glimpse of dark objects, men, gun-carriages, shelters etc." Artillerist Jenkin Lloyd Jones, still standing with his guns, reported, "All at once a dead heavy roll . . . and you could see nothing but a black cloud of dirt and powder smoke, throwing the earth 30 or 40 feet in the air, and about half of the wall rolled over the ditch as if turned by a ponderous plow." Waiting in the assault column, Corporal Wilber F. Crummer of the Forty-Fifth Illinois recalled that "the ground was shaken as by an earthquake."[28]

All around the siege lines, soldiers reported the fantastic sight that Hickenlooper's explosion had wrought. On Sherman's front, a soldier of the Fifty-Fifth Illinois later described the scene. At "about half-past three," the soldier stated, "the parapet was seen to heave, and instantly up rose a huge dark column of earth, mingled with timber, tools [and] bodies of men, in the center of which for a second gleamed a lurid flame wreathed in white smoke." To the south of the blast, on Brigadier General A. J. Smith's front, C. W. Gerard of the Eighty-Third Ohio reported after the war that "the tremor of the exploded mine was felt for miles; the solid ramparts surged outward, and a massive dusty cone, mingled with smoke, rose in air, followed by a thunder-clap of the liberated force."[29]

Meanwhile, in Brigadier General Alvin P. Hovey's front, Richard J. Fuller of the Twenty-Fourth Indiana later recalled seeing "a cloud of black smoke go up like the upheaval of a volcano. It carried with it to the height of a mile, hundreds of tons of earth, and debris and a great number of men. This was followed by a mighty shaking of earth, and the 'Queen of Vicksburg' was no more." Just then, within seconds of the explosion, Union guns all along the siege lines opened fire "as if they were all pulled off by one lanyard." According to William S. Morris of the Thirty-First Illinois, the concussion was awesome: "Blood spurted from the nose and ears of the men at the big guns. Some put their hands to their ears; the sound seemed to penetrate the brain." And, with that, the assault force amassed in Logan's Approach in front of the crater pressed forward.[30]

Hickenlooper, along with engineer Captain Stewart R. Tresilian, led the pioneer detachment into the crater and cleared the debris. The men of the Forty-Fifth Illinois, who followed close behind, entered the defile and initiated "the battle of Fort Hill . . . a hell within a radius of five hundred feet." Inside the crater, however, the men of the Forty-Fifth encountered a startling surprise. According to a member of Hickenlooper's pioneers, "This explosion was expected to create a very large breach in the works, which would destroy every impregnable defense and enable our troops to charge through the breach, capturing this impregnable position." This, however, did not turn out to be the case. "The explosion had destroyed about one-half of the redan," Hickenlooper later remembered, and "made of it an inverted cone-shaped crater about fifty feet in diameter and about twenty feet deep." Meanwhile, "the inner rim" of the crater "consisted of a parapet made by the descending earth." The Confederates, responding quickly, "brought a battery into position and manned the wings with a force of infantry," a decision that made "it impossible" for the Federals "to raise even a hand above the crest without having it pierced by a dozen bullets." Although there is no definitive proof that Hickenlooper used Mahan's equation, the resulting crater, with a line of least resistance of twenty feet and a radius of twenty-five feet, suggests that the Seventeenth Corps engineer overcharged his mine. This resulted in a shallow crater with a wide opening.[31]

The Confederates, well aware of the mining project that had proceeded over the previous days, had formed another earthen defensive wall that closed off the rearward mouth of the redan. Consequently, rather than creating a hole in the rebel defenses, the Union mine had simply blown off the forward face of the redan, leaving the Confederate line uninterrupted. The lead miners now faced another, unbroken defensive line manned by Confederates. Hickenlooper, however, was not fazed. Prior to the attack, the engineer had ordered the construction of prefabricated head-logs to be placed in the crater just in case the attack degenerated into a firefight. Seeing this unfortunate turn of events, Hickenlooper sent back for his logs.[32]

The men of Company K, Twentieth Illinois, made up Hickenlooper's special pioneer detachment. According to one member of the company, Private Jerome B. Dawn, the group "was selected to lead the charge and prepare the way for the assaulting column, but to go unarmed. The duty assigned them was to clear a passage through our side of the crater and put it in a defensable condition." Two days earlier, on June 23, Captain John A. Edmiston of Company E received orders that he was to be reassigned to Company K for "special duty." During the afternoon, Edmiston, as ordered, led his unarmed detachment, later dubbed the "forlorn hope," to its designated place on the right of Leggett's brigade already formed up in Logan's Approach. According to Captain Edmiston, "we were placed in charge of two logs already prepared, and, as I remember, about ten inches in diameter and 18 or 20 feet along with notches on the under side about every two feet. I divided the company in two platoons and placed a log in charge of each, with instructions to charge into the breach immediately after the explosion, first platoon filing to the left and the second to the right, and place the timbers on the top of the crater." Thus, they were to turn the crater into a defensive position, complete with headlogs. In theory, each log would lie on the lip of the crater with its notched side down. The notches would then form loopholes through which Union soldiers could fire their weapons with relative impunity.[33]

With the Union troops in trouble, Hickenlooper ordered that the men of Company K fetch the logs and cap the earthen redoubt that the explosion from the crater had made. According to one K Company member, R. M. Springer, "The perforated logs . . . brought from the rear and elevated to the crest dividing the contending forces, came up some time after the explosion, and not until more than one attempt had been made by the 45th, and then by the 20th [Illinois], to force their way into the interior of the Fort." Edmiston later recalled the arduous task of hauling up the head-logs. "After the explosion as soon as the debris and earth had some what settled," Edmiston remembered, "we passed into the crater, and under great difficulty, as we had to carry these heavy timbers up the side of the crater through crumbling earth and over obstacles. We succeeded in performing the duty assigned. We experienced no loss. . . . Having accomplished the duty assigned us, we returned to the 20th [Illinois] resumed our places in the line, and participated in the subsequent section in the crater with the regiment." After helping direct the placement of the loopholed timbers, Tresilian noticed that some of the Confederates appeared to be preparing to take the Union position by storm. The engineer acted quickly. He dashed to a nearby federal battery and obtained ten-pound Parrott shells that he rigged with "five-second fuses" and threw over at the enemy. Tresilian hurled his bombs one after the other, a feat that stopped the Confederate advance in its tracks.[34]

Hickenlooper's head-logs, however, met with only limited success. While adequate against small arms fire, the prefabricated head protection proved worthless against Confederate artillery that, upon striking the logs, would shatter the pieces, sending sharp splinters into the blue-clad troops. The Forty-Fifth, however, held until 6 P.M., when Leggett decided to withdraw the lead miners and replace them with the Twentieth Illinois. This process of regimental rotation for duty in what soldiers dubbed the "Slaughter Pen," the "Death Hole," "Fort Hell," or more simply the "Hell Hole," proceeded throughout the night and into the twenty-sixth of June. A bloody stalemate ensued for over twelve hours. Little was gained.[35]

Fight for the crater, sketched by A. E. Mathews of the Thirty-First Ohio Volunteer Infantry. *Lithograph by Middleton, Strobridge, and Company; Anne S. K. Brown Military Collection, Brown University Library.*

Although robbed of initial success, the federal troops of Leggett's brigade "were crowded into this frightful pit like sheep in a slaughter pen" and continued to hold the crater. The close proximity of the fighting and the bunching up of Union troops in the confined killing space of the crater led to horrific casualties. When the smoke cleared, 34 Union soldiers lay dead and another 209 were reported wounded.[36]

The exact size of the June 25 crater remains disputed. Those commenting on the precise measurements of the hole wrote their accounts years after the conflict, leaving one to question their accuracy. As previously stated, Hickenlooper, in his personal reminiscences, claimed the crater was "about fifty feet in diameter and about twenty feet deep." The testimony of other soldiers who served during the fight contradicts Hickenlooper. The Twentieth Illinois's John A. Edmiston wrote to William T. Rigby, Vicksburg's first park commissioner, on March 8, 1902, "As I remember, the crater was triangular in shape, the base line along the rebel works about 50 feet in length, the sides about 30; depth [of the crater] about 20 feet with sloping sides, very difficult to surmount." A member of Company K, Twentieth Illinois, more or less corroborated Edmiston's statement with regard to the crater's width, writing on March 18, 1902, "It [the crater] was about 50 feet from rim to rim, sloping like a large bowl from the bottom up, and quite regular in its interior." Similarly, S. C. Beck of the 124th Illinois and Wilber F. Crummer of the Forty-Fifth Illinois, both of whom participated in the crater fight, wrote after the war that the crater had a diameter of fifty feet. Yet on March 12, 1902, an unidentified member of Company K contradicted Edmiston's estimate of the crater's depth when he wrote to his former captain that "the pit being full of loose dirt and 10 to 15 feet from bottom to top was a hard thing to climb."[37]

Thus, although accounts pertaining to the exact dimensions of the crater differ, all of the dimensions would suggest that, at least according to Mahan's standards, Hickenlooper overcharged his mine. The resulting shallow hole, with gently sloping sides and a wide opening, appeared ideal. Nevertheless, circumstances beyond Hickenlooper's control turned the crater into a death-trap. The explosion pulverized the loess soil into a fine sand, making it nearly impossible for the Union assault force to climb out of the depression. At the same time, the Confederate defensive line at the base of the redan provided the rebels with a fixed defensive position from which they could pour plunging fire down onto the Union troops.

Meanwhile, others described the size of the crater in relative terms and avoided committing to numerical measurements altogether. Immediately after the fight, Grant wrote to Major General E. O. C. Ord that "the cavity made was sufficiently large to shelter two regiments." This, however, appears to be a mistake. William E. Strong, who lit the fuse with Hickenlooper, stated after the war, "The crater of the mine was cone-shaped, and very much exposed.... The cavity made by the explosion was not large enough to hold two regiments, and no formation whatever could be preserved." Other soldiers serving in Logan's division corroborated Strong's observation. According to Wilber Crummer of the Forty-Fifth Illinois, "The Crater was not large enough to hold more than two Companies at a time; between 60 and 80 men." Similarly, a member of the Thirty-First Illinois wrote after the war, "The crater would not admit more than two companies at once."[38]

Why did the federal attack fail? In his after-action report, Hickenlooper described the event as a "Perfect success." This terse statement, however, referred to the detonation of the mine and the fact that the Union assault party had been able to hold part of the crater. When perceived through this narrow lens, Hickenlooper's rosy view becomes justified. He ably carried out an engineering project that lacked precedent, and the assault force, while not able to exploit the breach, was able to consolidate some of its holdings. Hickenlooper, however, remained in the minority in celebrating the event. Most soldiers, both blue and gray, judged it a failure since the assaulting Union troops were unable to break through the Confederate line. As the Twentieth Ohio's Osborn Hamiline Oldroyd wrote on June 28, "Nothing, however, was gained by blowing up the fort, except planting the stars and stripes thereon."[39]

Those who perceived the event as a failure searched for reasons. Most blamed Hickenlooper and his pioneers. George Ditto, a pioneer in the Fifth Iowa, wrote on June 25, "The blowing up of the fort is not as complete as it was expected to be but is I learn satisfactory. The walls of the fort are very thick and the side was not fully blown out as the charge was not far enough under it." On the other side of the siege lines, Confederate engineer Major Samuel H. Lockett claimed that the mine failed because "the charge was too small to do much damage. Nevertheless, it tore off the vortex of the redan, and made what the federals thought was a practicable breach." Back on the Union side, Albert O. Marshall of the Thirty-Third Illinois drew the same conclusion as Lockett. According to Marshall, "The power-charge had not been large enough to have much effect upon the earth fort." That was of secondary importance, Marshall maintained, because "the real purpose of the experiment, which was to ascertain the effect and determine the amount of powder needed for such a purpose in such ground, was accomplished." Thus, in Marshall's estimation, with little precedent to draw on, the information that the trial yielded outweighed the limited nature of its results. Meanwhile, Frank W. Tupper, serving in Seventeenth Corps headquarters, reported a different reason for the June 25 failure, suggesting that the "powder [was not] put in properly and the hole [was not] closed as it should [have] been."[40]

Rather than simply search for what the Union did wrong, it is more profitable to explore what the Confederates did right. Hickenlooper's explosion and the subsequent charge into the crater did not doom the federal attack. Instead, Lockett's ingenuity and the foresight that spurred his decision to erect his last-ditch breastwork at the rear of the Third Louisiana Redan is what determined Union failure. As Lockett succinctly reported after the event, "An attempt was made to assault the work immediately after the explosion, but our men, having good cover behind the new parapet, repulsed the assailants with considerable slaughter."[41]

Grant, however, would not allow the crater fight to be a total loss, and after the engagement the Seventeenth Corps chief engineer received orders to construct a breaching battery in the middle of the crater. Although Hickenlooper began the project, it soon became clear that any guns placed in this defile would be dominated by Confederate fire. On learning this, Grant had McPherson bisect the crater with a line of field fortifications that allowed the Federals to hold their minuscule gains for the remainder of the siege. "The Pioneers," under Hickenlooper's "personal supervision," erected "a defensive line about midway across the crater," and "a ledge" was cut "along the face of the dividing parapet" in order to provide Union troops with a firing step. A "covered way or shelter in the center" was established with the aim of running "another gallery" toward the Confederate line. According to Hickenlooper, "The completion of our new line and shelter enabled us to withdraw the force from the face of the crater, and yet securely hold all that we had gained."[42]

Despite the fact that Leggett's brigade could not exploit the breach, Grant telegraphed back to Major General Henry W. Halleck the successful details of the ordeal. On June 26 he informed the commanding general in Washington, "Yesterday, a mine was sprung under the enemy's work most commanding the fort, producing a crater.... Our men took immediate possession and still hold it. The fight for it has been incessant, and thus far we have not been able to establish batteries in the breach—Expect to succeed."[43]

Some serving in the rank and file, however, questioned the logic of pressing the fight in the crater. Although Wilber Crummer of the Forty-Fifth Illinois conceded after the war that the Federals had successfully held the crater, he believed the cost of the engagement outweighed its benefits. Reflecting on the event in 1915, Crummer wrote, "It probably was alright to have made the charge into the crater after the explosion and try to make a breech [sic] inside the enemy's lines, but it surely was a serious mistake, either of Gen. Grant or Gen. McPherson, to cause that crater to be held for over 48 hours with the loss of brave men every hour." In retrospect, Grant did in fact make the best of the situation. He consolidated his line in the crater, held onto his limited gains, and kept moving forward toward his ultimate goal—Vicksburg's capitulation.[44]

With this fresh defensive position created, Hickenlooper received his new orders on June 27 to commence a second mine beginning on "the right-hand side of the crater." Anticipating such a directive, Hickenlooper actually had already begun a "covered gallery in [the] center of the crater" on the previous day for the purpose of launching "mines or counter-mines, as the case might require." This project he finished just before sunset on June 26 after suffering the loss of seven pioneers engaged in constructing the gallery. With new orders in hand, the energetic Hickenlooper continued to push his new mine forward in an attempt to blow a second mine underneath what remained of the Third Louisiana Redan. This new gallery ran "northwest from [the] covered gallery in [the] crater" toward the "left wing of the [Rebel] fort," the remaining "portion of the redan which had not been seriously affected by [the June 25] explosion."[45]

Despite the successful detonation of the mine, the siege began to take its toll on Hickenlooper. Over the course of the siege, the lack of engineers present with the army became an onerous reality that placed a steady, unrelenting strain on Hickenlooper. Sleep deprivation, exposure to the hot and humid Mississippi climate, and "nervous strain" finally broke the engineer's body, and he remained "sick and confined to tent" from June 29 to July 2. In short, Hickenlooper experienced "a total collapse," one that left him "incapable of physical exertion." While he was never able to pinpoint "the specific character of [his] disease," he attributed it to "nervous prostration." Medical personnel and staff officer colleagues doted over the ailing engineer captain as he slipped in and out of a "comatose condition." Unaware of the exact nature of the engineer officer's serious illness, attendants used common treatments. These included packing his head in ice, applying mustard plasters to his stomach, and administering a strict diet of beef, tea, and whiskey.[46]

Nevertheless, Hickenlooper's condition continued to decline, and several days after the collapse, McPherson informed Grant that the young engineer would probably expire. The commanding general of the Army of the Tennessee, concerned for the fate of the talented Seventeenth Corps engineer, decided to pay him a visit. The unassuming Grant quietly entered the tent and sat down beside the ailing Hickenlooper, who, though sick, was "perfectly conscious." Grant gingerly grasped one of the prostrated engineer's hands, felt his forehead, and asked, "Do you know who I am?" Hickenlooper replied, "Certainly I do, you are General Grant." To this, Grant solemnly responded, "I hope you will soon be better." With that brief exchange, Grant exited the engineer's tent and went about his daily business. Although the situation appeared desperate, Hickenlooper would live. Time out of the sun and confinement to quarters saved the young engineer's life, and on July 2 he was able once again to report for duty.[47]

During Hickenlooper's convalescence, the preparations for the second mine went forward, most likely under the direction of Captain Stewart R. Tresilian, Hickenlooper's right-hand man during the June 25 assault into the crater. By June 29 the federal miners were well underway on their second mine, which aimed to destroy the remnants of the Third Louisiana Redan. The Confederates continued to harass the blue-clad westerners, attempting to impede their progress. In order to protect those coming in and out of the mine, Edmund Newsome, along with seventy-four other members of the Eighty-First Illinois, began constructing "a timber shelter" out of "bundles of long cane" designed to shield workers at the base of the fort from enemy hand grenades. The improvised cane roof worked. According to Newsome, "The enemy continued to favor us with their explosive compliments until night, but our cane roof rolled them down . . . and no one was hurt."[48]

Lockett, seeing that the Confederate hand grenades were falling impotently to the wayside, decided to kick the rebel defensive measures up a notch. In order to deter those working under the remnants of the redan, he obtained an empty barrel, packed it with 125 pounds of powder, "rolled [it] over the parapet and exploded [the device] with a time-fuse of fifteen seconds." The resulting blast achieved its intended effect. According to Lockett, "The effect of the explosion was very severe, and fragments of sap-rollers, gabions and pieces of timber were thrown into the air, and, I think, some of the enemy's sappers must have been burned and smothered." Nevertheless, the resourceful Federals rebounded and finished their second mine under the remaining northwest segment of the redan on July 1.[49]

Participants in the siege did not record the dimensions of the second set of galleries and branches that formed the subterranean honeycomb under the Third Louisiana Redan. Nevertheless, on July 1, Union troops finished packing the mine's chambers with approximately eighteen hundred pounds of powder, some four hundred fewer pounds than the previous June 25 mine. On learning that the mine was ready, McPherson contacted Grant for further instructions. Grant, with his penchant for direct orders, responded promptly and succinctly. The Army of the Tennessee commander ordered the Seventeenth Corps commander to "explode the mines as soon as ready. . . . You need not do more than have rifle-pits filled with sharpshooters. Take all advantage you can, after the explosion, of the breach made, either to advance guns or your sharpshooters." The debacle the first explosion had wrought influenced Grant's orders on July 1. A quiet, practical man of intelligence, Grant would not make the same mistake twice.[50]

Union commanders settled on 3 P.M. as the detonation time, and McPherson handed down Grant's instructions to Logan. At around 11 A.M. on July 1, McPherson instructed Logan, "The mine in your front will be exploded as soon as the proper disposition of troops can be made. It is not intended to make any assault, but simply to have the rifle-pits lined with sharpshooters, and the command under arms, ready to take advantage of any chance in our favor or repel any sortie of the enemy." As ordered, Logan detonated the second mine on his front. This time, events went according to plan. Unlike during the June 25 explosion, the delay between setting match to powder trail to the explosion in the underground chamber did not include the tense extra half hour of waiting.[51]

The explosion obliterated the remainder of the Third Louisiana Redan at 3 P.M. as scheduled. "Oh my, what a sight it was," wrote S. C. Beck of the 124th Illinois. "Timbers, dirt, men all in the air at once." Farther to the south in the rifle pits that protected Carr's Approach, Albert O. Marshall of the Thirty-Third Illinois described the memorable event in greater detail. "The entire hill seemed to rise in the air," wrote Marshall. "The more compact pieces of earth and all solid bodies in the fort, such as magazine, timbers and artillery, and even men, were shot up into the air like rockets. The ground beneath our feet trembled as though a fierce earthquake was passing beneath us. As the force of the explosion ended, the loose earth and broken fragments of the destroyed fort fell back, into the opening made, a shapeless mass."[52]

Among those on the rebel side thrown into the air was a young African American slave named Abe who had been working on a Confederate countermine designed to disrupt Logan's second mining attempt. Of the rebels working in the countermine, Abe became the only one who "survived his transit." An instant camp celebrity, Abe became the subject of many soldiers' accounts of the siege. According to Seth J. Wells of the Seventeenth Illinois, the blast "threw out several people, one Negro was thrown a hundred and fifty feet, [landing] on his head and shoulders, scarcely hurting himself. He attempted to run back, but a half dozen [leveled] muskets brought him back." According to another version that R. L. Howard of the 124th Illinois penned after the war, Abe, on landing unharmed, "said he went up two miles, saw the stars, met his master—who was one of the white men killed—coming down, etc., the part of which—seeing stars—was doubtless true. He was the hero of the hour, and seemed to enjoy it vastly." News of the remarkable event eventually ascended the ranks, and Logan, on hearing of the miraculous incident, "had his [Abe's] wounds dressed and well cared for."[53]

Reports of the exact dimensions of the resulting July 1 crater vary. According to chief engineer Cyrus B. Comstock, who did not provide the depth of the hole, the blast generated a crater some "30 feet in diameter." Meanwhile, Confederate engineer Samuel H. Lockett in his report stated, "The charge must have been enormous, as the crater made was at least 20 feet deep, 30 feet across in one direction and 50 in another. The earth upheaved was thrown many yards around, but little of it falling back into the crater.... The original faces of the redan were almost completely destroyed." At the same time, Jenkin Lloyd Jones of the Sixth Wisconsin Battery, part of the Seventeenth Corps, simply recorded in his diary on July 1 that "a large volume was thrown inside making a much wider gap than before." Unfortunately, the conflicting information in Comstock's and Lockett's reports makes it difficult to determine the type of Mahanian mine detonated on July 1. Regardless, the blast proved devastating, and as McPherson would later report to Grant, the detonation "took the rebels by Surprise."[54]

In addition to the damage done to the remainder of the redan, the explosion also cut a large swath out of the retrenchment berm that Lockett had erected across the "gorge of the work"—that is, the extra section of breastwork across the rear of the redan that had stymied the June 25 assault. Fearing a replay of the unsuccessful June 25 attack, the Federals refused to mount another charge. Rather, they raked the new opening with murderous artillery fire.[55]

Lockett, expecting a Union charge into the breach, immediately sprang into action and set to work repairing the damages the mine had wrought to his last-ditch defense line, which now sported a large, gaping hole some twenty feet wide. The Confederate engineer ordered his shell-shocked gray-and-butternut-clad subordinates to obtain shovels and heave dirt into the breach. Union fire, however, proved too hot and negated this effort. Undaunted, Lockett called for sandbags, hoping that these, once filled, would plug the hole. This too failed. Union artillery and rifle fire tore holes in the bags and scattered their contents. With casualties mounting, Lockett improvised an ingenious solution. He scraped together an unspecified quantity of "tent flies and wagon covers," rolled them up with dirt inside, and pushed them into the hole. This solved the problem and sheltered the Confederates from federal fire. According to the Confederate engineer, "At last we had something between us and the deadly hail of shot and shell and minie-balls."[56]

If Lockett had only known that the Union did not intend to make an attack, he could have waited until nightfall in order to repair his earthworks under the cover of darkness, but he did not. As a result, when the smoke cleared, some one hundred Confederate casualties littered the field. Reflecting on the incident sometime after the war, Lockett wrote that the July 1 explosion "was really the last stirring incident of the siege." From this point forward, until the rebel garrison surrendered on July 4, the only sounds of war would come from the random report of a sniper's rifle, the belch of cannon and the subsequent thud as its ordnance lost velocity against the Vicksburg defenses, and the steady sound of pickaxes and shovels as approaches along the line continued to press forward toward the Gibraltar of the Confederacy.[57]

Nineteenth-century military mining was a pseudoscience rooted in assumption. While engineering theorists understood the basic principles of their art, the high cost associated with experimental mining led to a lack of empirical data. As a result, Mahan, beginning with the root assumption that all mines yielded a right truncated cone, derived equations that would allow engineers in the field to generate predictable results. Mahan's basis for comparison was the common mine, a crater where the line of least resistance was equal to the crater radius. Everything in Mahan's theoretical realm, from overcharging to undercharging mines, stemmed from this constant standard. Although modern engineers and scientists might scoff at Mahan's pseudoscience, his theories were cutting-edge during the antebellum period.

During the Vicksburg siege, Andrew Hickenlooper, a prewar civil engineer and self-taught military engineer, was the only one to successfully detonate a mine under the Confederate works. Sources do not indicate whether or not Hickenlooper applied Mahanian maxims to either his first mine, which he detonated on June 25, or his second mine, which was detonated by proxy on July 1. While Hickenlooper understood the basic principles of mining, he probably did not use Mahan's equations or exact methodology. Hickenlooper, a homespun frontier engineer and inherent problem-solver who lacked a formal military education, improvised. In addition, the nature of the local loess soil allowed Hickenlooper to skip the most difficult step in military mining—framing and shoring the shaft and subsequent galleries and chambers.

According to Mahanian definitions, Hickenlooper overcharged the June 25 mine. This, however, despite the negative connotation of its name, was not bad. The blast generated a shallow hole with a wide opening that appeared ideal. The crater's theoretical parameters, however, were deceptive. Behind the blast radius at the base of the redan, Confederate chief engineer Major Samuel H. Lockett had created a fixed defensive position that thwarted the federal advance. In addition, the explosion pulverized the loess soil, turning the crater's walls into a fine sand that made it difficult for the attackers to climb out of the hole. Thus, although Hickenlooper successfully detonated his first mine, the subsequent attack failed.

Following the failed assault on June 25, the Federals under Hickenlooper's command prepared a second mine, which was detonated on July 1. Conflicting accounts make it difficult to determine what type of Mahanian mine Hickenlooper created with his second blast. Although this explosion destroyed what remained of the Third Louisiana Redan, Grant feared a replay of the failed charge into the crater, and a subsequent attack never occurred. Hickenlooper's efforts, however, were not in vain. The detonation of this second mine confirmed Grant's belief that his neophyte western sappers could successfully undermine the Confederate defenses. Vicksburg's fate was almost sealed.

Conclusion:
Vicksburg Is Ours!

Despite the limited gains that the June 25 and July 1 mines offered, the efforts of the engineers on Major General John A. Logan's front provided a glimpse down an avenue of potential victory. The successful detonation of two mines underneath the Third Louisiana Redan proved to the Army of the Tennessee that it was possible to excavate and detonate other mines all along the Confederate line. Although the Confederate garrison refused to surrender, Major General Ulysses S. Grant had one final card to play. If exploding these mines could be coordinated with one large infantry assault, the Gibraltar of the Confederacy would surely fall.

The federal besieging army operated from a position of strength on July 1. At many places along the Union siege lines, only the width of the Confederate parapet separated the federal and rebel forces. As a result, close-quarter battle became the norm along the line, revealing that "little farther progress could be made by digging alone." According to Captains Frederick E. Prime and Cyrus B. Comstock, "At ten different points we could put the head of regiments under cover within from 5 to 100 yards of his line." Thus on July 1, Grant, realizing that to launch an "assault would be little easier if [the Federals] waited ten days more," decided that the final push to storm the Confederate works would take place on July 6.[1]

Preparations for the attack commenced in earnest. The heads of all Union approaches were to be prepared "for the easy debouch of troops" with those farthest advanced widened to accommodate artillery and assault columns four men wide. In addition, "planks and sand-bags, stuffed with pressed cotton," were to be prepared for crossing enemy trenches. Grant's orders trickled down the chain of command, leaving the army's division and brigade commanders,

along with their engineers, to hammer out the preparation details. For example, in the Fifteenth Corps sector, Grant ordered Major General Frederick
Steele to concentrate on making the approaches of Brigadier General John
M. Thayer, Brigadier General Joseph A. J. Lightburn, and Colonel Giles
Smith ready for the assault. Comstock, who replaced Prime as the Army
of the Tennessee's chief engineer on July 27, outlined the details for Steele
on July 2. "The heads of trenches, for 60 feet," Comstock ordered, "should
be cut with gentle steps, so that troops can leave the trenches rapidly and in
order." In addition, the engineer specified that "preparations should also be
made for crossing ditches; planks should be obtained and held in readiness,
and sand-bags, solidly stuffed with cotton, tried, to see if they will not make,
when thrown in ditches, a sufficiently solid roadway for infantry."[2]

To the south, on the Thirteenth Corps front, where First Lieutenant
Peter C. Hains reigned over engineering activities, similar preparations took
place. "In compliance with orders, the trenches are being prepared to allow
easy passage of troops over them for an assault," Hains wrote. "In order to
cross the ditches of the works at the point of attack, grain-sacks are being
prepared, filled with cotton, well stuffed. Planks 18 feet long are being prepared to throw across the ditch to allow the passage of an assaulting column."
Things progressed smoothly.[3]

Until this point, the different Union approaches had met with varying
degrees of success. Although ten of the Union approaches were "within five
to 100 yards of [the] enemy's" line," it is unclear how many of these saps would
have been ready to explode mines on July 6. On the Fifteenth Corps front,
Captain William Kossak sank a mine at the head of Ewing's Approach on
June 26 and had been involved in a game of mining and countermining with
Confederate forces since that date. Even so, despite the give-and-take between
blue and butternut at this point, Kossak's mine was ready to receive a charge
of twenty-two hundred pounds of powder on July 4. Meanwhile, Union sappers did not begin excavating mines at the heads of Thayer's, Lightburn's, and
Giles Smith's Approaches until July 3. Whether or not these mines would
have been ready in time for the July 6 assault is a matter of speculation.[4]

Nevertheless, Union engineers believed that an attack on July 6 would
succeed. The majority of the casualties that the Army of the Tennessee had
suffered on May 22 had resulted from launching a large-scale assault over open
ground. The carefully laid out Confederate works provided interlocking fields
of fire and created choke points covering the natural pathways leading up to

the rebel defenses. These factors, which had doomed the May 22 assault, no longer existed at this late stage in the siege. The efforts of the Army of the Tennessee's limited number of engineers, combined with the adaptability of its western soldiers, determined that by July 6, a labyrinth of approach trenches and parallels allowed Union troops to traverse no-man's-land unmolested to within a few yards of the Confederate earthworks. Now, when Grant ordered his grand charge on July 6, federal troops would be exposed for only a few moments before surmounting the rebel defenses.[5]

In the center of the Union line, only Logan's Approach might have been ready to spring a third mine. Just to Logan's north, mining operations at the head of Ransom's Approach had been abandoned on June 28 since the ground on that front did not facilitate easy mining operations. At the same time, on the Thirteenth Corps front, Major General E. O. C. Ord's approaches were within striking distance of the Confederate lines and preparing to sink mines when Grant's orders for the July 6 attack left his command tent. Federal troops in Brigadier General A. J. Smith's left approach began construction of a mine gallery on July 2. Meanwhile, just to the south of Smith, both Carr's and Slack's Approaches reached to within ten yards of their designated objectives on July 2 and July 3 respectively. Farther down the line, the head of Hovey's Approach extended to within twenty yards of the rebel Fort Garrott on July 3.[6]

Progress had been slow on the southernmost part of the Union line. Repeated Confederate sorties on Lauman's Approach distracted soldiers from forward excavation. Meanwhile, at the head of Herron's Approach, Union soldiers were some hundred yards distant from the Confederate works by July 3. Thus, as of this date, it was nearly impossible to know exactly how many Union mines would be ready for detonation on July 6. Grant, despite these uncertainties, had made up his mind. On July 6, those mines that were ready would be ignited, and a large-scale infantry assault all along the line would follow. As Albert O. Marshall of the Thirty-Third Illinois stated, "If our plans are consummated we will witness the grandest explosion the world ever knew."[7]

Throughout the siege, Grant worried that a Confederate relief expedition would attempt to save Lieutenant General John C. Pemberton's beleaguered garrison. To the east of the Union siege lines, General Joseph E. Johnston was amassing an army that could be used in an attempt to break the siege. This concern led Grant to request reinforcements from his superior Major General Henry W. Halleck, who by June 17 had inflated Grant's army to some seventy-seven thousand men. In late June, Grant placed thirty-four thousand men under Major General William T. Sherman's command with orders to protect the Army of the Tennessee's rear while the primary offensive besieging force, now approximately forty-three thousand strong, continued to advance methodically toward the Vicksburg defenses. Sherman dutifully obeyed and by the end on July 4 had fortified the key approaches to Vicksburg west of the Big Black River. Although Johnston eventually amassed a relief army of twenty-eight thousand men that could have been coordinated with Pemberton's garrison of some thirty thousand soldiers to attempt a breakout, Johnston acted with unwarranted caution and marked time around Yazoo City and Benton. As Grant's army grew and Johnston dallied, the odds that Vicksburg could hold out diminished with each passing day of the siege.[8]

The plan was hard to keep secret, and rumors of a final grand assault began to permeate the federal ranks. To many this was welcome news as Grant's weary westerners had become "tired of digging rifle pits." Those on picket duty used the rumors as an opportunity to taunt their rebel counterparts only a few yards away. As Lieutenant Henry R. Brinkerhoff of the Thirtieth Ohio related, "A rumor became quite prevalent that an assault would be made on the fourth of July, and our men took occasion to threaten the rebels, in conversation while on picket, that they would catch one of the entire future worlds, and the warmest one of that, on the coming fourth."[9]

Meanwhile, those back in the Union trenches commenced preparations for the July 6 attack. Soldiers took "large numbers of bags" and stuffed them "as tight as possible" with cotton. According to Frank Swigart of the Forty-Sixth Indiana serving in Brigadier General Alvin P. Hovey's division, "these were to be used first to shield and protect the men while they reached the ditch, as they had nothing but the rifle-bullets to guard against." Once they reached the ditches fronting the rebel works, Swigart continued, "these cotton bags could be used to fill it up, and make a bridge instantly on which the charging column could cross."[10]

While some rigged up these devices, others along the siege lines procured planks that could be used to traverse the rebel ditches. The remainder of the men sat on the sidelines and inspected their rifles or labored away widening the various approach trenches. According to William E. Strong, by July 2, "More than half the besieging army could be massed in order of battle within pistol-shot of the enemy's line, without the loss of a man." Confidence resonated throughout the Union ranks. According to Charles A. Hobbs of the Ninety-Ninth Illinois, "The different mines under the rebel forts were all to be fired at the same time. The grandly-terrific explosion would be the preliminary to the bloody and victorious charge . . . like the atmosphere before the burst of the tempest, the dread experience was at hand . . . the bloody day when Vicksburg should fall, taken by storm!"[11]

The final Union attack, however, never occurred. Lack of communication from Johnston made it clear to Pemberton that the Vicksburg garrison would not be relieved, a fact that devastated Confederate morale. In addition to news of the Union grand assault infiltrating the Confederate ranks via the scuttlebutt of blue and gray pickets, those rebels manning the parapets could clearly see the meticulous Union preparations that signaled a large-scale attack. Thus, the Confederates would not be surprised when the assault came but would be overwhelmed nonetheless. Pemberton, realizing that further resistance was futile, sought out Grant's terms of surrender.[12]

On the morning of July 3, Pemberton drafted a letter to Grant and charged Major General John Bowen and Lieutenant Colonel Louis M. Montgomery with the task of channeling the message to the Union commander and initiating Confederate surrender. The two men exited the Vicksburg defenses from the Second Texas Lunette and proceeded down the Baldwin's Ferry Road toward the Union lines. Captain Joseph Leonard commanding B Company of the Ninety-Sixth Ohio, then on picket duty in that sector, hailed the two riders as they approached and asked, "What is wanted?" Upon learning that Bowen and Montgomery intended to discuss surrender terms, Leonard blindfolded the two Confederates and handed them over to a sergeant who conducted them to A. J. Smith's headquarters. Upon arrival, guards untied their blindfolds, and the two proceeded to meet with the Union division commander in his tent. After a brief parlay, Smith exited, mounted his horse, and rode off to Grant's headquarters in order to relay Pemberton's message. While the two Confederate officers waited outside the tent, Bowen briefly surveyed the federal siege works and remarked that the blue-clad westerners "must have the whole damned country around them dug up."[13]

The Union commander received A. J. Smith, and the two mulled over the Confederate proposition. Interestingly, Grant and Bowen had been neighbors before the war. Nevertheless, despite this relationship, the Union commander refused him an audience. Grant would discuss surrender terms only with Pemberton. Bowen, upon hearing this, suggested that the two army commanders meet later that afternoon at 3 P.M. Grant, believing it was Pemberton's desire to initiate capitulation, agreed to meet the Confederate commander at a designated spot in front of Major General James B. McPherson's headquarters.[14]

While Bowen and Montgomery brought Grant's message back to Pemberton, the Union commander continued to apply pressure against the Vicksburg defenders. McPherson, relating Grant's orders to division commander John A. Logan, specified that during the interim, there was to be "no cessation of hostilities." He further directed that "artillery and infantry, will be kept at their usual posts, firing at the enemy, as has been the practice." Although it appeared that the Confederates intended to surrender, engineers, pioneers, and regular soldiers continued to excavate mines and build earthworks.[15]

Bowen and Montgomery rode back into the Confederate defenses and reported to Pemberton. At 3 P.M. Pemberton, accompanied by Bowen and Montgomery, emerged from the Confederate lines and met the Union commander and his entourage under an oak tree in no-man's-land south of the Jackson Road. Among Grant's party were Generals McPherson, Ord, Logan, and A. J. Smith. An interesting and awkward turn of events took place once Grant and Pemberton met face to face. Bowen, perhaps through tactical initiative and desiring Vicksburg's capitulation, implied in his report to Pemberton that Grant had called for the meeting. As a result, Pemberton believed that the Army of the Tennessee's commander would negotiate favorable terms. This was not the case. When Grant met Pemberton he immediately told the Confederate general that it was his understanding that Pemberton desired the meeting and would be willing to accept Grant's terms. The Union commander's harsh provisions compounded this awkwardness. Grant, although having served with Pemberton during the Mexican War, refused to soften his demand for the unconditional surrender of the city and its defenders. The Confederate commander was outraged. With Grant unwilling to bend, Pemberton declared that he was prepared to continue the siege.[16]

Despite Grant's commitment to the rebels' unconditional surrender, the Union commander, although prepared to storm the city's works, did not want to suffer unnecessary casualties. Luckily Bowen, the architect of this situation, suggested that representatives from the two commanding generals' respective entourages try to hammer out a settlement. Pemberton and Grant agreed, and the accompanying subordinates, namely Bowen and A. J. Smith, sketched out more lenient terms than Grant had initially demanded. Unwilling to be rushed, Grant decided that he and his generals would consider the new terms and forward a final proposal to Pemberton by 10 P.M. that night.[17]

Back in his command tent, Grant and his generals met in order to draft the new surrender terms. On the advice of his subordinates, Grant agreed to parole the Confederate defenders rather than absorb the cost in Union manpower and resources of transporting the rebels north as prisoners of war. The Confederate enlisted men were to forfeit their small arms while rebel officers were allowed to retain one horse each and keep their sidearms. In addition, Grant allotted the garrison thirty wagons in which the Confederates could tote foodstuffs, from their own stocks, on their journey home as parolees.[18]

While the Union troops awaited the Confederate reply, an eerie silence replaced the roar of cannon fire and the crack of riflery. For the first time during the siege, all was quiet. Despite the brief cessation in hostilities, plans to commemorate "the eighty-seventh anniversary of American Independence" commenced. Grant ordered his three corps commanders and Major General Francis J. Herron commanding the southernmost division on the Union siege line to "fire a national salute of thirty-four guns from each battery (not from each gun) . . . at 5 A.M." In the trenches, individual commanders celebrated in their own way. The Thirty-Third Wisconsin's Captain W. W. Warner "suggested that this was a good and appropriate time to read the Declaration of Independence." He leaped up on top of the Union works and "read it [the Declaration] a loud, clear and distinct." At the end of the reading, Warner invited the Confederates "to give with us three rousing cheers for the Declaration." They remained silent.[19]

Meanwhile, Pemberton received Grant's terms and, after conferring with his own generals, decided that this was the best they could expect from the Union general. As a result, Pemberton and the Confederate defenders formally surrendered to the Army of the Tennessee on July 4, 1863. Elation filled the Union ranks. Upon hearing the news of Vicksburg's surrender, Seth J. Wells of the Seventeenth Illinois recorded in his diary, "Vicksburg is ours! . . . Thus ends one of the most brilliant campaigns the world has ever known since the days of Austerlitz. No one but Napoleon could have equaled it. It has resulted in the complete destruction of the Rebel army at Vicksburg. . . . The boys are beginning to think Grant is a Napoleon."[20]

The Confederate soldiers also held a high opinion of Grant's army. Mingling after the surrender, a group of Confederates told soldiers in Brigadier General Jacob Lauman's division "that Grant had the best Army in the world." According to Lieutenant George B. Carter of the Thirty-Third Wisconsin, "They told us we beat the world at digging. . . . One of their officers, in talking to us, said in pointing to our works within 50 yards of theirs, 'Men who could . . . come up there to stand and build pits are good soldiers.'" Carter also reported that the Confederates told the Union troops "that they had no shame in surrendering to Grant's Army, but they would be damned if they would soon surrender to the Army of the Potomac."[21]

After approximately six weeks of siege warfare, the soldiers of the Army of the Tennessee were a rough sight. Determined to meet their defeated enemy with dignity, officers, where possible, ordered their men to blacken their boots and obtain paper collars and white gloves in preparation for the surrender ceremony. On the morning of America's eighty-seventh birthday, the Confederate defenders solemnly exited their defenses and surrendered their arms and standards. After the Confederates left their works, Union bands trumpeted "Hail Columbia" and "The Star-Spangled Banner" as the blue-clad westerners entered the city. The Forty-Fifth Illinois, which had received a bloodletting during the June 25 crater fight, led the way and concluded its triumphal procession by planting the Stars and Stripes atop the Vicksburg Court House.[22]

Victorious Union soldiers in Vicksburg after the siege. On the hill is the Old Court House as it appeared in 1863. *Frederic B. Schell, "Entering Vicksburg, July 4, 1863"; courtesy of the Becker Collection, Boston College.*

For the Army of the Tennessee's engineers, however, the siege of Vicksburg was not over. Now that the westerners held the Gibraltar of the Confederacy, their posture changed from an offensive force to that of a defensive garrison. The approaches and parallels, the perfect melding of Mahanian siege craft and soldier improvisation that made federal success possible, now became a liability. Should the Confederates decide to attempt to recapture Vicksburg, the same trenches that secured victory against the former rebel garrison could now be used against the city's new blue-clad keepers. As a result, on July 4 Grant ordered chief engineer Captain Comstock to fill in the Union approaches and parallels excavated outside of the city's defenses and prepare Vicksburg to adopt a defensive posture. With this final order, after some six weeks, the siege of Vicksburg, the largest siege in U.S. history, was over.[23]

The Vicksburg Campaign was the most significant campaign fought during the most significant war in American history. The loss of the Gibraltar of the Confederacy, combined with the rebel reverse at Gettysburg, struck at the heart of Confederate morale. Union success at Vicksburg, however, unlike the victory at Gettysburg, proved strategically decisive. Vicksburg's capitulation made the Union the undisputed master of the Mississippi River, while the victory at Gettysburg did not significantly alter the strategic situation in the eastern theater. According to Grant, "From that day to the close of the rebellion the Mississippi River, from its source to its mouth, remained in the control of the National troops." Similarly, George Ditto of the Fifth Iowa recorded on July 4 that "200 miles or more of the river are now open and the only obstruction to its navigation its whole length, is at Port Hudson and that will be able to hold out only a few days longer. . . . It will do very much to reduce the stock of supplies in the south as Texas was their main depot for beef and it is now cut of[f]." Federal domination of the Mississippi allowed trade with midwestern farmers to resume in earnest and denied the Confederacy access to invaluable trans-Mississippi resources. From Vicksburg, the Union could concentrate on striking east to conquer the Confederate heartland.[24]

In addition, federal success at Vicksburg elevated the reputation of Ulysses S. Grant. Although it would be the Chattanooga campaign that finally convinced Lincoln that Grant was the man to lead all of the federal armies, his success at Vicksburg contributed to his growing reputation. Considered a hero after the capture of Forts Henry and Donelson in 1862, many had begun to doubt Grant's ability after Albert Sidney Johnston launched a surprise

Union troops preparing to defend Vicksburg after the siege. *Frederic B. Schell, "Siege of Vicksburg: Soldiers at Work on the Fortifications," May–June 1863; courtesy of the Becker Collection, Boston College.*

attack that resulted in the two-day Battle of Shiloh (April 6–7, 1862). Although Grant drove Confederate forces back on the second day and secured a Union victory, some believed that Grant, due to the first day's reverses, was unfit for command. Vicksburg, however, changed all of this. The success caught the attention of those in Washington and, as one soldier estimated in his diary, "completely wiped out his Shiloh affair." Thus, Vicksburg confirmed Grant's reputation and brought him renewed recognition.[25]

The siege of Vicksburg proved the linchpin of the campaign. If the Army of the Tennessee had failed to take the city, then Grant's previous victories during this campaign would have been for nothing. The Confederacy would have maintained control of the Mississippi River and retained its link with the trans-Mississippi theater. In addition, what remained of Grant's reputation might have been destroyed. Rather than celebrate Grant's Vicksburg Campaign as a paradigm of maneuver warfare, later military theorists probably would have described it as a failure—an operational success sandwiched between the federal campaign reverses during the winter of 1862–63 and a botched siege. Luckily for the Union, and the United States as a whole, Grant succeeded. His army, while deficient in professionally trained military engineers, worked well thanks to the ingenuity of its soldiers. Through a perfect blend of theory and improvisation, they waged the largest and most successful siege in U.S. history. The Army of the Tennessee's success at Vicksburg ensured federal victory in the West and sealed the Confederacy's fate. As one beleaguered Confederate soldier wrote during the waning days of the siege, "Our existence, almost, as a nation, depends on holding this place." He was correct. Ultimate Union victory some two years later killed slavery once and for all in the United States and ended the debate over the practicality of secession. In short, Grant's engineers and the ingenuity of his western soldiers helped establish the course of U.S. history for the next one hundred and fifty years.[26]

An assessment of the significance of Union military engineering during the Vicksburg siege requires an examination of the Confederate garrison on the eve of surrender. More specifically, it becomes imperative to evaluate the role that the lack of provisions and starvation played in forcing capitulation.

Since the earliest days of the siege, Union soldiers reported that food shortages were taking their toll on the Confederate defenders. One Union soldier, after serving on picket duty in front of Brigadier General Eugene A. Carr's division, wrote to his wife on June 16, "Our Pickets stand guard at night within 20 feet of one another and have quite a time conversing with one another. . . . They are getting very hungry in Vicksburg and our Pickets give theirs crackers and coffee nearly every night as they seem almost starved." Similarly, James H. Wilson of Grant's staff wrote on June 30, "Deserters report that rations and mule meat are now issued to the garrison."[27]

The condition of the Confederate troops continued to decline as the siege entered its final days. On July 4, the official day of the surrender, George Ditto of the Fifth Iowa, after conversing with Confederate prisoners, wrote, "They [the Confederates] were almost entirely destitute of provisions and some of the regiments had already began to feed on mule beef which had risen to $1.00 per lb and but very little of any kind of food was issued to the citizens." "The officers fared no better than the men," Ditto wrote. "A days rations consisted of ¼th lb of meat and flour or corn meal, 2 oz of peas, beans and rice, other things in proportion but not coffee that by no means is enough for a man that is expected to fight under any hardships." Another Union soldier serving in the Forty-Third Illinois reported similar Confederate privations. After conversing with the rebels on July 7, three days after the surrender of the city, this particular Union soldier wrote, "But the Garrison was half starved, having for some weeks past been living on ¼ ration of bread and a nearly full ration of, however the meanest kind of, fresh meat. It might have held out a few days longer but they had nothing to gain, so they surrendered." These accounts of deficient Confederate provisions were reiterated in postwar regimental histories and permanently wedded to Vicksburg siege narratives as one of the primary reasons for rebel capitulation.[28]

Further investigation reveals that a shortage of food, while perhaps a contributing factor, was not the main reason for rebel defeat. According to Vicksburg historian Michael Ballard, the Confederates contained adequate food stores upon surrender. "Contrary to the tales of no food left," Ballard writes, "many Confederate supplies were available. These included 38,668 pounds of bacon . . . 5,000 bushels of peas, 51,241 pounds of rice, 82,234 pounds of sugar, 721 rations of flour, and 428,000 pounds of salt." The argument that lack of food forced Confederate surrender is a "Lost Cause" myth. Pemberton reduced the garrison's rations in order to hold Vicksburg for as long as possible. Rations, while meager, were still supplied to the rebel defenders throughout the siege. The fact that such a large number of supplies remained in rebel hands at the end of the siege indicates that Confederate soldiers' complaints were nothing more than the typical grumbling that soldiers have done throughout history—a fact that led Napoleon Bonaparte to affectionately refer to his elite Imperial Guard as "grognards" (grumblers).[29]

Deficiencies in food stocks did not determine the garrison's fate; rather, it was the efforts of the Union engineers and the westerners of the Army of the Tennessee that forced Pemberton to surrender the Gibraltar of the Confederacy. The melding of Mahanian engineering theory with soldier improvisation allowed the Federals to occupy positions along the siege lines only a few yards from the rebel parapets. General McPherson summarized this theme in his laudatory July 4 message to the Seventeenth Corps. "With tireless energy, with sleepless vigilance by night and by day, with battery and rifle-pit, with trench and mine," McPherson praised, "you made sure approaches, until, overcome by fatigue and driven to despair in the attempt to oppose your irresistible progress, the whole garrison of over 30,000 men, with all their arms and munitions of war, have, on this anniversary of our National Independence, surrendered to the invincible troops of the Army of the Tennessee."[30]

Although McPherson intended this message as a tribute to inflate morale, his declaration illustrates the western tenacity that allowed Grant's army to achieve victory. The efforts of the Army of the Tennessee's engineers, combined with the adaptability of the common soldiers in that army, allowed Union troops to prepare for a massed attack that would have taken Vicksburg by force. According to the chief engineer of the Fifteenth Corps, William L. B. Jenney, federal preparations for the July 6 attack, conducted within plain view of the Confederates, intimidated the garrison into surrendering. Confederate chief engineer Major Samuel H. Lockett confirmed Jenney's observation when he wrote, on the eve of the surrender, "Federal forces were within less than a minute of our defenses, so that a single dash could have precipitated them upon us in overwhelming numbers." Thus, Confederate knowledge of Grant's impending attack, the result of successful Union engineering, was the primary factor forcing Pemberton's surrender.[31]

Nevertheless, despite Grant's intention to assault the rebel works, the Confederates, in their writings about the siege, provide a host of factors that forced Pemberton's surrender. In addition to low stocks of consumables and the Union proximity to the Confederate lines at the end of the siege, Lockett claimed that shortages of ammunition, combined with a lack of manpower and artillery, contributed to the rebels' decision to capitulate. Yet according to evidence that William T. Sherman provided on July 4, some of Lockett's reasons for Confederate surrender are not supported. According to Sherman, "The number of prisoners as given by the rebels is 27,000. There is much more artillery than we thought; the field-pieces are given at 128, and about 100 siege guns." According to Prime and Comstock, it was the Confederates' inability to use these guns to stymie the systematic federal advance, the direct result of Union engineering, that facilitated the smooth blue-clad progress across no-man's-land. Thus the Confederates, at the end of the siege, had more than enough troops and artillery to hold the Vicksburg defenses. While Sherman reported on the state of Confederate artillery upon Vicksburg's surrender, chief engineers Prime and Comstock stated that, although some captured Confederate officers cited lack of ammunition as the main mover behind rebel surrender, Union troops "captured over 40,000 rounds of artillery ammunition."[32]

In truth, Johnston's refusal to relieve the beleaguered garrison early in the siege, before Grant received substantial reinforcements, combined with the Union ability to launch a large-scale attack on July 6, forced Pemberton's hand. By July 3, and perhaps even earlier, the fate of the Confederate garrison was sealed. As one Confederate soldier wrote on July 3, "Our affairs now seem to be getting desperate[.] No news from Johnson for many days. . . . While we grow weaker the enemy are reinforced." To the rear, Sherman commanded a large enough force to hold off Johnston. To the front, Grant's dogged engineers and the tenacity of his westerners negated the factor that had doomed the May 22 attack, crossing anywhere from three hundred to five hundred yards of rugged terrain completely exposed to Confederate fire. Unfortunately, to cite lack of food alone as the primary factor forcing the city's surrender would be to subscribe to the Lost Cause chimera that continues to infiltrate some Civil War histories. Simply stated, Grant's westerners bested Pemberton's garrison. The siege tactics that the Army of the Tennessee implemented, a successful combination of Mahanian maxims and soldier improvisation, severed the garrison's lines of supply and communication while tightening the ring around the Confederate defenses. Although Pemberton probably could have held out a little longer, the scheduled July 6 attack, which Grant's troops had engineered, combined with the reality that Johnston was not coming, forced his decision to surrender.[33]

Of course, it would be incorrect to conclude from this discourse that the blend of West Point training and soldier ingenuity that allowed Grant's siege to succeed was perfect. As one Confederate soldier quipped on June 28, "It is only owing to the total inefficiency of the enemy that we are not already captured." While this was clearly an overstatement, a subtle layer of truth existed below the curt surface. The West Point–trained engineers that served with the army often criticized the rank and file for their amateurish performance and techniques that paled in the light of professional standards. Despite the fact that the Union troops excavated a complicated trench network extending an "aggregate length" of twelve miles and erected some "89 batteries, with 220 guns in position," Grant's professionals remained critical of the army's overall performance. According to Prime and Comstock, "The amount of night work done by a given detail [depended] very much on the discipline of the command from which it [was] taken and on the energy of its officers. Under average circumstances, such details [did] not in a given time accomplish half of the work of which they [were capable]." They further stated that "from the lack of educated engineer officers, the approaches and parallels were in some places badly located and much unnecessary work done. The boyaus [*sic*] were often sunk to the depth of 5 or even 6 feet where the enemy's fire was heavy, largely increasing the amount of labor."[34]

Nevertheless, despite their harsh criticisms, Comstock and Prime praised the ingenuity of Grant's midwesterners. With only three engineer officers on duty at any given time to oversee the army's vast engineering enterprise, "only a general supervision was possible." This, according to the Union chief engineers, "gave to the siege one of its peculiar characteristics." The nature of the work carried out, its quality and style, "depended on officers, or even men, without either theoretical or practical knowledge of siege operations, and who had to rely upon their native good sense and ingenuity.... Officers and men had to learn to be engineers while the siege was going on." Through this process of trial and error, the resourceful men of the Army of the Tennessee waged an imperfect, yet successful, siege. According to the chief engineers, "Whether a battery was to be constructed by men who had never built one before, a sap-roller made by those who had never heard the name, or a ship's gun carriage to be built, it was done, and, after a few trials, was well done."[35]

Ultimately, despite the fact that the Army of the Tennessee's improvised siege craft succeeded and that Grant's handful of professionals praised the ingenuity of the army's enlisted personnel, the overall impression of those such as Comstock and Prime was that the westerners' siege techniques were rough. While the chief engineers conceded that the July 6 assault would have been successful, the army "might have been ready for an assault two or three weeks earlier, if there had been a sufficient supply of engineer officers to watch that no time was lost or useless work done; to see that every shovelful of earth thrown brought us nearer to the end, and personally to push and constantly supervise the special works to which they were assigned."[36]

Despite the criticisms that the army's professionals leveled, the rank and file believed that their ability to adapt and achieve tangible results outweighed any deficiencies in their performance. First Sergeant Charles A. Hobbs of the Ninety-Ninth Illinois praised the ingenuity and adaptability of his comrades that, when combined with scientific siege craft, facilitated Vicksburg's demise. According to Hobbs, the Army of the Tennessee embarked on a journey to master a steep learning curve after the May 22 assault failed. While the few professional engineers with the army in most cases proved to be well-trained professionals, the institution as a whole "knew very little . . . how to proceed." Yet, "when the white flags went up on July 4 we [the soldiers] had learned much . . . before the siege ended there were many volunteer officers who could have quickly chosen the best position, and with no little skill have constructed works of defense." The fact that the siege "was the longest at this time of any in our [American] history" and was "a new experience . . . having all of the power of first impressions" mandated that the siege obtained "an exceptional position in the minds not only of the participants, but . . . of the [Union] people at large."[37]

Accolades and the recognition of the monumental achievement were not limited to the soldier's pen. Even Admiral David Dixon Porter recognized that the Army of the Tennessee and its leader, Ulysses S. Grant, had overcome great odds in engineering Vicksburg's demise. "General Grant has gained a world-wide reputation for his military work," Porter wrote after the war, and that reputation was gained at Vicksburg, "the most formidable series of earthworks ever erected on the continent." According to Porter, "I saw the celebrated Malakoff and the Redan [at Sebastopol] two days after they fell into the hands of the allied English and French army, and they were nothing in comparison with the defenses of Vicksburg." The accomplishment of Grant and his midwesterners was great and their soaring reputation well deserved.[38]

Interestingly, the Vicksburg siege barely impacted the later sieges of the Civil War and represented the last Vauban-style siege in Western military history. After the Battle of Chickamauga (September 19–20, 1863), Braxton Bragg's victorious Army of Tennessee drove the Army of the Cumberland north into Chattanooga and besieged the blue-clad westerners. Although Bragg's Confederates had trapped this particular Union army, the situation did not allow them to prosecute scientific approaches and parallels bent on penetrating the federal defenses. Rather, from their entrenchments atop Missionary Ridge and their shallow rifle pits at its base, the Confederates simply watched the trapped Union troops in a frontier game of "hem them in and starve them out."

Meanwhile, the combat surrounding the "siege of Petersburg" in June 1864 stood closer to the trench warfare conducted during the Russo-Japanese War of 1904–5 and the Western Front in late 1914 than it did to the Vicksburg siege. Petersburg was not a siege. During this almost yearlong combat, Grant's forces in Virginia did not cut General Robert E. Lee's supply or communication lines, nor did they dig methodical approaches toward the beleaguered Confederate army. Rather, as with the Allied and German forces during the late summer and early fall of 1914, constant contact between Union and Confederate troops forced the belligerents to dig hasty entrenchments that evolved over the coming year into more elaborate trench-works. In fact, Grant's unsuccessful attempts to extend his line west and outflank Lee during the Petersburg incident were more foreshadowing of the operational maneuvering of the Race to the Sea in 1914 than it was a harkening back to his attack by regular approaches at Vicksburg. In addition, the only successful mine detonated during the Petersburg siege, exploded on

July 30, 1864, did not resemble Captain Andrew Hickenlooper's Vicksburg mining operations on either June 25 or July 1. While Hickenlooper sank his mine after weeks of prosecuting a Vaubanian-style approach, the Union coal miners of the Forty-Eighth Pennsylvania at Petersburg dug a tunnel under no-man's-land toward the Confederate line some 586 feet in length, a task similar to (although much smaller than) the British mining efforts underneath Hill 60 on the Ypres salient during the First World War.[39]

Viewing the Vicksburg siege through a wider lens leads to the conclusion that this monumental event along the banks of the Father of Waters was the last Vauban-style siege in Western military history. As previously stated, according to Dennis Hart Mahan, a siege was a methodical and scientific movement against a fortified place in which the attacker cut the defender's line of communications before attacking by regular approaches. The later "sieges" of the nineteenth century, when measured against Mahan's narrow definition that had been handed down since the age of Vauban, may not even be considered sieges at all. For example, the Germans, at the 1870 siege of Paris during the Franco-Prussian War, encircled that French city but did not attack via regular approaches. Rather, German general Count Helmuth von Molke relied upon the combination of starvation and bombardment to break French resistance. To the East, at Plevna (1877), located in modern-day Bulgaria, Russian forces favored a mixture of bombardment and assault against the trapped Turkish forces rather than wage a methodical, Vaubanian approach.[40]

Meanwhile, the "sieges" of the various colonial conflicts of the late nineteenth century, which featured small European and American contingents against large forces of indigenous warriors, resembled gunfights more than the sieges of Vauban's day. Refined breech-loading weapons and combats in which Anglo-Europeans were on the defensive decreed that Vauban's maxims would not fit practical circumstances. The Wagon Box Fight of 1866 in the American Great Plains, the Battle of Rorke's Drift in South Africa (1879), the Siege of Khartoum in the Sudan (1884–85), and the incident at Peking during the Boxer Rebellion (1900) all featured outnumbered imperial forces deadlocked against overwhelming native troops. Thus, the age of the Vauban-style attack by regular approaches died at Vicksburg. Combat against non-European peoples with their own respective warrior cultures distanced from the European Enlightenment dictated that far-off colonial conflicts would be sans Vauban. In addition, the emergence of modern armaments, such as heavy, long-range, breech-loading artillery, and the large conscript armies of the twentieth century rendered the French engineer's offensive maxims obsolete. Warfare had changed. Vauban was not to be a part of the future—and, for that matter, neither was Mahan.

The Vicksburg siege, while not acting as a harbinger of future warfare, was still significant. It was a transitional event that helped define the Civil War as a transitional war. Although it signaled the death of the Vaubanian-style siege of the Enlightenment, the type of tactical movement that brought the Army of the Tennessee to within a few feet of the Gibraltar of the Confederacy during the summer of 1863 reinforced the basic principles of siege craft that extended back to antiquity. Armies, as in the days of Napoleon, may have remained the targets of modern warfare, but places were still important strategic objectives. Interestingly, future "sieges," such as the investments of Paris in 1870–71, Leningrad (1941–44), and Dien Bien Phu (1954), stood closer to Julius Caesar's siege of Alesia (52 B.C.) and the frontier-style "hem them in, starve them out" mentality of static warfare than they did to the great sieges of the Enlightenment. High-yield explosives of twentieth-century artillery shells and the eventual widespread use of machine guns and aircraft led to the extinction of forward-moving zigzag approaches and parallels. Soldiers, in order to avoid these new weapons, dug deeper. Nevertheless, under specific circumstances, "digging in" under fire and "waiting out" an enemy occupying a strategic objective remained a permanent feature of future conflicts.[41]

In addition, the Vicksburg siege hardly changed Mahanian engineering theory as taught at West Point. On March 21, 1865, some nineteen days before Lee surrendered to Grant at Appomattox Courthouse in Virginia, Dennis Hart Mahan, still considered West Point's leading military engineering theorist, continued to pontificate over the present state of siege warfare. On that day Mahan, with Union and Confederate armies still deadlocked in Virginia, released an "enlarged and improved edition" of his seminal *Complete Treatise on Field Fortification*, "which for many years" had been one of the standard textbooks then in use at West Point. This new and expanded edition, though similar to its predecessor, attempted to "comprise . . . the subjects of Military Mining and Siege Operations, both of which have found such extensive applications in several of the late remarkable sieges, in this country and in Europe, where the chief defenses consisted of a simple line of field works."[42]

The siege of Vicksburg, though worthy of Mahan's assessment, received cursory treatment. He mentioned it last, in the treatise's sixth chapter, "Examples of Remarkable Military Mining Operations." Despite the chapter's title, Mahan commented on the unremarkable nature of the siege's mining operations. According to Mahan, while Grant's soldiers successfully conducted their excavations and detonated the resulting mines "without the aid of a thoroughly trained military mining corps," the army's mining operations, on the whole, contained "no particular features of interest . . . further than the aptitude shown by our troops for any work to which they may be put in devising a means from whatever may be found at hand." "The charges were mostly small," Mahan wrote, with "the lines of least resistance not exceeding some 28 feet." In short, with regard to military mining, the tenacity of the Army of the Tennessee's fighting men and their ability to improvise were, in Mahan's estimation, the most remarkable parts of this phase of the siege.[43]

Yet the lack of Mahan's commentary stemmed from the fact that, as of March 1865, "no official details of professional interest [had] thus far been published of this siege, which has had such important results." As a result, Mahan's description and analysis of the siege was both superficial and inaccurate. While his description of the ground and the terrain was correct, Mahan's statement that "the besiegers were provided with a suitable siege train, particularly in mortars, and regularly trained engineer troops" was grossly inaccurate.[44]

Grant, upon setting out from Milliken's Bend on March 29, 1863, had no intention of conducting a formal siege against Vicksburg. As a result, he did not trail a burdensome siege train. In addition, the Army of the Tennessee did not contain siege mortars, a fact that forced them to construct wooden imitations (a novelty that Mahan touched on briefly in his commentary). Nevertheless, Mahan made some astute observations pertaining to the Union's conduct of offensive siege warfare. He acknowledged that the westerners ably used the broken terrain to "open their first parallels at from 500 to 800 yards . . . from the [Confederate] defenses" and to erect their batteries in favorable positions. From these concealed points of origin, federal troops prosecuted sufficient approaches and parallels to facilitate the mining operations that ultimately placed the army in an advantageous position for a final grand assault.[45]

Unfortunately for Mahan, the majority of the sources describing the engineering details of the siege were just out of his grasp. When forced retirement from the United States Military Academy triggered his suicide in 1871, the Academy's leading military engineering theorist had not lived long enough to peruse the sources that outlined the details of the Vicksburg siege. In any event, even if Mahan had had access to these details, it is unlikely that they would have revolutionized the theory of offensive siege warfare. The stalemates and "sieges" of the future would more closely resemble the trench warfare prosecuted under Grant and Lee outside Petersburg than the methodical approaches and parallels of Vicksburg. Petersburg, unlike Vicksburg, became a battle of attrition in the style of the First World War. While one could argue that the Vicksburg siege stood closer to the sieges of the Enlightenment rather than served as a harbinger of future trench warfare, such a debate would prove moot and requires the historian to submit to the falsehood that warfare, whether during the Age of Marlborough, the American Civil War, or the First World War, is static. It is not. For example, no matter how closely the trench warfare and proclivity for rifle pits that Americans displayed in 1864 might resemble the temporary field fortifications and early trenches of late 1914, they stand in far contrast to the elaborate system of defense-in-depth that characterized the Western Front in 1918. Rather than attempt to perceive the American Civil War as the last Napoleonic War or the herald of modern warfare, it is best to view the event as a transitional war that had its own nature. The Vicksburg siege illustrates this. It was a touch of Vauban mixed with new technologies that, when wedded to western soldier improvisation, yielded the largest and most successful siege in American history.

Appendix

Glossary

Bibliographic Essay

List of Abbreviations

Notes

Bibliography

Index

Appendix:
How Many Union Engineer Officers Served during the Vicksburg Siege?

T he question is simple. How many Union engineer officers served during the Vicksburg siege? This seemingly basic question should contain a single, quantifiable answer. Unfortunately, it does not. Historians writing about the siege, as well as those who served during the campaign, do not provide a definitive answer. The question, however, like many historical inquiries, opens up a Pandora's box of other questions about the Vicksburg engineers. For example, how does one define an "engineer" during the Vicksburg siege? Is it someone who received formal instruction in military engineering and served in the Corps of Engineers? Was it simply an individual who acted in the capacity traditionally reserved for a professional? This brief appendix attempts to answer this deceptively simple yet very complicated question. Although engineers also served in the construction of Major General William T. Sherman's line of countervallation designed to repel Confederate attempts to lift the siege, only those engineers participating in the direct offensive siege craft against the Vicksburg defenses will be examined in this appendix.

Most turn to Major General Ulysses S. Grant's *Personal Memoirs* in order to quantify the number of Union engineers present during the Vicksburg siege. According to Grant, the Army of the Tennessee "had but four engineer officers." Unfortunately, Grant did not mention who all of these engineers were. Although Grant went on to state that "Captain [Frederick E.] Prime, of the Engineer Corps, was to be the chief, and the work at the beginning was mainly directed by him" and that Prime, due to ill health, "was succeeded by Captain Cyrus B. Comstock, also of the Engineer Corps," the commanding general failed to identify who the remaining engineers were. Grant's four original engineers probably included Prime, the original chief engineer of the

Army of the Tennessee, and the chief engineers assigned to the army's three corps: First Lieutenant Peter C. Hains of the Thirteenth Corps, Captain Andrew Hickenlooper of the Seventeenth Corps, and Captain William L. B. Jenney of the Fifteenth Corps. Only two of these men, Prime and Hains, were West Point graduates who entered the Corps of Engineers; Prime graduated with the class of 1850 and Hains with the class of 1861. Captain Cyrus B. Comstock, who did not arrive at the siege until June 15 and did not take over for Prime until the latter's health declined on June 27, graduated from the United States Military Academy as an engineer in 1855.[1]

The three chief engineers of the Army of the Tennessee's original three corps hailed from diverse educational backgrounds. Hickenlooper was an antebellum civil engineer and self-taught military engineer, while Jenney graduated from Paris's École Centrale des Arts et Manufactures in 1856. Thus, according to Grant's memoirs, only five engineers served during the Vicksburg siege (Prime, Comstock, and the three corps engineers). This deficiency prompted him to "direct" graduates of "West Point, where they had necessarily to study military engineering," to "assist in the work," in addition to their other duties. Unfortunately, Grant did not relate how many West Point graduates answered his request, and as Vicksburg historian Michael Ballard points out, their usefulness would be contingent upon "how much they remembered" from their prewar studies. In short, while one could perhaps quantify how many West Point graduates were present during the Vicksburg siege, the overall significance of such a number would be moot since there is no way to measure how much engineering knowledge these former cadets retained from their days at the USMA.[2]

The fact that West Point graduates served during the siege meant that some Army of the Tennessee men had been exposed to Dennis Hart Mahan's teachings. Mahan's forty-one-year career at the USMA ensured that all Civil War officers who graduated from West Point attended his classes and read his treatises. While some brilliant officers such as William T. Sherman clearly remembered their Mahanian experience, others did not. In one anecdote from Grant's memoirs, the chief commissary of the Army of the Tennessee, upon learning of Grant's request, comically stated that, although he was a West Point graduate, "there was nothing in engineering that he was good for unless he would do for a sap-roller." Thus, a more important topic to examine is not how many West Pointers were at the Vicksburg siege but rather how many engineer officers, the architects of Union victory, were present.[3]

The *Official Records* provides an answer to this question. Yet this answer, like the one found in Grant's memoirs, generates more queries. Tucked in the back of Prime and Comstock's joint official report "is a list of engineer officers who were present during the siege on engineer duty." This list cites eleven engineer officers who served during the Vicksburg siege: Captain Frederick E. Prime (USMA class of 1850); Captain Cyrus B. Comstock (USMA class of 1855); Captain Miles D. McAlester (USMA class of 1856, arrived at Vicksburg on June 28); First Lieutenant Peter C. Hains (USMA class of 1861); Lieutenant Clemens C. Chaffee of the Ordnance Corps (USMA class of 1862); Lieutenant Hopkins of the Third Infantry (first name and prewar education unknown), who "was also detailed on duty with the chief engineer for a few days"; Captain William L. B. Jenney (graduate of the École Centrale des Arts et Manufactures, class of 1856); Captain Henry C. Freeman (acting engineer officer, Fourth Division, Sixteenth Army Corps); Captain Arnold Hoeppner (aide-de-camp); Captain William Kossak (aide-de-camp); and Lieutenant Christian Lochbihler "and his pioneer company" of the Thirty-Fifth Missouri Regiment. In short, according to this report, the answer should be clear: there were eleven engineer officers who served during the Vicksburg siege.[4]

The consecutive chief engineers' attempt to list the number of engineer officers present at Vicksburg, however, generates more problems than it solves. First, Prime and Comstock stated in this segment that "additional aides-de-camp, were assigned, respectively, to Sherman's corps and Lauman's and Herron's Divisions." Unfortunately, Prime and Comstock did not tell who the aides were who served as acting engineers or even how many did so. Eight names of known persons who served as engineers during the siege do not appear on their list. These include Captain Andrew Hickenlooper, chief engineer of the Seventeenth Army Corps; Grant's aide-de-camp James H. Wilson (USMA class of 1860); Frank Holcomb Mason and Captain John M. Wilson (who served under Comstock); Captain Stewart R. Tresilian (engineer officer, Third Division, Seventeenth Army Corps); Captain Herman Klostermann (commander of the pioneer company of Major General Frederick Steele's division); Lieutenant Emmett Headington (a member of Brigadier General Hugh Ewing's staff who supervised Ewing's Approach until replaced by Clemens C. Chaffee); and Captain A. M. Powell (an artilleryman who oversaw Ransom's Approach). If these names are added to those in the Prime and Comstock report, nineteen engineers served during the Vicksburg siege.[5]

Yet not all of these men were professional military engineers. Although it is beyond the scope of this work to define professionalism, Comstock's individual addendum report, written on September 7, 1863, provides some insight into how West Point–educated engineers defined their art. According to Comstock, "After Captain Prime's departure, the only officers of engineers present on engineer duty were Capt. M. D. McAlester and First Lieut. P. C. Hains. Captain McAlester reported June 28, and was assigned to the charge of operations on the left, where he rendered efficient assistance till relieved on July 5." Thus, according to Comstock, after Prime departed, only three engineer officers were present for duty. These three men, including Comstock himself, were West Point graduates who had entered the Corps of Engineers. In addition, since McAlester did not arrive until June 28 and Comstock did not relieve Prime until June 27, there were still only three "engineer officers on duty" before Prime's departure. Comstock, in his report, omitted both Hickenlooper's name and those serving as engineers in the Fifteenth Corps sector. Whether this was a clerical error or an intentional omission due to Comstock's self-imposed definition of professionalism remains uncertain.[6]

Tension existed between professional engineers (those with West Point training who went from the USMA directly into the Corps of Engineers) and those who simply oversaw engineering tasks. According to Prime and Comstock's report, "When the siege commenced there were with the army two engineer officers doing engineer duty," a fact that made "superintendence at any particular point . . . impossible, without neglecting the more important general superintendence of the whole line." The authors' "two engineer officers" were Prime himself and Lieutenant Peter C. Hains, both of whom were USMA graduates and officially attached to the Corps of Engineers. Comstock, remaining critical of the army's volunteers, later wrote in his independent report that "from the lack of educated engineer officers, the approaches and parallels were in some places badly located and much unnecessary work done. The boyaus [sic] were often sunk to the depth of 5 or even 6 feet where the enemy's fire was heavy, largely increasing the amount of labor." Further highlighting their narrow definition of an engineer officer, the two consecutive chief engineers also wrote that "the want of engineers has already been referred to, there being at no time more than three on engineer duty." Thus, in Comstock's estimation (and Prime's, for that matter), only those who graduated from West Point and went on to serve in the Corps of Engineers were truly "educated engineer officers." To these men, a clear distinction existed between those who were professionals and others who simply directed engineering operations.[7]

This brief appendix is by no means definitive; however, it does provide a rough estimate designed to answer the original question. If one subscribes to Grant's memoirs, then the siege began with four engineer officers on duty. Prime and Comstock provide a list of twelve names, but that list can easily be expanded to twenty known officers who oversaw construction projects during the siege. If, however, one subscribes to Comstock and Prime's narrow definition of "educated engineer officers" present for duty—in effect, those who received a West Point education and entered the Corps of Engineers after graduation—then the number of engineer officers is certainly much smaller (somewhere between perhaps three and four, depending upon what period of the siege one is examining).[8]

Nevertheless, regardless of the actual number of engineers present during the siege, professionals such as Prime and Comstock believed that there simply were not enough. According to these two men, "The engineer organization here . . . was very deficient, if we judge either from the practice of nations wiser in the art of war than ourselves or from results. Thirty officers of engineers would have found full employment. . . . With so deficient an engineer organization was the siege to be carried on." The lack of engineers at Vicksburg created a different kind of siege. The shortage of engineer officers "gave the siege one of its peculiar characteristics," Prime and Comstock wrote, "namely that many times, at different places, the work that should be done, and the way it should be done, depended on officers, or even on men, without either theoretical or practical knowledge of siege operations, and who had to rely upon their native good sense and ingenuity." As a result of this shortage, those with West Point training and applicable mechanical skills were called upon to assist in engineering tasks. This combination of West Point professionalism and western improvisation sealed Vicksburg's fate.[9]

Glossary

----

approach trench. See **zigzag**.

attack by regular approaches. The process of methodically reducing an enemy fortress via siege techniques; primarily refers to the art of the attack using approach trenches and parallels.

bastion. A defensive structure protruding from a fortification's wall (curtain). It typically cut at angles in order to provide supporting fire for other bastions and the curtain.

boyaux. A communication trench excavated to connect two or more additional trenches.

branches. A nineteenth-century mining term referring to horizontal excavations with dimensions measuring less than three feet by four feet.

breaching batteries. Artillery batteries established for the purpose of battering holes in the enemy defenses that might be exploited by infantrymen.

camouflet. A detonated mine that does not break through to the surface. Typically used in countermining.

capital. Traditionally defined as the line bisecting the salient angle of a fortification. In this work, it refers to the tip of the salient.

chamber. The part of a mine where the powder charge is placed.

counter-batteries. Artillery batteries established for the purpose of targeting and destroying enemy artillery. A form of suppressing fire.

countermine. A defensive tactic in which a mine is dug underneath an attacker's mine with the purpose of detonating a camouflet. If properly executed, the attacker's mine will collapse.

covered way. A path for defending infantrymen on the far side of a fortification's defensive ditch.

defilade. Using cover, either artificial or natural, in order to protect against flanking fire.

demi-lune. A crescent-shaped or triangular outwork that guards either a curtain wall or the entrance to a fortification.

demi-parallel. A shorter version of the standard parallel.

double sap. An approach trench with two sap heads, two sap rollers, and a row of gabions (gabionade) on each side of the trench.

embrasure. An opening in the wall of a fortification or fieldwork for an artillery piece; a gunport.

enfilade. Flanking fire.

enfilading batteries. Artillery batteries situated so that they can fire down the length of the enemy's flank.

fascines. Tightly bound bundles of sticks used for revetment.

flying sap. A rapidly constructed approach trench that utilizes gabions.

full sap. An approach trench that contains fascines on top of the gabionade. This type of sap is supposed to be constructed by professional sappers.

gabion. A woven basket filled with earth and used for revetment in saps. Typically made out of pliable materials such as cane.

gabionade. A row of gabions.

galleries. A nineteenth-century mining term referring to horizontal excavations containing dimensions measuring more than three feet by four feet.

glacis. The outer slope of a defensive fortification.

half parallel. A shorter version of the standard parallel.

headlog. A form of head protection used in entrenchments.

howitzer. A medium-range artillery piece that lobs projectiles at a high trajectory.

invest. Action taking place early in the siege in which the besiegers (attackers) form a perimeter around the besieged in an attempt to cut their lines of communication and prevent escape.

investment. See **invest.**

line of circumvallation. A connected line of works facing the enemy; created by the besiegers (attackers) early in the siege after the investment of the enemy's fortification.

line of countervallation. A chain of detached works that protects the rear of the besieger from the possible approach of an army of relief attempting to lift the siege.

lunette. A defensive structure that typically cuts at angles and resembles a crescent moon. The back of the work, on the defender's side, is left open.

mantlets. Artillery blinds used to conceal gun crews.

mine. An underground chamber excavated, filled with gunpowder, and then detonated with the intention of breaching the enemy's works.

mortar. A short-range artillery piece that lobs projectiles at a high trajectory.

opening the trenches. The early phase of a siege when ground is broken on approach trenches.

parallel trench. A form of trench that branches off from a zigzag approach and runs parallel to the enemy's defensive line. These trenches support the approach trench.

parapet. An earthen wall that protects defenders from rifle and artillery fire.

redan. A V-shaped defensive fortification open on the side facing the garrison. It allows the defender to deliver flanking fire against an attacking enemy.

redoubt. An enclosed defensive structure that provides protection on all sides.

revetment. Material used to brace or strengthen an earthen wall.

rifle pit. A shallow entrenchment designed to protect either an individual or a small group of soldiers. During the Civil War, soldiers used the term to describe everything from rifle pits proper to trenches, parallels, and approaches.

salient. A protrusion in a line of defensive works.

sap. A trench that utilizes gabions.

sappers. Special troops trained to dig saps.

sap roller. A large woven structure that resembles a gabion turned on its side. Sap rollers are used at the head of approach trenches in order to provide protection for teams of excavators.

siege. An offensive tactic characterized by cutting the enemy's line of communications and prosecuting forward-moving approach trenches.

simple trench. A trench with a basic earthen embankment or parapet.

sortie. A raid.

terreplein. The floor beneath an artillery piece or battery. In more permanent fortifications, the terreplein typically refers to the level area behind the rampart.

traverse. Earthen walls used in the construction of artillery batteries to protect the flanks of a gun's position.

trench. An excavated defensive structure. According to nineteenth-century military manuals, trenches typically came in the form of approaches and parallels.

trench cavalier. Structures erected at the head of approach trenches or saps before mining operations are conducted. These mounds provide elevated platforms from which plunging fire can be poured onto the enemy.

zigzag. An approach trench dug toward the besieged fortification. It cuts at sharp angles in order to avoid enfilading (flanking) fire.

Bibliographic Essay

Since the Civil War ended in 1865, publishers, civilians, and veterans have displayed a bias toward the eastern theater of the conflict. The close proximity of the warring capitals, Washington and Richmond, combined with large-scale battles, better press coverage, and the epic showdown between Robert E. Lee and Ulysses S. Grant, determined that this theater would earn the unwarranted distinction as the war's decisive arena.

This bias toward the Virginia theater remains in both professional and popular histories despite the fact that prominent historians such as Thomas Connelly (*Army of the Heartland: The Army of Tennessee, 1861–1862*) have argued the contrary since the second half of the twentieth century. This eastern partiality, evident during the war itself, affected Vicksburg studies, relegating the topic to second-class status. Nevertheless, the demise of the principal Confederate bastion that guarded the Father of Waters proved one of the most significant campaigns in the Civil War. Its fall severed the Confederacy, depriving the South of the rich resources located in the trans-Mississippi theater, and placed the Union one large step closer to dominating the Mississippi Valley.[1]

It would be inaccurate, however, to imply that historians have entirely neglected the Vicksburg Campaign. In fact, one of the most valuable studies, including a lengthy segment on the siege, appeared shortly after the cessation of hostilities. Adam Badeau, a former aide-de-camp to Grant, published his three-volume study, *Military History of Ulysses S. Grant, from April, 1861 to April, 1865* during the 1880s. Although Badeau did not become one of the general's aides until later in the war and did not serve at the siege of Vicksburg, he provided a lengthy account of Union engineering and siege craft.

Badeau, in his segment on Vicksburg, related a history of engineering improvisation. Suffering from a lack of engineering professionals, "officers and men had to learn to be engineers while the siege was going on." As a result, "much valuable time was in this way lost and many a shovelful of earth was thrown that brought the siege no nearer to an end." But Union junior officers and enlisted men overcame this handicap. Over time, soldiers, often lacking formal engineering training, learned through a process of trial and error. According to Badeau, "The work to be done depended on officers and men without either theoretical or practical knowledge of siege operations, and who had, therefore, to rely, almost exclusively, on their native good sense and ingenuity." While Badeau made astute observations, his history is limited due to his sparse sources. Missing from Badeau's history is the soldier's perspective—the "thinking bayonets" who made Union success possible.[2]

In more recent years, Vicksburg historian Michael Ballard has noted the lack of Vicksburg studies. "As for the Vicksburg campaign and its place in history," Ballard writes, "it continues to languish in the shadows of the Eastern Theater. . . . Unless more historians are willing to change the paradigm of Civil War turning points from the Eastern to the Western Theater, Vicksburg is likely to remain overshadowed." In short, the glamour of the eastern theater, coupled with the duration and complexity of the Vicksburg operations, has deterred scholars from tackling this immense task.[3]

Nevertheless, popular Vicksburg histories dominated Civil War scholarship until more recent decades yielded professional studies such as Ballard's. Not until national park historian Edwin C. Bearss published on the Vicksburg Campaign did the event receive detailed analysis. Bearss's first dabbling in Union military engineering appeared in a 1962 edition of the *Military Engineer*. Yet this article, "Ewing's Approach in the Siege of Vicksburg," outlines only one of the thirteen known Union approaches to Vicksburg's defenses. The article foreshadows Bearss's treatment of Union engineering in his later 1980s magnum opus *The Campaign for Vicksburg*, a detailed three-volume reference work that spans Grant's earliest attempts to take Vicksburg in 1862 through the city's capitulation. His single chapter on the siege painstakingly examines, through the lens of each of the thirteen Union approaches, federal attempts to breach the city's defenses.[4]

Professional geographer Warren Grabau breathed new life into Vicksburg studies with his 2000 publication, *Ninety-Eight Days: A Geographer's View of the Vicksburg Campaign*. His trained eye for terrain features elicited a remarkable history that details the campaign from Union and Confederate perspectives and analyzes both Grant's maneuver campaign and the siege. His segment on the siege, due to the large scope of his study, remains relatively brief as he attempts to focus on both northern and southern operations.

William Shea and former Vicksburg National Military Park historian Terrence Winschel provide an excellent overview of the entire Vicksburg Campaign in *Vicksburg Is the Key: The Struggle for the Mississippi River.* Meanwhile, Winschel's 2004 book, *Triumph and Defeat: The Vicksburg Campaign,* briefly touches on Union engineering during the siege in the chapter "Spades Are Trump." This chapter, like Steven E. Woodworth's account of the siege in *Nothing but Victory: The Army of the Tennessee, 1861–1865,* emphasizes Logan's Approach as the prime example of Union siege operations. As both historians correctly note, this particular federal approach, due to its various levels of success, warrants special attention.[5]

Meanwhile, Michael Ballard has emerged as the foremost authority on all things Vicksburg. His 2004 book, *Vicksburg: The Campaign That Opened the Mississippi,* attempts to provide a "new military history" of the entire campaign. This blend of traditional military history and social history, though placing a strong emphasis on strategy and tactics, addresses the holistic experience of war. This results in a brief chapter on the Vicksburg siege that focuses predominantly on the experience of positional warfare. Ballard's most recent book, *Grant at Vicksburg: The General and the Siege,* examines the role of the Army of the Tennessee's commander during the siege. In this study, Ballard does an exceptional job explaining how the Vicksburg siege contributed to Grant's military development and dispels many defamatory myths about the general.[6]

Some have attempted to analyze engineering during the Vicksburg Campaign. For example, in 1992 Major Robert M. Puckett submitted his master's thesis, "Engineering Operations during the Vicksburg Campaign," to committee members at the Army Command and General Staff College at Fort Leavenworth. Puckett's paper examines both Union and Confederate military engineering throughout the entirety of the Vicksburg operations and concludes that successful Union engineering practices led to the downfall of the Gibraltar of the Confederacy. Meanwhile, David F. Bastian's monograph *Grant's Canal: The Union's Attempt to Bypass Vicksburg,* printed in 1995, details the Army of the Tennessee's failed effort to sidestep Vicksburg by means of digging a canal across DeSoto Point, on the opposite side of the Mississippi.

Historical commentary on Civil War engineering stretches back to the early twentieth century. The multivolume series *The Photographic History of the Civil War*, published in 1911 and edited by Francis Trevelyan Miller, attempted to bring together articles, photographs, and veterans' observations about various aspects of the Civil War. U.S. Army captain O. E. Hunt's two essays in the work, "Entrenchments and Fortifications" and "Engineer Corps of the Federal Army," detail both siege craft and Union engineering during the war. Meanwhile, T. M. R Talcott's "Reminiscences of the Confederate Engineer Service" provides a Confederate veteran's account of engineering. All of the essays in the series blend period photographs with narrative accounts and celebrate the sacrifice of both Union and Confederate soldiers.[7]

Periodically, Vicksburg makes a brief appearance in broader engineering studies. For example, James Lynn Nichols's 1957 book, *Confederate Engineers*, provides a short chapter that combines both the Vicksburg and Petersburg campaigns. The section on Vicksburg centers around Confederate engineer Samuel H. Lockett and relies heavily on Lockett's account of the siege, which appeared as an article in the late nineteenth-century *Battles and Leaders of the Civil War* series. Meanwhile, Phillip M. Thienel writes on Union bridge-building during Grant's maneuver campaign in *Mr. Lincoln's Bridge Builders*, and Philip Shiman refers to Vicksburg sporadically in his report "Army Engineers in the War for the Union, 1861–1865." Yet, as in Nichols's study, Vicksburg emerges in both Thienel's and Shiman's histories as a brief example within a broader topical study.[8]

War during the first half of the twentieth century contained unprecedented destructiveness and mass slaughter, leaving many to question the relationship of the Civil War to conflicts past and present. The Vicksburg siege figures into this larger ongoing debate. On the one hand, some historians assert that the American Civil War stands closer to earlier Napoleonic conflicts. On the other, there are those who declare that the contest harbingered the type of modern warfare that bloodied the fields of Western Europe during the First World War. Yet, regardless of this broad theoretical division, most agree that Vicksburg, despite its resemblance to siege craft conducted in the tradition of the French military engineer Sébastien Le Prestre de Vauban, foreshadowed the trench warfare of the future.[9]

Interestingly, observations that trench warfare made the Civil War unique appeared before European armies dug the labyrinth of trench systems that spanned from Belgium to Switzerland by the end of 1914. In 1911, U.S. Army captain O. E. Hunt described Civil War trench warfare as evolutionary and innovative. According to Hunt, neophyte soldiers were hesitant to use entrenchments during the early stages of the war. This changed, and as the conflict continued, veterans learned the advantages of temporary and permanent fieldworks, often digging in without orders from their superiors. In Hunt's analysis, the soldier's propensity to entrench came as a response to the improved weapons technology of the era.[10]

Hunt's commentary on the Civil War's modernity remained ingrained until the late twentieth century. For example, in 1988 Edward Hagerman published in an article, "From Jomini to Dennis Hart Mahan: The Evolution of Trench Warfare and the American Civil War," and later in his classic book *The American Civil War and the Origins of Modern Warfare: Ideas, Organization, and Field Command* that the American Civil War was a modern conflict that, by war's end, resembled World War I. While the United States originally followed in the French Napoleonic tradition at the outbreak of hostilities, "the rifled musket . . . [prompted a] devastating increase in firepower [that] doomed the open frontal assault and ushered in the entrenched battlefield . . . scenes of trench warfare [that] anticipated World War I." Thus, according to Hagerman, the siege of Vicksburg stood closer to modern trench warfare than to the sieges of the Enlightenment. "Grant's operations against the main Vicksburg fortifications constituted 'a conflict,' to quote the Comte de Paris, 'between two entrenched armies rather than a siege in the strictest acceptance of the term.'" But shortly after Hagerman published his book, historians began to question some of his assertions.[11]

British historian Paddy Griffith, also known for his writings on the First World War, has started a cottage industry of questioning the modernity of the American Civil War. According to Griffith, the War of the Rebellion was not a transitional modern war but rather a poorly fought Napoleonic War. The United States Military Academy at West Point, the country's premier engineering institution, produced excellent engineers but mediocre commanders. "It was perhaps significant that the Republic's only official military academy had been built as a college of engineering," Griffith writes, "a version of Napoleon's École Polytechnique which was never balanced, like his." Griffith states, "Graduates of West Point might not have been particularly well versed in the art of commanding infantry or cavalry in battle, but whatever else one might say about them, it is certain that they had a solid grounding in mathematics and military engineering." Griffith goes on to claim that entrenchments during the Civil War provided more psychological than physical protection. Although this British historian is critical of American entrenching, he concedes that the elaborate earthworks around Vicksburg, and later at Chattanooga, Petersburg, and Atlanta, "did indeed eventually come to outclass everything that had gone before" them, thereby suggesting that Civil War fieldworks, entrenchments, and sieges, like Vicksburg, reside in the interstices of Napoleonic and modern warfare.[12]

Some, in more recent years, yield to Griffith's interpretations. Earl Hess, in his trilogy on field fortifications in the eastern theater, borrows from both Griffith and Hunt, arguing that field fortifications evolved over the course of the Civil War and did not result from the widespread use of the rifle-musket during the conflict. Rather, Hess believes that the stress of battle coupled with consistent contact between opposing armies provided the impetus that drove soldiers to entrench. In short, Hess debunks the popular notion that field fortifications in the East originated with Grant's Wilderness Campaign. According to Hess, "There was no sharp break between the Virginia operations of 1861–63 and those of 1864–65."[13]

Debate also rages around the question of who initiated the use of entrenchments and fieldworks in the Union and Confederate armies. Hess deviates from the celebratory tone of Hunt's work, which lauds the ingenuity of the American soldier. "In no other feature of the military art has that same individuality impressed itself more," Hunt wrote, "than in the construction of devices of protection against . . . the enemy." Hess modifies this "bottom up" interpretation of fieldworks, suggesting that soldiers from all ranks initiated the implementation of field fortifications at different times throughout the war. In contrast to both Hess and Hunt, Anthony Saunders in his book *Trench Warfare: 1850–1950* proposes that the officer corps on both sides during the American Civil War spurred the use of entrenchments and thus hypothesizes that the rank and file did not instigate the transition to trench warfare.[14]

Saunders, studying the larger chronology of the evolution of trench fighting from the Crimean War through the early stages of the Korean War, helps situate the American Civil War on the larger spectrum of trench warfare. According to Saunders, the origins of modern trench warfare, which deviated from older forms of siege warfare, date to the investing of Sebastopol during the Crimean War. He defines trench warfare as "military operations between two entrenched armies. . . . In other words, it is mutual siege." Trench warfare, in Saunders's estimation, became a feature of the American Civil War for two reasons. Deviating from Griffith, Saunders believes that the lethality of Civil War firearms hastened the adoption of entrenchments. Saunders, however, riding a middle ground, also borrows from Griffith, writing that the emphasis on engineering and entrenchments taught to cadets at West Point, who later became Civil War officers, influenced their decisions to entrench. With regard to the Civil War, he concludes that this propensity to adopt sophisticated fixed positions both during sieges and in open battle placed this American war closer to the First World War than to its Crimean predecessor, a conflict that placed an emphasis on entrenchments primarily during sieges.[15]

More recently, Nicholas Murray in his book *The Rocky Road to the Great War: The Evolution of Trench Warfare to 1914* argues that the art and construction of field fortifications between 1877 and 1914 made great strides. Although he does not examine the field fortifications of the Civil War in much detail, he believes that they contrasted with later examples. Murray upholds that field fortifications during the post–Civil War period shifted from predominantly above-ground structures with shallow ditches to deeper trenches in response to new weapons innovations, such as more destructive artillery projectiles. He supports his thesis with four case studies: the Russo-Turkish War, the Second Anglo-Boer War, the Russo-Japanese War, and the Balkan Wars. While primarily concerned with more modern conflicts, in an appendix he maintains that the Civil War should still be considered "the last of the old-style wars."[16]

The debate concerning the modernity of the American Civil War continues. In addition to filling in a blank page in Vicksburg's historical record, I hope that this study, *Engineering Victory: The Union Siege of Vicksburg*, contributes to this ongoing discussion. It is my belief that the American Civil War was neither purely Napoleonic nor exclusively modern but rather a transitional period in military history that held to previous maxims while foreshadowing the future. In short, the war was its own military event with its own developmental trajectory.

Abbreviations

ALPL   Abraham Lincoln Presidential Library

CMC   Cincinnati Museum Center

DU   Duke University

LOC   Library of Congress

OCHM   Old Court House Museum

OR   U.S. War Department, *The War of the Rebellion: A Compilation of the Official Records of the Union and Confederate Armies.* All references are to Series I unless otherwise indicated.

ORN   U.S. War Department, *Official Records of the Union and Confederate Navies in the War of the Rebellion.* All references are to Series I unless otherwise indicated.

RBHPC   Rutherford B. Hayes Presidential Center

USMA   United States Military Academy, West Point

VNMP   Vicksburg National Military Park

Notes

Introduction:
With a Spade in One Hand and a Gun in the Other

1. Fowler and Miller, *History of the Thirtieth Iowa*, 29–30.
2. Wheeler, *Siege of Vicksburg*, 183; Charles A. Hobbs, "Vanquishing Vicksburg: The Campaign Which Ended in the Surrender of America's Gibraltar," *National Tribune*, March 10, 1892.
3. Hobbs, "Vanquishing Vicksburg," March 10, 1892; *OR*, vol. 24, pt. 2, 177.
4. Woodworth, *Nothing but Victory*, ix; Hagerman, *American Civil War*, 204; William Lucius Rand to his father, June 20, 1863, box 1, Rand Family Papers, ALPL.
5. "The Army in Crisis," *New York Times*, October 16, 1864.

1. The Engineer's Art

1. Greene, *Letters to My Wife*, 67.
2. Ballard, *Vicksburg*, 343–44.
3. Greene, *Letters to My Wife*, 344–49; Mahan, *Memoirs*, 124–25.
4. Scott, *History of the 67th*, 38.
5. I. Richards to unknown recipient, May 22, 1863, Seventeenth Ohio Light Artillery file, VNMP; Greene, *Letters to My Wife*, 69; Stockton, *War Diary*, 16; unidentified soldier's diary, May 22, 1863, Seventeenth Ohio Light Artillery file, VNMP.
6. Woodworth, *Nothing but Victory*, 315–31.
7. Ibid., 315–90; Woodworth, *Decision in the Heartland*, 58–64.
8. Woodworth, *Decision in the Heartland*, 66.
9. Shea and Winschel, *Vicksburg Is the Key*, 145–46; Sherman, *Memoirs*, 1:325–26.
10. *OR*, vol. 24, pt. 2, 170; Trimble, *History of the Ninety-Third*, 98.
11. *OR*, vol. 24, pt. 2, 181, 206–7; Stockton, *War Diary*, 16.

12. Scott, *History of the 67th*, 36–37; OR, vol. 24, pt. 2, 170; Ballard, *Vicksburg*, 348; Hopkins, *Under the Flag*, 65.

13. Howard, *History of the 124th*, 105; Crummer, *Grant at Fort Donelson*, 114; Hickenlooper, "Personal Reminiscences," folder 2, 135, CMC; Newland, "Surrender of Vicksburg"; Morris, Hartwell, and Kuykendall, *History 31st Regiment*, 70; Joel W. Strong, "Civil War Narrative of Captain Joel W. Strong," 14, Tenth Missouri Infantry file, OCHM.

14. Grant, *Personal Memoirs*, 1:532; Jefferson Brumback to Kate, May 23, 1863, Ninety-Fifth Ohio Infantry file, VNMP.

15. Weigley, *History of the United States Army*, 105; Morrison, *Best School*, 2.

16. Millett and Peter Maslowski, *For the Common Defense*, 134; Morrison, *Best School*, 3; James B. McPherson to Sardis Birchard, March 24, 1854, Sardis Birchard Collection, RBHPC; James B. McPherson to Catherine Stem, February 13, 1853, Stem Family Collection, RBHPC; Moten, *Delafield Commission*, 32, 68; Weigley, *History of the United States Army*, 106.

17. *Centennial*, 275–76.

18. Ibid., 276; Hagerman, "From Jomini," 199–201.

19. Guth, "Mahan, Dennis Hart"; Abbot, *Memoir of Dennis Hart Mahan*, 31–32; Millett and Maslowski, *For the Common Defense*, 133.

20. Abbot, *Memoir of Dennis Hart Mahan*, 35–36.

21. U.S. Military Academy, *Official Register*, 9; Comstock, *Diary*, 166.

22. Comstock, *Diary*, 166; U.S. Military Academy, *Official Register*, 9.

23. Comstock, *Diary*, 167, 200; Hagerman, "From Jomini," 203–4.

24. Abbot, *Memoir of Dennis Hart Mahan*, 32; Millett and Maslowski, *For the Common Defense*, 278; Guth, "Mahan, Dennis Hart."

25. Guth, "Mahan, Dennis Hart"; Abbot, *Memoir of Dennis Hart Mahan*, 34; Millett and Maslowski, *For the Common Defense*, 134; *Centennial*, 278–79.

26. Morrison, *Best School*, 91; Skelton, *American Profession*, 168.

27. Morrison, *Best School*, 94–95.

28. Mahan, *Complete Treatise*, 224–46; Mahan, *Summary*, 319–339.

29. Duffy, *Fire and Stone*, 11; Mahan, *Summary*, 228.

30. Mahan, *Complete Treatise*, 224–27.

31. Ibid., 227–28.

32. Ibid., 228–29.

33. Childs, *Warfare*, 144.

34. Mahan, *Complete Treatise*, 228–235; Childs, *Warfare*, 144.

35. Mahan, *Complete Treatise*, 229–31; J. C. Duane, *Manual*, 88–98.

36. Mahan, *Complete Treatise*, 233–34; Duane, *Manual*, 67–78.

37. Duane, *Manual*, 99; Mahan, *Complete Treatise*, 234–35.

38. Mahan, *Complete Treatise*, 236–39; Alger, *Definitions*, 54.

39. Mahan, *Complete Treatise*, 239; Duane, *Manual*, 207–30; Mahan, *Summary*, 250–56.

40. James B. McPherson to Catherine Stem, February 13, 1853; James B. McPherson to Sardis Birchard, March 24, 1854. For information on McPherson's brief stint teaching engineering at West Point, see Moten, *Delafield Commission*, 71.

41. *Centennial*, 415–16; Morrison, *Best School*, 97–98.

42. See editor's note in Comstock, *Diary*, 215, for Duane's class standing; Duane, *Manual*, 51–265.

43. Comstock, *Diary*, 155, 163, 193.

44. Morrison, *Best School*, 100–101.

45. Ibid., 115–21.

2. *America's Early Sieges*

1. Middlekauff, *Glorious Cause*, 559–68.

2. Martin, *Ordinary Courage*, 135; Middlekauff, *Glorious Cause*, 568.

3. Middlekauff, *Glorious Cause*, 568–69.

4. Ibid., 569–70; Martin, *Ordinary Courage*, 137–39.

5. Bauer, *Mexican War*, 232–36.

6. Ibid., 237–44; Johnson, *Gallant Little Army*, 35.

7. Bauer, *Mexican War*, 245; Johnson, *Gallant Little Army*, 25–26; McClellan, *Mexican War Diary*, 80–81; Warner, *Generals in Gray*, 180; Warner, *Generals in Blue*, 180; Moten, *Delafield Commission*, 102.

8. Johnson, *Gallant Little Army*, 27–28, 32; McClellan, *Mexican War Diary*, 84.

9. McClellan, *Mexican War Diary*, 91; Mahan, *Complete Treatise*, 227; Duane, *Manual*, 85–90.

10. Johnson, *Gallant Little Army*, 31–32; McClellan, *Mexican War Diary*, 88, 91–92.

11. Smith, *Company "A,"* 23.

12. McClellan, *Mexican War Diary*, 91, 93, 95, 98; Duane, *Manual*, 261; Duffy, *Fire and Stone*, 183–86.

13. McClellan, *Mexican War Diary*, 93; Bauer, *Mexican War*, 247; Johnson, *Gallant Little Army*, 32.

14. Johnson, *Gallant Little Army*, 32–33; Bauer, *Mexican War*, 250.

15. Johnson, *Gallant Little Army*, 37–38; McClellan, *Mexican War Diary*, 92, 96.

16. McClellan, *Mexican War Diary*, 97; Johnson, *Gallant Little Army*, 40, 42–46, 48–49; Bauer, *Mexican War*, 322.

17. Walter G. Bartholomew file, USMA.

18. Moten, *Delafield Commission*, 88–104.

19. Ibid., 108–41, 149–50; Watson, *Sieges*, 57–81.

20. Moten, *Delafield Commission*, 150–51; Mahan, *Summary*, 352; Mahan, *Elementary Course*, 270.

21. Moten, *Delafield Commission*, 149–55; Mahan, *Elementary Course*, 275; J. Black, *Age of Total War*, 35–36.

22. Mahan, *Elementary Course*, 351–52; Mahan, *Summary*, 351.

23. Mahan, *Elementary Course*, 266, 269.

24. Thienel, "Engineers," 36.

25. Woodworth, *This Great Struggle*, 36; Thienel, "Engineers," 36.

26. Thienel, "Engineers," 36.

27. Ibid., 36–38; Hess, *Field Armies*, 70.

28. Symonds, *Battlefield Atlas*, 25, 27; Hess, *Field Armies*, 69.

29. Hess, *Field Armies*, 71, 78–83; Alexander, *Fighting for the Confederacy*, 75.

30. Hess, *Field Armies*, 69–70; McClellan, *McClellan's Own Story*, 119; Barnard and Barry, *Report*, 13–69.

31. Sears, *To the Gates*, 42–62; Symonds, *Battlefield Atlas*, 29.

32. Mahan, *Complete Treatise*, 224; Hess, *Field Armies*, 73, 91.

33. Sears, *To the Gates*, 57; Hess, *Field Armies*, 74, 78, 87.

34. Hess, *Field Armies*, 77.

3. Preparing to Dig Them Out

1. Bently, *History of the 77th Illinois*, 162–63; Loop, "Campaigning with the Buckeyes"; Mahan, *Complete Treatise*, 224, 232.

2. Mahan, *Complete Treatise*, 226–27; Grant, *Personal Memoirs*, 1:536.

3. *OR*, vol. 24, pt. 2, 168; Mahan, *Complete Treatise*, 225; Badeau, *Military History*, 301.

4. Porter, *Naval History*, 320–22.

5. *OR*, vol. 24, pt. 2, 168; Grant, *Personal Memoirs*, 1:535–37, 543–46; Grabau, *Ninety-Eight Days*, 424, 613. Grant asserted that Herron's division arrived on June 11 while Grabau claims that Herron's division did not arrive until June 13.

6. Grant, *Personal Memoirs*, 1:536–38; Swigart, "Vicksburg Campaign."

7. Grant, *Personal Memoirs*, 1:536.

8. Morris, Hartwell, and Kuykendall, *History 31st Regiment*, 69–70; Baker, "Memoirs of Francis R. Baker," SC 69, ALPL; Bering and Montgomery, *History of the Forty-Eighth Ohio*, 88–89; Woodworth, *Nothing but Victory*, 425; *OR*, vol. 24, pt. 3, 341–42, 348; Sherman, *Memoirs*, 1:328; Simon, *Papers of Ulysses S. Grant*, 249; Grant, *Personal Memoirs*, 1:534.

9. *OR*, vol., 24, pt. 3, 343.

10. Giambrone, *Illustrated Guide*, 221; James H. Wilson Journal, May 23, 1863, Manuscript Division, LOC.

11. Greene, *Letters to My Wife*, 69; letter from I. Richards to unknown recipient, May 23, 1863, Seventeenth Ohio Light Artillery file, VNMP.

12. A. Marshall, *Army Life*, 245; *OR*, vol. 24, pt. 3, 348.

13. "Death List of a Day. Major Frederick E. Prime," *New York Times*, August 14, 1900.

14. Grant, *Personal Memoirs*, 1:536–37; Giambrone, *Illustrated Guide*, 181, 184, 186, 202; OR, vol. 24, pt. 2, 171; Bearss, *Unvexed to the Sea*, 885–86; Hickenlooper, "Our Volunteer Engineers," 304. A division headquarters staff typically contained a line officer serving in the capacity of an engineer.

15. Andrew Hickenlooper, "Personal Reminiscences," folder 3, 5–7, CMC.

16. Ibid., 8–12, 25–26.

17. Ibid., 12–13.

18. Ibid., 13–16, 22, 24–25.

19. Ibid., 33–38; 49–81; Hickenlooper, "Our Volunteer Engineers," 303–4; "Andrew Hickenlooper," 148–49.

20. Simpson, *Ulysses S. Grant*, 111; Hickenlooper, "Our Volunteer Engineers," 304; Grant, *Personal Memoirs*, 1:537; Badeau, *Military History*, 338; OR, vol. 24, pt. 2, 170, 177.

21. OR, vol. 24, pt. 2, 170, 177; Badeau, *Military History*, 338.

22. OR, vol. 24, pt. 2, 177–79.

23. Ibid.; "William L. Jenney," 169; Giambrone, *Illustrated Guide*, 186; Bearss, *Unvexed to the Sea*, 892.

24. OR, vol. 24, pt. 2, 177–78, 192; "Mustered Out," H. C. Freeman obituary, *National Tribune*, November 8, 1900; Bearss, *Unvexed to the Sea*, 892; Ballard, *Vicksburg*, 373; Mason, "Vicksburg Campaign."

25. Mason, *Forty-Second Ohio Infantry*, 227.

26. OR, vol. 24, pt. 2, 171; Grant, *Personal Memoirs*, 1:540–41; Hickenlooper, "Our Volunteer Engineers," 304.

27. Neal, *Illustrated History*, 9, 12, 15, 68; Dyer, *Compendium*, 1320.

28. Dyer, *Compendium*, 1197; Bearss, *Unvexed to the Sea*, 886; OR, vol. 24, pt. 2, 171; Dyer, *Compendium*, 1197; Bearss, *Unvexed to the Sea*, 886; OR, vol. 24, pt. 2, 171; OR, vol. 24, pt. 3, 370.

4. Earthworks Rose as by Magic

1. Morris, Hartwell, and Kuykendall, *History 31st Regiment*, 70.

2. Mahan, *Complete Treatise*, 226–27.

3. Badeau, *Military History*, 335; James H. Wilson Journal, May 29, 1863, Manuscript Division, LOC; Grant, *Personal Memoirs*, 1:538; A. Marshall, *Army Life*, 251; Gerard, *Diary*, 49.

4. Grant, *Personal Memoirs*, 1:546; Charles A. Hobbs, "Vanquishing Vicksburg: The Campaign Which Ended in the Surrender of America's Gibraltar," *National Tribune*, March 24, 1892.

5. Mahan, *Summary*, 309, 311; Grabau, *Ninety-Eight Days*, 421.

6. Mahan, *Summary*, 309, 311; S. Q. A. Diary, Tuesday, May 19, 1863, Fifth Iowa Infantry file, VNMP.

7. Mahan, Summary, 311; History of the Sixteenth Battery, 72–73.

8. Howard, *History of the 124th*, 112; Hobbs, "Vanquishing Vicksburg," March 24, 1892.

9. Mahan, *Summary*, 311; Hobbs, "Vanquishing Vicksburg," March 24, 1892; Badeau, *Military History*, 333–34; Grabau, *Ninety-Eight Days*, 419–28, 422; Simon, *Papers of Ulysses S. Grant*, 276, 281, 284–85; Brown, *History of the Fourth Regiment*, 228, 230; OR, vol. 24, pt. 3, 372; Isaiah Richards to all at home, May 30, 1863, Seventeenth Ohio Light Artillery file, VNMP; Bearss, *Unvexed to the Sea*, 1260.

10. Kellogg, *Vicksburg Campaign*, 49; Mason, *Forty-Second Ohio Infantry*, 228.

11. Lieutenant Antony B. Burton Diary, June 12, 1863, SC 2401, ALPL.

12. Ibid.

13. Mahan, *Summary*, 309–16; OR, vol. 24, pt. 2, 181; Fuller, *History of the Trials*, 70; Stockton, *War Diary*, 17; Mason, *Forty-Second Ohio Infantry*, 226–27; OR, vol. 24, pt. 2, 176, 181.

14. Unidentified soldier diary, May 23, 1863, Seventeenth Ohio Light Artillery file, VNMP; Isaiah Richards to dearly loved ones at home, May 19 and 21, 1863, and Isaiah Richards to Captain Wm. T. Rigby, November 27, 1903, Seventeenth Ohio Light Artillery file, VNMP; William H. Raynor to Captain Rigby, July 18, 1902, Fifty-Sixth Ohio Infantry file, VNMP; Grabau, *Ninety-Eight Days*, 20–22; OR, vol. 24, pt. 2, 169.

15. Grabau, *Ninety-Eight Days*, 48, 408; Burton Diary, Monday, June 1, 1863.

16. Jefferson Brumback to Kate, June 21, 1863, Ninety-Fifth Ohio Infantry file, VNMP; OR, vol. 24, pt. 2, 176; Hickenlooper, "Personal Reminiscences," 139, CMC.

17. Hobbs, "Vanquishing Vicksburg," March 24, 1892; OR, vol. 24, pt. 2, 176; Hickenlooper, "Personal Reminiscences," 139–40; Jefferson Brumback to Kate, June 21, 1863.

18. Hobbs, "Vanquishing Vicksburg," March 24, 1892.

19. Duane, *Manual*; Hickenlooper, "Personal Reminiscences," 139; Hobbs, "Vanquishing Vicksburg," March 24, 1892.

20. Sherman, *Memoirs*, 2:396; Sanborn, "Remarks on a Motion," 617–18.

21. Fletcher, *History of Company A*, 102.

22. Unidentified soldier diary, May 21, June 5, 1863, Seventeenth Ohio Light Artillery file, VNMP.

23. Howard, *History of the 124th*, 111; OR, vol. 24, pt. 3, 175; Joseph Bowker Diary, May 28, 1863, Forty-Second Ohio Infantry file, VNMP; Hicks, "Campaign and Capture," 104–5; W. R. Halsey Diary, May 27, 1863, Seventy-Second Ohio Infantry file, VNMP; Swigart, "Vicksburg Campaign"; Hobbs, "Vanquishing Vicksburg,"

March 24, 1892; A. Marshall, *Army Life*, 248; Jefferson Brumback to Kate, May 31, 1863, Ninety-Fifth Ohio Infantry file, VNMP; Isaiah Richards to Wm. T. Rigby, July 13, 1903, Seventeenth Ohio Light Artillery file, VNMP; unidentified soldier diary, May 23, 1863, Seventeenth Ohio Light Artillery file, VNMP.

24. I. Richards to all at home, June 15, 1863, Seventeenth Ohio Light Artillery file, VNMP; Joel W. Strong, "Civil War Narrative of Captain Joel W. Strong," Tenth Missouri Infantry file, OCHM.

25. S. C. Beck, *A True Sketch of His Army Life*, 124th Illinois Infantry file, OCHM.

26. Rood, *Story of the Service*, 191; Barney, *Recollections*, 190; S. Black, *Soldier's Recollections*, 51.

27. Unidentified soldier diary, May 20, 1863, Seventeenth Ohio Light Artillery file, VNMP; Morris, Hartwell, and Kuykendall, *History 31st Regiment*, 69; Crummer, *Grant at Fort Donelson*, 115; Wagner, "Hasty Intrenchments," 226; Charles A. Hobbs, "Vanquishing Vicksburg: The Campaign Which Ended in the Surrender of America's Gibraltar," *National Tribune*, March 17, 1892.

28. Mahan, *Complete Treatise*, 231; Morris, Hartwell, and Kuykendall, *History 31st Regiment*, 70; Hobbs, "Vanquishing Vicksburg," March 17, 1892; P. C. Hains to W. B. Scates, June 1, 1863, John McClernand Papers, box 24, ALPL; T. Marshall, *History of the Eighty-Third Ohio*, 89; Kellogg, *Vicksburg Campaign*, 47; Stockton, *War Diary*, 71; Elder, *Damned Iowa Greyhound*.

29. Barney, *Recollections*, 190; Grant, *Personal Memoirs*, 1:538.

30. W. F. Jones, "Besieging a Stronghold," *National Tribune*, February 15, 1900; "My Civil War Memoirs. And Other Reminiscences as Written by my Father. W. R. Eddington," p. 10, SC 441, W. R. Eddington Papers, ALPL.

31. Hobbs, "Vanquishing Vicksburg," March 17, 1892.

32. T. Marshall, *History of the Eighty-Third Ohio*, 90; Mahan, *Summary*, 294; *Reminiscences of a Boy's Service*, 57.

33. Raum, "With the Western Army"; Rood, *Story of the Service*, 193; Oldroyd, *Soldier's Story*, 34; Orange Perret Diary, Wednesday, June 3, 1863, Seventy-Seventh Illinois Infantry file, VNMP; Kiper, *Dear Catherine*, 114; Bro. William to "Dear Brother," May 27, 1863, Russell Family Papers, ALPL; McDonald, *History of the 30th Illinois*, 49; Fowler and Miller, *History of the Thirtieth Iowa*, 31; T. Williams, *Historical Sketch*, 54–55; Campbell, *Union Must Stand*, 105.

34. Oldroyd, *Soldier's Story*, 34; William Franklin Patterson to "My Own Dear Wife," May 28, 1863, Container No. 1, Manuscript Division, LOC; Beck, *A True Sketch of His Army Life*; Campbell, *Union Must Stand*, 103, 105; Hopkins, *Under the Flag*, 67; S. S. Massett to "Dear Companion," May 29, 1863, misc. file, DU; Charles A. Hobbs, "Vanquishing Vicksburg: The Campaign Which Ended in the Surrender of America's Gibraltar," *National Tribune*, April 7, 1892.

35. Hobbs, "Vanquishing Vicksburg," March 17, 1892; Jones, "Besieging a Stronghold," February 15, 1900.

36. Mahan, *Summary*, 294; *My Civil War Memoirs*, 10; Jones, "Besieging a Stronghold," February 15, 1900; Willison, *Reminiscences*, 57; Hobbs, "Vanquishing Vicksburg," March 17, 1892; Rood, *Story of the Service*, 191–92; Barney, *Recollections*, 190.

37. Grant, *Personal Memoirs*, 1:532; L. P. Jessup Diary, May 19, 1863, Twenty-Fourth Indiana Infantry file, VNMP.

38. Grant, *Personal Memoirs*, 1:532; L. P. Jessup Diary, May 19, 1863; McDonald, *History of the 30th Illinois*, 47; Jones, "Besieging a Stronghold," February 15, 1900; Morris, Hartwell, and Kuykendall, *History 31st Regiment*, 68.

39. Scott, *History of the 67th*, 36; Ira Blanchard, typescript of regimental history, Twentieth Illinois Infantry, folder 75-31, ALPL; William H. Raynor Diary, May 21, 1863, Fifty-Sixth Ohio Infantry file, VNMP; Grant, *Personal Memoirs*, 1:540.

40. *OR*, vol. 24, pt. 2, 187; Grant, *Personal Memoirs*, 1:534–35.

41. *OR*, vol. 24, pt. 2, 188.

42. Neal, *Illustrated History*, 98. Colonel Bissell resigned from command of Bissell's Engineer Regiment of the West on May 27, 1863. *OR*, vol. 24, pt. 2, 187–88; Loop, "Campaigning with the Buckeyes"; Fletcher, *History of Company A*, 99–100; Grabau, *Ninety-Eight Days*, 440; S. Black, *Soldier's Recollections*, 51–52; Hobbs, "Vanquishing Vicksburg," March 24, 1892.

43. For this entry, see Edmund Newsome memoir, *Experience in the War*, insert between May 31 and June 3, 1863, entry, and Eighty-First Illinois Infantry file, OCHM. Howe, *What Hath God Wrought*, 690–98; Wells, *Siege of Vicksburg*, 71; E. Williams. *Extracts*, 70–71.

44. Simon, *Papers of Ulysses S. Grant*, 264–65, 273; Simpson and Berlin, *Sherman's Civil War*, 472; Winters, *Musick of the Mocking Birds*, 56–57.

45. Hickenlooper, "Personal Reminiscences," 138; Mason, *Forty-Second Ohio Infantry*, 226; Crummer, *Grant at Fort Donelson*, 143.

46. Swigart, "Vicksburg Campaign"; Crummer, *Grant at Fort Donelson*, 143; Willison, *Reminiscences*, 57; Burt, "Letters from the Trenches."

47. Burt, "Letters from the Trenches"; Sergeant James H. Lewis to unknown recipient, June 5, 1863, Twenty-Fourth Iowa Infantry file, VNMP.

48. Kellogg, *Vicksburg Campaign*, 46–47; William H. Raynor Diary, May 24, 1863.

49. James H. Lewis to unknown recipient, June 5, 1863, Twenty-Fourth Iowa Infantry file, VNMP.

50. Newsome, *Experience in the War*, 18, Eighty-First Illinois Infantry file, OCHM; Mason, *Forty-Second Ohio Infantry*, 220; Mahan, *Complete Treatise*, 227.

51. Stockton, *War Diary*, 105; Morris, Hartwell, and Kuykendall, *History 31st Regiment*, 72; Sherman, *Memoirs*, 1:328; Grant, *Personal Memoirs*, 1:540; Simon, *Papers of Ulysses S. Grant*, 295.

5. More Roads to Rome Than One

1. National Park Service, Vicksburg National Military Park.
2. Mahan, *Complete Treatise*, 224, 227; Mahan, *Summary*, 294.
3. OR, vol. 24, pt. 2, 331; Grant, *Personal Memoirs*, 1:538; Badeau, *Military History*, 339; Mason, *Forty-Second Ohio Infantry*, 227; Mahan, *Complete Treatise*, 231–32.
4. OR, vol. 24, pt. 3, 343–44, 348; pt. 2, 188, 199; Simpson and Berlin, *Sherman's Civil War*, 471, 473; Raum, "With the Western Army"; Warner, *Generals in Blue*, 390–91; Mahan, *Complete Treatise*, 228.
5. Bearss, *Unvexed to the Sea*, 885–957; Mason, *Forty-Second Ohio Infantry*, 227; OR, vol. 24, pt. 2, 171.
6. OR, vol. 24, pt. 2, 171–75; Badeau, *Military History*, 338–39; Pryce. *Vanishing Footprints*, 132.
7. A. Marshall, *Army Life*, 252; Woods, *Services of the Ninety-Sixth Ohio*, 30; McDonald, *History of the 30th Illinois*, 50.
8. Loop, "Campaigning with the Buckeyes"; Charles A. Hobbs, "Vanquishing Vicksburg: The Campaign Which Ended in the Surrender of America's Gibraltar," *National Tribune*, March 17, 1892.
9. Mahan, *Complete Treatise*, 228; Jenney, "Personal Recollections of Vicksburg," 247–65; OR, vol. 24, pt. 2, 170; Mason, *Forty-Second Ohio Infantry*, 227; OR, vol. 24, pt. 3, 348.
10. Woodworth, *Nothing but Victory*, 425–55, 428–29; Simon, *Papers of Ulysses S. Grant*, 266; Andrew Hickenlooper, "Personal Reminiscences," folder 3, 137, CMC.
11. Kellogg, *Vicksburg Campaign*, 48; Lockett, "Defense of Vicksburg," 489; A. Marshall, *Army Life*, 245; Joseph Stockton Diary, May 25, 1863, ALPL.
12. Kellogg, *Vicksburg Campaign*, 48; Hickenlooper, "Vicksburg Mine, 540.
13. Duane, *Manual*, 85–92; Mahan, *Complete Treatise*, 231.
14. Hickenlooper, "Vicksburg Mine," 539.
15. Hickenlooper, "Personal Reminiscences," folder 3, 137–38.
16. Bearss, *Unvexed to the Sea*, 935; Hobbs, "Vanquishing Vicksburg," March 17, 1892.
17. Hickenlooper, "Personal Reminiscences," folder 3, 139.
18. Ibid.; Oldroyd, *Soldier's Story*, 36; Lockett, "Defense of Vicksburg," 490; Giambrone, *Illustrated Guide*, 240.
19. Lockett, "Defense of Vicksburg," 490.
20. Ibid., 484, 490.
21. Mason, *Forty-Second Ohio Infantry*, 227; unidentified soldier diary, May 19, 1863, Seventeenth Ohio Light Artillery file, VNMP; Willison, *Reminiscences*, 56; A. Marshall, *Army Life*, 251.

22. William E. Strong, "Campaign against Vicksburg," 313–54; J. Q. A. Campbell Diary, May 19, 1863, Fifth Iowa, VNMP.

23. Simpson and Berlin, *Sherman's Civil War*, 472.

24. Ibid.; Willison, *Reminiscences*, 56.

25. *OR*, vol. 24, pt. 2, 182; ibid., 183; Barber, *Army Memoirs*, 111; *OR*, vol. 24, pt. 2, 182–83.

26. Bearss, *Unvexed to the Sea*, 889.

27. Duane, *Manual*, 193–200; *OR*, vol. 24, pt. 2, 171–72.

28. Captain W. T. Rigby to C. A. Lucas, February 25, 1904, Twenty-Fourth Iowa file, VNMP; Downing, *Downing's Civil War Diary*, 120–21; Charles A. Hobbs, "Vanquishing Vicksburg: The Campaign Which Ended in the Surrender of America's Gibraltar," *National Tribune*, March 24, 1892; Crooke, *Twenty-First Regiment*, 108; Committee of the Regiment, *Story of the Fifty-Fifth Regiment*, 248. For examples of soldiers all along the front digging at night, see Daniel G. Wineger to Elvira, May 31, 1863, SC 2107, Daniel G. Winegar Letters, ALPL; and Cyrus E. Dickey to "My Dear Sister," June 17, 1863, Wallace-Dickey Papers, box 2, ALPL.

29. B. to "My dear Kate," June 21, 1863, Ninety-Fifth Ohio file, VNMP.

30. Grant, *Personal Memoirs*, 1:540; George Ditto Diary, June 11, 1863, SC 2192, ALPL; *OR*, vol. 24, pt. 2, 177.

31. Bearss, *Unvexed to the Sea*, 932; Remley qtd. in Holcomb, *Southern Sons*, 72.

32. "Your Soldier Boy" "to all at Home," no date, Seventeenth Ohio Light Artillery file, VNMP; *OR*, vol. 24, pt. 2, 177.

33. E. H. Ingraham to "Dear Aunt," June 16, 1863, SC 802, E. H. Ingraham Letters, ALPL.

6. The School of the Sap

1. *OR*, vol. 24, pt. 2, 176; Duane, *Manual*, 99, 148; Mahan, *Summary*, 295–98; Mahan, *Complete Treatise*, 234.

2. Mahan, *Complete Treatise*, 234; Duane, *Manual*, 148.

3. Mahan, *Summary*, 295–97.

4. Ibid., 296–97.

5. Ibid., 297; Duane, *Manual*, 147.

6. *OR*, vol. 24, pt. 2, 331; Mahan, *Complete Treatise*, 231–32; Grant, *Personal Memoirs*, 1:538; Badeau, *Military History*, 339.

7. *OR*, vol. 24, pt. 2, 176–77; Woods, *Services of the Ninety-Sixth Ohio*, 29–30.

8. *OR*, vol. 24, pt. 2, 333.

9. Simon, *Papers of Ulysses S. Grant*, 359; Hickenlooper, "Vicksburg Mine," 540–41.

10. Strong, "Campaign against Vicksburg," 338; S. C. Beck, *A True Sketch of His Army Life*, 124th Illinois Infantry file, OCHM.

11. Loop, "Campaigning with the Buckeyes"; Gerard, *Diary*, 52.

12. B. to "My dear Kate," June 21, 1863, Ninety-Fifth Ohio Infantry file, VNMP.

13. Bearss, *Unvexed to the Sea*, 942.

14. Woodworth, *Nothing but Victory*, 431; OR, vol. 24, pt. 1, 103; Kiper, *Major General John Alexander McClernand*, 270–71; Cresap, *Appomattox Commander*, 99.

15. *Register of the Officers and Cadets*, 6; OR, vol. 24, pt. 1, 107; Bearss, *Unvexed to the Sea*, 933.

16. Bearss, *Unvexed to the Sea*, 890–94, 910–12; Simpson and Berlin, *Sherman's Civil War*, 476, 478–79.

17. OR, vol. 24, pt. 1, 107.

18. Ibid.

19. P. C. Hains to W. B. Scates, June 8, 1863, box 24, John McClernand Papers, ALPL; OR, vol. 24, pt. 2, 183; Simon, *Papers of Ulysses S. Grant*, 371; Edward N. Potter Diary, May 29–June 7, 1863, Twenty-Ninth Wisconsin Infantry file, VNMP; Mason, *Forty-Second Ohio*, 227; Bearss, *Unvexed to the Sea*, 933, 941.

20. Swigart, "Vicksburg Campaign."

21. Ibid.

22. Mahan, *Complete Treatise*, 234–35.

23. Mahan, *Summary*, 293.

24. Crummer, *Grant at Fort Donelson*, 118; OR, vol. 24, pt. 2, 180; Hickenlooper, "Personal Reminiscences," folder 3, 140, CMC; Morris, Hartwell, and Kuykendall, *History 31st Regiment*, 71; unidentified soldier diary, May 23, 1863, Seventeenth Ohio Light Artillery file, VNMP.

25. OR, vol. 24, pt. 2, 183; Bearss, *Unvexed to the Sea*, 933; T. Marshall, *History of the Eighty-Third Ohio*, 91; C. A. Lucas to W. T. Rigby, February 25, 1904, Twenty-Fourth Iowa file, VNMP.

26. A. Marshall, *Army Life*, 256; Charles A. Hobbs, "Vanquishing Vicksburg: The Campaign Which Ended in the Surrender of America's Gibraltar," *National Tribune*, March 24, 1892.

27. Hobbs, "Vanquishing Vicksburg," March 24, 1892.

28. OR, vol. 24, pt. 2, 184; Hobbs, "Vanquishing Vicksburg," March 24, 1892.

29. Isaiah Richards to "Dearly loved ones at home," May 19 and 21, 1863, Seventeenth Ohio Light Artillery file, VNMP; "My Civil War Memoirs. And Other Reminiscences as Written by my Father. W. R. Eddington," SC 441, W. R. Eddington Papers, ALPL.

30. Bearss, *Unvexed to the Sea*, 908; OR, vol. 24, pt. 2, 199; Hickenlooper, "Personal Reminiscences," folder 3, 141.

31. Wells, *Siege of Vicksburg*, 76; Francis R. Baker, "Memoirs of Francis R. Baker," p. 18, SC 69, ALPL; LaBounty, *Civil War Diaries*, 3–24; W. A. Lorimer to William T. Rigby, May 16, 1904, Seventeenth Illinois Infantry file, VNMP; Campbell, *Union Must Stand*, 105; George Ditto Diary, June 20, 1863, SC 2192, ALPL.

32. Beck, *A True Sketch of His Army Life*; William A. Lorimer Memoir, June 1914, Seventeenth Illinois Infantry file, VNMP; Fletcher, *History of Company A*, 104–5.

33. Hickenlooper, "Personal Reminiscences," folder 3, 142; Mahan, *Summary*, 296.

34. Hickenlooper, "Personal Reminiscences," folder 3, 142.

35. Ibid.

36. Bearss, *Unvexed to the Sea*, 910; OR, vol. 24, pt. 2, 200.

37. Lockett, "Defense of Vicksburg," 491.

38. OR, vol. 24, pt. 2, 202, 332; Hickenlooper, "Vicksburg Mine," 540; Lockett, "Defense of Vicksburg," 491; Hickenlooper, "Personal Reminiscences," folder 3, 144–45.

39. Hickenlooper, "Personal Reminiscences," folder 3, 142–43.

40. Ibid., 143.

41. Ibid.

42. Simpson and Berlin, *Sherman's Civil War*, 479.

43. Grant, *Personal Memoirs*, 1:532.

7. The Body Snatchers

1. Pryce, *Vanishing Footprints*, 134; Chaplain W. M. Baker Diary, June 13, 1863, 116th Illinois Infantry file, VNMP.

2. Doughty and Gruber et al., *Warfare*, 36–39.

3. Mahan, *Complete Treatise*, 231–35.

4. These distances are approximations measured on satellite photos provided by Google Earth. Also see map in Bearss, *Unvexed to the Sea*, 906, for info on Logan's Approach. For distances of Carr's right and left approaches, see Bearss, *Unvexed to the Sea*, 935; for an example of the Third Louisiana Redan referred to as "Fort Hill," see OR, vol. 24, pt. 2, 200.

5. Mason, *Forty-Second Ohio Infantry*, 227.

6. Ibid.; Albert Chipman to "Dear Wife," June 2, 1863, Albert Chipman Papers, box 1, ALPL; OR, vol. 24, pt. 2, 183; Badeau, *Military History*, 347; OR, vol. 24, pt. 2, 185; Bearss, *Unvexed to the Sea*, 891–901, 936.

7. Morris, Hartwell, and Kuykendall, *History 31st Regiment*, 71; Kellogg, *Vicksburg Campaign*, 49.

8. Committee of the Regiment, *Story of the Fifty-Fifth Regiment*, 248–49; George Ditto Diary, June 7, 1863, SC 2192, ALPL; Charles A. Hobbs, "Vanquishing Vicksburg: The Campaign Which Ended in the Surrender of America's Gibraltar," *National Tribune*, March 24, 1892; Mason, *Forty-Second Ohio Infantry*, 228.

9. Mason, *Forty-Second Ohio Infantry*, 228; Barber, *Army Memoirs*, 113; Jefferson Brumback to Kate, June 7, 1863, Ninety-Fifth Ohio Infantry file, VNMP; Morris, Hartwell, and Kuykendall, *History 31st Regiment*, 71; Loop, "Campaigning with

the Buckeyes"; Charles A. Hobbs, "Vanquishing Vicksburg: The Campaign Which Ended in the Surrender of America's Gibraltar," *National Tribune*, March 17, 1892; Grant, *Personal Memoirs*, 1:538; Committee of the Regiment, *Story of the Fifty-Fifth Regiment*, 248–49; Badeau, *Military History*, 335–36.

10. Wescott, *Civil War Letters*, June 20, 1863; Committee of the Regiment, *Story of the Fifty-Fifth Regiment*, 248; Durham, *Three Years*, 141.

11. Duane, *Manual*, 110–34; Mahan, *Summary*, 294; Simon, *Papers of Ulysses S. Grant*, 358; Barney, *Recollections*, 190.

12. Duane, *Manual*, 130–32.

13. Ibid., 132.

14. Ibid.

15. Ibid., 130, 132.

16. Andrew Hickenlooper, "Personal Reminiscences," folder 2, 96, CMC.

17. Simpson and Berlin, *Sherman's Civil War*, 478–79; OR, vol. 24, pt. 1, 107.

18. OR, vol. 24, pt. 1, 107.

19. William to father, June 11, 1863, William Reid Diary, Fifteenth Illinois Infantry file, VNMP; Morris, Hartwell, and Kuykendall, *History 31st Regiment*, 69; Mahan, *Summary*, 352.

20. Comstock, *Diary*, 196; Barber, *Army Memoirs*, 113; Rood, *Story of the Service*, 195–96.

21. William Reid Diary, June 11, 1863; David W. Poak to Sadie, June 12, 1863, SC 2058, David W. Poak Letters, ALPL; OR, vol. 24, pt. 2, 322. S. C. Beck, *A True Sketch of His Army Life*, 124th Illinois Infantry file, OCHM.

22. Morris, Hartwell, and Kuykendall, *History 31st Regiment*, 71–72; "Fighting for Vicksburg," *National Tribune*, August 23, 1894.

23. "Fighting for Vicksburg"; Edward N. Potter Diary, June 17, 1863, Twenty-Ninth Wisconsin Infantry file, VNMP; Lieutenant Anthony B. Burton Diary, June 8, 1863, SC 2401, ALPL.

24. Joseph Stockton Diary, June 3, 1863, ALPL; Pryce, *Vanishing Footprints*, 134; Force, "Personal Recollections," 308; unknown author to Captain William T. Rigby, January 12, 1905, Forty-Fifth Illinois Infantry file, VNMP.

25. Hickenlooper, "Vicksburg Mine," 541; Ira Blanchard, typescript of regimental history, p. 93, Twentieth Illinois Infantry, folder 75-31, ALPL; Mary Anderson, *Civil War Diary*, 105; Hooper, *Historical Sketch*, 11; Brown, *History of the Fourth Regiment*, 230; Bearss, *Unvexed to the Sea*, 906; Loop, "Campaigning with the Buckeyes."

26. Blanchard, typescript of regimental history, p. 93; Oldroyd, *Soldier's Story*, 49; F. W. Tupper to "Dear Parents," June 30, 1863, SC 1567, F. W. Tupper Letters, ALPL; Newsome, *Experience in the War*, 22, Eighty-First Illinois Infantry file, OCHM; McDonald, *History of the 30th Illinois*, 50.

27. Loop, "Campaigning with the Buckeyes"; George Ditto Diary, Saturday, June 20, 1863; Beck, *A True Sketch of His Army Life*, 11; Hickenlooper, "Vicksburg Mine," 541; F. W. Tupper to "Dear Parents," June 30, 1863. Tupper enclosed a rough diagram of the tower in his letter. It depicts a three-sided figure (a square missing one side) with each side labeled (from left to right) 1, 2, and 3. There is a loophole in the middle of each numbered side for a total of three sharpshooter ports.

28. Blanchard, typescript of regimental history, p. 93; Hickenlooper, "Vicksburg Mine," 541.

29. Wells, *Siege of Vicksburg*, 84; Kellogg, *Vicksburg Campaign*, 59.

30. Kellogg, *Vicksburg Campaign*, 60; Brown, *History of the Fourth Regiment*, 230. Another version of this story appears in Brown's account.

31. Beck, *A True Sketch of His Army Life*, 11; F. W. Tupper to "Dear Parents," June 30, 1863; Blanchard, typescript of regimental history, p. 93; Miller, *Photographic History*, 209; Loop, "Campaigning with the Buckeyes"; National Park Service Soldiers and Sailors System, http://www.nps.gov/civilwar/search-soldiers-detail.htm?soldier_id=eb9b429e-dc7a-df11-bf36-b8ac6f5d926a (accessed on July 11, 2012); *Report of the Adjutant General*, 222. During the siege, Henry C. Foster served as a second lieutenant in Company B, Twenty-Third Indiana. He was promoted to first lieutenant on July 4, 1863.

32. Blanchard, typescript of regimental history, p. 93.

33. Kiper, *Dear Catherine*, 115; Joseph Bowker Diary, June 21, 1863, Forty-Second Ohio Infantry file, VNMP.

34. Michaels, *Civil War Letters*, 87; William Reid to father, June 24, 1863, William Reid Diary; Campbell, *Union Must Stand*, 105; Michaels, *Civil War Letters*, 87; Campbell, *Union Must Stand*, 105; William Reid to father, June 24, 1863; A. Marshall, *Army Life*, 257.

35. Burton Diary, Sunday, May 24, 1863; W. B. Smith Diary, Tuesday, May 26, 1863, Sixty-Eighth Ohio Infantry file, VNMP; J. A. Bering to "Dear Brother," June 7, 1863, Forty-Eighth Ohio Infantry file, VNMP; James H. Lewis to unknown recipient, June 11, 1863, Twenty-Fourth Iowa Infantry file, VNMP.

36. Simon, *Papers of Ulysses S. Grant*, 377; William Reid to father, June 8, 1863, William Reid Diary; Kiper, *Dear Catherine*, 115.

37. Raum, "Fighting for Vicksburg," *National Tribune*, August 23, 1894; Remley qtd. in Holcomb, *Southern Sons*, 77.

38. Holcomb, *Southern Sons*, 77; W. M. Baker Diary, May 28, 1863, 116th Illinois Infantry file, VNMP; David W. Poak to Sadie, June 12, 1863.

39. Pryce, *Vanishing Footprints*, 137–38; T. Williams, *Historical Sketch*, 55; Beck, *A True Sketch of His Army Life*, 12.

40. Pryce, *Vanishing Footprints*, 137–38; T. Williams, *Historical Sketch*, 55; Beck, *A True Sketch of His Army Life*, 12; Fowler and Miller, *History of the Thirtieth Iowa*, 31; Fuller, *History of the Trials*, 71. For references to federal precision sharpshooter fire, see Barber, *Army Memoirs*, 112; William Reid to father, June 24, 1863; and Campbell, *Union Must Stand*, 105.

41. Charles A. Hobbs, "Vanquishing Vicksburg: The Campaign Which Ended in the Surrender of America's Gibraltar," *National Tribune*, April 7, 1892; Barber, *Army Memoirs*, 112; George Ditto Diary, June 6, 1863; F. W. Tupper to "Dear Parents," June 30, 1863.

42. Fowler and Miller, *History of the Thirtieth Iowa*, 250; Kiper, *Dear Catherine*, 115; Jefferson Brumback to Kate, June 11, 1863.

43. Pryce, *Vanishing Footprints*, 133; William H. Raynor Diary, May 29, 1863, Fifty-Sixth Ohio Infantry file, VNMP.

44. *My Civil War Memoirs. And Other Reminiscences as Written by my Father. W. R. Eddington*, W. R. Eddington Papers, SC 441, ALPL.

45. W. M. Baker Diary, June 27, 1863; 116th Illinois Infantry Regiment History, http://civilwar.illinoisgenweb.org/history/116.html (accessed on December 30, 2013).

8. Turning Loose the Dogs of War

1. Scott, *History of the 67th*, 39.

2. "Fighting for Vicksburg," *National Tribune*, August 23, 1894; Lieutenant Anthony B. Burton Diary, June 6, 1863, SC 2401, ALPL.

3. Mahan, *Complete Treatise*, 234; Mahan, *Summary*, 309.

4. *OR*, vol. 24, pt. 2, 182, 184; Badeau, *Military History*, 349.

5. *OR*, vol. 24, pt. 2, 184; Joseph Bowker Diary, June 29, 1863, Forty-Second Ohio Infantry file, VNMP.

6. Mahan, *Summary*, 312–19.

7. George Ditto Diary, June 21, 1863, SC 2192, ALPL; Grant, *Personal Memoirs*, 1:540–41; P. C. Hains to W. B. Scates, June 8, 1863, box 24, John McClernand Papers, ALPL; George Ditto Diary, June 6 and June 15, 1863; Burton Diary, June 13, 1863.

8. Mahan, *Summary*, 309–19; *OR*, vol. 24, pt. 2, 176; Oscar Eugene Stewart, "Memoirs of the Civil War," Fifteenth Iowa Infantry file, OCHM; S. Q. A. Campbell Diary, June 16, 1863, Fifth Iowa Infantry file, VNMP; E. B. Bascom Diary, June 15, 1863, Fifth Iowa Infantry file, VNMP; *OR*, vol. 24, pt. 2, 176, 180.

9. Burton Diary, June 14, 1863.

10. Isaiah Richards to "Dearly loved ones at home," May 21, 1863, Seventeenth Ohio Light Artillery file, VNMP; Isaiah Richards to William T. Rigby, November 27, 1903, ibid.

11. Isaiah Richards to William T. Rigby, July 13, 1903, Seventeenth Ohio Light Artillery file.

12. Ibid.; Isaiah Richards to William T. Rigby, November 27, 1903. A diagram of this battery is included in this letter.

13. *OR*, vol. 24, pt. 2, 176; ibid., 176, 194; Burton Diary, June 1, 1863; *OR*, vol. 24, pt. 2, 194.

14. *OR*, vol. 24, pt. 2, 323.

15. Sanborn, "Remarks on a Motion," 617.

16. George Ditto Diary, July 1, 1863.

17. *OR*, vol. 24, pt. 3, 348.

18. Sherman, *Memoirs*, 1:328; Committee of the Regiment, *Story of the Fifty-Fifth Regiment*, 24; Sanborn, "Remarks on a Motion," 618; Farwell, *Queen Victoria's Little Wars*, 185–87.

19. Jones, *Artilleryman's Diary*, 71.

20. I. Richards to "all at home," June 15, 1863, Seventeenth Ohio Light Artillery file, VNMP; *OR*, vol. 24, pt. 2, 180.

21. *OR*, vol. 24, pt. 2, 185.

22. Jones, *Artilleryman's Diary*, 72; Force, "Personal Recollections," 307.

23. *OR*, vol. 24, pt. 2, 176.

24. Charles A. Hobbs, "Vanquishing Vicksburg: The Campaign Which Ended in the Surrender of America's Gibraltar," *National Tribune*, March 10, 1892; *OR*, vol. 24, pt. 2, 319; Mason, *Forty-Second Ohio Infantry*, 228.

25. Hopkins, *Under the Flag*, 70; W. B. Smith Diary, June 10, 1863, Sixty-Eighth Ohio Infantry file, VNMP; Andrew Hickenlooper, "Personal Reminiscences," folder 3, 144, CMC; George Ditto Diary, June 29, 1863; Wells, *Siege of Vicksburg*, 85.

26. Grabau, *Ninety-Eight Days*, 48, 408; *OR*, vol. 24, pt. 2, 180.

27. Bearss, *Unvexed to the Sea*, 909; Grabau, *Ninety-Eight Days*, 422; *OR*, vol. 24, pt. 2, 200; Hickenlooper, "Personal Reminiscences," folder 3, 144. Hickenlooper states in the *OR* that Battery Hickenlooper was finished on June 5. After the war, in his "Personal Reminiscences," he wrote that the battery was completed on June 6. *OR*, vol. 24, pt. 2, 200.

28. Hickenlooper, "Personal Reminiscences," folder 3, 144; W. A. Lorimer to William T. Rigby, May 16, 1904, Seventeenth Illinois Infantry file, file 278, VNMP. According to Lorimer of the Seventeenth Illinois, sharpshooters also operated from behind the protection of Battery Hickenlooper. S. C. Beck, *A True Sketch of His Army Life*, p. 11, 124th Illinois file, OCHM.

29. Joiner, *Mr. Lincoln's Brown Water Navy*, 138; Porter, *Naval History*, 322–23; *ORN*, 25:43.

30. Joiner, *Mr. Lincoln's Brown Water Navy*, 138; Porter, *Naval History*, 322–23.

31. Brown, *History of the Fourth Regiment*, 230; OR, vol. 24, pt. 2, 180; Mason, *Forty-Second Ohio Infantry*, 228.

32. Grant, *Personal Memoirs*, 1:540; OR, vol. 24, pt. 2, 323; Joseph Bowker Diary, June 15, 1863.

33. OR, vol. 24, pt. 2, 178–80.

34. Kiper, *Dear Catherine*, 116; Charles A. Hobbs, "Vanquishing Vicksburg: The Campaign Which Ended in the Surrender of America's Gibraltar," *National Tribune*, March 24, 1892; A. Marshall, *Army Life*, 258; Committee of the Regiment, *Story of the Fifty-Fifth Regiment*, 250.

35. OR, vol. 24, pt. 2, 175.

36. Fuller, *History of the Trials*, 76; Frank W. Tupper to his parents, June 30, 1863, SC 1567, F. W. Tupper Letters, ALPL; Jefferson Brumback to Kate, May 31, 1863, Ninety-Fifth Ohio Infantry file, VNMP.

37. I. Richards to "all at home," June 15, 1863; Burton Diary, June 16, 1863; "Your Bro. Wm to Spencer," June 15, 1863, box 2, Russell Family Papers, ALPL.

38. OR, vol. 24, pt. 3, 418.

39. Ibid., 418–19.

40. Burt, "Letters from the Trenches"; Committee of the Regiment, *Story of the Fifty-Fifth Regiment*, 249; Michaels, *Civil War Letters*, 93; Campbell, *Union Must Stand*, 107.

41. Blake, *Succinct History*, 19; Committee of the Regiment, *Story of the Fifty-Fifth Regiment*, 250.

9. Toiling Day and Night

1. Simon, *Papers of Ulysses S. Grant*, 304; "Fighting for Vicksburg," *National Tribune*, August 23, 1894; T. Marshall, *History of the Eighty-Third Ohio*, 90; Simpson and Berlin, *Sherman's Civil War*, 488.

2. B. to "my Dear Kate," June 21, 1863, Ninety-Fifth Ohio file, VNMP; OR, vol. 24, pt. 2, 178–79; Albert Chipman to "Dear Wife," June 22, 1863, Albert Chipman Papers, box 1, ALPL; Cyrus E. Dickey to "My dear Sister," June 28, 1863, Wallace-Dickey Papers, box 2, ALPL.

3. A. Marshall, *Army Life*, 256; Woods, *Services of the Ninety-Sixth Ohio*, 32.

4. OR, vol. 24, pt. 1, 107.

5. Bearss, *Unvexed to the Sea*, 933, 936–37, 942; I. Richards to "all at home," June 15, 1863, Seventeenth Ohio Light Battery, VNMP.

6. OR, vol. 24, pt. 2, 240; William H. Raynor Diary, Fifty-Sixth Ohio file, VNMP.

7. Simon, *Papers of Ulysses S. Grant*, 321; U. S. Grant to Major General John A. McClernand, June 15, 1863, John McClernand Papers, box 24, ALPL.

8. Bearss, *Unvexed to the Sea*, 942. The exact date that Hovey opened his approach is debated. Bearss states that Hovey began his approach on the night of June 23, while C. A. Lucas of the Twenty-Fourth Iowa wrote to Captain W. T. Rigby, chairman of the Vicksburg National Military Park Commission, on February 25, 1904, that the approach began on June 24. C. A. Lucas to Captain W. T. Rigby, February 25, 1904, Twenty-Fourth Iowa file, VNMP; William H. Raynor Diary, June 26, 1863; Fuller, *History of the Trials*, 75; ; OR, vol. 24, pt. 2, 186; William H. Raynor Diary, July 1, 1863.

9. Bearss, *Unvexed to the Sea*, 946–47, 951–52; William Orme to "My Dear Sir," July 1, 1863, William Orme Papers, box 1, ALPL.

10. Bearss, *Unvexed to the Sea*, 889, 891, 893, 898, 905, 912; Your Bro. William to "Dear Spencer," June 15, 1863, Russell Family Papers, box 2, ALPL. On June 15, Giles Smith's Approach was eighty yards of the Confederate defenses.

11. William Franklin Patterson to "My Own Dear Wife," June 22, 1863, LOC; S. C. Beck, *A True Sketch of His Army Life*, pp. 13–14, 124th Illinois file, OCHM; Haydon, "Grant's Wooden Mortars," 30–31.

12. Mahan, *Complete Treatise*, 237; OR, vol. 24, pt. 3, 422.

13. Lockett, "Defense of Vicksburg," 492; George Cooper to S. L. Cooper, June 28, 1863, Forty-Sixth Illinois Infantry file, OCHM; Oscar Eugene Stewart, "Memories of the Civil War," Fifteenth Iowa Infantry file, OCHM.

14. Haydon, "Grant's Wooden Mortars," 33; OR, vol. 24, pt. 2, 181.

15. Haydon, "Grant's Wooden Mortars," 33; OR, vol. 24, pt. 2, 181, 186; W. F. Jones, "Besieging a Stronghold," *National Tribune*, February 22, 1900.

16. "Fighting for Vicksburg," *National Tribune*, August 23, 1894; OR, vol. 24, pt. 2, 178, 185.

17. Haydon, "Grant's Wooden Mortars," 33; McElroy, "Wilderness Campaign."

18. Haydon, "Grant's Wooden Mortars," 35; Andrew Hickenlooper, "Personal Reminiscences," folder 3, 145, CMC.

19. OR, vol. 24, pt. 2, 179, 208.

20. Brown, *History of the Fourth Regiment*, 228; Loop, "Campaigning with the Buckeyes"; Force, "Personal Recollections," 293–309; McElroy, "Wilderness Campaign."

21. OR, vol. 24, pt. 2, 186.

22. Hickenlooper, "Vicksburg Mine," 540; Oldroyd, *Soldier's Story*, 63; Newsome, *Experience in the War*, 22, Eighty-First Illinois Infantry file, OCHM; Francis R. Baker, "Memoirs of Francis R. Baker," SC 69, ALPL.

23. OR, vol. 24, pt. 2, 334.

24. Mahan, *Summary*, 304.

25. Ibid., 297, 304.

26. Ibid., 305–6; Duane, *Manual*, 184–89.

27. OR, vol. 24, pt. 3, 419; William C. Clements Library, Manuscripts Division Finding Aids, http://quod.lib.umich.edu/c/clementsmss/umich-wcl-M-1730kos?view=text (accessed on July 10, 2012).

28. OR, vol. 24, pt. 2, 189, 191. See "Sketch of Bastion in Front of Brig. Gen. Ewing."

29. Ibid., 186.

30. Ibid., 184.

31. Durham, *Three Years*, 142–43; Mason, *Forty-Second Ohio Infantry*, 229–30; Kellogg, *Vicksburg Campaign*, 60; Crummer, *Grant at Fort Donelson*, 118–19; William H. Raynor Diary, June 12, 1863; Jefferson Brumback to Kate, June 7, 1863, Ninety-Fifth Ohio Infantry file, VNMP; Ira Blanchard, typescript of regimental history, Twentieth Illinois Infantry, folder 75-31, ALPL; Swigart, "Vicksburg Campaign"; A. Marshall, *Army Life*, 250–51; Committee of the Regiment, *Story of the Fifty-Fifth Regiment*, 251.

32. William Franklin Patterson to "My Own Dear Wife," June 22, 1863.

33. A. Marshall, *Army Life*, 253.

34. Ibid., 254.

35. Mahan, *Complete Treatise*, 238–39.

36. OR, vol. 24, pt. 3, 420; Simpson and Berlin, *Sherman's Civil War*, 484–85; OR, vol. 24, pt. 2, 189–90.

37. OR, vol. 24, pt. 2, 190.

38. Hickenlooper, "Personal Reminiscences," folder 3, 141; OR, vol. 24, pt. 2, 200, 202; Campbell, *Union Must Stand*, 107.

10. The Key to Vicksburg

1. Wiggins, *Siege Mines*, 5–26.

2. Ibid., 30–47; Chandler, *Art of War*, 234–71; Doughty and Gruber et al., *Warfare in the Western World*, 36–39.

3. A. Marshall, *Army Life*, 258.

4. Crummer, *Grant at Fort Donelson*, 136.

5. Hickenlooper, "Our Volunteer Engineers," 311; OR, vol. 24, pt. 2, 202. According to the *Official Records*, Hickenlooper reached the Third Louisiana Redan on June 22, but harassment from Confederates grenades forced him to begin mining operations on June 23. Hickenlooper, "Vicksburg Mine," 541. After the war, Hickenlooper stated that mining operations commenced on the night of June 22. Mahan, *Summary*, 251; Duane, *Manual*, 208; A. Marshall, *Army Life*, 256.

6. A. Marshall, *Army Life*, 258; Hickenlooper, "Our Volunteer Engineers," 311; Strong, "Campaign against Vicksburg," 338.

7. Andrew Hickenlooper, "Personal Reminiscences," folder 3, 145–46; Crummer, *Grant at Fort Donelson*, 136; Newland, "Surrender of Vicksburg"; *OR*, vol. 24, pt. 2, 202. Hickenlooper's report in the *OR* states that thirty-five miners volunteered. After the war, Hickenlooper wrote in his "Personal Reminiscences" that forty men stepped forward. Hickenlooper, "Vicksburg Mine," 541; Stevenson, *History of the 78th Regiment*, 252.

8. Bently, *History of the 77th Illinois*, 173; Hickenlooper, "Vicksburg Mine," 541. Here, Hickenlooper stated that the gallery was 4 feet wide and 5 feet high; *OR*, vol. 24, pt. 2, 202; Hickenlooper, "Personal Reminiscences," folder 3, 146. Hickenlooper later claimed in his "Personal Reminiscences" that this gallery was 3½ feet wide by 4½ feet high.

9. Duane, *Manual*, 207.

10. *OR*, vol. 24, pt. 2, 177; Hickenlooper, "Personal Reminiscences," folder 3, 146.

11. Hickenlooper, "Personal Reminiscences," folder 3, 146; Lockett, "Defense of Vicksburg," 491.

12. *OR*, vol. 24, pt. 2, 202; Hickenlooper, "Personal Reminiscences," folder 3, 146.

13. Hickenlooper, "Personal Reminiscences," folder 3, 146.

14. Mahan, *Summary*, 252.

15. Walter G. Bartholomew file, USMA.

16. Mahan, *Summary*, 254.

17. Ibid., 251.

18. Ibid.

19. Ibid., 256.

20. Ibid., 251, 254–58.

21. Ibid., 256.

22. *OR*, vol. 24, pt. 2, 202; Andrew Hickenlooper to "My Dear Sister," CMC.

23. Woodworth, *Nothing but Victory*, 358; *OR*, vol. 24, pt. 3, 438–41.

24. Brown, *History of the Fourth Regiment*, 227; *OR*, vol. 24, pt. 3, 440.

25. Hickenlooper, "Vicksburg Mine," 542; *OR*, vol. 24, pt. 2, 294; Hickenlooper, "Personal Reminiscences," folder 3, 147.

26. Strong, "Campaign against Vicksburg," 339; Hickenlooper, "Personal Reminiscences," folder 3, 148; Jerome B. Dawn to unknown recipient, March 13, 1902, Twentieth Illinois Infantry file, VNMP; Jones, *Artilleryman's Diary*, 73.

27. Hickenlooper, "Personal Reminiscences," folder 3, 147–48; Hickenlooper, "Vicksburg Mine," 542; Strong, "Campaign against Vicksburg," 341.

28. Strong, "Campaign against Vicksburg," 341; Hickenlooper, "Personal Reminiscences," folder 3, 140; Jones, *Artilleryman's Diary*, 73; Crummer, *Grant at Fort Donelson*, 137.

29. Committee of the Regiment, *Story of the Fifty-Fifth Regiment*, 252; Gerard, *Diary*, 51.

30. Fuller, *History of the Trials*, 74; Jones, *Artilleryman's Diary*, 73; Morris, Hartwell, and Kuykendall, *History 31st Regiment*, 73.

31. Morris, Hartwell, and Kuykendall, *History 31st Regiment*, 74; James F. Coyle to Captain John A. Edmiston, April 11, 1902, Twentieth Illinois Infantry file, VNMP; Hickenlooper, "Personal Reminiscences," folder 3, 148.

32. Woodworth, *Nothing but Victory*, 442.

33. Jerome B. Dawn to unknown recipient, March 13, 1902; unknown soldier to "Comrade Edmiston," March 1, 1902, Twentieth Illinois Infantry file, VNMP; John A. Edmiston to Wm. T. Rigby, March 8, 1902, Twentieth Illinois Infantry file, VNMP.

34. R. M. Springer to Captain J. A. Edmiston, March 18, 1902, Twentieth Illinois Infantry file, VNMP; John A. Edmiston to Wm. T. Rigby, March 8, 1902; *OR*, vol. 24, pt. 2, 208.

35. Woodworth, *Nothing but Victory*, 444; Howard, *History of the 124th*, 116; Strong, "Campaign against Vicksburg," 342; Crummer, *Grant at Fort Donelson*, 139; R. M. Springer to Captain J. A. Edmiston, March 18, 1902; Woodworth, *Nothing but Victory*, 445; Raum, "With the Western Army."

36. Strong, "Campaign against Vicksburg," 342; Woodworth, *Nothing but Victory*, 445.

37. Hickenlooper, "Personal Reminiscences," folder 3, 148; John A. Edmiston to Wm. T. Rigby, March 8, 1902 VNMP; R. M. Springer to Captain J. A. Edmiston, March 18, 1902; S. C. Beck, *A True Sketch of His Army Life*, p. 14, 124th Illinois file, OCHM; Wilber F. Crummer to Captain W. T. Rigby, October 21, 1902, Forty-Fifth Illinois file, VNMP; unknown to J. A. Edmiston, March 12, 1902, Twentieth Illinois Infantry file, VNMP.

38. *OR*, vol. 24, pt. 3, 441; Strong, "Campaign against Vicksburg," 341; Wilber F. Crummer to Captain W. T. Rigby, October 21, 1902, Forty-Fifth Illinois Infantry file, VNMP; Crummer, *Grant at Fort Donelson*, 137; Morris, Hartwell, and Kuykendall, *History 31st Regiment*, 73–74.

39. *OR*, vol. 24, pt. 2, 202; Oldroyd, *Soldier's Story*, 68.

40. George Ditto Diary, June 25, 1863, SC 2192, ALPL; Lockett, "Defense of Vicksburg," 491; A. Marshall, *Army Life*, 258; F. W. Tupper to "Dear Parents," June 30, 1863, SC 1567, F. W. Tupper Letters, ALPL.

41. *OR*, vol. 24, pt. 2, 333.

42. Woodworth, *Nothing but Victory*, 445; *OR*, vol. 24, pt. 2, 202; Hickenlooper, "Personal Reminiscences," folder 3, 149–50.

43. Simon, *Papers of Ulysses S. Grant*, 431–32.

44. Crummer, *Grant at Fort Donelson*, 142.

45. *OR*, vol. 24, pt. 3, 444; ibid., pt. 2, 202–3; Hickenlooper, "Vicksburg Mine," 542; Hickenlooper, "Personal Reminiscences," folder 3, 150.

46. Hickenlooper, "Personal Reminiscences," folder 3, 150–51; *OR*, vol. 24, pt. 2, 203.

47. Hickenlooper, "Personal Reminiscences," folder 3, 150–51; *OR*, vol. 24, pt. 2, 203.

48. *OR*, vol. 24, pt. 2, 334; Newsome, *Experience in the War*, Eighty-First Illinois Infantry file, 21–22, OCHM.

49. *OR*, vol. 24, pt. 2, 334–35.

50. Ibid., 178; *OR*, vol. 24, pt. 3, 456.

51. *OR*, vol. 24, pt. 2, 178; ibid., pt. 3, 456–57.

52. Ibid., pt. 2, 178; Beck, *A True Sketch of His Army Life*, 15; A. Marshall, *Army Life*, 259.

53. Howard, *History of the 124th*, 118; Wells, *Siege of Vicksburg*, 85; Stevenson, *History of the 78th Regiment*, 252; Beck, *A True Sketch of His Army Life*, 16; A. Newland, "Surrender of Vicksburg"; Stockton, *War Diary*, 18.

54. *OR*, vol. 24, pt. 2, 178, 334; Jones, *Artilleryman's Diary*, 75; Simon, *Papers of Ulysses S. Grant*, 449.

55. *OR*, vol. 24, pt. 2, 334; Lockett, "Defense of Vicksburg," 491–92.

56. *OR*, vol. 24, pt. 2, 334; Lockett, "Defense of Vicksburg," 491–92.

57. Lockett, "Defense of Vicksburg," 491–92.

Conclusion: Vicksburg Is Ours!

1. Lockett, "Defense of Vicksburg"; *OR*, vol. 24, pt. 2, 175.

2. *OR*, vol. 24, pt. 2, 175; pt. 3, 458–59.

3. Ibid., pt. 2, 186.

4. Bearss, *Unvexed to the Sea*, 891, 898–901, 904.

5. *OR*, vol. 24, pt. 2, 177.

6. Bearss, *Unvexed to the Sea*, 907, 934, 937, 940, 942.

7. *OR*, vol. 24, pt. 2, 174; A. Marshall, *Army Life*, 259.

8. Ballard, *Vicksburg*, 388–95.

9. Bently, *History of the 77th Illinois*, 177–78; C. A. Lucas to Captain W. T. Rigby, February 25, 1904, Twenty-Fourth Iowa file, VNMP; Kellogg, *Vicksburg Campaign*, 61; Brinkerhoff, *History of the Thirtieth Regiment*, 79.

10. Swigart, "Vicksburg Campaign."

11. Charles A. Hobbs, "Vanquishing Vicksburg: The Campaign Which Ended in the Surrender of America's Gibraltar," *National Tribune*, April 14, 1892; Swigart, "Vicksburg Campaign"; Strong, "Campaign against Vicksburg," 343.

12. Grabau, *Ninety-Eight Days*, 493–94; Strong, "Campaign against Vicksburg," 343.

13. Grabau, *Ninety-Eight Days*, 495; Craven, "Fighting Them Over"; T. Marshall, *History of the Eighty-Third Ohio*, 93.

14. Grabau, *Ninety-Eight Days*, 495–96; Grant, *Personal Memoirs*, 1:555–58.

15. *OR*, vol. 24, pt. 3, 446; Chaplain N. M. Baker, July 3, 1863, 116th Illinois file, VNMP.

16. Grabau, *Ninety-Eight Days*, 496; Howard, *History of the 124th*, 120.

17. Grabau, *Ninety-Eight Days*, 496–97; Grant, *Personal Memoirs*, 1:558–60.

18. Grabau, *Ninety-Eight Days*, 497–99; Grant, *Personal Memoirs*, 1:543–63; Ballard, *Grant at Vicksburg*, 149.

19. Francis R. Baker, "Memoirs of Francis R. Baker," p. 22, SC 69, ALPL; Holcomb, *Southern Sons*, 81; Howard, *History of the 124th*, 119; OR, vol. 24, pt. 3, 467; Lieutenant George Hale, *Diary of Lieut. Geo. Hale*, July 4, 1863, Thirty-Third Wisconsin file, VNMP.

20. Grabau, *Ninety-Eight Days*, 497–99; Wells, *Siege of Vicksburg*, 87.

21. Lieutenant George B. Carter to Bill, July 6, 1863, Thirty-Third Wisconsin file, VNMP.

22. Howard, *History of the 124th*, 121; Kellogg, *Vicksburg Campaign*, 62–63; Brinkerhoff, *History of the Thirtieth Regiment*, 80.

23. OR, vol. 24, pt. 3, 477; Simon, *Papers of Ulysses S. Grant*, 464–65; Isaiah Richards to Wm. T. Rigby, July 13, 1903, Seventeenth Ohio Light Artillery file, VNMP.

24. Grant, *Personal Memoirs*, 1:568; George Ditto Diary, July 4, 1863, SC 2192, ALPL; Woodworth, *Decision in the Heartland*, 66.

25. Ballard, *U.S. Grant*, 44, 56–62, 147–49; Ballard, *Grant at Vicksburg*, 172; Wells, *Siege of Vicksburg*, 87.

26. Richard and Richard, *Defense of Vicksburg*, 216.

27. Ballard, *Grant at Vicksburg*, 144; Kiper, *Dear Catherine*, 116; James H. Wilson Journal, May 23, 1863, Manuscript Division, LOC.

28. George Ditto Diary, July 4, 1863; Dear Mina from "Your Adolph," July 7, 1863, Englemann-Kircher Papers, box 3, ALPL; Morris, Hartwell, and Kuykendall, *History 31st Illinois*, 74; Committee of the Regiment, *Story of the Fifty-Fifth Regiment*, 253; Ira Blanchard, typescript of regimental history, Twentieth Illinois Infantry, folder 75-31, ALPL.

29. Ballard, *Grant at Vicksburg*, 149; Richard and Richard, *Defense of Vicksburg*, 217; Uffindell, *Napoleon's Immortals*, 30.

30. OR, vol. 24, pt. 3, 477.

31. Jenney, "Personal Recollections of Vicksburg," 264–65; Lockett, "Defense of Vicksburg," 492.

32. Lockett, "Defense of Vicksburg," 492; OR, vol. 24, pt. 3, 474; pt. 2, 179–80.

33. Lockett, "Defense of Vicksburg," 492; Richard and Richard, *Defense of Vicksburg*, 223.

34. Richard and Richard, *Defense of Vicksburg*, 216; OR, vol. 24, pt. 2, 177, 180.

35. OR, vol. 24, pt. 2, 177.

36 Ibid.

37. Charles A. Hobbs, "Vanquishing Vicksburg: The Campaign Which Ended in the Surrender of America's Gibraltar," *National Tribune*, March 17, 1892.

38. Porter, *Incidents and Anecdotes*, 132.

39. Mahan, *Elementary Course*, 177; Mahan, *Complete Treatise*, 224; Murray, *Rocky Road*, 123–69; Hess, *Union Soldier*, 65; Long and Long, *Civil War*, 548; Wiggins, *Siege Mines*, 46–51.

40. Davis, *Besieged*, 254–55, 258–59; Murray, *Rocky Road*, 45–80.

41. Murray, *Rocky Road*, 44, 225–37; ibid., 44, 225–37.

42. Mahan, *Elementary Course*, preface.

43. Ibid., 180.

44. Ibid., 277.

45. Ibid., 180.

Appendix:
How Many Union Engineer Officers Served during the Vicksburg Siege?

1. Grant, *Personal Memoirs*, 1:536–37; Badeau, *Military History*, 285; OR, vol. 24, pt. 2, 178.

2. Grant, *Personal Memoirs*, 1:537; Ballard, *Vicksburg*, 258.

3. Grant, *Personal Memoirs*, 1:537.

4. OR, vol. 24, pt. 2, 177–78.

5. Ibid., 178; Mason, *Forty-Second Ohio Infantry*, 227. According to Private Frank Holcomb Mason, McClernand charged him with the responsibility of managing engineering tasks on the Thirteenth Army Corps' left flank, a service that would later earn him a promotion to the rank of captain and aide-de-camp. Mason also stated that "Colonel Harry Wilson," referring to James H. Wilson, who served on Grant's staff, provided "informal oversight over the operations in front of the Thirteenth Corps."

6. OR, vol. 24, pt. 2, 180.

7. Ibid., 170, 177, 180.

8. Ibid., 180.

9. Ibid., 170–71.

Bibliographic Essay

1. Woodworth, *Decision in the Heartland*, 66.

2. Badeau, *Military History*, 337–38; "The Army in Crisis," *New York Times*, October 16, 1864.

3. Ballard, *Vicksburg*, 430.

4. Bearss, "Ewing's Approach in the Siege of Vicksburg"; Bearss, *Unvexed to the Sea*, 885–968.

5. Winschel, *Triumph and Defeat*, 129–38; Woodworth, *Nothing but Victory*, 425–55.

6. Ballard, *Grant at Vicksburg*, 170–72.

7. Hunt, "Entrenchments and Fortifications"; Hunt, "Engineer Corps of the Federal Army"; Talcott, "Reminiscences."

8. Nichols, *Confederate Engineers*, 102–10; Lockett, "Defense of Vicksburg"; Shiman, "Army Engineers," 49–51, 53, 63, 76, 86–87; Thienel, *Mr. Lincoln's Bridge Builders*, 113–34.

9. Griffith, *Battle Tactics*, 130; Hagerman, *American Civil War*, 206–7; Saunders, *Trench Warfare*, 58.

10. Hunt, "Entrenchments and Fortifications," 194, 196.

11. Hagerman, *American Civil War*, xi–xii, 202.

12. Griffith, *Battle Tactics*, 124, 129, 130, 132.

13. Hess, *Field Armies*, xvi–xviii.

14. Hunt, "Entrenchments and Fortifications," 218; Hess, *Field Armies*, xvii; Saunders, *Trench Warfare*, 50.

15. Saunders, *Trench Warfare*, 8, 49, 51, 54.

16. Murray, *Rocky Road*, 243.

Bibliography

----

*Included here are separate sections for manuscripts; primary sources;
printed secondary sources; theses, reports, and maps; and electronic sources.*

Manuscripts

Abraham Lincoln Presidential Library, Springfield, Illinois
    Baker, Francis R. "Memoirs of Francis R. Baker."
    Blanchard, Ira. Typescript of regimental history, Twentieth Illinois Infantry.
    Burton, Lieutenant Anthony B., Diary.
    Chipman, Albert, Papers.
    Ditto, George, Diary.
    Eddington, W. R., Papers.
    Englemann-Kircher Papers.
    Ingraham, E. H., Letters.
    McClernand, John, Papers.
    Orme, William, Letters.
    Poak, David W., Letters.
    Rand Family Papers.
    Russell Family Papers.
    Stockton, Joseph, Diary.
    Tupper, F. W., Letters.
    Wallace-Dickey Papers.
    Winegar, Daniel G., Letters.
Cincinnati Museum Center, Cincinnati, Ohio
    Andrew Hickenlooper to "My Dear Sister," June 26, 1863, Hickenlooper Collection, MSS fH628, box 11, folder 12.
    Hickenlooper, Andrew. "Personal Reminiscences," volume 1, Hickenlooper Collection, MSS fH628, box 1, folders 2–3.

Duke University, Durham, North Carolina
> S. S. Massett to "Dear Companion," Special Collections.

Library of Congress, Manuscript Division, Washington, D.C.
> William Franklin Patterson to "My Own Dear Wife."
> Wilson, James H., Journal.

Old Court House Museum, Vicksburg, Mississippi
> Regimental Files
>> Illinois
>>> Infantry, Forty-Fifth, Forty-Sixth, Eighty-First, 116th, 124th
>> Iowa
>>> Infantry, Fifteenth
>> Missouri (Union)
>>> Infantry, Tenth

Rutherford B. Hayes Presidential Center, Fremont, Ohio
> Birchard, Sardis, Collection.
> Stem Family Collection.

United States Military Academy, West Point, New York
> Walter G. Bartholomew file, Corps of Engineers, USMA Library, Special Collections.

Vicksburg National Military Park, Vicksburg, Mississippi
> Diaries and Letters Files
>> Reid, William, Diary.
> U.S. Regimental Files
>> Illinois
>>> Infantry, Fifteenth, Seventeenth, Twentieth, Forty-Fifth, Seventy-Seventh, 116th
>> Indiana
>>> Infantry, Twenty-Fourth
>> Iowa
>>> Infantry, Fifth, Twenty-Fourth
>> Ohio
>>> Artillery, Seventeenth
>>> Infantry, Forty-Second, Forty-Eighth, Fifty-Sixth, Sixty-Eighth, Seventy-Second, Ninety-Fifth
>> Wisconsin
>>> Infantry, Twenty-Ninth, Thirty-Third

Primary Sources

Abbot, Henry L. *Memoir of Dennis Hart Mahan 1802–1871, Read before the National Academy, Nov. 7, 1878.* Washington, D.C.: Judd and Detweiler, Printers, n.d.

Alexander, Edward Porter. *Fighting for the Confederacy: The Personal Recollections of General Edward Porter Alexander.* Edited by Gary W. Gallagher. Chapel Hill: University of North Carolina Press, 1989.

Anderson, Mary Ann, ed. *The Civil War Diary of Morgan Geer, Twentieth Regiment, Illinois Volunteers.* New York: Cosmos Press, 1977.

Barber, Lucius W. *Army Memoirs of Lucius W. Barber, Company D. 15th Illinois Volunteer Infantry. May 24 to Sept. 30, 1865.* Chicago: J. M. Jones Stationery and Printing Co., 1984.

Barnard, Brigadier General J. G., and Brigadier General W. F. Barry. *Report of the Engineer and Artillery Operations of the Army of the Potomac, from Its Organization to the Close of the Peninsular Campaign.* New York: D. Van Nostrand, 1863.

Barney, Captain C. *Recollections of Field Service with the Twentieth Iowa Infantry Volunteers; or What I Saw in the Army.* Davenport: Printed for the author at the Gazette job rooms, 1865.

Bently, Lieutenant William H. *History of the 77th Illinois Volunteer Infantry. Sept. 2, 1862–July 10, 1865.* Peoria, Ill.: Edward Hine, 1883.

Bering, John A., and Thomas Montgomery. *History of the Forty-Eighth Ohio Vet. Vol. Inf.* Hillsboro, Ohio: Printed at the Highland News Office, 1880.

Black, Samuel. *A Soldier's Recollections of the Civil War.* Minco, Okla.: n.p., 1911.

Blake, Ephraim E. *A Succinct History of the 28th Iowa Volunteer Infantry.* Belle Plaine, Iowa: Union Press, 1896.

Brinkerhoff, Henry R. *History of the Thirtieth Regiment Ohio Volunteer Infantry, from Its Organization, to the Fall of Vicksburg, Miss.* Columbus: James W. Osgood, 1863.

Brown, Alonzo. *History of the Fourth Regiment of Minnesota Infantry Volunteers during the Great Rebellion 1861–1865.* St. Paul, Minn.: Pioneer Press Company, 1892.

Burt, Lieutenant R. W. "Letters from the Trenches. A Contemporaneous Account of the Investment and Surrender of Vicksburg." *National Tribune,* July 3, 1902.

Campbell, John Quincy Adams. *The Union Must Stand: The Civil War Diary of John Quincy Adams Campbell, Fifth Iowa Volunteer Infantry.* Edited by Mark Grimsley and Todd D. Miller. Voices of the Civil War, edited by Frank L. Bryne. Knoxville: University of Tennessee Press, 2000.

A Committee of the Regiment. *The Story of the Fifty-Fifth Regiment Illinois Volunteer Infantry in the Civil War 1861–1865.* N.p., 1887.

Comstock, Cyrus B. *The Diary of Cyrus B. Comstock.* Edited by Merlin E. Sumner. Dayton, Ohio: Morningside House, 1987.

Craven, J. H. "Fighting Them Over. What Our Veterans Have to Say about Their Old Campaigns. Vicksburg. The Offer to Surrender." *National Tribune,* October 30, 1884.

Crooke, George. *The Twenty-First Regiment of Iowa Volunteer Infantry. A Narrative of Its Experience in Active Service, Including a Military Record of Each Officer, Non-commissioned Officer, and Private Soldier of the Organization.* Milwaukee: King, Fowle, and Co., 1891.

Crooker, Lucien Bonaparte. "Episodes and Characters in an Illinois Regiment." In *Military Order of the Loyal Legion of the United States*, 10:33–49. Wilmington, N.C.: Broadfoot, 1992.

Crummer, Wilber F. *Grant at Fort Donelson, Shiloh and Vicksburg and an Appreciation of General U. S. Grant*. Oak Park, Ill.: E. C. Crummer and Co., 1915.

Downing, Alexander G. *Downing's Civil War Diary*. Edited by Olynthus B. Clark. Des Moines: Historical Department of Iowa, 1916.

Duane, J. C. *Manual for Engineer Troops*. New York: D. Van Nostrand, 1862.

Durham, Thomas Wise. *Three Years with Wallace's Zouaves: The Civil War Memoirs of Thomas Wise Durham*. Edited by Jeffrey L. Patrick. Macon, Ga.: Mercer University Press, 2003.

Elder, Donald C., III, ed. *A Damned Iowa Greyhound: The Civil War Letters of William Henry Harrison Clayton*. Iowa City: University of Iowa Press, 1998.

Fletcher, Samuel H. *The History of Company A, Second Illinois Cavalry*. Chicago: D. H. Fletcher, 1912.

Force, Manning M. "Personal Recollections of the Vicksburg Campaign." In *Military Order of the Loyal Legion of the United States*, 1:293–309. Wilmington, N.C.: Broadfoot, 1991.

Fowler, James A., and Miles M. Miller. *History of the Thirtieth Iowa Infantry Volunteers. Giving a Complete Record of the Regiment from Its Organization until Mustered Out*. Mediapolis, Iowa: T. A. Merrill, 1908.

Fuller, Richard J. *A History of the Trials and Hardships of the Twenty-Fourth Indiana Volunteer Infantry*. Indianapolis: Indianapolis Printing Co., 1913.

Gerard, Clinton W. *A Diary: The Eighty-Third Ohio Vol. Inf. in the War. 1862–1865*. Cincinnati, 1890.

Grant, Ulysses S. *Personal Memoirs of U. S. Grant*. 2 vols. New York: Charles L. Webster, 1885.

Greene, Harvey J. *Letters to My Wife: A Civil War Diary from the Western Front*. Compiled by Sharon L. D. Kraynek. Apollo, Penn.: n.p., 1995.

Hickenlooper, Andrew. "Our Volunteer Engineers." In *Military Order of the Loyal Legion of the United States*, 3:301–18. Wilmington, N.C.: Broadfoot, 1991.

———. "The Vicksburg Mine." In *Battles and Leaders of the Civil War*, 3:539–42. New York: Thomas Yoseloff, 1956.

Hicks, Henry G. "The Campaign and Capture of Vicksburg." In *Military Order of the Loyal Legion of the United States*, 31:82–107. Wilmington, N.C.: Broadfoot, 1992.

History of the Sixteenth Battery of Ohio Volunteer Light Artillery U.S.S. from Enlistment, August 20, 1861 to Muster Out, August 2, 1865. N.p., n.d.

Holcomb, Julie, ed. *Southern Sons, Northern Soldiers: The Civil War Letters of the Remley Brothers, 22nd Iowa Infantry*. DeKalb: Northern Illinois University Press, 2004.

Hooper, Shadrach K. *A Historical Sketch of the 23rd Indiana Volunteer Infantry July 29th 1861 to July 23rd 1865*. New Albany, Ind.: Indiana-Vicksburg Military Park Commission, 1910.

Hopkins, Owen Johnston. *Under the Flag of the Nation: Diaries and Letters of Owen Johnston Hopkins, a Yankee Volunteer in the Civil War*. Edited by Otto F. Bond. Columbus: Ohio State University Press, 1998.

Howard, Richard L. *History of the 124th Regiment Illinois Infantry, Volunteers, Otherwise Known as the Hundred and Two Dozen, from August, 1862 to August, 1865*. Springfield, Ill.: Printed and bound by H. W. Rokker, 1880.

Jenney, William B. "Personal Recollections of Vicksburg." In *Military Order of the Loyal Legion of the United States*, 12:247–65. Wilmington, N.C.: Broadfoot, 1992.

Jones, Jenkin Lloyd. *An Artilleryman's Diary*. Madison: Wisconsin Historical Commission, 1914.

Kellogg, John Jackson. *The Vicksburg Campaign and Reminiscences from Milliken's Bend to July 4, 1863*. Washington, Iowa: Evening Journal, 1913.

Kiper, Richard L., ed. *Dear Catherine, Dear Taylor: The Civil War Letters of a Union Soldier and His Wife*. Transcribed by Donna B. Vaughn. Lawrence: University Press of Kansas, 2002.

LaBounty, William P., ed. *Civil War Diaries of James W. Jessee 1861–1865 Company K, 8th Regiment Illinois Volunteer Infantry*. Normal, Ill.: McLean County Genealogical Society, 1997.

Lockett, S. H. "The Defense of Vicksburg." In *Battles and Leaders of the Civil War*, 3:482–92. New York: Thomas Yoseloff, 1956.

Loop, M. B. "Campaigning with the Buckeyes. Ten Thousand Miles with the 68th Ohio. In the Trenches before Vicksburg." *National Tribune*, November 15, 1900.

Mahan, D. H. *A Complete Treatise on Field Fortification, with the General Outlines of the Principles Regulating the Arrangement, the Attack, and the Defense of Permanent Works*. New York: Wiley and Long, 1836.

———. *An Elementary Course of Military Engineering. Part I. Comprising Field Fortification, Military Mining, and Siege Operations*. New York: John Wiley and Sons, 1867.

———. *Summary of the Course of Permanent Fortification and the Attack and Defense of Permanent Works, for the Use of the Cadets of the U.S. Military Academy*. Richmond, Va.: West and Johnston, 1863.

———. *A Treatise on Field Fortification, Containing Instructions on the Methods of Laying Out, Constructing, Defending, and Attacking Intrenchments; with the General Outlines Also of the Arrangement, the Attack and Defence of Permanent Fortifications*. Richmond, Va.: West and Johnston, 1862.

Mahan, James Curtis. *Memoirs of James Curtis Mahan*. Lincoln, Neb.: Franklin Press, 1919.

Marshall, Albert O. *Army Life; From a Soldier's Journal.* 2nd ed. Joliet, Ill.: printed for the author, 1884.

Marshall, T. B. *History of the Eighty-Third Ohio Volunteer Infantry: The Greyhound Regiment.* Cincinnati: Published by the Eighty-Third Ohio Volunteer Infantry Association, 1912.

Martin, Joseph Plum. *Ordinary Courage: The Revolutionary War Adventures of Joseph Plum Martin.* Edited by James Kirby Martin. St. James, N.Y.: Brandywine Press, 1995.

Mason, Frank Holcomb. *Forty-Second Ohio Infantry: A History of the Organization and Services of That Regiment in the War of the Rebellion with Biographical Sketches of Its Field Officers and a Full Roster of the Regiment.* Cleveland: Cobb, Andrews and Co., 1876.

———. "Vicksburg Campaign." *National Tribune*, October 9, 1884.

McClellan, George B. *McClellan's Own Story.* New York: Charles L. Webster, 1887.

———. *The Mexican War Diary and Correspondence of George B. McClellan.* Edited by Thomas W. Cutrer. Baton Rouge: Louisiana State University Press, 2009.

McDonald, Granville B. *History of the 30th Illinois Veteran Volunteer Regiment of Infantry.* Sparta, Ill.: Printed by Sparta News, 1916.

McElroy, John. "The Wilderness Campaign." *National Tribune*, September 15, 1910.

Michaels, Edward Rynearson, ed., *The Civil War Letters of Sylvester Rynearson 1861–1865.* San Rafael, Calif.: E. R. Michaels, 1981.

Morris, W. S., L. D. Hartwell Jr., and J. B. Kuykendall. *History 31st Regiment: Illinois Volunteers Organized by John A. Logan.* Carbondale: Southern Illinois University Press, 1998.

Neal, W. A., ed. *An Illustrated History of the Missouri Engineer and the 25th Infantry Regiments Together with a Roster of Both Regiments and the Last Known Address of All That Could Be Obtained.* Chicago: Donohue and Henneberry, 1889.

Newland, A. "Surrender of Vicksburg. Marching into the City on the Glorious Fourth, 1863." *National Tribune*, August 27, 1903.

Newsome, Edmund. *Experience in the War of the Great Rebellion by a Soldier of the Eighty First Regiment Illinois Volunteer Infantry August 1862–August 1865.* 2nd ed. Carbondale, Ill.: n.p., 1880.

Oldroyd, Osborn Hamiline. *A Soldier's Story of the Siege of Vicksburg.* Springfield, Ill.: H. W. Rokker, 1885.

Patrick, Jeffrey L., ed. *Three Years with Wallace's Zouaves: The Civil War Memoirs of Thomas Wise Durham.* Macon, Ga.: Mercer University Press, 2003.

Porter, David D. *Incidents and Anecdotes of the Civil War.* New York: D. Appleton, 1885.

———. *The Naval History of the Civil War.* New York: Sherman Publishing, 1886.

Pryce, Samuel D. *Vanishing Footprints: The Twenty-Second Iowa Volunteer Infantry in the Civil War.* Edited by Jeffrey C. Burden. Iowa City: Camp Pope Bookshop, 2008.

Raum, General Green B. "With the Western Army. Tightening the Coils." *National Tribune*, January 16, 1902.

Register of the Officers and Cadets of the U.S. Military Academy. June 1839.

Reminiscences of a Boy's Service, with the 76th Ohio in the Fifteenth Army Corps, under General Sherman, during the Civil War, by that "Boy" at Three Score. Menasha, Ohio: n.p., 1908.

Report of the Adjutant General of the State of New Indiana. Vol. 2. Indianapolis: W. R. Holloway, 1865.

Richard, Allan C., Jr., and Mary Margaret Higginbotham Richard. *The Defense of Vicksburg: A Louisiana Chronicle.* Texas A&M Military History Series, edited by Joseph G. Dawson III. College Station: Texas A&M University Press, 2004.

Rood, Hosea W. *The Story of the Service of Company E, and the Twelfth Wisconsin Regiment, Veteran Volunteer Infantry, in the War of the Rebellion.* Milwaukee: Swain and Tate, 1903.

Sanborn, John B. "Remarks on a Motion to Extend a Vote of Thanks to General Marshall for Above Paper." In *Military Order of the Loyal Legion of the United States*, 29:615–22. Wilmington, N.C.: Broadfoot, 1992.

Scott, Reuben B. *The History of the 67th Regiment Indiana Infantry Volunteers.* Bedford, Ind.: n.p., 1892.

Sherman, William T. *Memoirs of General William T. Sherman. By Himself.* 2 vols. New York: D. Appleton, 1875.

Simon, John Y., ed. *The Papers of Ulysses S. Grant.* Vol. 8. Carbondale: Southern Illinois University Press, 1979.

Simpson, Brooks D., and Jean V. Berlin, eds. *Sherman's Civil War: Selected Correspondence of William T. Sherman, 1860–1865.* Chapel Hill: University of North Carolina Press, 1999.

Smith, Gustavus Woodson. *Company "A" Corps of Engineers, U.S.A., 1846–1848, in the Mexican War.* Edited by Leonne M. Hudson. Kent, Ohio: Kent State University Press, 2001.

Stevenson, Thomas M. *History of the 78th Regiment O.V.V.I. from Its Muster In to Its Muster Out Comprising Its Organization, Marches and Skirmishes.* Zanesville, Ohio: Hugh Dunne, 1865.

Stockton, Joseph. *War Diary of Brevet Brigadier General Joseph Stockton.* Chicago: John T. Stockton, 1910.

Strong, William E. "The Campaign against Vicksburg." In *Military Order of the Loyal Legion of the United States*, 11:313–54. Wilmington, N.C.: Broadfoot, 1992.

Swigart, Captain Frank. "Vicksburg Campaign." *National Tribune*, August 9, 1888.

Trimble, Harvey M., ed. *History of the Ninety-Third Illinois Volunteer Infantry from Organization to Muster Out.* Chicago: Blakly Printing, 1898.

U.S. Military Academy. *Official Register of the Officers and Cadets of the U.S. Military Academy.* West Point, N.Y., 1855.

U.S. War Department. *Official Records of the Union and Confederate Navies in the War of the Rebellion.* 31 vols. Washington, D.C.: Government Printing Office, 1890–1901.

———. *The War of the Rebellion: A Compilation of the Official Records of the Union and Confederate Armies.* 128 vols. Washington, D.C.: Government Printing Office, 1880–1901.

Wells, Seth J. *The Siege of Vicksburg from the Diary of Seth J. Wells.* Detroit: Wm. H. Rowe, 1915.

Wescott, Morgan Ebenezer. *Civil War Letters Written to My Mother.* N.p.: n.p., 1909.

Williams, Edward P. *Extracts from Letters to A. B. T. from Edward P. Williams during His Service in the Civil War, 1862–1864.* New York: for private distribution, 1903.

Williams, Thomas D. *An Historical Sketch of the 46th Ohio Volunteer Infantry during the Great Civil War from 1861 to 1866.* Columbus: Lawrence Press, 1899.

Willison, Charles A. *Reminiscences of a Boy's Service with the 76th Ohio in the Fifteenth Army Corps, under General Sherman, during the War.* Menasha, Ohio: n.p., 1908.

Winters, William. *The Musick of the Mocking Birds, the Roar of the Cannon: The Civil War Diary of William Winters.* Edited by Steven E. Woodworth. Lincoln: University of Nebraska, 1998.

Woods, J. T. *Services of the Ninety-Sixth Ohio Volunteers.* Toledo: Blade Printing and Paper Co., 1874.

Printed Secondary Sources

Alger, John I. *Definitions and Doctrine of the Military Art Past and Present.* The West Point Military History Series, edited by Thomas E. Griess. Wayne, N.J.: Avery, 1985.

"Andrew Hickenlooper." In *Biographical Sketches of the Contributors to the Military Order of the Loyal Legion of the United States.* Suppl. 1. Compiled by William Marvel, 149–49. Wilmington, N.C.: Broadfoot, 1995.

Arnold, James R. *The Armies of U. S. Grant.* London: Arms and Armour Press, 1995.

Badeau, Adam. *Military History of Ulysses S. Grant, from April, 1861 to April, 1865.* Vol. 1. New York: D. Appleton, 1881.

Ballard, Michael B. *Grant at Vicksburg: The General and the Siege.* Carbondale: Southern Illinois University Press, 2013.

———. *U. S. Grant: The Making of a General, 1861–1863.* The American Crisis Series, edited by Steven E. Woodworth. Lanham, Md.: Rowman and Littlefield, 2005.

———. *Vicksburg: The Campaign That Opened the Mississippi.* Chapel Hill: University of North Carolina Press, 2004.

Bastian, David F. *Grant's Canal: The Union's Attempt to Bypass Vicksburg.* Shippensburg, Penn.: Burd Street Press, 1995.

Bauer, K. Jack. *The Mexican War: 1846–1848*. New York: Macmillan, 1974.

Bearss, Edwin C. "Ewing's Approach in the Siege of Vicksburg." *Military Engineer*, January–February 1962, 26–28.

———. *Unvexed to the Sea*. Vol. 3 of *The Campaign for Vicksburg*. Dayton: Morningside House, 1996.

Black, Jeremy. *The Age of Total War, 1860–1945*. Lanham, Md.: Rowman and Littlefield, 2006.

The Centennial of the United States Military Academy at West Point. Vol. 1. Washington, D.C.: Government Printing Office, 1904.

Chandler, David. *The Art of War in the Age of Marlborough*. Kent, UK: Spellmount Limited, 1990.

Childs, John. *Warfare in the Seventeenth Century*. Cassell's History of Warfare, edited by John Keegan. London: Cassell, 2001.

Connelly, Thomas Lawrence. *Army of the Heartland: The Army of Tennessee, 1861–1862*. Baton Rouge: Louisiana State University Press, 2001.

Cresap, Bernarr. *Appomattox Commander: The Story of General E. O. C. Ord*. San Diego: A. S. Barnes, 1981.

Davis, Paul K. *Besieged: An Encyclopedia of Great Sieges from Ancient Times to the Present*. Santa Barbara: ABC-CLIO, 2001.

Doughty, Robert A., and Ira D. Gruber et al. *Warfare in the Western World: Military Operations from 1600 to 1700*. Vol. 1. Lexington, Mass.: Heath, 1996.

Duffy, Christopher. *Fire and Stone: The Science of Fortress Warfare 1660–1862*. New York: Hippocrene Books, 1975.

Dyer, Frederick H. *A Compendium of the War of the Rebellion Compiled and Arranged from Official Records of the Federal and Confederate Armies Reports of the Adjutant Generals of the Several States, and Army Registers and Other Reliable Documents and Sources*. Vol. 2. Dayton, Ohio: Broadfoot Publishing Company, Morningside Press, 1994.

Farwell, Byron. *Queen Victoria's Little Wars*. New York: Harper and Row, 1972.

Giambrone, Jeff. *An Illustrated Guide to the Vicksburg Campaign and National Military Park*. Jackson, Miss.: Communication Arts, 2001.

Grabau, Warren E. *Ninety-Eight Days: A Geographer's View of the Vicksburg Campaign*. Knoxville: University of Tennessee Press, 2000.

Griffith, Paddy. *Battle Tactics of the Civil War*. New Haven: Yale University Press, 1989.

Hagerman, Edward. *The American Civil War and the Origins of Modern Warfare: Ideas, Organization, and Field Command*. Bloomington: Indiana University Press, 1992.

———. "From Jomini to Dennis Hart Mahan: The Evolution of Trench Warfare and the American Civil War." *Civil War History* 13, no. 3 (September 1967): 197–220.

Haydon, F. Stansbury. "Grant's Wooden Mortars and Some Incidents of the Siege of Vicksburg." *Journal of the American Military Institute* 4, no. 1 (Spring 1940): 30–38.

Hess, Earl J. *Field Armies and Fortifications in the Civil War: The Eastern Campaigns, 1861–1865.* Chapel Hill: University of North Carolina Press, 2005.

———. *In the Trenches at Petersburg: Field Fortifications and Confederate Defeat.* Chapel Hill: University of North Carolina Press, 2009.

———. *Trench Warfare under Grant and Lee: The Field Fortifications in the Overland Campaign.* Chapel Hill: University of North Carolina Press, 2007.

———. *The Union Soldier in Battle, Enduring the Ordeal of Combat.* Lawrence: University Press of Kansas, 1997.

Howe, Daniel Walker. *What Hath God Wrought: The Transformation of America, 1815–1848.* Oxford: Oxford University Press, 2007.

Hunt, O. E. "Engineer Corps of the Federal Army." In *The Photographic History of the Civil War: Forts and Artillery,* edited by Francis Trevelyan Miller, 222–54. New York: Castle Books, 1957.

———. "Entrenchments and Fortifications." In *The Photographic History of the Civil War: Forts and Artillery,* edited by Francis Trevelyan Miller, 194–218. New York: Castle Books, 1957.

Johnson, Timothy. *A Gallant Little Army: The Mexico City Campaign.* Lawrence: University Press of Kansas, 2007.

Joiner, Gary D. *Mr. Lincoln's Brown Water Navy: The Mississippi Squadron.* Lanham, Md.: Rowman and Littlefield, 2007.

Kiper, Richard L. *Major General John Alexander McClernand: Politician in Uniform.* Kent: Kent State University Press, 1999.

Long, E. B., and Barbara Long. *The Civil War Day by Day: An Almanac, 1861–1865.* Garden City, N.Y.: Doubleday, 1971.

Middlekauff, Robert. *The Glorious Cause: The American Revolution 1763–1789.* New York: Oxford University Press, 1982.

Miller, Francis Trevelyan, ed. *The Photographic History of the Civil War: Forts and Artillery.* New York: Castle Books, 1957.

Miller, William J. "I Only Wait for the River: McClellan and His Engineers on the Chickahominy." In *The Richmond Campaign of 1862: The Peninsula and the Seven Days,* edited by Gary W. Gallagher, 44–65. Chapel Hill: University of North Carolina Press, 2000.

Millett, Allan R., and Peter Maslowski. *For the Common Defense: A Military History of the United States of America.* Rev. and exp. ed. New York: Free Press, 1994.

Morrison, James L., Jr. *The Best School in the World: West Point, 1833–1866.* Kent, Ohio: Kent State University Press, 1998.

Moten, Matthew. *The Delafield Commission and the American Military Profession.* College Station: Texas A&M University Press, 2000.

Murray, Nicholas. *The Rocky Road to the Great War: The Evolution of Trench Warfare to 1914.* Washington, D.C.: Potomac Books, 2013.

Nichols, James Lynn. *Confederate Engineers*. Tuscaloosa, Ala.: Confederate Publishing, 1957.

Saunders, Anthony. *Trench Warfare: 1850–1950*. Barnsley, South Yorkshire: Pen and Sword Military, 2012.

Sears, Stephen W. *To the Gates of Richmond: The Peninsula Campaign*. New York: Ticknor and Fields, 1992.

Shea, William L., and Terrence J. Winschel. *Vicksburg Is the Key: The Struggle for the Mississippi River*. Lincoln: University of Nebraska Press, 2003.

Simpson, Brooks D. *Ulysses S. Grant: Triumph over Adversity, 1822–1865*. Boston: Houghton Mifflin, 2000.

Skelton, William B. *An American Profession of Arms: The Army Officer Corps, 1784–1861*. Lawrence: University Press of Kansas, 1992.

Symonds, Craig. *A Battlefield Atlas of the Civil War*. Baltimore: Nautical and Aviation Publishing Company of America, 1983.

Talcott, T. M. R. "Reminiscences of the Confederate Engineer Service." In *The Photographic History of the Civil War: Forts and Artillery*, edited by Francis Trevelyan Miller, 255–70. New York: Castle Books, 1957.

Thienel, Phillip M. "Engineers in the Union Army, 1861–1865." *Military Engineer* 47 (January 1955): 36–41.

———. *Mr. Lincoln's Bridge Builders: The Right Hand of an American Genius*. Shippensburg, Penn.: White Mane Books, 2000.

Uffindell, Andrew. *Napoleon's Immortals: The Imperial Guard and Its Battles, 1804–1815*. Gloucestershire: Spellmount Limited, 2007.

Wagner, Major A. L. "Hasty Intrenchments in the War of Secession." *Journal of the Military Service Institution of the United States* 22 (February 1898): 225–46.

Warner, Ezra J. *Generals in Blue: Lives of the Union Commanders*. Baton Rouge: Louisiana State University Press, 1992.

———. *Generals in Gray: Lives of the Confederate Commanders*. Baton Rouge: Louisiana State University Press, 1992.

Watson, Bruce Allen. *Sieges: A Comparative Study*. Westport, Conn.: Praeger, 1993.

Weigley, Russell F. *History of the United States Army*. New York: Macmillan, 1967.

Wheeler, Richard. *The Siege of Vicksburg*. New York: Harper and Perennial, 1991.

Wiggins, Kenneth. *Siege Mines and Underground Warfare*. Buckinghamshire, UK: Shire Publications, 2003.

"William L. Jenney." In *Biographical Sketches of the Contributors to the Military Order of the Loyal Legion of the United States*. Suppl. 1. Compiled by William Marvel, 169. Wilmington, N.C.: Broadfoot, 1995.

Winschel, Terrence J. *Triumph and Defeat: The Vicksburg Campaign*. Vol. 1. New York Savas Beatie, 2004.

Woodworth, Steven E. *Decision in the Heartland: The Civil War in the West*. West-port, Conn.: Praeger, 2008.

———. *Nothing but Victory: The Army of the Tennessee, 1861–1865*. New York: Knopf, 2005.

———. *This Great Struggle: America's Civil War*. New York: Rowman and Little-field, 2001.

Theses, Reports, and Maps

Battle maps, drawn by Edwin C. Bears, Vicksburg National Military Park.

Puckett, Robert M. "Engineer Operations during the Vicksburg Campaign." Master's thesis, Fort Leavenworth, 1992.

Shiman, Philip L. "Army Engineers in the War for the Union, 1861–1865." A report presented to the Office of the Chief of Engineers, U.S. Army Corps of Engineers, May 31, 1995.

Electronic Sources

Guth, Peter L. "Mahan, Dennis Hart." *American National Biography Online*. www.anb.org/ (accessed May 6, 2011).

116th Illinois Infantry Regiment History. http://civilwar.illinoisgenweb.org /history/116.html (accessed on December 30, 2013).

National Park Service Soldiers and Sailors System. www.nps.gov/civilwar (accessed July 11, 2012).

———. Vicksburg National Military Park. www.nps.gov/vick/historyculture /illinois-memorial.htm (accessed June 6, 2012).

William C. Clements Library, Manuscripts Division Finding Aids, http://quod.lib .umich.edu (accessed July 10, 2012).

Index

Italicized page numbers indicate figures.

Justin S. Solonick is an adjunct instructor in the Department of History and Geography at Texas Christian University. His most recent publication, "Saving the Army of Tennessee: The Confederate Rear Guard at Ringgold Gap," appeared in *The Chattanooga Campaign*, edited by Steven E. Woodworth and Charles D. Grear. He has also published numerous book reviews pertaining to Civil War topics.